Knowing and Serving Diverse Families

VERNA HILDEBRAND
Michigan State University

LILLIAN AOTAKI PHENICE
Michigan State University

MARY McPHAIL GRAY
Kansas State University

REBECCA PEÑA HINES
Neighborhood Centers, Inc., Houston

Merrill,
an imprint of Prentice Hall
Upper Saddle River, New Jersey   *Columbus, Ohio*

Library of Congress Cataloging-in-Publication Data

Knowing and serving diverse families / Verna Hildebrand . . . [et al.].
   p. cm.
   Includes bibliographical references (p.) and index.
   ISBN 0-02 354537-2
   1. Family services—United States. 2. Family social work—United States. 3. Multiculturalism—United States.   I. Hildebrand, Verna.
   HV699.K59 1996
   362.82'0973—dc20
                              95-34928
                                  CIP

Cover photo: Sherri Silverman/Superstock
Editor: Kevin M. Davis
Developmental Editor: Carol S. Sykes
Production Editor: Christine M. Harrington
Photo Editor: Anne Vega
Design Coordinator: Julia Zonneveld Van Hook
Cover Designer: Thomas Mack
Production Manager: Laura Messerly
Electronic Text Management: Marilyn Wilson Phelps, Matthew Williams, Karen L. Bretz, Tracey Ward

This book was set in Century Schoolbook by Prentice Hall and was printed and bound by Book Press. The cover was printed by Phoenix Color Corp.

 © 1996 by Prentice-Hall, Inc.
Simon & Schuster/A Viacom Company
Upper Saddle River, New Jersey 07458

Photo Credits: Scott Cunningham, Merrill/Prentice Hall, pp. 18, 54, 208; Anne Vega, pp. 70, 156, 172 326; Todd Yarrington, Merrill/Prentice Hall, pp. 51, 169, 264, 298; Authors, pp. 1, 5, 34, 94, 120, 136, 238, 323.

Printed in the United States of America

10 9 8 7 6 5 4 3

ISBN: 0-02-354537-2

Prentice-Hall International (UK) Limited, *London*
Prentice-Hall of Australia Pty. Limited, *Sydney*
Prentice-Hall of Canada, Inc., *Toronto*
Prentice-Hall Hispanoamericana, S. A., *Mexico*
Prentice-Hall of India Private Limited, *New Delhi*
Prentice-Hall of Japan, Inc., *Tokyo*
Simon & Schuster Asia Pte. Ltd., *Singapore*
Editora Prentice-Hall do Brasil, Ltda., *Rio de Janeiro*

The authors wish to dedicate this book to the millions of concerned students who, recognizing the common humanity of all families will make the world a healthy place for diverse families to live and raise their children.

And to John R. Hildebrand, whose commitment to world peace and human diversity was actualized in his unfailing support for the vision and reality of this book.

An Affirmation of Human Oneness

I am a member of the human family.
My home is the earth.
The achievements of men and women
    throughout the ages are my heritage.
My destiny is bound to that of all my
    fellow human beings.
What we jointly create forms our
    bequest to future generations.
May my life serve the good of my family.
May our use of the earth preserve it
    for those yet to come.

—Dr. Joseph E. Schwartzberg,
Professor of Geography,
University of Minnesota

Preface

*K*nowing and Serving Diverse Families is designed as an introductory text to meet a growing need for course offerings in the multicultural area of study at two- and four-year colleges and universities. These course additions are far more than cosmetic changes in the curricula. The intention is to begin early to prepare students to work comfortably with all people and to help solve critical societal problems of relating to people at home, in the community, the nation, and the world.

This book is written especially for undergraduate college and university students in the early years of their college experience. Most professional careers require meeting and working with diverse people. Students planning to enter the helping professions are encouraged to learn to understand the family background of their clients, patients, students, or customers and develop the knowledge and experience through courses, internships, and field experiences throughout their college years to enable them as graduates to work with all persons.

Developing and utilizing the knowledge, ideas, abilities, skills, and energy of all diverse individuals are essential if the twenty-first century is to become most effectively an era of greater peace, prosperity, and progress. The many individuals and families in our pluralistic society can make important contributions to their families and to their local, national, and world communities through their strengths and diversity when they are understood, encouraged, and welcomed into the mainstream of societal activities.

Information presented will also assist currently active helping professionals, such as social service, health, and law enforcement professionals, teachers, counselors, business people, and many others who want to become more sensitive and more aware of the similarities, differences, and concerns of various families and individuals. The effectiveness of private and public helping agencies will depend largely on whether helping professionals are serving all persons in a high-quality manner, upholding basic constitutional rights, and respecting the human dignity of all.

Knowing and Serving Diverse Families is based on up-to-date research and years of practice. Part I introduces the concern for basic human rights, recognition of the oneness of the entire human family, and the use of intercultural communication information, the human ecosystem, empowerment, and human capital concepts to help understand families and the environments within which families function. Constitutional and legal rights are highlighted.

Part II illustrates the diversity of families racially, ethnically, and religiously, and suggests systems for study of additional families that the helping professional may be serving.

Part III features families with specific structures, memberships, or challenges. The choice to include these diverse families in an undergraduate text represents a commitment to inclusiveness and to an understanding of existing family units that are found in society and that helping professionals must learn to serve appropriately.

Part IV summarizes the realities of diverse families and the responsibilities of helping professionals in promoting progress, harmony, peace with justice, and human rights for every family.

Following each chapter are study questions to help students review chapter content. Also, each chapter has separate application suggestions for students seeking experiences, extension of knowledge, and opportunities for stating their own views. Media suggestions and additional readings are also provided.

ACKNOWLEDGMENTS

We extend our appreciation to Editor Kevin Davis of Prentice Hall for support and guidance throughout the writing of this text. We also thank the reviewers of this text for comments and suggestions: William A. Anderson, Mankato State University; Linda Padou Burkett, University of Minnesota; Gayle J. Cox, Indiana University; Gladys H. Hildreth, Texas Woman's University; Brij Mohan, Louisiana State University; Sharon H. Price, University of Georgia; Gwenneth Rae, University of Rhode Island, Felix G. Rivera, San Francisco State University; Carol Seefeldt, University of Maryland; Lynda Henley Walters, University of Georgia; and Emmadene T. Winston, University of Alabama. Special appreciation is given to Gena Wagaman for editing and word processing support.

Contents

CHAPTER 6

Asian-American Families   93

CHAPTER 11

Divorced Single-Parent Families   207

CHAPTER 12

Stepfamilies   237

CHAPTER 13

Families with Challenged Members   263

PART I

Introduction

CHAPTER 1

Knowing and Serving the Human Family: An Introduction

Key Concepts

◆ Human Rights
◆ *E Pluribus Unum*
◆ Pluralistic
◆ Synergy
◆ Diversity

Recognition of the inherent dignity and the equal and inalienable rights of all members of the human family is the foundation of freedom, justice and peace in the world.

— United Nations Universal Declaration of Human Rights

Providing service to people is the hallmark of many careers today. How can you, as a future helping professional, best serve individuals and families? This book focuses on the diversities inherent in families and reveals ways of relating to family members who may differ from you in age, race, ethnicity, economics and family form.

It is clear that there is a need to think about the professional challenges that lie ahead in your career. Preparing to work with individuals and families is a long-range educational objective requiring much of your attention during your entire educational program. Proper study and experience will ready you for service to families following graduation, something that cannot be easily learned the day before your first job begins.

FAMILIES IN YOUR CAREER

As professionals in careers ranging from Accounting to Zookeeping, you will deal with individuals or customers and, either directly or indirectly, their families.

Talk It Over

What is your definition of a family? Explore this concept with your classmates. On what points do you agree?

Many families, if not most, will differ radically from the family and members of the community in which you grew up.

You may question the importance of a course that emphasizes families when your future career requires only that you relate to individuals. Experience shows, however, that individuals are best served by professionals who understand the family, social milieu and personal dynamics of their individual client, customer, patient or student.

DIVERSITY MAKES LIFE INTERESTING

Diversity is exciting. You may know people who travel, study abroad, or read and ask questions in order to become aware of the ways people are alike and how they differ from themselves. Listen when a friend meets a foreigner and begins talking about how "we" do something here in the United States. Your impression may be that your friend is self-centered. However, good conversationalists often consciously seek common ground with other people, a technique that can lead to interesting ideas and friendships.

A close look at our own hometowns, where much common ground exists, will reveal that individuals and families are unique and different from us as well as each other. How can you prepare yourself to serve those in your hometown, as well as people on the other side of the world?

Perhaps you've had the experience of relating a problem to a friend, then having that person suggest solutions that would never work for you—mostly due to your individual family circumstances. You may have been prompted to comment, "That would never fly in my family." Such experiences point to our need to learn more about the differences that exist in families.

 Talk It Over

List the characteristics of three families that you know best. What are the ages of members? How many years apart, and of which gender are any children? What are their goals, values and economic and other resources? Draw conclusions from your analysis regarding their diversity.

SERVING UNIQUE FAMILIES

A family is like no other family,
Like some other families and
Like all other families.

These assertions will help you think about the many facets of your education concerning families, and each will be examined briefly.

Like No Other Family

By now you have learned that individual people are unique. No two are alike! In the same way, individuals both come from and form families that are also unique and unlike any other family. Think of the fact that the 5.6 billion people in today's world came from approximately 1 billion families. Or, think of the prediction that, by the year 2010, the world will contain 7 billion people and that, by the year 2035, that figure will increase to 8.3 billion (Population Reference Bureau, Inc., 1994). This rich diversity is amazing and makes for a much more interesting world than if we were all similar.

The population of the United States is expected to increase from 260 million people in 1993 to 300 million in 2010 and to 338 million by 2035 (Population Reference Bureau, Inc., 1994). Figure 1-1 shows the population change by states, with California gaining the most people, followed by Texas and Florida, according to projections for the year 2020 derived from the 1990 census. Also, the census projections show that the racial and ethnic mix of the United States will change over the next thirty years. The Asian population will increase faster than any other racial group, followed by African-Americans. The Hispanic population will account for one-third of the increase in the nation's population. The proportion of youth and elderly in the population will remain about the same as in 1993. The dependency ratio, or the ratio of young and elderly, as compared to working Americans, will show a slight increase by the year 2000. According to the Bureau of the Census (1994), one of our largest cities, Los Angeles, will be comprised of 60 percent minorities and 40 percent Caucasian by the year 2010. It has been reported that 94 different languages are part of the English as a Second Language program in Los Angeles schools today (Dunn, 1994).

According to Kalish (1994) at the Population Reference Bureau,

> In 1993, 26.7 percent of children under the age of 18 were currently living with one parent, up from 11.9 percent in 1970. Many children are likely to spend some time in a single-parent home. These changes affect all U.S. racial and ethnic groups and all educational levels, but are more intensified for some. In 1993, 64 percent of white adults were currently married (down from 73 percent in 1970). The proportion of married African-American adults plunged from 64 percent in 1970 to 43 percent. The married proportion of Hispanics fell from 72 percent to 60 percent during the same period. Or, from a different perspective, the proportion of never-married adults age 18 and older has risen to 20 percent of whites, 38 percent of blacks, and 28 percent of Hispanics. (p. 3)

The sciences devoted to the study of individuals include genetics, psychology, and human development. Each family's uniqueness occurs because individual family members contribute to the distinctiveness of the whole family. Thus, each family constellation differs. For example, every family is unique in the ages of the partners, the number and gender of any children, the years between siblings, the unique characteristics of each individual, the variation in structure of the family, and many other aspects (Caldwell, 1983).

If individuals and families are so unique, how is it possible to develop sufficient background to serve them in a professional capacity? The answer is that your understanding of families will be a long-range proposition to be gained both from your education and your experience. Through your formal and informal studies, you will begin to understand characteristics that are especially unique to the family groups you will be serving. You will develop a certain sensitivity and learn how to search for facts about new individuals and their families when you encounter them.

Actually, some of the very experience you'll need can be gained by taking every opportunity to volunteer in community agencies while you are still enrolled in college. By doing so you'll learn how individuals and families pursue their lives and solve problems. You'll also be making an important contribution to your community. Later, you'll draw upon this rich reservoir of experience with individuals and their families when you become a new professional.

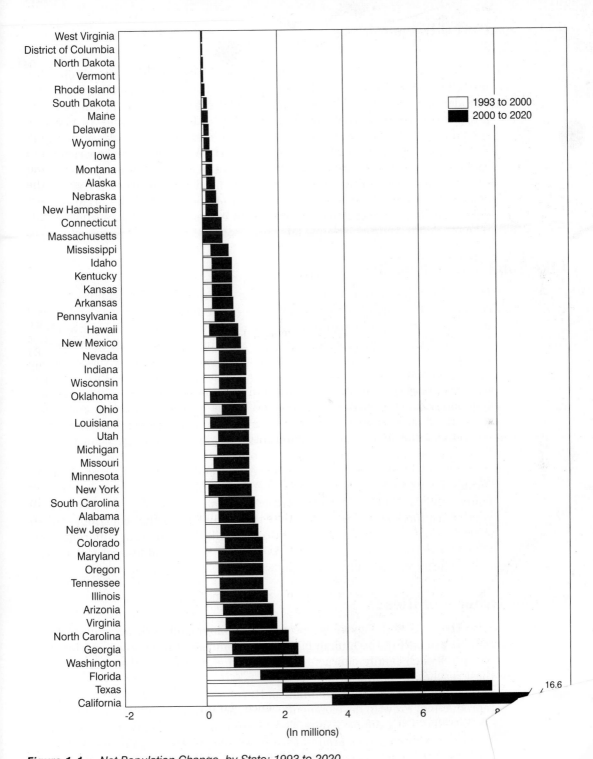

Figure 1–1. *Net Population Change, by State: 1993 to 2020*

Source: Preferred series, Table 1. Washington, DC: U.S. Department of Commerce, Bureau of the Census, 1994.

For example, volunteering in a Head Start program will give you opportunities to meet the parents of the small children you serve, which will give you confidence in dealing with those parents you meet when you attain your full professional degree, even though you are not a parent yourself. To help you search for volunteer and, sometimes, paid experiences, the end of each chapter of this book contains suggestions for application or volunteer experiences to consider. You can research your own community for volunteer possibilities, through such organizations as United Way funded agencies or a community volunteer office. Be sure to keep a record of the name of the organization, dates and hours worked, types of activities engaged in, and your supervisor's name to add to your job resume later on.

Like Some Other Families

In certain respects, your own family is like other families. For example, we are somewhat like our neighbors, simply due to the fact of being born and reared in similar communities within the same country. As Americans we live under the same Constitution and the same laws giving us shared values of freedom and liberty. Americans have many common experiences such as voting, education, and popular culture. We learn some common assumptions, such as knowing we have a right to be heard at a public meeting and have access to some common resources, such as schools and media of communication. Foreigners even say we have some common personality traits! These commonalities make individuals and families in a community more like each other than they are like families on the other side of the country or the world.

These shared characteristics are called culture and are studied in the social sciences we know as sociology, social psychology, cultural psychology, and family studies. Culture is continuously in a state of slow change. Throughout your education you will come to know the many factors that contribute to our shared values and characteristics. Also, you will learn to argue different viewpoints to remind others that there is another view or additional fact to consider before coming to any conclusions.

Like All Other Families

With the help of the social sciences of archeology and anthropology we know that we are part of the human family and members of the human species. This fact gives each family characteristics in common with families from the farthest reaches of the world.

Human beings have common patterns of genetics, biology, physiology, reproduction, growth, development, speech acquisition, problem solving, aging and the like. For example, researchers have even found commonalities in how children learn languages around the world (Slobin, 1972). Your task will be to learn as much as you can and gain different perspectives from those who study families in detail.

Talk It Over

Suggest ways that separatism is alarming and dangerous for a peaceful, just, and happy human community. What actions have been taken in your college or larger community to bring people together? State some steps that persons in your future profession can take to end separatism.

OUT OF MANY, ONE

"E Pluribus Unum" (Out of many, one) is the motto of the United States. This motto, which appears on our coins, states one of the values of the founders of our democratic form of government. When foreigners arrive on our soil, it isn't long before they begin to think of themselves as Americans, rather than French, or Haitian, or Irish, as they might if they had immigrated to some other countries. Americans have developed a pluralistic society. That is, people with differing backgrounds have come together to form a society in common, the United States of America.

BUILDING ON THE IDEAL

What are some steps that we, as helping professionals and today's citizens, can take to build on the ideal of *E Pluribus Unum* and help end the cycles of misunderstanding, conflict, and violence among families and individuals in the United States and within and among countries of the entire world? In a world full of many diverse cultures and countries, are there ways families and individuals can more effectively seek peaceful, democratic, and pluralistic means of living together in harmony with all human beings?

YOUR MEMBERSHIP IN A MINORITY GROUP

Like every citizen, you are a member of a minority group. If this sounds far-fetched to you, consider that, according to some estimates, there are about 5,000 distinct ethnic groups and about 1,000 languages in the world. Taking a global perspective, with a total human population of over 5.6 billion diverse peoples, it appears, by various definitions, that there is no majority race, culture, or lifestyle. Consequently, each of us has a vested interest in minority rights. Minority rights are those basic human rights of equal protection and equal opportunity enshrined in those cherished United States documents, the Constitution, the Bill of Rights and other amendments to the Constitution.

These rights and values are the glue that hold this nation of diverse peoples together. Laws, regulations, and agreements at the local, state, national, and international levels help provide additional glue, making it possible for peoples of all backgrounds to cooperate. A selection of these laws and two special amendments will be described in Chapter 2.

It is essential to prepare professionals to serve and promote harmony among diverse families if improvements in relations are to be significant and rapid. Avoiding oppression and victimization, providing equal protection and equal opportunity for every individual becomes crucial to every one of us. Cross-cultural contacts, study, interaction, cooperation, and service seem necessary if bridges of understanding and friendship are to be built in the ongoing American and global experiments of learning to thrive within and gain from multicultural and other forms of diversity.

PEACEFUL ACCOMMODATION

Peace is cheaper than war or strife in terms of costs, whether in lives or materials. Peaceful resolution of difficulties of many kinds often results from free competition in the marketplace of ideas—from discussions by "friend" and "foe" alike. The role of freedom of expression and freedom of inquiry in producing healthy change merits serious attention as the new millennium approaches.

Decades ago, President Woodrow Wilson said, "I have always been among those who believed that the freedom of speech was the greatest safety, because if a man is a fool, the best thing to do is to encourage him to advertise that fact by speaking" (Dority, 1992, p. 31).

Exposing bigotry concerning any minority group is best done by debate and reason. The answer to a poor idea is a good idea that can be arrived at best by more, not less, free speech. Discrimination against any ethnic group or culture must be exposed in order to enlighten people. Bridges can be built between cultures, races and religions. Free speech and thus the free exchange of ideas provide a peaceful way of achieving perpetual revisions and improvements in the light of new understanding. In a democracy, dissent is not viewed as treason, heresy, or disloyalty. Thoughtful opposition is preferred over thoughtless agreement. Reform is a neverending process and requires constant discussion.

If two people each exchange a good idea in a discussion, they have doubled their wealth of useful knowledge. Indeed, *synergy* often occurs, with the result becoming greater than the single contribution of each party. Furthermore, new insights may also be stimulated by the exchange of ideas. For example, an issue may arise in a discussion group that might cause you to think and later alter your perspective.

With many cultural variations on national and global levels, peaceful accommodation becomes essential. Different ethnic and cultural groups often choose different ways in which to live. A pluralistic society with a pluralism of values can contribute greatly to progress as continual discussion is stimulated. Diversity can be a strength. Though each of us views a situation through eye-

---

 Talk It Over

List and give details of some recent national or international dialogues between historically hostile groups or countries that give the world hope of peaceful reconciliation. How did these breakthroughs happen? What role do you think free speech played?

---

glasses colored by the culture within which we were born and reared, understanding gradually comes through cross-cultural contacts, studies, and observations, and a more enlightened and objective view generally develops. Harmful separatism or tribalism can gradually be replaced by a general bonding among the human species, a bonding transcending borders surrounding each group of seemingly diverse people. A wider cooperating community of diverse peoples will be the result—perhaps best summarized as a "community of communities."

A GLOBAL COMMUNITY

More people are becoming aware of the global nature of our lives. Markets are global, and even the plague that struck India in 1994 was said to be related to a similar outbreak in the United States a year earlier. Many different forms of communication are now instantaneous, and rapid modes of transportation move individuals from one continent to another in a matter of hours. English has become a language utilized by commerce and governments in many areas. Even so, many more Americans in our global economy are feeling the need to learn another language.

The United Nations (UN) is one major global attempt to build bridges connecting all countries of the world. As indicated in the opening quotation of this chapter, the UN provides a forum for developing a global respect for human rights. It is hoped that, through efforts like these, the future will hold no place for unjust oppressors or suffering victims. Humans seem to be learning through trial and error that differences among individuals need not make a difference. Diversity enriches our lives, for example, through art, literature and music, and need not divide people.

Strangely, the human species is the only animal species known that systematically wages wars to destroy its own kind on a massive scale! After billions of years should the human species contrive its own self-destruction? One great strength of the United Nations is that people in countries outside specific local, regional, cultural or lifestyle conflict generally are able to take a more rational and objective perspective than those directly involved in a conflict. This follows because people and countries outside certain areas of conflict are less likely to be captives of or subject to the same current or historical societal conditioning or emotional pressure. The many diverse people of our planet have the power to develop new visions, to make changes, and to remove destructive myths or superstitions that have kept us apart.

Societal problems needing serious attention were strikingly stated recently in a lead story in *The Wall Street Journal* by Dennis Farney:

National Paradox

In Los Angeles, the nation's worst riots in more than a century erupt in the streets. Some of the country's most thoughtful observers see a nation curdling like sour milk into racial and ethnic groups: Separate, unequal and often hostile.

"The United States or Yugoslavia—what's the difference?" asks author Peter Drucker. Mr. Drucker says, "an upsurge of tribalism" threatens to dissolve the shared values that once held Americans together. (Farney, 1992)

Cooperation, friendship, safety, and perhaps even love, will develop as we learn to share and enjoy life together. That is the civilized way. Violent bloody conflicts and wars are too deadly to tolerate. Global institutions of governance to help settle disagreements peacefully and with justice are a vital world-wide resource. While the merits of such organizations as the United Nations, the World Court, and the UN peace-keeping units in the post-Soviet world are recognized, the supervised disarming of opposing forces and the overseeing of honest and peaceful elections will need skillful international negotiation.

CONCLUSIONS

Think of your career path and begin to prepare yourself by taking advantage of experiences with many different individuals and families. In a real sense you are a minority person in certain environments. You can surely recognize a self-serving interest in being respected and treated with respect for your intellect and ability. However, the modern idea that all human beings are born equal and should, as global citizens, enjoy basic liberties and rights, is gaining wider acceptance. With the foundation given in this book, the authors believe that respect, hope, self-esteem, and development for every member of the human family will be stimulated. Our world, at times referred to as "a global apartment house" because we live so closely together in terms of time, can be made safe not only for participatory democracy, but, also, safe for diversity where families of all kinds are welcomed, valued, and even cherished.

STUDY QUESTIONS

(Reviewing the Study Questions for each chapter will help you focus on particular concepts presented in each chapter and clarify the ways in which the authors apply those concepts.)

1. Name the organization that sponsors the Universal Declaration of Human Rights.
2. The present population of the world is_____. In 15 years the world population is expected to reach_____. How will the racial and ethnic mix in the United States change in the next 15 years?
3. What does the statistic termed *dependency ratio* show? How does that ratio relate to a study of families?
4. According to the latest census reports, what was the percentage of U.S. children living in single-parent homes in 1993? What has been the trend since 1970?
5. List three sciences that focus on individual development.
6. List the social sciences that study groups of people and families.
7. *E Pluribus Unum* is the motto of the United States. Give its meaning. How does it apply to your study of families?
8. What does *pluralistic* mean? How is it applied in your text?
9. What does *synergy* mean? How is it applied in your text?

APPLICATIONS

(Students: Each chapter contains a list of Applications, encouraging more in-depth study of concepts learned earlier. Complete one or several of these suggestions to gain experience applying concepts discussed in each chapter. The purpose of the Applications is to make the chapter more relevant to your particular situation. The exercises are open-ended and individual and the outcomes will vary. Discussing them with your classmates will aid in learning how each of the Applications relates to the topics.)

1. Write out and discuss your definition of a family.
2. List the characteristics of three families you know best. What are the ages of each family member? How many years apart and of which gender are any children? In describing themselves, do they use racial or ethnic characteristics? What can you conclude about your sample of three families?
3. In considering the population and demographic statistics provided, list statistics that apply particularly to your home community. Were there any surprises? If so, what are they?
4. As you consider your future career, write a one-page essay about the types of individuals and families with whom you expect to interact. State how you are preparing or expect to prepare yourself for this interaction.
5. Suggest ways that separatism is alarming and dangerous. What steps have been taken in your college or community to bring people together? State what people in your future profession can do to end separatism.

6. List and give details of recent national or international dialogues between historically hostile groups that give the world hope of peaceful reconciliation. State some ways your personal interests might be affected by these dialogues.

7. Write down your thoughts on controversial points of view in a one-page essay, then prepare to discuss them in your class.

8. Write a one-page essay on how the United Nations facilitates understanding among the peoples of the world.

9. Peter Drucker is quoted earlier in the text as saying the United States has had an "upsurge of tribalism." Write a one-page essay discussing the meaning of his statement and your reaction to it.

10. Talk to three persons, on or off campus, whom you recognize as being different from yourself. Ask their views on current issues, families, and the relationship of families to their career. Summarize in a two-page report the three views and your own view on the topics.

VOLUNTEERING

Canvass your community for an opportunity to volunteer to work with people on a weekly basis in order to have relevant personal experiences you can apply to your courses. Ask your local United Way fund for a list of agencies needing volunteers. Your instructor can also guide your search and selection of a volunteering site. College credit is sometimes attached to a specific volunteering experience, so it might be worth your while to look into it.

Keep a daily log or diary of your work, complete with time spent, dates, names and addresses of supervising personnel. At graduation, this record can help you develop an item on your employment resume or vita to substantiate your volunteer experience. A record of volunteer experience is viewed favorably by most employers.

REFERENCES

Caldwell, Bettye. (1983). Keynote address at the World Assembly of the World Association for Early Childhood Education, August 1983, Geneva, Switzerland.

Day, Jennifer Cheeseman. (1993, November). Population Projections of the United States by Age, Sex, Race, and Hispanic Origin: 1993–2050, Current Population Reports, P25–1104, U.S. Census Bureau.

Dority, Barbara. (1992, March–April). Civil liberties watch. *The Humanist,* *52*(2), p. 31.

Dunn, Ashley. (1994). In California, the numbers add up to anxiety. *The New York Times, CXLIV,* Section 4, p. 3.

Farney, Dennis. (1992). National paradox: As America triumphs, Americans are awash in doubt, pessimism. *The Wall Street Journal, CCXX*(19), July 27, 1992, p. 1.

Kalish, S. (1994, November). Fewer and fewer "traditional" U.S. households. *Population Today,* p. 3.

Population Reference Bureau, Inc. (1994). *1994 Population Data Sheet,* Washington, DC: author.

Slobin, Dan I. (1972, July). They learn the same way all around the world. *Psychology Today.* In Anne Kilbride (Ed.), *Human development 76–77* (p. 272). Guilford, CT: Dushkin Publishing Group.

FURTHER READING

Eldering, L. and Leserman, P. (1993). *Early intervention and culture.* The Hague: National Commission for UNESCO.

Ferencz, Benjamin, and Keyes, Jr., Ken. (1991). *Planethood.* Coos Bay, OR: Love Line Books.

Gonzalez-Mena, Janet. (1993). *The child in the family and the community.* Washington, DC: The National Association for the Education of Young Children.

McCracken, Janet Brown. (1993). *Valuing diversity: The primary years.* Washington, DC: The National Association for the Education of Young Children.

MEDIA RESOURCES

What Rights Has the Child? (16mm film, 20 minutes). New York, NY: United Nations Publications.

CHAPTER 2

Serving Individuals and Families: Equal Protection

Key Concepts

◆ Defining a Family
◆ Legal Rights
◆ Being Professional
◆ Strengths versus Deficits

An African-American family was involved in a car accident on a highway near a small Midwestern town. The accident victims were moved to a small hospital nearby for observation and treatment. Later, the mother wrote to the head nurse, thanking the nurse and the staff for their caring attitude toward her and her family. "Our greatest fear was that we might be refused desperately needed services," the mother wrote.

The helping professionals in this small hospital are remembered for their quick, professional, and nonprejudicial service to this family. The mother's statement shows that she is fully aware that in some localities her family might not have received the prompt, thorough treatment needed. Mistreatment or nontreatment may have been her prior experience.

Diversity is one thing to be aware of in serving families. Even your particular family is diverse within itself. At any one time, a given family can differ from one to several members, with people of different ages and with differing relationships. Diversity is a vital part of families, even families in your particular town, state, region, or nation. Families are far from being all alike.

WHAT IS A FAMILY?

Most people have their own definition of a family and it is likely to coincide with the family in which they grew up. Most young children believe their family is like everyone else's family. To some, the family is a place as well as a group of people. One young man wrote, "A family is where, when you go there, they have to let you in."

There are legal definitions, political definitions, sociological definitions, and personal definitions of the family. Family scholars Bubolz and Sontag (1993) have developed the following inclusive definition:

> We define families in an inclusive sense to be composed not only of persons related by blood, marriage, or adoption, but also sets of interdependent but independent persons who share some common goals, resources, and a commitment to each other over time. (p. 435)

Note the important features of the above definition: composition, goals, resources, commitment, and interdependent and independent people.

Current news stories often feature discussions about single parents. Figure 2–1 shows that there are nearly as many never-married single parents with children as divorced single parents (Kalish, 1994, p. 3). These all fall under our definition of a family. Think about what this set of statistics means to you as a

---

  Talk It Over

Are college roommates a family? Is an unmarried couple without children a family? Is your elderly great-grandparent who lives alone a family? Is a single parent rearing a child a family? Is a parent who lives with a son and his family part of the son's family? Discuss.

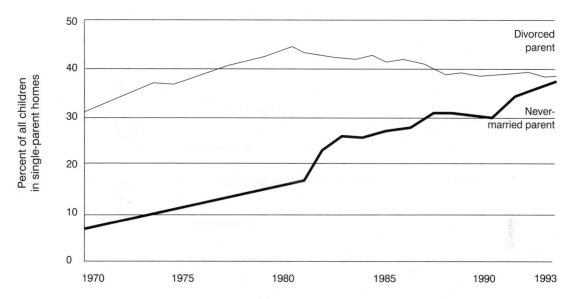

Figure 2–1.   *Nearly as Many Never-Married as Divorced Single Parents*
Source: Census Bureau, *Marital Status and Living Arrangements: March 1993.*

helping professional, and how it affects children, certain parents, and even yourself, personally. Single parents vary according to age and circumstances and will be discussed in detail in Part III.

Using the Bubolz-Sontag definition of the family you would include many individuals today living in social groups, whether they are a couple in the family formation stage or a grandparent in his or her waning years. The family is the most common social group among the world's peoples.

SERVING FAMILIES

Some agencies and programs are developed to be support services for families. Child (day) care centers, for example, are developed to help families care for and educate their children while parents are working. In order for families to remain strong, society must have high standards of care with regard to children's centers, so that children will develop appropriately. These are the formative years for young children and less than high quality care could have damaging effects. Current professional efforts are devoted to improving standards for child care. Child care, formerly referred to as day care, has been available in the United States since the 1800s, and thus is not a new support service for families. Today there are many types of child care ranging from family child care in homes, to nonprofit centers, to centers operated by industries for their employees' children. The concept of dependent care during the day is also used to provide care for the elderly and is a growing service available to American families. Occasionally, the child and elder care are in the same facilities.

If your future work involves adult educational programs, you may be involved with individuals who must arrange your program around the needs of their family. A program leader must be sensitive to family demands of participants in setting location, needs for child care, and times for meetings. Certain programs are currently being designed to help unemployed parents obtain job training for future employment. Helpful attitudes toward family circumstances on the part of directors and instructors in such programs will largely determine whether the participating parent succeeds or fails in the new schooling endeavor.

Children's needs are a priority for parents taking classes. A babysitter who cancels on a class night or a sick child at exam time are devastating situations for any parent. Patience, understanding, helpfulness, and procedures that accommodate these emergencies are hallmarks of service in those who work with parents, particularly parents of young children.

Being "family friendly" has become a mark of excellence for some American corporations. These companies have developed programs that help their employees deal with family concerns while interfering little with their work. For example, numerous on-site child care centers have been established in industries across the country. "Flex-time," wherein employees are able to select a work schedule different from the typical 8 to 5, has become a possibility in cooperation with other employees. Some people may begin working at 7 A.M. and leave at 4 P.M. Others may work 10 hours a day for four days a week, rather than 8 hours for five. Two people may actually fill one position or "job share." Through the use of interactive communications and computers, many employees are able to conduct a part, perhaps even a substantial portion, of their work from a home office. Family friendly employers are being recognized for encouraging parents, both mothers and fathers, to use their family leave when a baby is born or adopted. You may already be part of an organization that is considered supportive of families. Or, you may want to select your professional career from such a family friendly setting. Each fall *Working Mother* magazine identifies "family friendly" corporations and work places.

Whatever your career choice, you'll surely have contact with families, if not in your job, perhaps in your neighborhood or in your own extended family. Many careers involve opportunities to serve individuals who are part of families. Other careers may serve the whole family as a unit. Whether serving individuals or families as a whole, being informed about families can only contribute to your success.

For instance, you'll likely have immediate interaction with parents if you are a teacher of children, a physician maintaining the health of children, or a law enforcement officer taking juveniles into custody. You can logically assume that these children or youths have parents who are expected to be responsible for them and whom you'll need to contact. Indeed, in the first two cases, parents are likely to contact you.

Suppose that your career deals with products, for example, engineering or agricultural products. Though you may actually be designing structures or producing various products, people in families will use them. And people from families will help produce them. You may serve in your spare time on a school board, or on a Chamber of Commerce committee where service to the community's families is a goal. Also, your employees, friends, neighbors, coworkers, and others generally live in family groups. This course will aid you in understanding families of different kinds.

RIGHTS OF INDIVIDUALS AND FAMILIES

The United States Constitution provides the very foundation for the rights or protections for individuals and, therefore, their families. Any professional interaction as well as other interpersonal relationships with individuals and families must conform to these Constitutional protections. Two amendments stand out as being significant for everyone. These are the first and fourteenth amendments.

First Amendment

Congress shall make no law respecting an establishment of religion, or prohibiting the free exercise thereof; or abridging the freedom of speech, or of the press, or the right of the people peaceably to assemble, and to petition the Government for a redress of grievances.

The First Amendment instructs us as citizens to allow others to have their say and exercise our own rights to speak up for the good of all. The organization you become involved in must assure people that they can exercise their freedom of religion and be confident that it neither gains them favors nor causes them to be excluded. Planning for the free exercise of these rights needs to be part of any organization's bylaws, policies, and practices.

Fourteenth Amendment

. . . No state shall make or enforce any law which shall abridge the privileges or immunities of citizens of the United States; nor shall any State deprive any person of life, liberty, or property, without due process of law; nor deny to any person within its jurisdiction the equal protection of the laws. . . .

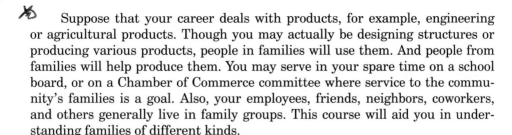

◆ Talk It Over ◆

Discuss specific ways the First Amendment applies to you and your family. Recall any instance in your community or in a news story where an individual tested this amendment. Discuss why Americans might accept these rights casually.

Talk It Over

What due process procedures exist in your college or in your housing arrangement to protect your rights? Discuss.

Most organizations have written bylaws, policies, and procedures for providing due process to those they serve or hire. That is, if a problem occurs on the job or with regard to the service, there is an established written procedure for the individual or family to express their concern and an opportunity for those responsible to make constructive suggestions and work out acceptable remedies. Without proper procedures within the policies of businesses, institutions, and other organizations, the courts become the last resort for due process as legal action is taken.

FEDERAL LAWS

A number of federal laws, in addition to the Constitution, offer various protections to individuals and directly or indirectly to families. A few of the primary laws will be described briefly. Your librarian can help you gain more information about a specific law or a certain type of legal protection. Laws of this type are continuously being evaluated and may be amended. As professionals you must become aware of the laws that apply within your professional arena. Certain laws are usually on the books that authorize the service in the first place. You should know about those laws and read the standards for your particular service and discuss them with your supervisor, especially any laws or standards you do not understand. You are obligated to follow the laws governing your service.

Later, as a professional, you may be in a position to make recommendations for changes in laws. The laws listed and briefly described are the more prominent ones. However, there are literally hundreds of laws that affect individuals and families in their homes and places of work. Your librarian can help you find out details of laws on any topic, as well as the history of the legislation, including the social conditions that led to the passage of the laws.

EXAMPLES OF U.S. LAWS THAT APPLY WIDELY

1.   *Civil Rights Act of 1964—Title VII (amended in 1972 and 1978).*

This act, when passed, was the most comprehensive civil rights legislation in U.S. history. It contains provisions for parity in the use and enjoyment of public accommodations, facilities, and education, as well as federally assisted programs and employment. It prohibits discrimination because of race, color, religion, sex, or national origin (*The Guide to American Law,* Vol. 2, pp. 339–349). The Pregnancy Discrimination Act of 1978 was an amendment to the Civil Rights Act, Title VII, that prevented the practice of firing workers because of pregnancy (*The Guide to American Law,* Vol. 4, p. 334).

2.   *Voting Rights Act of 1965 and Voter Registration Act of 1993.*

The 1965 Act established guidelines for courts to follow in cases involving voting rights discrimination. It provided that no policy or procedure may be adapted or maintained by state officials for discriminatory purposes (*The Guide to American Law,* 1987 Supplement, p. 334). The 1993 Act allows a citizen who has reached age 18 or older to register to vote while obtaining a driver's license or to send in a voter registration by mail (*The Guide to American Law,* 1994 Supplement, p. 475). Both acts help individuals gain fuller access to the voting process, one of the hallmarks of a democracy.

3.   *1968 Fair Housing Act.*

A fair housing program was part of the Civil Rights Act of 1968 that focused on discrimination in public housing and created the mandate for equal access to housing for persons and families regardless of race, color, creed, sex, or national origin. Efforts to reach this goal still continue, including a ruling in 1991 that pertained to advertisements in *The New York Times* for rental or sale of housing stating that it was unlawful to "publish any . . . advertisement, with respect to the sale or rental of a dwelling that indicates any preference . . . based on race" (*The Guide to American Law,* 1992 Supplement, pp. 308–309). Accepting diversity in housing has been a long time coming in America.

4.   *Equal Pay Act of 1963.*

This act requires equal pay for men and women performing similar work (*The Guide to American Law,* Vol. 9, p. 230).

5.   *The Fair Labor Standards Act of 1938 (1972 amendments).*

Often referred to as the "Wage and Hour Law," the act established a minimum wage, equal pay, and recordkeeping requirements. It forbade the use of child labor under the age of 16, and prohibited the use of workers under the age of 18 in those occupations deemed dangerous (*The Guide to American Law,* Vol. 5, p. 137).

6.   *Vietnam Era Veterans' Readjustment Assistance Act of 1974.*

Prohibits job discrimination and requires affirmative action to employ and advance in employment qualified Vietnam veterans.

7.   *Executive Orders 11246 and 11375 (of President Lyndon Johnson).*

Both Executive Orders relate to providing equal opportunity in employment. This mandate began with employment in Federal Government positions, over which President Johnson had the most control, and expanded over the years. The above listed executive orders require an affirmative action program by all federal contractors and subcontractors with a contract of $10,000 or more (Johnson, 1946–1965, p. 334 and p. 684).

8.   *Rehabilitation Act of 1973 (Amended 1974).*

Prohibits job discrimination because of disability and requires affirmative action to employ and advance in employment qualified disabled workers. The amendments of 1974 required modification of public buildings or facilities financed by Federal Aid to provide physically handicapped individuals with means of access to them. This act is a forerunner of the 1990 Americans with Disabilities Act (*Guide to American Law,* Vol. 6, pp. 3–4).

9.   *Education for All Handicapped Children Act of 1975.*

This act provided the incentive for making available to handicapped individuals opportunities formerly denied to them. A "free and appropriate public education" must be available to handicapped children comparable to the educational opportunities provided to other children in the public schools (*Guide to American Law,* Vol. 6, pp. 3–4).

10.   *Social Security Act (Social Security Act of 1935 and Federal Insurance Contributions Act).*

Provides retirement, disability, burial, and survivor benefits to eligible employees and self-employed individuals. In 1939, Congress created a separate benefit for the dependent wives, children, widows, and parents of wage earners—to soften the economic hardship created when a family loses a wage earner's support. Today, fathers left with dependent children may receive the benefit, too. In 1935 the law reached only workers in industry and commerce; however, in the 1950s, the act was extended to most self-employed individuals, and nearly all jobs are covered by Social Security today. The spouse of a retired worker who reaches sixty-two can receive benefits equal to one-half of the worker's benefits. Supplemental Security Income (SSI) provides extra payments for those who are blind, over sixty-five, or disabled (*The Guide to American Law,* Vol. 9, pp. 286–298).

11.   *Occupational Safety and Health Act of 1970.*

Requires that employers shall furnish employees a safe place to work. Under this act, standards are promulgated, penalties are established for noncompliance and investigations are made of hazardous working conditions (*The Guide to American Law,* Vol. 7, p. 37).

12.   *The Age Discrimination in Employment Act of 1967 (amended in 1978).*

Prohibits discrimination against persons 40–70 years of age in any area of employment (*The Guide to American Law,* Vol. 4, p. 337).

13. *National Research Act of 1974.*

An act requiring anyone doing research with human subjects of any age to give informed consent without undue influence, force, or deceit (*The Guide to American Law,* Vol. 8, p. 151). This act requires a board to screen all research projects to assure that an individual's rights are protected.

14. *Americans with Disabilities Act of 1990.*

Title I prohibits discrimination against individuals with disabilities by requiring equal employment opportunities.

Title II requires equal availability and accessibility in state and local government programs and services, including transportation.

Title III prohibits discrimination in public accommodations and services, such as hotels, restaurants, grocery stores, retail stores, service establishments, and other public facilities.

Title IV addresses communication, particularly telecommunications.

Title V contains miscellaneous provisions regarding the continued viability of state or other federal laws providing people with disabilities with greater protection, various generally applicable rules, and provisions of the Architectural and Transportation Barriers Compliance Board (Cross et al., 1993, p. 32).

15. *Family and Medical Leave Act of 1993.*

The act permits workers to take up to twelve weeks of unpaid leave of absence each year for family illness, childbirth, or adoption, and requires employers to maintain the worker's insurance benefits and assure their job return after their leave. This act is considered a significant advance in employee rights and the strengthening of families and places them somewhat on par with families in other advanced industrial nations (*The Guide to American Law,* 1994 Supplement, p. 455).

16. *Government in the Sunshine Act.*

This act requires that boards of public decision-making bodies shall give adequate public notice of the forthcoming meetings of these committees, councils, and the like and conduct their meetings in public. This act has brought many decisions "out in the sunshine" when formerly they might have been made secretly in political deals. More democracy, fairness, and representation have thus become available to all citizens (*Federal Register,* [1992] Vol. 56: 160, p. 61. Washington, DC: Government Printing Office).

STATE AND LOCAL LAWS

Laws vary considerably among the various states and localities. These laws must extend federal benefits and not provide less than the federal legislation and the rulings of the United States Supreme Court. For information or free

Talk It Over

Considering these laws and amendments, are there any that you think are unnecessary? Discuss a law that you have had personal experience with.

brochures regarding protections under your local or state laws, contact your local and state governmental agencies.

As a professional or a citizen affected by any of these laws, you can make a contribution by recommending amendments to or enforcement of laws. Your local or state bodies will hold hearings when new amendments are offered to laws or new laws are being discussed. You are welcome to attend such hearings. You can learn about the hearings through the appropriate legislative committee. Also, you are free to testify in the time allotted for testimony if you have information that would be helpful. Students often find such hearings very informative.

YOUR CAREER GOALS

Sometimes students, upon graduation, expect to return to their own communities and serve. Of course, this goal can indicate a personal dedication to service and an understanding of the needs in their own communities. However, it can also indicate a desire for a safe haven, a place where clients will be more like them. Remember, even in your own home town, you'll find diversity among families. Very few families could be expected to have your exact background. Each professional with a career in a helping profession will be a member of some minority group that some clients won't readily identify with. Additional information about families will be essential to your service, even in your home town. A broader professional career objective would be to serve families in a culturally sensitive manner, regardless of any particular individual characteristics.

Knowledge, skill, and professional expertise are paramount in any career. Surely another goal is to be accepted as a professional offering expertise to families without necessarily having the personal experience. For example, a single person can be called upon to serve married persons. A person of one race or religion can be called upon to serve persons of other races or religions. Persons from cities can work with people from rural areas and vice versa. Individuals without children can serve those with children, and so on.

At a recent university graduation when the medical school degrees were presented, a member of the audience whispered to her friend in the next seat, "I wouldn't want to go to them." "Why?" asked her friend, wondering if it was because many were women. "Because they are so young," came the reply. If such a biased attitude prevails, new young physicians have much work ahead of them to gain the confidence of older people many will serve.

BEING PROFESSIONAL

Being both professional and excellent in your specialization requires objective, empathetic, yet controlled, emotional responses to a client's needs. You'll need methods, sensitivity, and experience to be both empathetic and professional simultaneously. When an individual needs a professional service, the diversity between himself or herself and the professional sought should matter little. For example, like the employees in the hospital emergency room described in the opening anecdote, all professionals need to fulfill their responsibilities in rapid sequence without regard for the racial, ethnic, or other characteristics of those individuals needing emergency care. While close family members or friends may display emotion, professionals must be in control of their emotions and proceed quietly, methodically, thoroughly, and objectively in performing the services for which they were trained and licensed.

Families and individuals have many legal protections as they seek the services of professionals. Through study and experience you'll learn to recognize and appreciate the differing characteristics of individuals and families and be better able to help them obtain the services needed.

Many professionals are doing an excellent job today serving as role models for pre-professionals like yourself who are preparing to join them in the work force. Many professional organizations have worked hard for years to bring more equity and diversity into their workplace. There is still much to be done before the goal of equity is achieved. The role you will play is an important one.

FAMILY-RELATED SCIENCES

A variety of family-related sciences will help provide the information you will receive in this course. The authors draw upon scientific studies, their own professional experiences and those of professionals in many fields. The goal of the authors is to help you study, analyze, and understand more fully the wide variety of families you may encounter in your career. This course will teach you frameworks for looking at each family and ways of analyzing any new type of family that presents itself. With your greater understanding, your services will reach more families successfully and have a positive impact on society. As a result, you will find satisfaction in the services you are able to render.

STRENGTHS OF FAMILIES

Your study will focus on the strengths of families. This approach contrasts with a tendency to focus on the pathologies or deficits of certain families, implying that the pathologies are associated with the entire group.

Talk It Over

What are the strengths of the family you grew up in? How did those strengths facilitate your entry into college?

"What are family strengths?" you may be asking. Strengths might include the family's willingness and ability to manage limited resources tightly to make them cover essentials. Or, a strength can be a family's mutual love and respect for each member. Parents sacrificing for their children's education might be another strength. Another family strength would be parents who exercise strong control over their children's whereabouts, education, or goals. Still another strength might involve the cohesion within the family and the extended family, exhibiting shared effort among family members, perhaps of several generations.

"What are family deficits or pathologies?" The deficit or pathological approach might focus on the family's impoverished situation, an absent parent, lack of job skills, or poor housing.

Funding agencies, attempting to "fix" certain problems, may pressure professionals to utilize a "pathological" approach to any problems. For example, a Mexican-American educator was asked to participate in a study that focused on the deficits of people in her community. She asked the psychologists why they could not focus on the strengths the people brought to their families. The psychologist replied, "Because you can't get funding for that type of research." The woman's professional experience showed her that many of the families had strengths which, if documented, could lead to positive suggestions for the troubled families of the community.

Another project used a door-to-door survey to describe the characteristics of an inner-city neighborhood. When the results were presented, the negative or problem statistics were emphasized. Yet, looking at the data, one could see that a sizable percentage of people were "making it" in that community. Why not ask, "How do these people make it? What are their strengths?" The answers to these questions may give clues to help those who fall by the wayside.

 Talk It Over

What are pathologies of a family you know or have recently read about? Have those pathologies hindered the family members meeting goals? (To protect privacy, avoid using any real names in your discussion.)

Biographies are good sources of success stories, giving insights into the strengths of individuals, often showing the family support, and sometimes sacrifice, that helped the individual persevere to greatness. You can ask your own professors, for example, about any mentors who made a difference in their careers. Behind their cloak of prestige often lies a very humble beginning with key models or supporters encouraging them along the way.

AVOIDING STEREOTYPING

Every family group that can be named prompts a stereotype in the mind of someone. While stereotypes are usually harmful, a general composite picture can play a valid role in seeking useful information and adding to your knowledge—knowledge that will serve you all the years of your life.

This book will bring to your attention information based on professional research and experience. Some information will be aimed at helping you understand and avoid stereotyping. We hope you will always carefully question sources of information and ideas. Also, remember to question and extend your inquiry beyond these pages. Read a variety of articles and books on families and discuss family issues with other students, faculty, parents, and others.

CONCLUSIONS

Families differ widely throughout our country, primarily because they are composed of groups of unique individuals that do not fit some preconceived model. Our Constitution and many laws are designed to protect individuals and families from being discriminated against. Professionals must be conscientiously aware of these legal protections, be ready to defend them, and avoid interfering at all costs.

As you discuss issues presented in this chapter, you may find you disagree with your classmates or the instructor. In a democracy, dissent is not treason. However, learning to disagree agreeably and respectfully is essential. Like your senator on the floor of the Senate, learn to argue with decorum. The person you disagree with today may be a powerful ally tomorrow. What is needed is an orderly, thoughtful discussion of the various ideas, the separation of facts and myths, and a sharing of views concerning the many issues on the table. Those of you who have had the experience of taking various sides in debate classes or on debate teams can help your classmates learn the technique of effective debating.

Clearly, the need to discuss diversity and discrimination is immediate, and the responsibility for serious thinking and the development of some creative solutions rests upon us all. Let your study of knowing and serving families with their many ethnic and structural variations proceed rapidly, thus preparing you to help solve pressing societal problems.

STUDY QUESTIONS

1. Define a family.
2. Make a list of 10 ways different professionals help families.
3. (a) Write down the First Amendment to the U.S. Constitution.
   (b) Think about, then explain, how this amendment relates to family rights.
4. (a) Write down the Fourteenth Amendment to the U.S. Constitution.
   (b) Think about, then explain, how this amendment relates to family rights.
5. (a) List the 16 federal laws described in the chapter that assure special rights to individuals.
   (b) Paraphrase the essential right provided by each one, especially how each law applies to a family. Describe family life without this protection. Share your views with your classmates. If you have had special experience with a law, be sure to share your experience with others.
6. Indicate the positive and negative aspects of the statement, "I want to work with my own people."
7. List 10 major characteristics of a professional. Star those that you have achieved. Place a # symbol before ones you are working on presently. Discuss.
8. (a) Think of a family you know. Write a paragraph differentiating between studying that family from a *strengths* perspective and studying that family from a *deficit* or *pathological* perspective.
   (b) Give examples of how a deficit usually does not include the whole person or a whole family and why this fact can be a strength.
9. (a) Describe how our senators and congresspeople argue with decorum.
   (b) Explain how this style can facilitate class discussion. (Watch a session of C-Span Television for examples.)

APPLICATIONS

1. Analyze the features of the Bubolz-Sontag definition of family. Select your own or another family you know well and, using pseudonyms, state
   (a) Who makes up the family?
   (b) What would be "common goals and resources"?
   (c) What would be "commitment"?
   (d) What does "over time" mean?
   State your definition of family. Discuss how the Bubolz-Sontag definition differs or agrees with your own definition.

2. (a) State your present proposed profession or career.
   (b) Write a two- to three-page analysis of how a person in that career/ profession will have contact with or serve families, or individuals who are part of families. State at least three laws that would be prominent in your work with families. Describe a typical work day for your professional person.

3. Reread the First Amendment to the U.S. Constitution quoted in the text above. Write a two-page essay on how you think that amendment applies to the content of this book. (See Table of Contents, Dedication, and Preface.)

4. Reread the Fourteenth Amendment to the U.S. Constitution quoted in the text above. Write a two-page essay on how you think that amendment applies to the content of this book. (See the Table of Contents, Dedication, and Preface.)

5. Reread the sample of laws relating to individual rights. Select one law and write a 100-word essay on how it affects families.

6. Interview three people from three different families. Ask them to evaluate their contact with a helping professional in recent months. Using pseudonyms, write a two-page report on the positive and negative aspects of what these people encountered in their contact with professionals and the help or lack thereof they received. Discuss.

7. From a newspaper or magazine, clip or copy a story involving a family or individual *and* a professional person. Describe the interaction with the professional depicted in the article. Write down your own opinions regarding the interaction and connect your views with those mentioned in the chapter.

REFERENCES

Bubolz, M. M., and Sontag, M. S. (1993). *Human ecology theory.* In P. G. Boss, W. J. Doherty, R. LaRossa, W. R. Schumm, and S. K. Steinmetz (Eds.), *Sourcebook of family theories and methods: A contextual approach* (pp. 419–448). New York, NY: Plenum Press.

Cross, E. W., Cantwell, M., and Summers, T. (Summer, 1993). The Americans with disabilities act: Increasing awareness through human ecology/home economics education. *Journal of Home Economics, 85*(2), p. 32. (See also The Americans with Disabilities Act, P.L. 101–336, 42 U.S. Congress 12101 [1990].)

Federal Register. (1992). Vol. 56, No. 160, p. 61. Washington, DC: Government Printing Office.

The Guide to American Law. (1983, 1992, 1994). Vols. 2–9, 1983, plus 1992 and 1994 Supplements. New York, NY: West Publishers.

Johnson, Lyndon. (1964–1965). *Code of Federal Register.* Executive Orders 11246 and 11375 (1966). Washington, DC: Office of the Federal Register. 1964–1965, pp. 339–348 and l966–70, pp. 684–686.

Kalish, S. (November, 1994). Fewer and fewer "traditional" U.S. households. *Population Today,* p. 3.

FURTHER READING

Dorris, Michael. (1990). *The broken cord.* New York, NY: Harper Perennial.

O'Connell, Martin. (1993). *"Where's papa?" Fathers' role in child care.* Washington, DC: Population Reference Bureau, Inc.

Pruett, Kyle D. (1987). *The nurturing father.* New York, NY: Warner Books, Inc.

CHAPTER 3

Systems for Knowing Families

Key Concepts

◆ Intercultural Communication
◆ Family System
◆ Family Ecosystem
◆ Principles of Empowerment
◆ Human Capital
◆ Family Functions

Kim went out to the garage to start her car for the twenty-minute trip to work. The car failed to respond to the touch of the key in the ignition. "Now what's wrong?" exclaimed Kim in a panicky voice. After trying the lights, Kim made a quick diagnosis, "The battery is DEAD!" Kim's quick test showed that the car's electrical system was without energy.

Investigating various systems is routine in diagnosing mechanical difficulties in equipment and even social problems in modern society. A *system* is defined as *a group of devices or an organization forming a network for a common purpose.* For instance, a secretary congratulated herself on how much work she had accomplished one morning and realized that there had not been the usual telephone calls that interrupted her work. Picking up the phone, she heard no dial tone and concluded that the telephone system was not working. "No wonder things were quiet," she exclaimed. The telephone is an important part of a modern communication system.

When the telephone, water, or electrical system temporarily fails, one realizes how dependent modern society is on various systems that are all linked together in a maze of interconnections. Individuals and families confront many such systems every day of their lives.

Your body has numerous systems as well. You know that there are interconnections between systems from your study of the skeletal, respiratory, reproductive, and cardiac systems in biology class.

As you go about your daily routine, take time to think about the various systems you use each day. Knowing about a system helps you learn how to get the most out of that system and how to fix it if problems arise. For example, the starter on Kim's car responded when she properly attached jumper cables from another car's battery to her car's battery. This activated the electrical system to start the car.

COMMUNICATION FOR HELPING PROFESSIONALS

Communication with diverse individuals and families will become a necessity as you move into your volunteer and career roles in the helping professions. Communication is a two-way street between you and your clients, customers, patients, students or others. Communication probably requires some reorientation and new learning for you, as it does for most persons who branch out to serve others in the helping professions. Recall that, in a certain sense, we are all minorities to some of those we will serve, thus bridging the communication gap is essential.

Intercultural communication has become an important science as business and political leaders have moved into the international arena. The skills they are learning have meaning for any of us working with people who are different from ourselves.

Striving for *shared meaning* will be our goal. Shared meaning involves understanding each other in both written and spoken language, in body language, and in concepts.]Achieving shared meaning will take time and effort on your part. Even if we speak the same basic language we may not fully understand another person. Humor is a case in point. With shared meaning we can laugh heartily; without shared meaning many things are simply not funny. However discouraged we become, we must still keep trying to communicate. "Meanings are in people" and striving for shared meaning is fundamental to building positive relationships.

Every act of communication is in some sense an intercultural one, according to Sarbaugh (1988), a specialist in intercultural communication. Studies show that the more alike you and another person are in terms of feelings, beliefs, materials, helping with tasks, or working together on a common activity, the more positive the relationship will be perceived. Thus, being aware of the differences between yourself and another individual or family will encourage you to work hard to create a positive relationship and arrive at shared meanings. Rather than give up your personal integrity, you increase it as you develop new ways of interacting with and understanding others.

Studying communication and racism, Teun (1987) found that persons within a group tended to stress differences between themselves, whereas when talking to or discussing members of other groups, people stress similarities or common ground. The in-group members tended to minimize differences between ethnic groups and between ethnic group members. That is, Asian-Americans might discuss their similarities to Hispanics, and note their differences among all other Asian groups.

In studying new information of any kind, individuals who discriminate typically tend to look for *similarities,* but when looking at members of their own group tend to look at the *differences,* according to Teun (1987). For clearer reciprocal interaction, it is necessary to observe both the similarities and differences you find in your clients, customers, patients, students, or the like.

A helping professional must look beyond the social, cultural, selective focusing and attention-getting veneer of a new client or even a coworker, and attempt to understand what is really going on. A thorough and critical look at one's own biases is a necessary step. To this end, some organizations have routine workshops to help people discuss their own ethnic, racial, gender, or age biases so they can move on to new levels of service.

Old stereotypes and ethnocentric ideas often get in the way of progress. Some of these are reinforced in the media. The most subtle stereotypes provide models of ethnic groups in negative behaviors or situations. Classic examples are the social topics of urban decay and run-down neighborhoods. Indirectly, this negative image is attributed to a given ethnic group. As you study many aspects of American life, you'll learn that stereotypes are often unfounded. The effort you'll make in this course will be an important step in overcoming stereotypical biases.

Communication is a two-way street where you can learn something every day and still have much to learn. Many clients may speak languages other than English, so you'll have additional avenues to explore to be able to communicate with them effectively. Learning to communicate in another language is a long-range effort that is worthy of your time and attention. If you have the interest and take time to learn a single word or phrase, that effort will be rewarded by someone longing for empathetic support.

A SYSTEMS APPROACH TO STUDYING FAMILIES

A number of approaches are used in understanding and describing the family. The *functional family* is one defined by shared activities: shared household living, shared responsibility for daily life, and shared child rearing. The *legal family* is defined by legal structures that are altered by divorce or adoption of children. The *biological family* is defined by blood relationships between parents and children, between siblings, and between and among blood relatives of present and former generations. The *interpersonal family* is defined by the perceptions of its members.

A *systems approach* for studying the family uses an integrative method that is holistic, dynamic, and adaptable to change. A systems approach can be used with any of the definitions of the family. The main reason for studying the family system, for you as helping professionals, is because the family is assumed to be economically responsible for and socially and emotionally influential in the care, treatment, and education of individuals in the family. A good plan for regaining the health of an individual can become sidetracked if the family does not understand the plan or is unable to follow through. Or, on the other hand, the family can be so successful with a plan that recovery is swift and thorough.

The Human Ecological System

The *human ecological system* is a holistic approach to studying the family advocated by psychologist Urie Bronfenbrenner (1979). In his view, the individual is linked to the family, the community, and the influence of each on the other. He describes four entities or systems that influence individuals: *microsystems, mesosystems, exosystems,* and *macrosystems*. These systems are envisioned as concentric circles around the individual, the community, and the larger environments. The closest are *microsystems,* the immediate settings containing the individual, such as the family. The *mesosystems* consist of the various microsystems regularly involving the individual. For example, for a school-age child the family microsystem and the school microsystem are linked together as the mesosystem of the child. However, for the family members who are not regularly involved in the school, the child's mesosystem becomes an *exosystem*. The *macrosystem* refers to the outside institutions of the culture, such as religious beliefs and practices, and the political and economic influences of society. These four systems form the "context" in which the individual and child function and Bronfenbrenner advocates analyzing the total context when planning programs for or facing difficulties with children.

The individual's and family's interactions with the physical-biological and the social-cultural environments make up the *human ecosystem*. For example, in the human ecological approach, the teacher or physician planning strategies for helping a child must connect with the parents who are responsible for the child and who will, in all likelihood, be in charge of carrying out the plan. Scientists studying and serving humans have borrowed from natural scientists to show the extent to which the individual is affected by the environment.

The Family as an Ecosystem

The *family as an ecosystem* is a conceptual framework for studying the family that builds on Bronfenbrenner's human ecological approach and on other approaches from natural science. Hook and Paolucci (1970) emphasized the mutual transactions that link people and environments, and the creative decisions families make to adapt to the environment and to foster human development. The family ecosystem is an *open system* with interactions flowing between and among (1) the *natural physical-biological environment,* (2) the *human-built environment,* and (3) the *social-cultural environment.* The family interacts with and is interdependent on the total environment (Bubolz & Sontag, 1993, pp. 28–31).

Natural Physical-Biological Environment. The natural environment includes the climate, rainfall, water, land, forests, plants, animals, minerals and other physical-biological resources available to the family or influencing the family's economic situation through the type of jobs available for the family's livelihood. The natural resources available will affect the family and the systems that serve families. One example might be a small village where most people make their living working in a gold mine in round-the-clock shifts. The big concern for such a village is what to do for a livelihood when the gold ore has all been processed.

Human-Built Environment. The human-built environment includes all alterations and transformations of the natural physical-biological environment made by people over the centuries as they have served human needs. Urban settlements, buildings, cultivated land, medicine, and material artifacts such as school books are only a few examples of alterations and transformations made over time in the natural environment by human beings. Every community is now becoming aware of the toxic by-products from these alterations and transformations of the environment. The problems created by these changes, such as polluted air and water, are now becoming prominent social issues demanding action.

Systems have been developed in every segment of life, for instance, in agriculture, transportation, education, medicine, business, government, and religion. Such systems have altered and transformed the natural physical-biological environment over the centuries. The early American pioneers, for example, strongly supported the establishment of schools for their children. Schools were often created as soon as a settlement was staked out. In many instances, one pioneer mother or daughter served as a teacher in a simple one-room school built by neighbors out of local materials. This high value placed on education made the American rural population highly literate compared to rural populations in other societies.

Socio-Cultural Environment.   The socio-cultural environment includes the other human beings, community organizations, language, laws, values, and patterns. The high value pioneer families placed on education made public schools and literacy a unique feature compared to typical rural populations of the world. Public schools were established for the children of Americans on the frontier, and the wife or daughter of a settler was often the first teacher. The socio-cultural environment also includes human population levels, family size, family structure, and the communications among family members, kinship groups and the greater society. In the family ecosystem approach, understanding situations facing families contributes to the success of any venture purporting to improve life for children.

You can think of the above three environments as three concentric or embedded circles with the family at the point enclosed by each of the three circles. This conceptualization indicates that each of the three environments affects the family and, also, that the family affects each of the three environments. Imagine a waterbed as you think of these interacting forces. Any pressure at one point will cause movement in other parts of the system.

ADAPTATION

Individuals and families interacting with and modifying the environment in which they function can help create an improved quality of life. Individual values and goals are often framed and reframed as people strive together to invent ways to address family concerns. As in a natural ecosystem, the family adapts and changes the state or structure of the family system. According to Bubolz and Sontag (1993, p. 433), the family modifies its environment to meet goals, detect information, select from a range of possible alternative responses, and respond. Through feedback, the family modifies its structure and organization. This requires knowledge, commitment, creativity, and energy from family members.

VALUES

Values are defined as those things you hold most dear. They are conceptions of what is good, right, or worthwhile and direct your actions as well as those of other family members. When you hear someone say, "You ought to. . . . " you are hearing them state a value.

Talk it Over

Write down the "Ought to. . . . " statements you have heard your parents or others make. What "Ought to. . . . " statements are easiest for you to follow? Discuss.

As you study families throughout this course, think about your own family as a system and the various systems within which the members of your family interact. You can think about your family's values—those things they hold most dear. How do these values guide your behavior and the behavior of your parents? You'll begin to recognize how families use their values, goals, and human and nonhuman resources to make decisions and fulfill the objectives they set for their family members individually and for the family collectively.

As you begin your interaction with families, you can diagram their ecosystem in order to consider methodically the various environments that affect their behavior. This analysis will help you design a process for interacting with the family members.

PHILOSOPHY OF EMPOWERING FAMILIES

Many of you are studying for professional careers involving service to people. Or perhaps you are already working with families. That is one reason you've embarked on reading this book. Others may be interested on a non-professional level, expecting to apply the ideas to their own family or neighborhood.

The *empowering philosophy* is this book's philosophy. *Empowering* means helping individuals and families take charge of their future by encouraging their decision-making confidence as they weigh the alternatives available to them. The authors developed this philosophy over the years while working with families and individuals. Using this philosophy in dealing with individuals and families can help to create healthy families that can impact their systems. Many of the careers of the twenty-first century will be focused on keeping people healthy, responsible, and fully functioning.

Principles of Empowering Families

As a helping professional, there are four simple principles to consider in the empowering philosophy. The principles will permeate many of the following chapters. They include:

1.   *The professional's task is one of identifying a family's strengths and building upon those strengths for the good of the individual family member as well as the family as a whole.* As you work with individuals and families you

will find some successful families that, by all odds, should have problems. As one divorced mother said of her family, "I insist we not have a 'broken home,' whatever that means. We are stronger than ever." She had marshaled the family's resources and worked on relating to her two children consistently and comfortably in order to make this statement with assurance.

The empowering principle can be contrasted with one that focuses on the family's problems or deficits, for example, a family's homelessness or ill health. Typically, if a problem exists in a family, the family members are seldom the entire cause of the problem. The cause of the problem lies partly in another system, perhaps the economic system. When families recognize their own strengths and that they can make a difference through their efforts, they are empowered to act and to carry out plans for making changes within their own family system, in their interaction with other systems, and within other systems.

2.   *The methods and strategies selected by professionals to achieve goals will enable and empower families to make informed decisions themselves.* Differences in cultural background and the adults' stage of life within a family may have an impact on how problems are understood, faced, and solved. Solutions that fit one type of family may be wrong for another type of family. An example is the housing expert who, speaking to a group of women senior citizens, told them how families could make furniture out of boxes or purchase it at garage sales. Had the professional considered the backgrounds of the women she was speaking to, she would have realized that these women were sizing down their households, giving away furnishings accumulated over many years. They needed helpful information on how to divide up their treasures fairly among family members wanting their antiques.

As a professional who is new to a community of families, you can learn from other more experienced professionals which methods and strategies they find most useful within the community. You also can find ways to learn from the families themselves regarding their needs. Then, by using your experience and professional knowledge, you can help families develop meaningful programs to fit their needs. Solutions must be developed with the full participation of the family. Understanding the diverse cultures of different families is necessary to deal most effectively with the complexities of each community of families.

This empowerment principle contrasts with one where the professional makes people feel incompetent, or fails to develop their decision-making ability by making decisions for them. To succeed with any program for families, the professional must take the time and have patience while learning the values, goals, and interaction processes typical of the cultural group. Competent professionals treat clients—young or old—as equals with valuable opinions. Choices are established clearly so that families or individuals can make informed decisions.

3.   *The approach will be one of a cooperative partnership with families, as families recognize their own needs and decide what steps they want to take to fulfill their needs.* Encouraging families to state what *they* need and exploring

ways *they* might fulfill those needs fit this principle. When future problems arise, the family will have learned an improved method of analysis and decision-making. This principle contrasts with one where a professional assumes an authoritative role and decrees what must be done without consulting the family.

4.   *The goal is to strengthen the available human and material resources in the total community—within the individual, family, school, service clubs, religious organizations, and neighborhood.* There is a Chinese proverb that says, "Give a man a fish and you feed him for a day; teach him how to fish and you feed him for a lifetime." Teaching skills to help people cope with their problems is an important role for the helping professional. Additional resources can be provided at minimum costs. Many a service club has cleared a vacant lot for a baseball diamond or put up basketball hoops in order to provide young people a healthful place for recreation (Dunst & Trivette, 1987, p. 451).

As you study the following chapters focusing on families with their various ethnic, structural characteristics and challenges, consider how the four principles of empowering families apply. Positive relationships with families that help them feel strong and able to act wisely are important, not only to the families, but also to the future of the society on the local, national, and global levels.

Professionals must work on the assumption that, if they are truly successful, the families they help will be able to continue progressing alone. The autonomy of families in their communities is a major objective. Also, the notion of continuing or life-long education should be stressed to families to help them accept the idea of progressive learning throughout life. With the fast pace of modern life, each person must be prepared to retool from time to time. Professionals can expect to complete their jobs with particular families and turn their attention to other families in need.

FAMILY FUNCTIONS

What functions do families perform? You might ask, "Where among these functions would a helping professional serve?"

The family is viewed as being part of the social system. As such, the family is expected to contribute to society by performing the following functions:

Reproductive Function

The family unit is responsible for perpetuating the human species. Small families and thoughtful family planning are considered essential by demographers in order to preserve the quality of life for future generations. The developed world has been criticized often for utilizing more than their share of the world's natural resources and fostering pollution. Many helping professionals assist families with family-planning information, decisions, and services. These decisions have important ramifications for the child, the family, the society, the environment, and the balance of productive resources relative to population in each country throughout the world. Some couples may choose not to have children or to use their energy to support and care for children in their communities or in their extended family.

Socialization and Caregiving Function

The family is responsible for the physical care and nurturing of children and family members. The family unit is expected to socialize children to interact appropriately in kinship groups and in the larger society. Due to rising economic and other pressures for both parents to work outside the home, large numbers of children are also cared for by others—often in infant, toddler, and child care centers. In addition, families with school-aged children often seek the help of professionals as they guide the education and care of their children. This natural linkage with families must be facilitated by teachers, aides, and administrators of every school group from infant care through high school. In addition, this socializing and caregiving function must be supported by the community in a demonstrable way to help stem the violence being fostered when children are neglected by families and others.

The care of the elderly will be an increasing family responsibility as our population ages in the coming years. Like child care centers, elder care centers are becoming more widespread in some localities. Protected environments allowing elderly citizens to remain self-sufficient in their own homes, with assistance from health care workers with regard to personal care and medications, offer another alternative. These tasks promote careers for a new group of health care workers.

Emotional Support Function

The family is expected to foster the healthy emotional development and emotional ties among family members. Family members all need trust, love, security, and safety. The family home is expected to be a private secluded environment for individual expression of affection and for protection at all times. Assisting in maintaining the emotional health of families is one role the professional can play. Helping some families find the appropriate therapeutic service and aiding with that treatment at times may be another essential function of the professional. Family goals of strengthening emotional ties between family members are achieved gradually. Any stigma attached to seeking professional help should be removed, especially at crucial transition times, such as birth, divorce, remarriage, retirement, and the like.

Economic Function

The family's economic function is ever present. Families need jobs to survive. Jobs are directly related to both the natural and human resources available. The family of today buys most items it consumes. Historically, the household was largely a self-sufficient production unit, producing many of the personal

Talk it Over

Consider what preparation you received in your own family for learning to become an economic support person for a family. What small steps and large steps were part of your family experience? What did adults tell you and what did their behavior show you? Discuss.

and household items needed for daily living. Even today, many families could thrive better economically if they had the skills and motivation to do more production within the home. Making nutritious meals, caring for clothing, doing home repairs and renovation, or raising vegetables, are examples of home production. One important economic skill today is the family's ability to make decisions based on a selection of needed and desired goods and services and their relationship to family goals.

In fulfilling its economic function, the family is expected to prepare its members to contribute to the economic life of society. Families need jobs, skills for job advancement, and the cultivation of appropriate job behaviors, all of which may require help from professionals. Methods of searching for jobs may be taught to adults and adolescents, as well as counseling students and their parents about future jobs. Professional help may be essential to prepare families to confront gender or racial discrimination.

Depending on your professional specialty, you may be called upon to serve families or individual family members concerning one or more of these four family functions—reproductive, socializing and caregiving, emotional support, or economic. How will you go about it? What useful skills are you learning now?

HUMAN CAPITAL

The concept of *human capital* is useful for helping professionals as they argue for support of funds and carry out programs to serve individuals and families. As an economic concept it may attract an audience of funders who might not otherwise find an argument for equity or human development appealing.

Human capital includes the knowledge, skills, abilities, and attitudes that we each possess to enable us to function in society and to produce needed goods and services. Such services range from a personal level of self care to helping one's children acquire the skills and attitudes necessary for life outside the home, as well as the development of skills and knowledge that are economically valued in the marketplace.

Human capital contributes to a country's economic development as surely as physical capital or natural resources contribute to the overall economic health and wealth of a country measured by the Gross Domestic Product (GDP).

Educating the New Hands

You will often hear the statement that each new person contributes a new pair of hands for working. Yet one must consider that long before the infant's hands become a worker's hands, the family, the school, and the community must develop the infant's inborn potential to become a worker by nourishing, caring for, and educating the child at home and at school. There are large costs connected with this health and education service. Some societies are more able and willing to assist families to do their part than others. The effort to transform a baby into a worker demands tremendous physical capital outlays (money and materials), as well as the skills of many parents, teachers and others. The community and nation must be willing and able to make this investment. Human capital development is severely hampered when large numbers of births outstrip the funds available for human capital investments in families and schools. This fact is evident today in the developing world where in some countries the population is doubling in less than twenty years.

The U.S., for example, had a period of population pressure on resources for developing human capital that occurred following World War II in 1945. Since all available resources were directed toward the war effort, the U.S. had to catch up from about a decade of being unable to build schools. Los Angeles, for example, experienced a period of rapid growth that necessitated the building of numerous schools. A large number of people had migrated to the region during the Great Depression of the 1930s and during the war to work in war industries. The post-war "baby boomers" were reaching school age in 1945–50. The city reportedly was dedicating a school nearly every day of the year in those post-war years.

Of course, the high costs of building and staffing all those schools were borne by the taxpayers and were considered overall essential. The investments in education and other human services contributed to the economic progress that followed. During that time, the educational program known as the G.I. Bill gave World War II veterans an opportunity to further the schooling they were deprived of because of their required military service. The government invested heavily in the human capital of its youth and young adults. This cadre of well-educated, former military-service people who were now trained to take jobs that needed doing encouraged the out-migration from agriculture that was necessary for economic growth after the war.

 Talk it Over

What might have happened if U.S. taxpayers had not shouldered the burden of funding schools, teachers, and the G.I. Bill after World War II?

Up until fairly recently, in an agrarian developing country the family was able to teach children what was necessary to know to carry on the family work in the future. However, in today's world, most parents are unaware of the needs of the next decade, let alone the next three decades. And parents usually do not have the technical knowledge, skills, or materials necessary to prepare their own children. This is as true among poor Americans as it is among poor people in many other countries. Thus, all parents need community support to succeed in developing their children's human capital. Parents' own human capital must also be updated in most societies today, due to the rapidly changing employment scene.

Nutritional Improvements

T. Paul Schultz (1994), of Yale University, in analyzing world-wide studies of human capital, indicated that mothers with schooling are able to provide more adequate nutrition for their children than mothers without schooling. Since child care is the province of females in most societies today, male education does not show the same statistical connection to children's well-being as does female education, Schultz claims. Yet many societies place high priority on the education of sons. In addition, mothers who have had some schooling have fewer children and experience fewer infant deaths. Of course, adequate nutrition is essential for life as well as for a sustained level of child growth and development and employment later as adults. (Schooling in Schultz's studies refers to minimal levels of literacy in developing countries, pp. 50–51.)

Life Expectancy

Another human capital statistic analyzed by Schultz (1994) is the longer life expectancy of females than males. Since about 1930, female life expectancy has improved as families in many countries moved to urban centers from rural areas. The urban environment provides females increased opportunities for schooling as well as opportunities to enter the labor force and earn money for their own care and the care of their families. Females also have benefited from improved health services, including family planning services, more readily available in health centers located in urban areas. Fertility control, which is in part responsible for the reduction in maternal deaths, also makes a significant difference in female life expectancy statistics (p. 18). That is, if birth spacing occurs, if mothers with problem pregnancies can prevent them, and if women can stop having babies when they have reached their desired family size and their older ages, their health and life expectancy improve. By avoiding frequent pregnancies, women can devote more of their own human capital and family resources to educate and nurture current children.

Human capital is first developed in the families of the world as children are cared for by parents and others in the community. The analysis done by

Schultz (1994) found that the investment in women (who have been woefully neglected in some societies) who in turn can nurture children adequately is an excellent long-range economic investment. Mothers with an education are more likely to see that their children become educated than women or men without an education.

Most countries and families have a history of dedicating more resources to educating males than females. This is especially true where education is not compulsory, children need to work, and costs are a private expense for the family. The Schultz (1994) analysis showed that:

> Social subsidies for investments in female children and adults may be justified by:
>
> (1) efficiency, such as high individual private market returns;
> (2) social externalities, such as reduced child mortality and [female] fertility;
> (3) intergenerational redistribution, such as better health and education of children and a slower growth in population; and
> (4) equity, that is, an increase in the productive capability of poorer individuals relative to richer individuals. (p. 48)

The Equal Pay Act of 1963 makes an equity argument in stating that males and females should be paid the same wages for doing the same job. The Schultz (1994) analysis shows that the long history of lower investment in female education is largely responsible for females topping out in low-paying positions. Statistics from the 1970s showing the percentages of females and males admitted to a given class in professional schools of law or medicine can be compared to statistics on 1994 admissions for two stark examples. Only since the 1970s has a legion of female students entered many of the higher-paying professions. Thus, for generations, females have missed out on state subsidies for their educations that males have long enjoyed, not to mention the traditional private family contributions of greater subsidies for sons than for daughters. The same would likely be true if an analysis were done of minorities and education in the U.S. White Americans have received governmental subsidies for their educations for generations, which explains the lower wage categories for most minorities, at least up until 1972 when the Civil Rights Act began to take effect in higher education.

Higher rates of investment in the human capital of females by a widening circle of industrial developed countries show that these countries have been more successful in stimulating modern economic growth, even though most adult females' wage rates are still far below male rates. Furthermore, placing emphasis on the education of females provides many external benefits to society, as measured by reduced child mortality and morbidity, improved child nutrition and schooling, and decreased fertility and population growth. Schultz' (1994) studies show a shortfall in female education and health services compared to that of males, particularly in South and West Asia and in

Talk it Over

Select a family you know and list examples of human capital development that you think occurred within the family. Give examples of parents or friends as mentors for the children.

Africa. He believes that in these areas of the world, the family decision-making process and parents' own traditionally defined interests attach less value to the future productivity of daughters than sons. (This finding should be recalled when the preference for sons is discussed in later chapters.)

APPLICATION TO DIVERSE FAMILIES

The Schultz (1994) analysis of the differences in human capital investment between women and men suggests that females be given adequate schooling and health supports as efforts are made to render our society gender neutral, as well as racially and ethnically equal. Additional investments in girls' and women's education and health care will create human capital and are certain to produce monetary and private and social returns needed by society.

In the forthcoming chapters, American family groups with varied ethnic backgrounds and family structures and challenges will be presented. You can develop a process of analyzing family characteristics based on the family ecosystem framework, the empowerment model, the family functions, or the human capital concept. Thus, as a helping professional encountering a family, you can select a system for planning your interaction with its members. Think of your family analysis as descriptive, instead of either good or bad, or right or wrong. The question to ask yourself is, "How can these family members be empowered or find the strengths to achieve goals on their own?"

 Talk it Over

In considering male and female children of all racial and ethnic groups, do you think the argument that "equity in subsidies to improve economic efficiency" would be heard more favorably in the halls of Congress and legislatures than the argument that "equity is desirable because it is right"? Discuss your arguments in class or in a written paper.

CONCLUSIONS

Several analytical frameworks have been presented for you to use in working with families in your professional career. The ecological system, the four major family functions, the four principles for empowering families and the concept of developing human capital are all frameworks that a helping professional can utilize in analyzing situations facing families. These frameworks should be kept in mind as you study families and their ethnic, racial, religious, and family structures. There is no one best approach to use in helping a particular family. Remain sensitive to the fact that families change over time and will require new approaches as family members gain experience and reach new stages in their life cycle. The empowerment of families is your objective.

STUDY QUESTIONS

1. Define a systems approach to studying families. Give examples of systems.
2. Explain the human ecosystem as identified by Urie Bronfenbrenner.
3. Identify the three parts of the human ecosystem as defined by Bubolz and Sontag. Explain in your own words the relationships among the three environments.
4. Define the role adaptation plays in a human ecosystem.
5. State the four principles of empowering families and give examples.
6. State the four major functions of families and give examples.
7. Define human capital.
8. Describe the findings of the T. Paul Schultz analysis with regard to investment in women and how it impacts the economic development of a family or a country.
9. How does the Schultz analysis give substance to the statement "When you educate a female, you educate a family"?
10. Discuss findings of studies by Teun and Sarbaugh on intercultural communication.

APPLICATIONS

1. Using the three environments of the human ecosystem, diagram your own family and label the various parts of the system. Discuss adaptation among the environments as you analyze your family.
2. Using the human ecosystem framework, diagram the interaction that a family with two young children might have with the systems outside the family.
3. State the four principles of empowering families and give an example of each principle in relation to some interaction you experienced at college. Discuss.

4. Look up statistics of females entering the professional fields during the late 1970s in the U.S. Compare your data with statistics from a decade earlier. How many more females were admitted to professional schools such as law and medicine in the later decade? What does this suggest about family and governmental subsidies for education and the differences in availability to females and males?

5. Discuss with your classmates the Talk it Over questions in the chapter.

6. Reflect on someone you've known a long time. In describing that individual, would you describe similarities or differences with yourself? Reflect on someone you've met recently who is very different from yourself. How would you describe that person? How does your behavior fit Teun's research described in the chapter?

REFERENCES

Bronfenbrenner, Urie. (1979). *The ecology of human development*. Cambridge, MA: Harvard University Press.

Bubolz, M. M., and Sontag, S. (1993). Human ecology theory. In P. G. Boss, W. J. Doherty, R. LaRossa, W. R. Schumm and S. K. Steinmetz (Eds.), *Sourcebook of family theories and methods: A contextual approach* (pp. 419–448). New York, NY: Plenum Press.

Bubolz, M. M., Eicher, J. B., and Sontag, S. (1979). Human ecosystem: A model. *Journal of Home Economics, 71*(1), pp. 28–31.

Dunst, Carl J., and Trivette, Carol M. (1987). Enabling and empowering families: Conceptual and intervention issues. *School Psychology Review, 16*(4), p. 451.

Hook, Nancy, and Paolucci, Beatrice. (1970, May). The family as an ecosystem. *Journal of Home Economics, 62*(5), pp. 315–318.

Sarbaugh, L. (1988). A taxonomic approach to intercultural communication. In Young Yun Kim and William B. Gudykunst (Eds.), *Theories in intercultural communication* (pp. 22–38). Newbury Park, CA: Sage Publications Inc.

Schultz, T. P. (1994). *Human capital investment in women and men*. San Francisco, CA: Institute for Contemporary Studies.

Teun, A. van Dijk. (1987). *Communicating racism*. Newbury Park, CA: Sage Publications, Inc.

FURTHER READING

Paolucci, Beatrice, Hall, Olive A., and Axinn, Nancy. (1977). *Family decision making: An ecosystem approach*.

Schultz, T. P. (1994, August). *Human capital and economic development*. Presentation to the International Association of Agricultural Economists, Harare, Zimbabwe.

Schultz, T. P., and Tansel, A. (1992). *Measurement of returns to adult health: Morbidity effects on wage rates in Cote d'Iovoire and Ghana.* (Discussion Paper No. 663), New Haven, CT: Yale University, Economic Growth Center.

Schultz, T. W. (1967). The rate of return in allocating investments to education. *Journal of Human Resources, 2*(3), pp. 293–309.

PART II

Ethnic Diversity Among American Families

CHAPTER 4

African-American Families

Key Concepts

◆ Holistic
◆ Ethnic
◆ Minority
◆ Bondage

I am the darker brother
They send me to sit in the kitchen
When company comes,
But I laugh,
And eat well,
And grow strong.

Tomorrow,
I'll sit at the table
When company comes.
Nobody'll dare
Say to me,
"Eat in the kitchen,"
Then.

Besides,
They'll see how beautiful I am
And be ashamed.

    — Langston Hughes (1902–1967)

Langston Hughes, the award-winning African-American poet, understood the tragedies faced by Black people. Hughes believed that Blacks must first learn to accept themselves as beautiful, have self-esteem, and celebrate their own individuality in order to release their creativity and achieve their potential.

As we look at African-American families, the complex web of relationships between families and their environments is touched upon. As in all human systems, the specific African-American family structures arise from the interactions and interdependence of their parts and their environments. This chapter emphasizes general relationships rather than isolated relationships

within a variety of family styles or individuals. Therefore, the emergence of identifiable African-American family patterns is fundamentally different from the consecutive stacking of building blocks of information and data. A reductionist view of Black families can be useful, and may in some cases be necessary. However, reductionism and *holism* are complementary approaches and, when used in proper balance, help us obtain a deeper knowledge of the life of today's Black family.

African-Americans or Blacks represent the largest ethnic minority group in the United States. The term *ethnic* is used in the sociological sense of common ancestry, being born in a particular community or culture, and following a particular social pattern that gives one a sense of belonging, such as speaking a particular language or even a dialect of a language. According to Mindel, Habenstein, and Wright (1988), an ethnic group consists of people who share a historically unique social and cultural heritage that is passed on from generation to generation. The term *minority* is also used in the sociological sense and refers to unequal access to power in relationships which translates into access to opportunities, such as having less political and economic power than the majority (Wilkinson, 1993).

HISTORICAL BACKGROUND

For African-American families, whether their American lineage stemmed from the 225,000 "free" individuals in the North after the American Revolution, or from slavery in the South, their painful legacy cannot be adequately addressed here. Blacks have had one of the most unfortunate family life histories from which to build a viable ethnic American culture.

Black families adapted, evolved, and survived in spite of historical and statistical distortions to segregate and discriminate against them. Billingsley (1968) identified four distinct cultural traits that separate Blacks from other immigrants to the United States that help to define the special sense of people-hood. These are (1) Blacks came from a country with norms and values that were different from the American way of life; (2) Blacks came from different tribes with different cultures, languages, and traditions; (3) Black men came first, without women; and (4) Blacks came in bondage.

Much has been written about the destruction of the Black family as a result of slavery and the consequent weakening of the Black male's traditional functions. There are also scholars who support the notion that the Black family, as a social unit during slavery, provided an important survival mechanism for African-American people. The family was the haven for companionship, love, empathy for one's suffering, and the socialization of the children.

A tour of Colonial Williamsburg, Virginia, would be of help in understanding the American Black family during the period of slavery. In 1979, the Black historical and cultural experience was introduced into the historical replica of Colonial Williamsburg. The museum tour, called "The Other Half," depicts the daily life of slaves and freed Blacks and how they lived during that period. Lectures on the slave trade, urban and rural slavery, education, religion, and music are also introduced.

The authors strongly encourage you to read further about Black families. The resources suggested at the end of the chapter provide a short list of worthwhile information available. When reading further, it is important to study the research data, historical information, articles, and books with a knowledge of the applied major theoretical approaches which have, historically and presently, influenced the field of social science in the study of Black families.

Billingsley (1968) noted a significant mistreatment of Black families by social scientists in the past that contributed to the negative and distorted image of Black families in America today. Because Black family behavior patterns were seen as different from the majority, the behaviors were often described as deviant. He suggests that the misinformation, generated and perpetuated by social scientists, is partially responsible for the self-fulfilling prophecy.

DEMOGRAPHIC INFORMATION

In 1991, there were 30 million (12.1 percent) African-Americans in the United States. This represents the largest and most visible ethnic minority group in America (*Population Bulletin,* 1991). During the 1950s through the 1970s, Blacks made gains in education, health, living conditions, political access, and incomes. However, according to all demographic indications, the 1980s to the 1990s were not as favorable as the previous decades, and there were even some regressions in socioeconomic areas.

The movement of middle-class African-Americans to the suburbs has been on the increase. This trend has created an isolated and poorer inner-city community with insufficient material and human resources and institutions to support families adequately. Most African-Americans live in large metropolitan areas such as New York, Chicago, Detroit, Philadelphia, Los Angeles, Houston, Baltimore, and Washington.

In 1990, 84 percent of African-Americans lived in metropolitan areas. There is much concern about an increasing number of Blacks living in high poverty areas with the associated high crime rates and other social ills (O'Hare, et al., 1991). With the decline of manufacturing and blue-collar jobs in inner cities, many urban poor face even more isolation and unemployment, further undermining the strength of the Black family.

The median age of the Black population is 27.7 years, while that of the total U.S. population is 32 years. With higher birth rates of 2.4 children per woman, compared with 1.8 per white woman, there is a momentum for future population growth as the large number of Blacks in the childbearing ages will continue well into the twenty-first century. Birth rates for unmarried women increased dramatically in the 1980s. In 1988, 64 percent of Black infants born during that year were born out of wedlock—many to teenage mothers (Bureau of the Census, 1990).

An African-American male child born in 1988 can expect to live an average of 64.9 years, about eight years less than a Black female child. In comparison, an average white male child born in 1988 can expect to live an average of 72.3 years. Since 1985, there has been an actual decline in life expectancy for Blacks, especially Black males. For whites, there are continued gains in life expectancy. At every age, Blacks die at higher rates than whites (National Center for Health Statistics, 1987).

A particular problem facing the Black community is the unbalanced sex ratio, which creates competition for mates among Black women. This will continue to deny large numbers of Black women suitable mates.

THE ECOLOGY OF AFRICAN-AMERICAN FAMILIES

Using the holistic ecological system framework presented in Chapter 3 helps us look at various systems that impact families. Systems will include those within the family and those impacting families.

Family Structure

"The Black Family Nobody Knows," an article published in *Ebony* magazine by Massaquoi (1993), states, "Despite the fact that most Black families are close-knit, loving, hardworking, law-abiding, and stable, there is a widespread tendency to write Black families off as dysfunctional . . . and in disarray." What is often not reported is the fact that "the Black family has survived and continues to survive" (pp. 28–31). In A. Billingsley's (1993) book, *Climbing Jacob's Ladder*, he counters some of the most common myths, stereotypes, and misinformation that have been written about the Black family. Stable Black families are found in all economic classes; however, the largest group of predominantly stable Black families is the "non-poor working class." Dr. Billingsley identifies this group as the economic, social and political backbone of the Black community.

Like families of other ethnic groups, Black families have undergone dramatic evolutionary changes. While the traditional Black family, consisting of a married couple and children, is prevalent, there are other types of relationships that constitute a family and a feeling of belonging. More and more Black families are opting to remain childless in order to pursue their dual career goals.

Approximately 5 percent of Black adults are living together, without marriage, in stable, economically viable relationships (Massaquoi, 1993). Some of these relationships are a prelude to marriage and others are a substitute for marriage. Such living together has been rapidly increasing among Black Americans, reflecting a general trend in America.

The African-American community is experiencing dramatic and fundamental changes with a growing number of female-headed households living in poverty. According to a study by Lindblad-Goldberg (1986), Black single-parent households that function well have a number of characteristics in common, such as:

1. more internal organization with the single parent being clearly the one in charge,
2. mothers more responsive to their children's needs for authority,
3. less conflict between individuals within the household,
4. see themselves as quite adaptable to the ways of the outside world,
5. are cohesive and integrative in their relationships with each other, and
6. have control over their life space and can assert control over their living environment.

According to Lindblad-Goldberg, well-functioning, single-parent families see that the most important source of income for the family is employment. According to Sudarkasa (1993), Black women have adopted unique family forms of organization in response to the demographic, economic, and political realities of Black life in America.

Family scholars have argued that African-American families have always differed from the traditional European-American families and should not be expected to conform to the nuclear couple pattern. There are analysts who argue that the weak family structure resulted from the legacy of slavery when marriages among Blacks were not legally recognized. Other social scientists trace some of the family structure back to ancestral homes in African countries (Farley and Allen, 1991). An aspect most scholars agree upon is that kinship structures are interdependent and multigenerational. According to H. McAdoo (1979),

Black families are characterized by involvement with each other and adhere to a set of unwritten obligations and reciprocity to relatives regardless of age.

Gender Roles

There is a growing trend among Black women to remain single. According to Staples (1988), the institutional confinement of many Black males is one factor in this unprecedented number of single females. There are also other sociocultural factors that have impacted the relationship between Black males and females. Staples (1988) argues that the conflict between Black men and women is traced to incompatible roles. The societal prescription is for Black women to be passive and Black men dominant. However, Black women resist Black men's dominance. Often Black men who wish to be accorded the superior male role cannot fulfill the economic provider role due to unemployment. Income superiority helps support the dominance of men in American families. Black women with good jobs are more able to define their own status and gain more independence.

According to Coontz (1992), African-American working women have made the largest income gains relative to men of any ethnic group, thereby producing new options for women both inside and outside of marriage. Many Black women are models of strength, courage, and independence.

Black Children

There are many examples throughout history of the impenetrable bond between the African-American mother and her children (Brown and Forde, 1967; Bell, 1971; and Ladner, 1971). Rooted in African heritage, a mother's children hold a special value because they represent the continuity of life. Most Black mothers share a similar desire to give the very best to their children. All mothers want their children to grow up in a safe environment, get a good education, and make a contribution to their community and society. Black parents realize that for a Black child to survive and achieve, the child must develop an extensive set of different behavior repertoires concerning social relationships. According to McAdoo and McAdoo (1985), Black children's interactions are very complex because they need to interact in many different environments, each with differences in values, social expectations, and social relationships. Therefore, Black children must be able to demonstrate flexibility in many situations.

The child-rearing techniques of Black parents are often designed to prepare children to survive in environments foreign to most middle-class Americans. According to Staples (1988), Black parents are more likely than whites to use physical punishment, rather than verbal reasoning, to enforce discipline.

There is considerable current debate on the effect of the absence of a positive male role model for a majority of Black children today. However, studies fail to support a direct relationship between a father's absence and children's problem behaviors. Many Black children experience growing up without a father living in the home. Yet many are in contact with warm, nurturing male role models among relatives and friends in the extended family system.

For generations, Black families taught their children to be polite, submissive and to always conform to the larger society. Today, more and more Black families are challenging their children to take risks, accept their past heritage, and push for improvements in racial equality. Some parents place extraordinary demands on their youth to question and to challenge the role society plays concerning their struggles against marginality.

AFRICAN-AMERICAN VALUES

According to Guess (1990), the progress of African-Americans has been attributed historically to the role played by the African Church and the influence of Black ministers. Even today we hear the calls of ministers like Dr. E. Jones, President of the National Baptist Convention of America, Inc. (1993), who reminds the Black community that, "Black people need to come back to the Church where family values and morals are extolled . . . " (p. 98). The Black church is a by-product of slavery and has been considered the backbone of Black families.

According to Dr. Franklin Frazier (1932), during slavery, any African who was baptized was not considered a slave, but an indentured servant. However, this practice was quickly abandoned as a result of laws passed and decisions passed down by the courts. It was declared that there was no relationship between acceptance of the Christian faith, baptism, and the conferring of free status upon Africans. Today, many believe that Christianity is a liberating theology, and that, with God's help, people can endure and overcome life's pains.

Endurance of suffering while moving ahead is a major theme found in Black families. This theme is eloquently portrayed in the poem "Mother to Son" by Langston Hughes, the noted prize-winning Black poet. Many Black social scientists agree that various themes give coherence to Black families. The synthesis of these themes forms unique constellations of Black families and includes (1) strong kinship bonds among a variety of family households, (2) strong work, education, and achievement orientation, (3) high level of flexibility in family roles, (4) strong commitment to religious values and church participation, and (5) a humanistic orientation for perceiving the world and relationships.

AFRICAN-AMERICANS AND THE EDUCATIONAL SYSTEM

For many Black families, the message is clear. Education, even in times of economic uncertainty, will enhance the quality of their lives. There is a strong belief among Black families that education in the long run can eliminate discrimination and provide a certain measure of economic security.

Black children make up about 16 percent of the nation's public school students. Black children are the majority in a number of our largest school districts, comprising as much as 90 percent in cities like Atlanta, Detroit, and Washington, D.C. Although educational levels have risen for Blacks, Blacks are more likely to drop out of school than whites, except in suburban areas where the drop-out rates are nearly equal (National Center for Education Statistics, 1989).

Studies show that students are more likely to drop out of school when their grades are poor, or when they are older than their classmates. They are also at higher risk of dropping out when they come from single-parent households, live in the center of metropolitan areas, or have parents who never finished school themselves. All these factors have been statistically attributed to poverty. Coontz (1992), in her book, *The Way We Never Were,* asks ironically, "Why launch new school reforms when . . . the real key to educational performance is whether a child comes from a two-parent family? Why experiment with new anti-poverty programs when . . . the most important indicator of poverty is whether there are two parents at home?" When this argument is used, blame is placed on the single-parent family. The solution is simple. "Marriage is the ticket out of poverty" (p. 256).

There is evidence suggesting that the prevailing negative social climate of schools can lead to good students performing below their ability and poor students being discouraged from improving. Complex social issues and unequal access to quality learning environments in the home, neighborhood, and school are sometimes overlooked as possible reasons for poor academic achievement and low graduation rates.

According to Kunjufu (1982), there is a discrepancy between what the inner-city Black male learns in his neighborhood environment and the required behavior for success in the educational system and workplace. Kunjufu further states that a number of young men have skills that serve them well on the streets, but poorly in the rest of society. For example, aggressive interpersonal skills necessary for street survival contribute to high rates of suspensions and other disciplinary actions in school. The results are often lower academic achievement, or high dropout rates.

Meanwhile, Black women tend to be more highly educated than Black men at all levels, except at the doctoral level. According to the U.S. Bureau of the Census (1991), Black men continue to lag behind Black women educationally. Achieving a higher level of education has helped Black women become involved in the workplace and has placed them at an economic advantage. The service and high technology sectors of the U.S. economy are continually growing and Black women are becoming more competitive in the expanding economy. However, Black men with less education than women are often unable to secure employment in a shrinking industrial marketplace.

AFRICAN-AMERICANS AND THE HEALTH CARE SYSTEM

The eight major killers and disablers of African-Americans are: cardiovascular disease, cancer, diabetes, substance abuse or chemical dependency (including heavy alcohol use and smoking), violence (homicide and suicide), accidents, infant mortality, and AIDS (acquired immune deficiency syndrome) (Goodwin, 1990).

There are alarming indications that some of these health risks are increasing. For example, cancer rates for Black males and females are higher than the rates for white counterparts. The cancer rate is 17 percent for Black males compared to 5.9 percent for white males, and 8.3 percent for Black females, compared to 6.5 percent for white females (National Cancer Institute, 1986). Dr. Freeman, President of the American Cancer Society, estimates that approximately one-third of Black Americans either don't have the money or insurance to see a doctor, or are so fearful of cancer they are likely to put off a physical exam until it is too late (Barrow, 1990).

The elderly, who form the fastest growing segment of the Black population, are undergoing a crisis in medical care. The Black elderly are more likely to be sick and disabled than the white elderly. They have higher rates of chronic disease, functional impairment, high blood pressure, and other indicators of risk.

A large portion of elderly Blacks no longer live in the same city as relatives, and are thus deprived of needed in-home care and support. There is the ideal notion that the Black elderly will be taken care of by relatives and will never need to be placed in a nursing home. The use of nursing homes by Blacks may seem relatively new; however, nursing home care for the Black elderly has been around since the slave era. According to Barrows (1990), there were between two to three hundred homes for the Black aged established since 1860. Today, there is a shortage of Black professionals in the field of gerontology.

One of the most disturbing differences between Blacks and whites is the fact that Black infants die at twice the rate of white infants in the United States (O'Hare, et al., 1991). Much of this disparity is associated with low birth-weight, placing infants at higher risk of death. Low birth-weight is attributed to poor nutrition, poor health, poor prenatal care, smoking, preteen and early teen pregnancy, and other harmful lifestyle habits of mothers during pregnancy. Preteen and teen pregnancies, being very high in the Black community, are a significant factor hampering healthy development and survival of infants and mothers.

AFRICAN-AMERICANS AND THE GOVERNMENT

Prior to the passage of the Voting Rights Act of 1965, Blacks, especially in the southern states, were discouraged and even barred from voting in elections. Poll taxes and literacy tests were both used to discourage or actually prevent Black voter registration. Today, all Blacks can vote. In fact, Blacks are becoming more involved in politics, running for office, getting elected, and serving in government at all levels, including the President's cabinet and the Supreme Court. In some states, Blacks constitute a significant number of voters, largely supporting the Democratic Party. Blacks tend to support African-American candidates. An example of the strength of the collective Black and liberal vote was witnessed recently in Virginia where Lawrence Douglas Wilder became the first African-American elected governor of any state in the history of the U.S.

AFRICAN-AMERICANS AND THE CRIMINAL JUSTICE SYSTEM

A vast majority of the Black community believes that the criminal justice system discriminates against them, especially against the Black male. A look at the 8 to 1 per capita ratio of Blacks to whites in prison needs further investigation. It is time for social scientists interested in social justice to explore the probability of institutional racism within the various levels of the judiciary system (Mann, 1993).

Americans are confronted daily with numerous negative stereotypes labeling and demeaning the status of Black men. Television and other media perpetuate the destructive images. Society must be reminded that a majority of Black men function responsibly and in ways that gain the respect of their families and communities.

AFRICAN-AMERICANS AND THE ECONOMIC SYSTEM

During the period 1970 to 1990, African-Americans made tremendous progress toward becoming active participants in the economic system of the U.S. More than a third of African-Americans are now earning middle-class or higher incomes. In 1989, one in seven Black families, about one million, had a yearly income of $50,000 or more. Affluent Black families tend to be well educated (32 percent are college graduates), homeowners (77 percent), in their prime earning ages (66 percent are age 35 to 55), married (79 percent), and living in suburban areas (U.S. Bureau of the Census, 1990).

Black-owned businesses increased 126 percent within 15 years, according to the Bureau of the Census (1991). Many of these new businesses were very small firms with only 17 percent having paid employees. There are Black-owned companies, as identified on the Black Enterprise 100s, that are competing successfully in corporate America. For example, Honeywell's Senior Vice President, Manny Jackson, organized an investor group to purchase controlling interest in the Harlem Globetrotters (Graves, 1993). This is one example of business investments and ownership opportunities undertaken by African-Americans. At the same time, many top-level Black executives in corporate America have found that, beyond the glass ceiling, there are often barriers of spiked steel (Graves, 1993), for example, intimidation and unjustified denial of credit-worthiness when applying for mortgage, business, or personal loans.

Over the past decade, however, African-American workers have lost economic ground and are faced again with high unemployment, intermittent work, and low pay. This sporadic work history often leads to lack of health care and adequate retirement benefits for Blacks. Older Blacks often live in poverty, retire early due to poor health, or work past normal retirement age in order to maintain some economic security (Allen, 1988). Elderly Blacks earn approximately one-third less retirement income than the majority of Americans.

According to researchers, elderly Blacks see themselves in three groups: (1) workers, 55 and over who are working 20 or more hours a week; (2) retirees, who are not working at all, or working less than 20 hours a week; and (3) non-retirees, those not working or those working less than 20 hours a week but who do not see themselves as being retired (Allen, 1988). Those particularly disadvantaged are the "non-retired" who are financially less secure, less educated, and less healthy. A significant percentage of "non-retired" are female heads of households who tend to live in rural areas.

Between 1990 and the year 2000, it is expected that Blacks will comprise up to 20 percent of the new entrants into the labor force. This labor force will divide Blacks along educational and socioeconomic lines. If present trends continue, a disproportionate number of Blacks will form an underclass, lacking the educational training required for upward mobility and remaining in low-paying jobs such as those found in the service sectors (O'Hare, et al., 1991). The inappropriate early tracking of many African-Americans into dead-end jobs often produces low-paid workers and low-income retirees.

According to a study by Joe and Yu (1984), the decrease of Black men of working age in the labor force corresponds closely to the percentage increase of black women heading families alone. In 1989, Black female-headed households had only a third of the annual income of Black married couple families, $11,600 compared to $30,700 (O'Hare, et al., 1991).

SERVING AFRICAN-AMERICAN FAMILIES

As helping professionals in your chosen career, you will meet many African-American families. With the increase of African-Americans in higher education, many Black professionals will be working side by side with you. Service rendered must be of high standard. Black and other helping professionals will serve many clients of all diverse groups. Professional ethics and the licensing of agencies require nondiscrimination and high standards of performance.

Cooperating with Black churches, Black sororities and fraternities, and a variety of other organizations will facilitate service to Black families. The same approach may work well with other ethnic and multi-cultural groups. Many community groups are willing to contribute services, mentoring, and money to help Black youth and others, for example. In part, your role will be one of activating various community resources.

CONCLUSIONS

African-Americans have made remarkable gains in one generation. No other ethnic minority group can claim the achievements made in this short time.

However, what does the future hold? There are many indications that Black families will become bipolar in economic distribution; that is, the span between affluent Blacks and poor Blacks is widening, with little evidence of a growing Black middle class bridging the gap.

A majority of Black children live in one-parent households. The income available to these families is insufficient to move them out of poverty. Especially vulnerable is the young Black male who is struggling to achieve a higher quality of life without good strategies for success. However, even with many odds against them, many Black children from poor families become successful adults.

Derrick Bell (1992) leaves us with a powerful message in his national best seller, *Faces at the Bottom of the Well:* "We yearn that our civil rights work will be crowned with success, but what we really want—want even more than success—is meaning. . . . It is a story less of success than of survival through an unremitting struggle that leaves no room for giving up. We are all part of that history and it is still unfolding . . . " (pp. 198, 200).

STUDY QUESTIONS

1. Define the terms: ethnic, minority, discrimination, prejudice, holistic, segregation.
2. Billingsley believes social scientists have misrepresented African-Americans. List three of his reasons.
3. List at least 10 demographic findings from Census Data about Black citizens and Black families.
4. Describe the family structure of African-American families.
5. Describe Black gender roles as described by researchers.
6. State evidence of African-American family values.
7. List 10 findings from studies of Black children and adults in the educational system.
8. Summarize the findings regarding the health and involvement of Blacks within the health care system.
9. List findings regarding elderly Black people.
10. List evidence of Black Americans' involvement with the governmental system.
11. List findings from data showing participation of Black Americans in the economic system.

APPLICATIONS

1. Is it true that the best studies of Black families have been done by Black scholars? List five reasons why you believe this statement is true and five reasons why it is not true.

2. What are some basic *similarities* between Black children and their families, and majority children and their families? Describe these similarities in a two-page essay.

3. What are some basic *differences* between Black children and their families, and majority children and their families? Describe these differences in a two-page essay.

4. Assume that you and your children are recipients of unequal treatment. Write a one-page essay stating how you would feel and how you would react as a parent.

5. List five examples of practices and behaviors that demonstrate institutional racism. State in a one-page essay how each institution in question should correct the behavior.

6. Review an encyclopedia of prominent Black Americans from your library. Select one individual and write a one-page essay on the factors that contributed to that individual's success.

REFERENCES

Allen, R. (Ed.). (1988, May/June). Older minorities in work and retirement. *Working Age, 3*(6), 1.

Barrow, L. (1990, November). Yes, cancer kills! But it doesn't have to kill you. *The Crisis Magazine* (pp. 11-15). Baltimore, MD: National Association for the Advancement of Colored People.

Bell, R. (1971). The relative importance of mother and wife roles among Negro lower-class women. In R. Staples (Ed.), *The Black family: Essays and studies* (pp. 248–256). Belmont, CA: Wadsworth.

Bell, R. (1992). *Faces at the bottom of the well*. New York, NY: Basic Books.

Bennett, L. (1993, August). Changing church confronts the changing black family. *Ebony, 18*(10), 94–100.

Billingsley, A. (1968). *Black families in white America*. Englewood Cliffs, NJ: Prentice-Hall.

Billingsley, A. (1970). Black families and white social science. *Journal of Social Issues, 26*(3), 127–142.

Billingsley, A. (1993). *Climbing Jacob's ladder*. Englewood Cliffs, NJ: Prentice-Hall.

Brown, A., and Forde, D. (1967). *African systems of kinship and marriage*. New York, NY: Oxford Press.

Bureau of the Census. (1990 and 1991). Department of Commerce, Washington, DC: U.S. Government Printing Office.

Coontz, S. (1992). *The way we never were*. New York, NY: Basic Books.

Farley, R., and Allen, W. (1991). Education strategies for the 90s. In J. Dewart (Ed.), *The State of Black America 1991* (pp. 95–110). New York, NY: National Urban League, Inc.

Frazier, Franklin. (1932). *The free Negro family.* Nashville, TN: Fisk University Press.

Gidding, P. (1990, March/April). Education, race, and reality: A legacy of the 60s. *Change,* pp. 13–17.

Goodwin, N. (1990, November). Heart disease and stroke—The leading killer of African-Americans. *The Crisis Magazine* (pp. 10, 30). Baltimore, MD: National Association for the Advancement of Colored People.

Graves, E. (Ed.). (1993, July). No time to rest. *Black Enterprise,* p. 9.

Guess, J. (1990, June/July). Freedom's warriors—The fighting Black clergy: An historical overview. *The Crisis Magazine* (pp. 14–30). National Association for the Advancement of Colored People.

Hughes, Langston, and Bontemps, Arna. (Eds.). (1951). *The poetry of the Negro, 1746–1949.* Garden City, NY: Doubleday.

Joe, T., and Yu, P. (1984). *The "flip side" of Black families headed by women: The economic status of Black men.* Washington, DC: The Center for the Study of Social Policy.

Jones, E. (1993, August). An interview on the topic, "Changing Church Confronts the Changing Black Family." *Ebony, 18*(10), pp. 94–100.

Kunjufu, J. (1982). *Counteracting the conspiracy to destroy young Black boys* (Vol. 1). Chicago, IL: African American Images.

Lindblad-Goldberg, M. (1986). Results of a federal study of Black single parent families. *Behavior Today, 17*(34), 2–3.

Mann, C. R. (1994). The reality of a racist criminal justice system. In R. C. Monk (Ed.), *Taking sides.* Guilford, CT: The Dushkin Publishing Group Inc.

McAdoo, H. (1979). *American ethnic family.* Racine, WI: The Johnson Foundation.

McAdoo, H. Pipes, and McAdoo, J. Lewis. (1985). *Black children and social and educational and parental environments.* Beverly Hills, CA: Sage Publications.

Massaquoi, H. (1993, August). The Black family nobody knows. *Ebony,* pp. 28–31.

Mindel, C., Habenstein, R., and Wright, R. (Eds.). (1988). *Ethnic families in America.* New York, NY: Elsevier.

National Cancer Institute. (1986). *Cancer among Blacks and other minorities: Statistical profiles.* U.S. Department of Health and Human Services, Public Health Services. Washington, DC: U.S. Government Printing Office.

National Center for Health Statistics. (1987). *Vital Statistics of the United States.* Washington, DC: U.S. Government Printing Office.

O'Hare, W., Pollard, K., Mann, T., and Kent, M. (1991, July). African-Americans in the 1990s. *Population Bulletin.*

Staples, R. (1988). The Black American family. In C. Mindel, R. Habenstein, and R. Wright (Eds.), *Ethnic Families in America* (pp. 303–324). New York, NY: Elsevier.

Sudarkasa, N. (1993). Female-headed African-American households: Some neglected dimensions. In H. McAdoo (Ed.), *Family ethnicity: Strength in diversity* (pp. 81–89). New York: Sage Publications.

Wilkinson, D. (1993). Family ethnicity in America. In H. McAdoo (Ed.), *Family ethnicity: Strength in diversity* (pp. 15–59). New York, NY: Sage Publications.

FURTHER READING

McAdoo, Harriet, and McAdoo, John Lewis. (Eds.). (1985). *Black children.* Beverly Hills, CA: Sage Publications, Inc.

Ploski, Harry A., and Williams, James. (Eds.). (1989). *The Negro almanac: A reference work on African-Americans* (5th ed.). Detroit, MI: Gale Research, Inc.

MEDIA RECOMMENDATIONS

A Question of Color. (1992). 58 minutes, 16 mm. Resolution, Inc., California Newsreel, 149 Ninth St., Suite 420, San Francisco, CA 94103.

Black History: Lost, Stolen, or Strayed. (1965). 60 minutes, video. Insight Media, 2162 Broadway, New York, NY 10024.

I'll Fly Away. PBS Television Series, Video. (Available in some libraries and from local TV stations.) Washington Educational Television Association, Box 2626, Washington, DC. Phone: 703-998-2600.

CHAPTER 5

Hispanic-American Families

Key Concepts

◆ Hispanics

◆ Anglos

◆ Three Rs of Hispanic Values

Six-year-old Gloria skipped into her grandfather's corner grocery store. She carried her first reader under her arm and exclaimed as she embraced her grandfather, "Abuelito, Abuelito, I learned to write my name today!"

Grandfather Martinez stopped arranging shelves and embraced Gloria, saying in his native Spanish, "¿Verdad? Aqui. ¿Puede mostrarme?" ("Is that true? Can you show me?"). He tore a corner off some wrapping paper and handed her a stubby pencil he carried in his apron.

Gloria wrote the letters G L O R I A in her six-year-old script and proudly showed Grandfather Abuelito. "¡Que Bueno!" ("How Great!"), he exclaimed, admiring her work. Then he opened his wallet, tucked the scrap of paper in for safekeeping, and carried it for many years.

Gloria felt the warmth of her grandfather's love and his appreciation of her success for all her growing-up years.

Family support for education, as indicated in the above story of Gloria and her grandfather, is evident in many Hispanic parents and grandparents. They are often even more overtly persistent in their encouragement of education for their children and grandchildren when they themselves have missed out on educational opportunities.

BRIEF HISTORY OF THREE MAJOR HISPANIC GROUPS

There are three Hispanic groups that comprise the majority of Hispanics in the United States. These are Mexican, Puerto Rican, and Cuban Hispanics. Combined, they make up 75 percent of all U.S. Hispanics (Bureau of the Census, 1990). Most of the remainder come from Central and South American countries and the Caribbean. Geographically, Hispanics live in every corner of this nation. However, heavy concentrations can be found in certain regions, with

Puerto Ricans living in the East and Northeast, Cubans in Florida and the Southeast, Mexicans in Texas and the Southwest, and South and Central Americans in the West and the Southwest.

Population Data

The U.S. Bureau of the Census (1990) reports that the number of Hispanics living in the U.S. soared from 9.1 million (4.5 percent of the population) in 1970, to an estimated 24.1 million (9.5 percent) by 1992, and is expected to reach 80.7 million (21.1 percent) by 2050. About three of five U.S. Hispanics are of Mexican descent, and seven of ten live in four states: California (34 percent of the total), Texas (19 percent), New York (10 percent), and Florida (7 percent).

Comparing Hispanics to non-Hispanic whites or "Anglos," the Census Bureau (1990) reports (Figure 5–1) that, on the whole, Hispanics are younger and less educated than non-Hispanic whites. The median age for Hispanics is 26 years and for Anglos 35 years. Eleven percent of Hispanic children are under age five, as compared to seven percent of Anglo children. Five percent of Hispanics are over age 65, while 14 percent of non-Hispanic whites are 65 or older. Educationally, 27 percent of Hispanic youth complete high school as compared to 37 percent of Anglos. Hispanics with associate or bachelor's degrees number 10 percent as compared to 21 percent for Anglos.

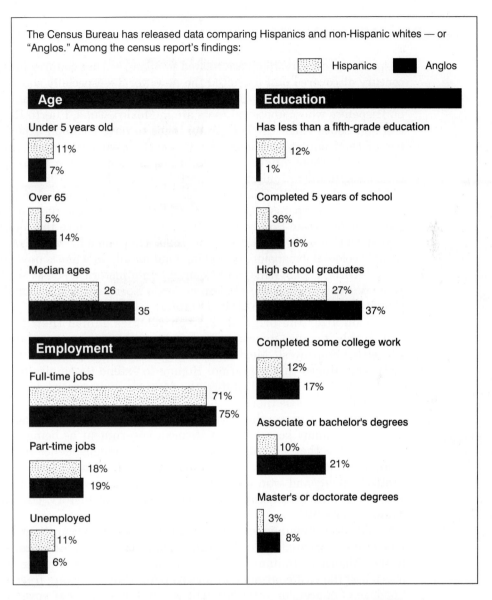

The Census Bureau has released data comparing Hispanics and non-Hispanic whites — or "Anglos." Among the census report's findings:

Hispanics   Anglos

Age

Under 5 years old
11%
7%

Over 65
5%
14%

Median ages
26
35

Employment

Full-time jobs
71%
75%

Part-time jobs
18%
19%

Unemployed
11%
6%

Education

Has less than a fifth-grade education
12%
1%

Completed 5 years of school
36%
16%

High school graduates
27%
37%

Completed some college work
12%
17%

Associate or bachelor's degrees
10%
21%

Master's or doctorate degrees
3%
8%

Figure 5–1. *Comparing Hispanics and Anglos: Age, Employment, and Education (percentages)*

Source: Bureau of the Census, U.S. Department of Commerce, 1990.

WHO ARE THE HISPANICS?

Hispanic-Americans' roots are related to Spain, as that country in the fifteenth century discovered and exploited the new world—especially southern parts of the U.S., Mexico, Central America, and South America. This chapter will focus on Hispanics whose ancestral roots are in Mexico, Cuba, Puerto Rico, and Central and South America. This group tends to have common experience in the use of the Spanish language. However, the diversity among the groups is grounded in their different points of origin, immigration history, and social class backgrounds (Goldscheider, 1991; Bean and Tienda, 1987).

As early as 1565, Spanish explorers and colonists settled in parts of what is now Florida. Spanish-speaking peoples, also, were the first to migrate into the great American Southwest, settling there even before the founding of the Plymouth Colony by the Pilgrims in 1620. They came by way of Mexico during Spain's colonial expansion, occupying land mainly in what is now New Mexico, Texas, Arizona, California, and Colorado. In a historical sense, settlers of Hispanic descent predate the settlers of Anglo-European origin, populating what is today the Southwestern United States.

Soon after the original thirteen colonies gained their freedom from British rule, massive migration began across the continent and into the Spanish-settled Southwest. Mexico, having gained its independence from Spain in 1821, encouraged this migration. Hoping to extend its empire to what is now the Southwestern United States, the Mexican government promised land to those willing to settle there.

After many years, those who settled there became increasingly difficult to govern, and many perceived the Mexican government as being so unjust and intrusive that they were driven to declare their independence from its oppression. In 1836, against what appeared to be insurmountable odds, Texans united, fought, and won their freedom in the decisive battle of San Jacinto. And thus came into being, for a brief moment in history, the "Republic of Texas" (Nava, 1972).

The new Republic encompassed the Great American Southwest, a conglomerate of original Spanish settlers, pioneering Anglo-Americans, as well as native American Indians. During the ensuing decades, migration from the south and the east continued at a swift pace. People seeking freedom from the bondage of oppression often brought with them a legacy of poverty. Mexicans, desirous of better economic and social environments, traveled north to settle and start anew. They entered the new republic freely—with no legal restraints—to join relatives, find work, and, thus, create a better existence. In the words of Abalos (1986), "our forbearers came to this country seeking a new life, a better life, at the cost of great personal suffering and risk" (p. 9).

Occurring simultaneously with the Spanish invasion of the mainland in the 1500s was the invasion of the Caribbean island now known as Puerto Rico. Spanish conquerors brought their language, literature, food preferences, and life values with them. They brought African slaves to the Island to work in the production of sugar cane. Over time, the native Taino Indian way of life became inextricably meshed with the Spanish and African influences.

Another invasion of Puerto Rico occurred in 1898 when the island became the property of the United States as a result of the Spanish-American War. In 1917, Puerto Ricans were granted U.S. citizenship, which greatly facilitated migration between the island and the mainland. It is believed that the strong influence of colonization by the United States and the ease of passage between the two greatly affected the lack of stability in Puerto Rican family life (Garcia-Preto, 1982).

The Caribbean island of Cuba, like Puerto Rico, was also invaded and colonized by Spanish conquistadors in the 1500s. Unlike Puerto Rico, Cuba was able to gain independence from United States' rule resulting from the Spanish-American War, and remained tied to the U.S. only through limited political and economic interest until the Cuban Revolution in 1959.

The course of economic development in Cuba since its independence resulted in the bulk of the wealth being in the hands of a small percentage of its citizens. After decades of exploitation, a large underclass was ripe for revolution and triumphed under Fidel Castro's socialist leadership. An immediate exodus from the island by the elite class ensued, with thousands choosing to migrate to the state of Florida, just 90 miles across the water.

While Cuban migration to the United States has occurred over many decades, the vast migration after 1959 consisted of the well-educated middle and upper classes. They were welcomed by Americans with "open arms" because they were "fleeing from communism" (Bernal, 1982, p. 188).

Prejudice

The reception of Hispanics by the original settlers in virtually all cases was less than enthusiastic, however. The newcomers were unwelcome and were treated with disdain and intolerable prejudice. Today it might seem unthinkable that human beings would begrudge other human beings the right to pursue a better existence for themselves and family; but Mexicans and other immigrants were—and are still today—scorned by those who arrived here first. Discrimination seems to be a common plight of new immigrants. Perhaps the fact that some migrated from Mexico, a country with which the U.S. had had military conflicts, or the fact that many immigrants were so culturally, ethnically, and linguistically distinct, encouraged the prejudice toward immigrants arriving in the "new republic."

Today, throughout the land areas that border Mexico, prejudice persists in various forms and degrees, not only toward Mexicans, but toward other Hispanics who immigrate from Central and South America as well. Pressure exerted by the majority culture on immigrants to become assimilated into a homogeneous national culture is pervasive and not always subtle. Many Hispanics—superbly proud of their roots and distinct national heritages—tenaciously resist this pressure. It is today ironic that some Hispanics who have become citizens and acculturated often speak against the immigration of others, even those from their own country of origin. Unlike Anglo-European Americans, Hispanic-Americans sustain and reinforce their culture largely due to the geographic proximity of their ancestral countries and islands.

HISPANICS: LIKENESSES AND DIFFERENCES

Even though geographic origins are varied, Hispanics have in common several salient cultural characteristics that facilitate their examination as a group. Many Hispanics will attest to the fact that they are more alike than different in areas that really matter, and for that reason will allow themselves—with inclusive pride—to be referred to as Hispanics.

Yet Hispanics are fiercely proud of their diversity. Each group is unique due to several factors, such as national ancestry, degree of acculturation, socioeconomic status, degree of bilingualism, and number of generations living in this country.

Most Hispanics prefer to be identified and called by their country of origin, such as Mexican-American, Cuban-American, or Spanish-American, rather than by such pan-ethnic terms like Latino or even Hispanic (Mann and Kalish, 1991, p. 4). Many Mexican-Americans prefer the term Chicano, because it is a self-chosen identifying term that connotes pride in the unique bicultural heritage of an American of Mexican descent. *Boricua, Latino,* and *La Raza* are also words which, according to Abalos (1986, p. 9), "represent a political decision to create an autonomous and self-determining life for Latinos." The personal decision of how to refer to the different groups lies ultimately with the individuals and their distinct preference. Some may prefer to be called Americans. Of course, a large percentage have been born in the United States and are Americans, while others are in various stages of becoming American citizens in the legal sense.

The Spanish Language

The Spanish language is one of the most salient characteristics of all the Hispanic people whose roots are ultimately from Spain. The beautiful, melodious Spanish language has been preserved by many American Hispanics, making it one of the proud characteristics held in common across groups. One's native language is an intimate, integral, and very personal part of the self. To have it recognized and valued is a boost to one's self-esteem. Conversely, to have one's language discredited or negated can be an assault on one's personhood.

The language of the home is the thread that tangibly connects individuals to loved ones. To eradicate the language, or even to suggest such an action, can have immediate—as well as long-term—deleterious effects on individuals and families (Fillmore and Britsch, 1988). To be stripped totally of one's mother tongue and culture is tantamount to negating one's personal identity—alas, one's own personhood. Though there are some who deny this (Chavez, 1991; and Rodriguez, 1981), obliteration of one's native language should not be sought or expected of any cultural group or individual. Many more choices exist for those with the ability to use both languages.

It is incumbent upon educational institutions, particularly those serving the young, to make efforts to value and help preserve students' mother tongues, even while encouraging children to learn English. Weakening of the mother tongue may contribute to the weakening of the family. Disparaging one's language may add to the alienation of the individual (Fillmore and Britsch, 1988).

The Spanish language is, of course, a language spoken by about 500 million people in Spain and in the Western Hemisphere. There is a large body of Spanish literature spanning many centuries. Until 1967, when the Bilingual Education Act became law, children were penalized in schools if they spoke a language other than English. Despite the educational intent of this practice, it served to discourage most children and to plant doubts in their minds about the value of their language, sometimes resulting in their partial or total avoidance of the language.

Since the implementation of the Bilingual Education Act, schools have provided teachers who can help children build on their native language while learning English. Introducing the children's cultures as well as their languages into the school and class environment is considered a more appropriate approach in a multicultural world. Under the old system, many Hispanics never learned to write or read Spanish or to understand its structure, even though they used the language in their most intimate associations. Modern approaches in the schools today maintain respect for the Spanish language and culture.

In contrast, some Hispanic parents still insist that schools teach their children English, and only English. They may equate proficiency in English with success in obtaining good jobs in the future, unaware of the effect on the child's self-image, and overlooking the advantages of fluent bilingual abilities. Some parents will even ask that no Spanish be spoken to their children in school, and will not allow their children to be placed in a bilingual class, fearing that their learning of English will be impeded. Some parents desire that their children maintain and preserve their native Spanish, but see this as a parental responsibility. Parental attitudes may be colored by their own struggle to learn English and the opportunity to obtain better jobs because of their English language proficiency. Professionals can help children by working closely with parents to clarify the immediate and long-term benefits of having bilingual and bicultural expertise.

State and national efforts to legislate "English-only" as the "official language of the government" tend to surface occasionally. While the intent of such bills may be to speed the learning of English, to expedite assimilation of language minorities into the mainstream culture, and to maintain the efficiency and cohesiveness of a single common language, they are considered by proponents of bilingual education to be restrictive of the civil rights and opportunities of non-English-speaking Americans, as well as unnecessary (Lyons, 1993).

THE ECOLOGY OF HISPANIC-AMERICAN FAMILIES

Although there is much diversity among Hispanic-Americans, certain important values are held in common by all groups (Diaz-Guerrero, 1976). Hispanics are traditional in orientation and affiliative in nature. Values rooted in the Judeo-Christian religious tradition strongly affect male and female roles and how these roles are played out within the family. Many Hispanics' views of work, people, and life are affected in many of the same ways as similarly rooted traditional cultures.

RELIGIOUS FOUNDATION OF HISPANIC FAMILIES

Hispanics have lived and functioned with the pronounced influence of Judeo-Christian principles on family roles and interpersonal relationships. Spaniards first introduced the Roman Catholic faith to the indigenous peoples of the new world. Through the centuries, a mingling of the old world religion with the beliefs of native peoples resulted in Christian converts who practiced the religion but still held on to some indigenous beliefs, such as *ojo* ("evil eye") and *enbrujo* ("witchcraft") (Falicov, 1982, p. 135).

When helping professionals learn of the beliefs held by clients they serve, it is important to withhold judgment and avoid making insensitive comments, no matter how unusual or different the belief may be or how much one disagrees with it. A nonjudgmental attitude allows a rapport to develop, which, in turn, facilitates a better understanding of the individual's functioning.

Catholicism is the professed religion of the majority of Hispanics, even though many do not actively practice the faith. Today, however, significant numbers of Hispanics are leaving Catholicism to join Protestant denominations, and some are simply rejecting religious affiliation altogether. The appeal of some Protestant denominations to Hispanics is due to the fact that the ministers generally come from a Latino background, speak Spanish, share the daily hardships of the community, and provide more of an egalitarian church service based on Scripture (Abalos, 1986).

Today, however, the Catholic church is facing many changes. In 1993, a committee of U.S. Catholic bishops developed a document on marriage that encourages Roman Catholics to move beyond the sexual stereotypes they grew up with and to strive toward equality of the sexes. Stating that "marriage is a partnership of man and woman equal in dignity and value," the statement was developed for presentation at the annual meeting of the National Conference of Catholic Bishops (*The Houston Chronicle*, November 6, 1993).

As change takes place, many Hispanics profess to be Catholic as an automatic response instead of a practicing reality in their lives. As individual Hispanics consider traditions and practices that tend to bind more than liberate, they may choose from other belief systems or religious options, including the option of practicing no formal religion at all.

HISPANIC FAMILY STRUCTURES

In searching for new economic opportunities and accepting new realities, Hispanics make efforts to maintain contact with their families of origin. The sanctity of the family is particularly emphasized in traditional Hispanic culture. It is within the context of the family that the individual finds security and "overwhelming strength" (Abalos, 1986).

"There's No Question: Family Comes First," declares a newspaper headline about Dr. Chad Richardson's (1993) research on Mexican families living in Northern Mexico along the United States border. Adults in these families enter the U.S. daily to work. In search of employment, some venture deeper into the United States and stay longer, leaving family behind. "Most people in Mexico do not want to leave their families, their homes and their country behind," says Dr. Richardson, a sociology professor and director of the Border Life Project at the University of Texas at Brownsville. "Awfully strong pressures, economic and otherwise, force them to go," he states. He continues, "The family is much more important in Mexico than in the United States" (p. 10). Financial needs often force children to drop out of school to help support the family. Individual goals become subordinated to the needs of the family.

Likewise, Mexican-Americans—especially the more recent immigrants—are oriented strongly toward the family, which is considered to be the "dominant source of advice and help in all generations" (Griswold del Castillo, 1984, p. 132).

While the notion that Hispanics are more family-oriented than Anglos has been a consistent theme in the social science literature for decades, the recent rise in the number of disrupted families headed by females is seen as an outcome of highly stressful environments (Frisbie, 1993). Census data show that, between 1960 and 1980, while the average size of Hispanic households decreased, marital disruption simultaneously increased (Bean and Tienda, 1987).

Nearly 23 percent of all Hispanic families are headed by single females, compared to 16 percent of white families. The percentage of single-parent families amongst Puerto Rican Hispanics is 44 percent, or double the Hispanic percentage, and triple the non-Hispanic Anglo average (Valdivieso and Davis, 1988).

Specifically, among Mexican-Americans and Cuban-Americans, statistics show that marital stability is inversely related to educational attainment. That is, the more education achieved, the less marital stability. Among Puerto Rican Hispanics, however, marital stability increases with educational attainment (Frisbie, 1993). Furthermore, even though Puerto Ricans have the highest fertility rate of all Hispanic groups, statistics show that for all groups, lower educational levels are positively correlated with higher fertility rates (Bean and Tienda, 1987). In short, fertility decreases for all groups with increases in education; however, marital stability increases for Puerto Ricans and decreases for Mexican- and Cuban-Americans with increases in education.

To be sure, Hispanic families have not escaped the societal assaults that negatively affect families of all cultural groups today. Divorce has taken its toll

Talk It Over

Mr. Santos, appearing upset, requested a conference with Mrs. Angella, the teacher of his four-year-old son, Jorge. While talking with the teacher, Mr. Santos thanked her for all she had done for Jorge since he enrolled in the preschool only six months before. The boy was now speaking English well and seemed to be on his way to becoming thoroughly bilingual. But the fact that Jorge had learned a great deal did not detract from Mr. Santos' distress. He wanted to address the gnawing concern that was on his mind. He was disturbed as he watched his son "playing house" in the home center of the classroom. It seemed that Jorge enjoyed dressing up like a "Mommy" as he played with the other children. "What are you going to do about it?" he emphatically asked the teacher.

Mrs. Angella, the teacher, believed that children gained perspective and understanding by playing out many roles in the classroom. She was challenged to explain why by the traditionally oriented father. What would you say and do if you were the teacher?

on Hispanic families and has seriously challenged the traditional, strongly held concept of family as a sacred institution and marriage as a life-long proposition.

MALE ROLES IN THE HISPANIC FAMILY

The authority of the husband as head of the wife and household is defined in the Bible, and is literally lived out in the traditional Hispanic nuclear family unit. The authority of the husband and father is seldom questioned or disputed. The father's role is expected to be one of breadwinner and protector of the family. He provides for the family's physical needs and monitors and controls all members' participation in the world outside the home. This sovereign role is often perceived by the society at large as "macho" or chauvinistic and extremely undemocratic. However, in the Hispanic culture, machismo refers to a role that carries major responsibility for others, namely the family. The concept of "manliness" is more synonymous with "macho" for most Hispanics. Such a definition is devoid of arrogance or chauvinistic characteristics often ascribed to the term by mainstream society. To Hispanics, the male role commands respect and significant regard, not because of the individual who plays the role but because of what the role involves.

FEMALE ROLES IN THE HISPANIC FAMILY

The Hispanic woman's self-sacrificing, self-effacing role as wife and mother is derived from the strict, traditional biblical interpretation of submissiveness. In this light, the woman is expected to serve her husband and nurture her children, often at the expense of her own needs and desires. Throughout most of the Hispanic world, the role of mother is venerated as the giver and perpetuator of life and love within the family.

Like the male role, however, the Hispanic married woman's traditional role is affected in the United States by values of individual equality regardless of gender and by tremendous societal pressures and opposing expectations. Women of today are educated and expect to be equal in power. Societal factors that impact male and female roles—such as the need for women to work outside of the home—have confronted the Hispanic family with an often unwelcomed need for change. The family's resistance to such fundamental change has resulted in difficult struggles. From all sides the message seems clear: the traditional Hispanic way of family functioning is at odds with the American way of life.

Thus, a cultural dilemma arises for the traditional Hispanic family. Economic pressures alone are often great enough to cause the mother to work outside the home, something diametrically opposed to strongly held convictions about obligations to home and family. Both males and females of younger and older generations are learning to adjust to new social forces.

As the Hispanic woman goes to work outside the home, she usually does so with much ambivalence about leaving her children in the care of others. Doubts about the decision are minimized when the caregiver happens to be the grandmother. However, more and more grandmothers are unavailable due to their own need to be involved in the work force or because families live long distances from each other.

Working outside the home is advantageous, if the family's economic situation necessitates it and the woman can command a decent salary. Lack of skills and education often limits the Hispanic woman's chances for a well-paying job, however. Unless the woman has sufficient education and qualifications, any wages that are earned may merely cover the cost of paid child care. But educated or not, the decision to work outside the home when children are young is a very difficult decision for many women. Generating income in her own right, causing a woman to expect to have more power in the family, often conflicts with the traditional role of the female as nurturer of the family and the male as the power-wielding head of the household.

CHILDREN'S ROLES IN THE HISPANIC FAMILY

Children are highly valued in Hispanic families, especially at younger ages. As infants, children are highly indulged, not only by parents but by older siblings and relatives as well. As children grow, however, they are expected to contribute to the family by performing chores, running errands, accompanying parents on shopping trips to help with English interpretation, and caring for younger siblings. Teens and young adults are expected to contribute financially to the family by working after school and on weekends. Such family obligations may interfere with the child's full participation in school, thereby resulting in poor academic performance. Poor school performance may contribute to the child's dropping out of school to work full time to help the family. Until they marry and leave the home, young adult children are expected to work and contribute some or all of their earnings to the family.

Children at School

In the school, the Hispanic child seems acutely sensitive to environmental, social, and psychological cues. Working with peers in small groups or pairs and receiving individual attention from the teacher are important. An environment that is psychologically cold, detached, and extremely task-oriented may actually impede Hispanic children's learning. On the other hand, an accepting atmosphere that enhances rapport between child and teacher, and that fosters supportive peer relationships, will greatly facilitate learning.

Obligations to the Extended Family

Caring for family members, including extended family, such as grandparents, aunts, uncles, and cousins, is a priority in Hispanic families. Placing elderly parents in nursing homes or centers for the aged is virtually unknown. To do so may be looked upon as abandonment or rejection of a loved one, and serious shirking of family responsibility. The wisdom of elder family members is highly respected, sought, and valued. The extended family functions as support and a stabilizing force for individual members. According to Abalos (1986, p. 9), "Our families must serve as crucibles that prepare us for selfhood."

Many Hispanics live in *colonias* or *barrios* with a majority of other Hispanics. Family members, relatives, and other members of the community share responsibility for the upbringing and socialization of the children. Close-knit communities collectively watch over their children by taking an interest in and participating, not only in accepting and nurturing them, but in guiding and disciplining them as well. The birth of a child is a cherished event celebrated by the family and community. In the Roman Catholic faith, the christening of the infant child is cherished as well. The adults chosen to be the child's godparents literally become a second set of parents for that child. They assume a significant role in the upbringing of the child and vow to take full and complete responsibility for the child if the parents die. For the older child, religious and nonreligious events, such as confirmation, and the *quinceañera,* a coming-out event for adolescent females, are significant events also celebrated by the community.

Out of care and concern, even neighbors assume the role of "family" and may report to parents any observed inappropriate behavior or social infractions, causing children and youth to behave more circumspectly than they might otherwise. Children demonstrate respect for the authority of elders, whether related or not, by referring to them as "aunt" or "uncle" and demonstrating the same deference they would give to family members.

PROMINENT VALUES OF HISPANIC FAMILIES

We can gain a better understanding of Hispanics if we examine closely the more significant values held by them that have persisted over time. Cultural values, by definition, are positive attributes that are held in esteem by the group and practiced, consciously or unconsciously, in everyday life. Such values are ones that will be addressed here.

Cultural values dictate people's day-to-day actions and decisions about life. They are passed down from generation to generation and are slow to change. Cultural values are such an integral part of a group's identity, that to be forced to change or pressured to relinquish them can be at best demoralizing and even psychologically detrimental.

Cultural groups have characteristics that distinguish them in unique ways. These may include foods they eat, manner of dressing, special holidays observed, and, in many cases, language. Cultural characteristics can be considered to be neutral, positive, or negative in terms of value.

Hispanic cultural values, which will be explored here, cut across socioeconomic boundaries and national origin. We need to pay attention to the fact that Hispanics comprise a disproportionate number of the poor in the United States. The various national groups that make up the Hispanic-Americans are differentially poor as well. Keeping in mind that poverty is an economic condition and not a cultural value, the purpose of this chapter is to emphasize the attributes that make the Hispanic culture special and to consider the positive contribution Hispanic values can make to a society that often seems insensitive, materialistic, and ethnophobic.

Focusing on the positive attributes of a people can work to counteract the negative, debilitating, deficit perspective so prevalent in the literature, where Hispanics are depicted as problematic, and as an enigma to society.

America is a conglomerate of diverse cultural groups from all over the world. Indeed, it is this rich diversity of people that contributes to the very strength of this nation. When each group lends its strongest, most positive values to the whole, something likened to a rich tapestry is created, woven in a beautiful, unique pattern to be admired, enjoyed, and valued. It is in this spirit that some of the values that Hispanics hold dear are addressed herein, and offered for consideration and appreciation.

Placing importance on personal relationships, respect, and responsibility are three values that Hispanics hold most dear, and are sometimes referred to as the "Three Rs" of Hispanic values. More than other values, these seem to cut across nationalities, as well as across all the socioeconomic levels of Hispanic groups. Two related values are cooperation (as opposed to competition) and other-centeredness (as opposed to self-centeredness).

Some social scientists say that the Spanish language is the "glue" that binds Hispanics to one another, and that may well be true. Clearly, a magnetism seems to draw speakers of Spanish to each other, establishing an instantaneous rapport and connectedness between them. However, as strong as the language bond is, family relationships, respect, and responsibility are so important that, even when language has been forgotten, abandoned, or inadvertently lost, the internalization of these values by the individual may result in a manner of being that is not easily altered or discarded.

In mainstream society, which values competition and rugged individualism, the values of relationships, respect, and responsibility offer such contrasts that Hispanics may find it difficult to adjust. Further discussion of how these values are lived out in everyday life may result in a better understanding for the reader.

Relationships in Families

First, among most Hispanic groups, family relationships are of paramount importance. Reported high divorce rates notwithstanding, Hispanics make decisions based primarily on how they will affect the family. In the last two decades, assimilation and other societal pressures have caused an increase in family disruption, but by and large, family still takes priority above all else. No sacrifice is considered too great to make for one's family. For example, it is very common for more recently immigrated families to spend all their hard-earned savings to travel great distances for extended visits to family members, particularly to see parents, siblings, and grandparents.

Further, if the choice is between spending money to purchase much-needed furniture for the home, and making a trip to visit family, the latter will always win out. In such a case as this, there is hardly a choice involved. For Hispanics, "people before things" is the operating principle.

The valuing of human relationships is clearly demonstrated by parents over and over in daily family life, in large and small ways. Children learn early and firsthand that people matter, above all. All children—but particularly very young children—are regarded with respect and affection. Respect is not only demonstrated but expected from each family member toward others. This creates strong emotional ties that transcend even great geographical distances. A feeling of belonging and strong emotional ties helps sustain many Hispanics through life's difficult and trying situations. An appropriate phrase to describe this phenomenon may come from the popular song: "People who need people, are the luckiest people in the world."

Loyalty to family is demonstrated by and expected from all family members. For example, older children may be kept home from school in order to help care for ill siblings or parents. Teachers may find that older Hispanic students who are frequently absent from school may be attending to family obligations, such as accompanying a parent on community shopping trips to help with language interpretation, or going on regular, extended, out-of-town visits to the grandparents' home. Likewise, adult wage earners may risk losing their jobs when they fail to return to work on time, because trips to visit relatives had to be prolonged for reasons deemed important to sustaining family ties and providing family support.

The high value placed on family relationships affects how individuals relate to those outside the family as well. Most Hispanics relate to the world from a familiar and comfortable people-oriented standpoint. They demonstrate gentleness and respect, and expect it in return. If this response is not reciprocated, they are likely to withdraw psychologically or avoid similar situations. Barriers are created, negatively affecting any future interaction.

Education is highly valued by Hispanics. But valued as it is, if education is perceived to contradict or come between the individual and his or her allegiance to the family, it may be promptly relegated to a low-priority status. Education is valued only to the extent that its attainment will enhance the family group, not merely for how it will aggrandize the individual. The well-known Spanish proverb, *La escuela instruye, mientras el hogar educa,* or, "the school instructs, while the home educates," well illustrates the order in which priorities are maintained. Stated differently, the individual who is *bien educado,* or "well-educated," is not the one who is clever and quick with book-learned facts and intellectual verbiage. Rather, it is the child who is respectful and responsible, first to his or her family and then to others as well. These behaviors are learned in the Hispanic home, where the most important "education" is believed to take place.

Most Hispanics believe that if the instruction of the school causes the individual to "put on airs," to consider oneself better than others, or in any way to exhibit conceit or vain behavior, then the school is considered to have failed in its purpose. Should a person's educational pursuits—as laudable and valued as they might be—cause her or him to disregard family, that individual is regarded as one whose priorities have gone awry. It is then incumbent upon the person to demonstrate convincingly that family loyalties can never be displaced. When an educated family member is able to maintain a balance between educational attainment and familial attentiveness, this individual is considered worthy of praise and emulation.

The apparent conflict between educational dedication and family attentiveness can pose quite a dilemma for the Hispanic individual. Is family deliberately disregarded? The family may perceive it as such. It may be very difficult for the individual to strike a balance between the two values of family and education. When the educated Hispanic moves away to serve in a job, the family and the individual are usually both distressed.

Higher Education

The attainment of a college education may be a mixed blessing for Hispanics, since such an accomplishment may result in being separated from family by great distances. Opportunities, economic and otherwise, increase greatly for Hispanics who hold college degrees, but often those opportunities exist far away from home. Statistics show that ten percent of Hispanics hold associate or bachelor's degrees as compared to twenty-one percent of Anglos. During the 1980s, Hispanic enrollment in institutions of higher learning increased by 84 percent, from 472,000 in 1980 to 867,000 in 1991 (Bureau of the Census, 1993). Despite this encouraging increase, however, Hispanics' participation in higher education is disproportionately low compared to the overall growth in their numbers. Pursuit of these appealing opportunities may mean increased vulnerability to the dangers of cultural assimilation.

Bicultural and Bilingual Attainment

Though education is valued, it is very difficult emotionally for the Hispanic family to be deprived of the proximity and loyalty of the family member who leaves to pursue that education. The goal is not for the individual to make the values of family and educational attainment mutually exclusive, but to maintain a balance or embrace both simultaneously. The most realistic solution is to become bicultural—that is, to be able to function with skill, ease, and comfort in two cultures. It means that the individual embodies the unique blending of two cultures, without sacrificing one for the other. As a prominent author expressed it, "bilingual/bicultural . . . implies and demands a synthesis, a coming together of opposite cultures and languages out of which emerges a third enriched reality that was not there before" (Chavez, 1991).

Others, like Richard Rodriguez (1993), author of *Hunger of Memory,* believe biculturalism to be an impossibility. Rodriguez and many others have found that living out one value system is usually at the expense of others, making biculturality, for them, quite unattainable.

For educators, helping children become truly bicultural does them a great service. To examine the two cultures critically and integrate the best of both into one's own unique lifestyle seems to be the most desirable solution for the individual and society as well. An increasing number of Hispanics are becoming successful bicultural professionals, providing observable models for children, parents, and others.

Respect

To Hispanics, respect means something quite different than it does to the majority culture. To ascertain the different ways in which respect is defined, Diaz-Guerrero and Peck (1976, p. 132) studied two student groups—one Anglo and one Mexican—who were presented with a list of 20 meanings typically ascribed to the word "respect." They were asked to check the statements that represented appropriate uses of the word and to leave blank those that did not. The list consisted of the following:

1. To look up to somebody with admiration.
2. To look up to somebody with awe.
3. To fear somebody.
4. To love somebody.
5. To be willing to treat somebody else on an equal footing.

6. To give someone else a chance.
7. To feel affection.
8. To feel admiration for somebody.
9. To anticipate a certain amount of protection from the respected person.
10. To anticipate the possibility of punishment from the respected person.
11. To feel a certain degree of protectiveness toward the respected person.
12. To dislike somebody.
13. To keep from trespassing on somebody else's rights.
14. To feel you like to obey someone.
15. To feel you have to obey someone.
16. To feel it is your duty to obey someone.
17. To be considerate of somebody else's feelings.
18. To be considerate of somebody else's ideas.
19. Not to invade someone else's privacy.
20. To avoid interfering in somebody else's life.

According to Diaz-Guerrero and Peck (1976), clear differences were found between the two groups. To Anglos, to respect meant to admire someone who is considered superior, to treat someone on an equal basis, or to grant others equal opportunity. To Mexicans, to respect means to show affection, to love someone, and to give and receive protection.

Diaz-Guerrero and Peck (1976) further examined the concept of respect as perceived by the Mexican and American cultures. A list of 60 different roles typically held by individuals in society was presented to 298 Mexican students and to 340 American students. The various roles included professional and educational occupations, as well as roles played within the family or other societal institutions, like the church. It also included personal attributes such as age and sex. Students were asked to indicate the people to whom the word "respect" might apply. The results showed significant differences between the cultures as to which roles in society or which stations in life are worthy of respect. For example, Mexicans respect people at the extremes of age, whereas Americans seem to respect youth. Beggars and poor people are more highly respected in Mexico and receive only medium respect in the United States. In summarizing the study, Diaz-Guerrero and Peck concluded that, in American society, respect is accorded on the basis of "what individuals perform or produce, and in Mexican culture, respect is bestowed on the mere basis of a person's humanity or for just being" (p. 176). Stated another way, a person's station in life has little or no bearing on the degree of respect that he or she might command in Mexican society. The famous Mexican leader and President, Benito Juarez, spoke of respect saying, *El respeto al derecho ajeno, es la paz* ("Respect for the rights of others is peace").

Responsibility

The third value that typifies Hispanic-Americans is responsibility. Responsibility toward the group is instilled diligently and early. The individual is expected to contribute to the group in whatever ways are appropriate to age and gender. For example, the father's responsibility to provide for his family by honest work constitutes the model for other male family members. Work is viewed as a utilitarian function that enables one to provide sustenance for the family and for self. One does not work for the sake of working, but to provide for those for whom one is responsible. Among Hispanics, "workaholism," or an enslavement to work for work's sake, is not likely to occur. The accumulation of material possessions is not the Hispanic's primary motive for working. Rather, it is to meet family responsibilities.

The Hispanics' spirit of cooperation is related to the sense of responsibility. All family members work together for the good of the group and not for individual gain. If the individual achieves in any area, the group receives the glory. An example may be swimmer Pablo Morales, the winner of the Olympic gold medal, who dedicated his gold medal to his mother who died of cancer just prior to the 1992 Olympics. Morales publicly attributed his drive and motivation to his mother's strong and persistent support. Touching scenes of demonstrable family closeness and pride were televised worldwide as Morales triumphed in Barcelona.

In similar fashion, young children may decide to behave or do well at school in order to please their parents. The family's blessing and sanction are very important to the Hispanic child.

HISPANIC FAMILIES AND THE GOVERNMENT SYSTEM

Many Hispanics value highly the American protection of rights and the freedoms afforded to the individual under the Constitution of this country. A desire for less oppressed lives and economic opportunity are primary reasons for Hispanic immigration to this country. Many are enjoying the right to vote and even running for public office. More than ever before, Hispanic names are appearing on election ballots, thanks to the redistricting brought about by more accurate accounting for Hispanics in the 1990 census. According to Rodriquez (1993), "Hispanics stand on the verge of making a quantum leap into [the] realm of political participation" (p. 10).

HISPANIC FAMILIES AND THE ECONOMIC SYSTEM

Perceiving the United States as a land of opportunity, Hispanics view the abundant resources as blessings to be shared, not hoarded. Though poor in material possessions, Hispanics will sincerely say, *Mi casa es su casa*—"My house is your house"— and really mean it. They offer the humblest of possessions, including their own home, to guests, as a gesture of generosity. But generosity notwithstanding, Hispanics do not readily accept "handouts," and often refuse to seek out needed welfare benefits to which they may be entitled.

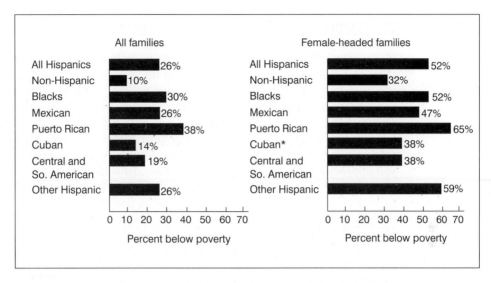

Figure 5–2.   *U.S. Families below poverty by race or ethnic group, 1987.*

Source: Bureau of the Census, U.S. Department of Commerce, 1990

* May be of any race.

Proud of their self-sufficiency and belief in hard work, they accept responsibility in the economic arena. They labor with diligence and integrity.

   The Cuban experience has made that group of Hispanics unique in America. In the 1960s, the educated elite left Cuba to escape the Castro regime. They have prospered economically in Florida. As a group, their income levels are higher than other Hispanics, according to the Bureau of the Census (1990).

HISPANIC FAMILIES AND THE HEALTH CARE SYSTEM

Hispanics often do not take advantage of health care services primarily due to language, economic, and other reasons, such as inconvenient location of services and the impersonal and frustrating treatment they often receive at public clinics.

   High rates of unimmunized children and poor prenatal care are very common among Hispanics, particularly among recent immigrants. A recent study shows that 17 percent of the nation's AIDS cases are Hispanics, and that they are contracting the disease faster than any other ethnic group (Office of the U.S. Surgeon General, 1993). Health care professionals with a real desire to serve Hispanics need to involve the family, speak Spanish when essential for real communication and understanding, meet people in their own communities, and foster participation of Hispanics in the health provider organizations and agencies.

RECOMMENDATIONS FOR SERVING HISPANIC FAMILIES

If you speak Spanish, you'll feel at home with Hispanics, even though many of them will speak English as well as you do. However, if you don't speak Spanish, you can start learning the language to gain rapport with the people you hope to serve. Ask Spanish-speaking friends for help in making word and phrase lists, develop techniques for remembering them, then work hard to learn more. Hispanics will appreciate your effort to learn. Many of them are working very hard to learn English and your effort to learn Spanish can help you appreciate the complexity of their task. In addition, Hispanics are learning many new things about a new culture. It is true that many Hispanics may not be able to read or write Spanish, not having had the opportunity to learn these skills. One can simply ask which language they prefer to use without making assumptions either way.

Hispanics thrive and respond positively in environments where their cultural values are understood, lived out, and affirmed. Rapport between Hispanics and helping professionals can be more readily established if respect and regard are demonstrated in personal relationships.

In today's society where everything is mechanized, computerized, and depersonalized for efficiency's sake, respect and meaningful relationships are rare commodities. Environments that are solely production-oriented are not conducive to relationships unless care is taken to make them so. A condescending or prejudicial attitude builds barriers to relationships and breeds disrespect. The implied message is "things above people," and nothing discourages Hispanics more than this mode of thinking. Depersonalized treatment of this nature alienates Hispanics, making it impossible to establish any degree of rapport. This is true, even among the youngest children within educational settings.

Valuing the Hispanic child's family and home enhances the child's positive feeling about herself or himself. The child's cultural values and traditions must be preserved and built upon. The development of personal abilities that enable the person to preserve the best of the family's culture while adding on the best of the majority culture must begin in the earliest educational experiences.

Hispanics thrive in warm, nurturing environments. In places characterized by sensitivity and acceptance, and by respectful relationships, the message is loud and strong: "People matter here; I am valued." Only by living in a society that encourages and supports their cultural uniqueness can Hispanics preserve their dignity and achieve success.

CONCLUSIONS

Knowing and serving Hispanic families will be an enriching and fulfilling experience for persons who understand and value— through word and action—the strengths and uniqueness of the culture and individuality of Hispanics themselves. Demonstrating warm respect and sincere interest will likely result in mutually beneficial interpersonal experiences that will contribute positively to peoples' lives and, ultimately, to stronger communities.

STUDY QUESTIONS

1. List historical facts about the three major groups of Hispanic families in the U.S. Explain how the accident of history affects the three groups today.
2. Study the statistics given in the chapter and list at least two statistics that apply to each of the three Hispanic groups.
3. What is meant by the terms bicultural and bilingual? List the benefits of being one or both.
4. What were the provisions of the Bilingual Education Act?
5. What is meant by "English-only" legislation?
6. Name and describe the predominant family structure of Hispanics.
7. Tell how the religious system affects a majority of Hispanic families.
8. Tell how the government system affects Hispanics.
9. Contrast male and female roles in the Hispanic family.
10. Tell how the economic system affects the three Hispanic groups.
11. State the statistics for the three Hispanic groups that show the relationships between education and fertility, and between education and marital stability.
12. State the primary arguments for helping people maintain their mother tongue.
13. What are the "Three Rs" of Hispanic family values?
14. What attitudes are important for helping professionals to develop in working with Hispanic families?

APPLICATIONS

1. Focus on the word Hispanic and write down the first twenty words that come to mind.
2. Relate the word stereotype to the list you have made for item 1. Are there harmful or prejudicial words in your list? What would happen if you acted on those stereotypes?
3. Write a description of a Hispanic friend or acquaintance of yours (or a Hispanic public figure if you do not personally know any Hispanics). Tell how that person is bicultural and/or bilingual. Interview that person by telephone or in person if possible. Ask questions to learn about early history of family and education and of career goals. Write a two- or three-page report.

4. Read newspapers and magazines to discover names of two Hispanic contemporary artists, authors, or musicians. Research the figures in appropriate periodicals and write a one-page essay on the early life, education, and experiences of each one. Conclude with one or two paragraphs about how you think their early life affected their art form.

5. Read a major newspaper in your state or inquire through a politician's office in your state to learn about what is being done legislatively to insure that Hispanic children's educational needs are being addressed. Citing your sources of information, write a two-page report.

6. Interview a person who came to the United States and learned English. Learn all you can about the person's age, motivation, obstacles or opportunities, and outcomes. Giving references, write a report drawing your own conclusions.

7. List the values a large majority of Hispanics hold in common regardless of socioeconomic status. Discuss variations you have read or heard about.

8. Write a two-page report addressing the question: Why do Hispanic-Americans face a difficult adjustment to the larger society? Make five recommendations that you think would help.

9. Make a list of ten commandments for non-Hispanics to follow in order to help Hispanics of all ages adjust to our society more successfully. Use your own career area, if you like.

10. Write an essay on how the cultural traits of the Hispanic culture can contribute to our global perspective today.

11. Write a two-page report on information resources on a topic of interest regarding Hispanics. Some examples might include bilingualism, immigration, international trade, liberation theology, the Spanish Inquisition, Cuban or Mexican Revolution, Agency for International Development, etc. Question your librarian for appropriate sources to research.

12. Suppose you were going to visit a Hispanic majority country for a summer service/educational experience. List in chronological order the tasks you would need to accomplish in order to prepare yourself to leave next June. State the country or region you'll visit and your primary goal. Conclude by giving your rationale for your list.

REFERENCES

Abalos, David T. (1986). *Latinos in the United States: The sacred and the political*. Notre Dame, Indiana: University of Notre Dame Press.

Bean, Frank, and Tienda, Marta. (1987). *The Hispanic population of the U.S.* New York: Russell Sage Foundation.

Bernal, Guillermo. (1982). Cuban families. In Monica McGoldbrick, et al. (Eds.), *Ethnicity and family therapy* (pp. 187–207). New York, NY: The Guilford Press.

Briggs, David. (1993, November 6). National Conference of Catholic Bishops, p. 1a. *The Houston Chronicle.*

Bureau of the Census. (1983). Conditions of Hispanics in America today. Washington, DC: U.S. Department of Commerce.

Bureau of the Census. (1990). Census Report. Washington, DC: U.S. Department of Commerce.

Chavez, Linda. (1991). *Out of the barrio: Toward a new politics of Hispanic assimilation.* New York, NY: HarperCollins Publishers.

Diaz-Guerrero, Rogelio, and Peck, Alonzo. (1976). *Psychology of the Mexican: Culture and personality.* Austin, TX: University of Texas Press.

Falicov, Celia Jaes. (1982). Mexican families. In Monica McGoldbrick, John K. Pearce, and Joseph Giordano (Eds.), *Ethnicity and family therapy* (pp. 134–163). New York, NY: The Guilford Press.

Fillmore, Lily Wong, and Britsch, Susan. (1988, June). *Early education for children from linguistic and cultural minority families.* Paper prepared for the Early Education Task Force of the National Association of State Boards of Education.

Frisbie, W. Parker. (1993). Variation in patterns of marital stability among Hispanics. *Journal of Marriage and the Family, 48,* pp. 99–106.

Garcia-Preto, Nydia. (1982). Puerto Rican families. In Monica McGoldbrick, et al. (Eds.), *Ethnicity and family therapy* (pp. 164–186). New York, NY: The Guilford Press.

Goldscheider, Calvin. (1991, November). Census monographs on ethnicity. *Demography, 28*(4), p. 663.

Griswold del Castillo, Richard. (1984). *La familia.* Notre Dame, IN: University of Notre Dame Press.

Lyons, James J. (1993, February 15). The view from Washington: English-only extremism, p. 1. *National Association for Bilingual Education News.*

Mann, Taynia, and Kalish, Susan. (1991, November). Mexican and Cuban Americans hold mainstream views. *Population Today, 19*(11), p. 4.

Nava, Julian. (1972). *Los Mexicano-Americanos pasado, presente, y futuro.* New York, NY: American Book Company.

Office of The U.S. Surgeon General. (1993, June). *The Surgeon General's Report on HIV and AIDS.* Washington, DC: author.

Richardson, Chad. (1993, August 23). The border life project. *The Houston Chronicle,* p. 10.

Rodriguez, Richard. (1981). *Hunger for memory: An autobiography.* Boston, MA: D. R. Godine.

Rodriquez, Lori. (1993, May 3). One vote. One voice. *The Houston Chronicle,* p. 10.

Valdivieso, Rafael, and Davis, Cary. (1988). U.S. Hispanics: Challenging issues for the 1990s. *Population Trends and Public Policy,* 17. Washington, DC: Population Reference Bureau.

FURTHER READING

Careaga, Rudy. (1988, Fall). Keeping limited English proficient students in school: Strategies for dropout prevention. *Program Information Guide Series,* 7. National Clearinghouse for Bilingual Education, 1118 22nd Street, NW, Washington, D.C. 20037.

Careaga, Rudy. (1988, Fall). Parent involvement: A resource for the education of limited English proficient students. *Program Information Guide Series,* 8. National Clearinghouse for Bilingual Education, 1118 22nd Street, NW, Washington, D.C. 20037

De Leon, Arnoldo. (1989). *Ethnicity in the sunbelt: A history of Mexican Americans in Houston.* Houston, TX: University of Houston Mexican American Studies.

Gingras, Rosario C., and Careaga, Rudy C. (1989, Spring). *Limited English proficient students at risk: Issues and prevention strategies.* New FOCUS, Occasional Papers in Bilingual Education, No. 10. The National Clearinghouse for Bilingual Education, 1118 22nd Street, NW, Washington, DC 20037.

Maril, Robert Lee. (1988). *Poorest of Americans: The Mexican-Americans of the lower Rio Grande valley of Texas.* Notre Dame, Indiana: Gardner Press.

Moore, Joan, and Pachon, Harry. (1985). *Hispanics in the United States.* Englewood Cliffs, NJ: Prentice-Hall.

Saracho, Olivia N., and Hancock, Frances Martinez. (1983). Mexican American culture. In Olivia Saracho and Bernard Spodek (Eds.), *Understanding the multi-cultural experience in early childhood education.* Washington, DC: National Association for the Education of Young Children.

Sotomayor, Marta. (Ed.). (1991). *Empowering Hispanic families: A critical issue for the 90s.* Milwaukee, WI: Family Service America.

Violand-Sanchez, Emma, Sutton, Christine P., and Ware, Herbert W. (1991, Summer). *Fostering home-school cooperation: Involving language families as partners in education.* Program Information Guide Series No. 6. Washington DC: National Clearinghouse for Bilingual Education, 1118 22nd Street, NW, Washington, DC 20037.

MEDIA RESOURCES

The Status of Latina Women. (1993). Video, 26 minutes, color.
Films for the Humanities, Inc., P.O. Box 2053, Princeton, New Jersey. 1-800-257-5126 or 609-275-1400.

CHAPTER 6

Asian-American Families

Key Concepts

◆ Chinese Exclusion Act
◆ World War II Detention of Japanese-Americans
◆ Issei
◆ Nisei
◆ Amerasians

The mountain moving day is coming.
I say so, yet others doubt.
Only a while the mountain sleeps.
In the past
All mountains moved in fire,
Yet you may not believe it.
Oh man, this alone believe
All sleeping women now will awake and move.

— Yasano Akiko (1911)

Asian-American women and men have been equally involved in every step of the growing Asian-American experience. The old, limiting perceptions held by Asian-Americans, influenced by remnants of the patriarchal Asian family traditions and expectations, are undergoing radical change due to contact with Western cultures. As Akiko (1911) predicted in the opening verse, Asian-American women—and men, too—are now awake and changing as they become aware of new options.

WHO ARE THE ASIAN-AMERICANS?

Subgroups of the Asian-American population have been in the United States for at least five generations, while others are new to America. The experience encountered by each ethnic Asian subgroup is unique. Each group represents a different cultural system of values and behaviors, as well as differing degrees of acculturation. To individuals not of Asian ancestry, the subgroups may all seem alike.

The term Asian-American is often used to refer to both Asians and Pacific Islanders. Asian-Americans are many people, rather than one. The term Asian-American identifies people who have origins in 26 countries, such as: Bangladesh, Bhutan, Burma, Cambodia, China, Hong Kong, India, Indonesia, Japan, Laos, Macao, Malaysia, Maldives, Mongolia, North Korea, South Korea, Nepal, Pakistan, Philippines, Singapore, Sri Lanka, Taiwan, Thailand, and many Pacific Islands. Asian-Americans may be one of the more diverse of America's major minority groups. This chapter will focus on some commonalities, then give details of two groups, the Japanese-Americans and the Vietnamese-Americans. You can use a similar procedure to learn about additional groups of Asian-Americans.

Historical Background

Asians came to the United States at different times for a variety of reasons. Earlier immigrants were processed through Angel Island in California. According to Lai, Lim and Yung (1981), many of the immigrants experienced a prisoner-like welcome in the United States. America's outstretched arms of welcome were not offered to Asians as they were to the "huddled masses" of European immigrants entering Ellis Island in New York harbor.

Early laws encouraged unequal treatment of the Chinese. For example, in 1882, Congress passed the Chinese Exclusion Act, which was the first law prohibiting immigration based on nationality (Takaki, 1993). This law banned Chinese immigrants, except those scholars, diplomats, and merchants who could obtain certificates from the U.S. consul and the Chinese government.

However, in a step toward equal treatment, the 1965 amendment to the Immigration and Nationality Act reopened the door for large-scale Asian immigration. Today anti-Asian hostility is less than was endured during those earlier periods (Chan, 1991).

Many earlier immigrants were fortune hunters seeking the golden fleece. For example, the early Chinese immigrants were seeking economic prosperity by working as sugar cane laborers in Hawaii, as gold miners in California, and as railroad workers across parts of the United States. Later Chinese immigrants moved into the service industry as cooks, servants, and launderers (Mei, 1984).

More recent immigrants come to the U.S. for political freedom and asylum, to escape from family pressures, and to fulfill personal aspirations. For example, many Chinese immigrated to escape Chinese Communism in the late 1940s, and, for similar reasons, many Vietnamese came to the U.S. during and after the Vietnam War.

Demographic Information

Today, Asian-Americans are the fastest growing minority group in the United States. Asian-Americans number about 7.3 million or 3 percent of the population. The growth rate between 1980 to 1990 was 95 percent, surpassing all groups in the United States. It is estimated that by the year 2020, Asian-Americans will number 20 million or more (LEAP, 1993).

The Chinese are the largest Asian-American ethnic group, comprising 22 percent; Filipino-Americans, 21 percent; Japanese- Americans, 19 percent; Indian- and Korean-Americans, 10 percent each; and Vietnamese-Americans, 7 percent. Each group grew by 100 percent between 1980 and 1990, except for the Japanese-Americans, who increased their numbers by only 21 percent (O'Hare and Felt, 1991).

In 1989, the median family income of Asian-American families was $35,000. Over a third (39 percent) of all Asian-Americans lived in households that had incomes of $50,000 or more. This may be a misleading picture of economic well-being, given that most Asian-Americans live in high-cost areas, such as Honolulu, Los Angeles, and San Francisco. Asian-Americans also tend to pool resources by living in large households where most family members work. This results in Asian-Americans having a lower per capita income than the non-Hispanic white population (O'Hare and Felt, 1991).

There are two distinct groups of Asians in the United States today. One group is well educated and advancing into the middle and upper-middle class, while the other group lacks the necessary skills and education to escape poverty. The poverty rate at 8 percent for Asian-American populations is approximately twice that of the non-Hispanic whites. According to the Population Reference Bureau, Inc. (1991), at least 59 percent of poor Asian-Americans live in households that participate in one of four governmental welfare programs: cash public assistance, Medicaid, Food Stamps, or Low Income Energy Assistance.

THE ECOLOGY OF ASIAN-AMERICAN FAMILIES

Family Structure

There is a great variability among Asian-American families; however, many are still strongly influenced by the male-dominated patriarchal Asian family tradition. Often the patriarchal lineage and hierarchical relationships, sometimes called *vertical,* fall into the patterns of: (1) father to son, (2) elder brother to younger brother, or (3) husband to wife. The only *horizontal* relationship, that of equal status, is that found between friends. Such traditional practices are based upon the teachings of Confucius.

Women in households, following these ancient traditions, are expected to play a passive role. This is particularly true of older Asian women and those born in their native land. Women are expected to be housewives and mothers, yet a large proportion of Asian-American women are in the work force. Younger educated Asian-American women often encounter problems with their parents, spouses, or other Asians as they become acculturated in American ways that encourage equality between the sexes (True, 1990). By actively participating in the majority culture, they are sometimes deeply troubled upon perceiving themselves to be unfairly treated at home.

ASIAN-AMERICAN FAMILY VALUES

The Asian people and their cultures have been influenced by religious beliefs such as Buddhism, Confucianism, Hinduism, and Islamism. However, there are certain common value systems that identify the group. Of course there are distinct differences in behavioral interpretations of these characteristics among the various Asian groups. Some of the more distinct characteristics are group orientation, family relationship and responsibility, self-control and personal discipline, emphasis on educational achievement, respect for authority, reverence for the elderly, and the use of shame as a behavioral influence (Tsui & Schultz, 1985; Chung, 1992). These characteristics and values contribute to a strong sense of self-reliance and interdependence in Asian families and individuals.

ASIAN-AMERICAN FAMILIES AND THE EDUCATIONAL SYSTEM

The current popular image of Asian-Americans as hardworking and successful is a turnabout from the earlier depictions of the group as the "Yellow Peril," seen by some as a threat to the American way of life. It wasn't until the 1960s that successful Asian-Americans became the popular model of achievement. Protests of other ethnic minority groups seeking social justice were discredited by the majority society in its emphasis on following the Asian-American success pattern.

Asian-Americans were viewed as a group who overcame racism and achieved success by hard work, uncomplaining perseverance, and quiet accommodation. Like any stereotype, this became an idealized view, to the extent that many Asian-Americans themselves felt an obligation to live up to this prescribed American vision of the group.

Today, Asian-Americans have become the largest ethnic minority group in many career fields and at many elite colleges. In 1980, when Asian-Americans comprised only 1.5 percent of the population, they consisted of 5 percent of the engineers and 8 percent of all doctors in the United States. Asian-Americans enrolled in elite colleges show the most significant evidence of the importance of education. For example, in 1987, Asian-Americans consisted of 13 percent of admitted freshmen at Harvard, and 25 percent of freshmen at the University of California at Berkeley. Asian-American women comprised 30 percent of entering female students at Massachusetts Institute of Technology (MIT), and over half of newly admitted women engineering students at the University of California at Berkeley (Hu, 1988).

Although Asian-Americans have taken full advantage of the benefits of our educational system, there are still problems for Asian-American students who do not fit the stereotype created by society. Asian-American students usually major in engineering, computer technology, or science. What about those students who decide on careers in the social sciences or arts and letters?

What is happening with respect to recent immigrants from Southeast Asia and their children? There is growing evidence from public schools in a number of Midwestern cities of high drop-out rates among Khmer, Hmong, and Laotian students. Their drop-out rates approach the high rate of a number of ethnic minorities (Hsia & Nakanishi, 1989). The Asian-American community is polarized along extreme ends of the continuum with many students needing special assistance at one end and others exceeding all expectations at the opposite end, leaving few in the middle.

ASIAN-AMERICAN FAMILIES AND THE HEALTH CARE SYSTEM

Health problems vary among Asian-American groups. For example, Filipinos have a high incidence of hypertension; Southeast Asians have a high prevalence of tuberculosis infection and Hepatitis B; the Chinese-, Japanese-, and Filipino-Americans have problems with cancer and cerebrovascular disease (LEAP, 1993).

Access to adequate health care is fragmented due to issues of language and culture, especially for the elderly, women, Southeast Asian refugees, and recent immigrants. There is evidence that increasing numbers of Asian-Americans are utilizing mental health services. Such data indicate that Asian-Americans are increasingly finding appropriate cultural and linguistic assistance at mental health agencies (True, 1990).

ASIAN-AMERICAN FAMILIES AND THE GOVERNMENTAL SYSTEM

The past relationship between local, state, and national governments and the Asian-American community has not been a harmonious one, but one plagued with struggles of acceptance and rejection. However, the once passive role of Asian-Americans in U.S. politics is changing. Several Asian-Americans have been elected to various offices, including those at the federal level.

Asian-Americans are becoming more active participants in the political arena. They are not easily characterized as Democrats or Republicans. According to studies carried out at the University of California at Los Angeles, Asian-Pacific-American voters are almost evenly divided between the Democratic and Republican parties in their registration and voting behavior (Nakanishi, 1989).

Both political parties have attempted to win Asian-American voters to their side because many are major financial contributors. During the 1988 presidential election, approximately $10 million from Asian-American contributors was evenly divided between the two parties. Republican and Democratic Asian-American leaders are working together to address issues related to Asian-American admission to institutes of higher education. Asian-Americans perform so well on college entrance examinations that there is pressure to limit their admissions. Debate continues about appropriate affirmative action.

ASIAN-AMERICAN FAMILIES AND THE ECONOMIC SYSTEM

Traditionally, running a small family business was common among Asian-Americans. For example, a Korean-American family and their relatives might assist in running a small grocery store. Japanese-American family members might own a grocery store or a truck farm. Chinese families might operate restaurants or laundries. During times of economic crisis, Asian community organizations pool their resources to bail out some of their members. As a result, many Asian-American credit associations were founded to provide loans to those within the community.

Leong and Hayes (1990) found that many Asian-American students become engineers, mathematicians, and computer scientists. The presence of occupational stereotyping has created a social reality for the Asian-American community. Over recent decades, the socioeconomic position of Asian-American families in American society has improved due to the high investment in educational credentials. Asian-Americans believe that family members must work and pool their resources to invest in higher education.

According to the U.S. Bureau of the Census *Source* (1990), Asian-Americans are more likely than whites to work in the manufacturing and trade industries and in professional positions, and less likely than whites to work in blue collar jobs. However, immigrant women from Bangladesh, Burma, Cambodia, Pakistan, Sri Lanka, Thailand, Indonesia, India, and China often work in low-wage jobs in garment factories or electronic assembly lines (LEAP, 1993).

JAPANESE-AMERICAN FAMILIES

In order not to mask differences that exist among various subgroups, we will focus now on two groups, the Japanese-American and the Vietnamese-American families.

The Japanese-American community is made up of generations of mostly native-born Americans, with other Asian-American ethnic groups having more recent immigrants.

The internment of Japanese-Americans during World War II must not be forgotten. It provides evidence and a reminder that any person or any ethnic group can be discriminated against unless there is vigilance in protecting basic human rights as enshrined in the U.S. Constitution.

Vietnamese-American families are examples of more recent Asian-Americans who immigrated for political reasons. Many are experiencing cultural conflicts and struggles as they accommodate and acculturate to the mainstream society.

THE ECOLOGY OF JAPANESE-AMERICAN FAMILIES

To understand Japanese-Americans, one must look at the human ecological changes throughout history from one generation to the next. You should recall the discussion of human ecology in Chapter 2. According to Suzuki and Yamashiro (1980), different environments affected the Japanese ability to transfer an ethnic world view from one generation to another. This finding is especially important given the nature of the Japanese personality and culture.

The Japanese have been characterized as being a situational people. This means they tend to accommodate to the present situation and make the best of it. According to Hall (1966 and 1983), the traditional Japanese culture is considered a high context culture. This means the context or environment in which the individual is living, working, and interacting is important in determining the adaptive strategy used in relating to others while still maintaining aspects of traditional values. The surrounding cultural and social conditions influence the life of the individual, organization, and community.

For example, the Japanese in Hawaii are embedded in an ethnically dominated geographic setting, whereas those in the continental United States typically reside within the majority community. Those who live in an ethnic community reinforce their cultural values and processes, while those residing outside the community find their values reinforced by a different system. The community environment influences a family's ability to instill particular values and practices.

Although the largest concentration of Japanese-Americans is found in California (261,800), followed by Hawaii with a Japanese-American population of 239,700, the acculturation process for each group is uniquely different (U.S. Bureau of the Census, 1991). The history of Japanese-American life in Hawaii is different from that of Japanese-Americans in the mainland United States. It is important to keep in mind the contextual milieu of Hawaii and the West Coast of the United States at the time of the original immigration and the much later context during and after World War II. These two eras are significant in Japanese-American history.

In Hawaii, most Japanese-Americans were confined to the islands during World War II. Those who were interned were perceived as a potential threat to the United States government. Most Japanese-Americans who lived along the western United States were treated as prisoners and forced into internment camps.

Family Structure

The first Japanese immigrants to the United States were students who arrived under two separate financial arrangements. One group was given scholarships to study in New England and Europe so they could return to the Meiji government and assume high government service posts. The other group consisted of private students who paid their own expenses. However, most of these students returned to Japan and are not considered to be the original pioneers (Ichioka, 1988).

Between 1861–1870, Japanese immigrants to the United States numbered only 186 individuals. Immigration increased after agreements were made in 1885 between the Japanese government and the Hawaiian sugar plantation owners. This agreement enabled Japanese contract laborers to leave Japan to work in the sugar cane fields in Hawaii (U.S. Department of Justice, 1964–1980; Immigration and Naturalization Service, 1984). Many of these were young, single men who came temporarily, fueled by dreams of making money and returning home to live more comfortably. Facing hardship and discrimination was perceived as short-term and many felt they could *gaman shi te* ("stick it out"). Over time, as some families adjusted to the culture, returning to Japan presented difficulties. Many families chose to remain in Hawaii.

Japanese immigration to the continental United States began in the 1890s. Most of the immigrants' work ranged from domestic and agricultural work, to jobs in mining and logging. From 1880 to 1890 most of the immigrants were unskilled single males. In 1908 a "Gentlemen's Agreement" was reached with the Japanese Government to restrict immigration from Japan. During the period 1907 to 1920, most of the immigrants were women who came as contractual "picture brides" for Japanese men already in the United States. With the 1924 Immigration Act, all Asian immigration to the United States was banned, leaving more than 42 percent of adult Japanese males without wives and with little hopes of marriage to Japanese women.

In 1940, 88 percent of the Japanese-Americans on the mainland lived on the West Coast, with 83 percent in California. A small percent lived in New York and Chicago. The Japanese attack on Pearl Harbor in 1941 was followed with the relocation of more than 110,000 Japanese-Americans from the West Coast to concentration camp sites in Arizona, Arkansas, California, Colorado, Idaho, Utah, and Wyoming with some being arrested and sent to prison camps as enemy aliens (Daniels, 1981). Only in 1992, fifty years later, did Congress attempt to correct this wrong by paying a token sum of $20,000 to each survivor of this World War II infringement on citizen's rights.

Some Japanese-Americans experienced arrest. Surrounded by barbed wire, individual freedom was restricted in camps. People were policed by soldiers carrying guns and following official directives. According to Broom and Kitsuse (1956), priority in these sites was given to daily routine and little to long-term planning for the future. Many used their skills and creativity to grow vegetables and decorate their quarters. Scholars have suggested that individuals who are reared in prison conditions, such as these, experience later adaptive struggles once they leave the prison camp and enter society again.

After World War II came the second relocation of Japanese-Americans. Most could not return to their former homes. Reports show that 268,814 or 37.5 percent were living in California; 9.4 percent were in the Pacific and Mountain states; 6.5 percent in the Northeast; 6.5 percent in the Midwest; and 6.6 percent in the South (U.S. Bureau of the Census, 1980). The families faced the difficult task of rebuilding their lives, as they experienced opposition and prejudice in the communities. The Japanese-Americans used their energies to blend into society and live as inconspicuously as possible. Children were urged into gaining educational achievements and young adults were pressured into occupational mobility by their families.

FAMILIES AND ACCULTURATION

Today, Japanese-Americans are generally perceived as successful, middle-class people who have been well integrated into American society. This gradual acculturation and adaptation into American society is best seen in generational terms. Individuals are commonly asked, "What generation do you belong to?" The practice of naming each generation using Japanese terminology honors the original immigrants, but gradually loses significance with each successive generation.

There are specific terms—*Issei, Nisei, Sansei,* and *Yonsei*—identifying individual generations since Japanese families first immigrated to the United States. The first generation immigrating to the U.S. is called "Issei." The first-born or second generation in the United States is called "Nisei." Offspring of the Nisei are called the "Sansei." The fourth generation is often simply termed the "fourth generation," although if one were to follow appropriate Japanese terminology, the term "Yonsei" would be used. By the fifth generation, most people see themselves as five generations removed from their immigrant ancestors and probably could not tell you the Japanese terminology for the fifth generation.

The Generational Model

Generational terms determine largely the degree of acculturation embodied by a Japanese-American individual. The first generation has minimal acculturation while the fourth or fifth generation is almost fully acculturated. The process of retaining the traditional culture or acculturating to the larger society depends to a large extent on whether an individual (1) seeks out other Japanese-Americans, (2) lives in a rural or urban area, or (3) belongs to the first generation or subsequent generations.

Issei.   Issei is the term for the first generation of Japanese individuals who immigrated to the United States. The Issei usually began life in the United States as single young adult males who arrived with the intent of returning to Japan after accumulating some wealth (Kitano, 1988). According to Strong (1934), the Issei were ambitious, intelligent, and probably the only early American immigrant group with the equivalent of an eighth-grade education.

The Issei formed ethnic communities that were a mixture of Old World traits and accommodative and acculturative institutions (Marden, Meyer and Engel, 1992). The community functioned as an extended family support unit. Investments, leisure activities, Tanomoshi (a credit system), restaurants, shops, real estate, and other businesses could all be found in the Japanese-American community. The Issei community was tightly committed to the ways of Japan.

In order to begin families, the Issei men turned to their family, friends, and matchmakers in Japan to secure future Japanese wives. Thus, the traditional Japanese custom of marriages arranged between households found its way to the United States. The practice of exchanging pictures of the prospective bride and groom was developed and added to the institutionalized and traditionally arranged marriages. The women were called "picture brides."

Although the marriage process was altered and hybridized, the concept of a patriarchal family and kin relationships continued unbroken from Japan to the United States (Yanagisako, 1985). Family rights almost always predominated over individual rights and family loyalty, duty, and responsibility took precedence over personal desires. A high value was placed on prescribed roles for males and females, with variations depending on age, status, and gender. The family was hierarchical in structure, with husbands holding most of the authority. There was a strong preference for male heirs.

The social structure of families was based on traditional Japanese interpretations of Confucian ideals of the superiority of old over young and male over female regarding all interpersonal relationships. The practice of the eldest son inheriting the property and power was also a link to the old country.

The pre-World War II Issei generation established clear boundaries of who was inside the family and who was considered an outsider. The Issei family system was an extension of the ethnic community. The norms, values, and behaviors of families were reinforced by the ethnic community at large. These communities provided the family with socio-emotional and economic support. Ethnic food stores, businesses, service organizations, newspapers, and other activities all helped create a secure familiar atmosphere for the Issei.

Japanese-American Issei families relied heavily upon family customs concerning marriages, deaths, births, anniversaries, holidays, picnics, and recreation as a means of insuring and solidifying Japanese family customs and traditions from generation to generation.

The phrase *kodomo no tame ni* ("for the sake of the children") (Ogawa, 1978) was a common Issei phrase meaning sacrificing one's needs for the children. High hopes and expectations for gaining success and acceptance were placed on the American-born children of Japanese parents.

With World War II and the evacuation of 110,000 Japanese-Americans living along the west coast of the U.S., life drastically changed for Issei families. Families were forced into hurriedly built internment camps in isolated areas, often desert areas of states such as California, Idaho, Utah, Wyoming, Colorado, Arkansas, and Arizona. According to Kitano (1988, p. 265), the Issei "learned to live by official directives, learned to respond to announcements, and learned the importance of adjusting to the whims of government-appointed white administrators. . . . Families were housed in one room units in modified barracks . . . almost all noise could be heard throughout the unit. . . . Community mess halls, lavatories, showers, and washrooms meant adjust to communal living."

The Issei family was severely challenged by being uprooted and incarcerated. Their freedom was taken from them and they were placed in a cultural context that was completely alien. It was unlike their ancestral community, unlike their American ethnic community, and unlike the majority white community. It was an environment wrought with fear and crisis.

The first generation (1800s) Issei could not marry a Caucasian according to family values as well as societal rules of disapproval. Neither could they own land after the Alien Land laws were passed in California and other states. They were limited in the types of neighborhoods in which they could live, the types of jobs they could hold, and the types of social and recreational opportunities available to them. The Issei were discriminated against and prevented from attending public schools. They had to struggle for the right to public education. These situations created great psychological stress for the Issei. They responded by resisting acculturation (Ichioka, 1988).

Nisei.   Nisei are the children of Issei. They are the second-generation Japanese-Americans. The Nisei represented to the Issei what they felt they could not achieve, success through education.

Outside of Hawaii, many second-generation Nisei attained a middle-class stature, moved out of the old Japanese ethnic neighborhoods into suburban America, and blended into the mainstream of social activity. Nisei were children and youth during World War II and spent years in the isolated environments of internment camps. One college-age Nisei student who was released from a desert area camp to attend college, told a seatmate on a long distance bus ride, "You can't imagine how it makes you feel to have your loyalty to the United States questioned." Her seatmate, a majority college student, listened in shocked disbelief at the student's personal account of the internment.

Nisei assimilation into the majority culture was more common among mainland Nisei than among the more traditional Japanese-Americans of Hawaii. The Nisei generation is now of senior-citizen age. According to Kitano (1988), the Nisei practiced American-type activities, such as dating, outings, retreats, conferences, and dances within their own peer group and were culturally closer to the American way of life than the Issei lifestyle.

The differences between the two generations are easily seen in the changes in marriage customs and rituals. For example, the Issei marriage was a model from Japan characterized by the following (Yanagisako, 1985):

1. marriages were arranged,
2. interaction of couples was based on obligations,
3. family bonds were more important than spousal bonds,
4. male domination,
5. labor differed by gender,
6. emphasis was on compassion, respect, and consideration,
7. emotional restraint and stability were expected,
8. little verbal communication occurred between spouses, and
9. family involvement was high in relationships.

The Nisei made a choice between the opportunities presented by the American model and the traditional ways of the Issei. This meant freedom of choice in choosing a spouse, allowing for romantic love, greater equality of the sexes, more overt emotional expressions, more verbal communication between spouses, prioritizing the spousal bond as more important than the family bond, an attachment to family relationships defined as opportunity rather than obligation, and freedom from negative sanctions concerning marriage and family stability.

The Nisei adapted to the bicultural dilemma by incorporating some of the old traditions and some of the new ways. English was their first language. Each individual and family selected those ideals that best fitted their cultural experiences and context. Today there exists a variety of family forms and customs, ranging from the traditional ideals of the Issei to the American ideals of individual freedom of choice.

What has remained important to the generations is the family, its past, its present, and its future with roots in both the Japanese and American dreams. Family gatherings, such as New Year's celebrations, weddings, and funerals, are important functions that serve to rekindle the ties of the cultural heritage.

An example of this cultural synthesis is the mixture of the old traditional foods, such as mochi, rice cakes, sushi, and sashimi, which are served along with American cookies, cakes, and soft drinks. Today monetary wedding gifts are given as well as bridal shower gifts. Envelopes containing a ten-dollar bill as well as a sympathy card are considered appropriate for funerals. Such behavioral practices all create the delicate balancing act of the second generation of Nisei with the new times and the places in which they reside.

Sansei.   The third generation, the Sansei, is a mixture of holding on and letting go of the ways of the older generations. Sometimes Sansei have been labeled "the bumblebee generation" because they are striped with yellow and black and deliver a sting. The Sansei have brought to the nation's consciousness the human rights issues of the U.S. internment camps for Japanese-Americans during World War II. Most Sansei have almost completely assimilated into the mainstream majority culture. They see no semblance of Japanese traditions in their own socialization or self-identity, except for their outward physical appearance.

The Sansei have integrated more American ways into the definition of self than the Nisei, just as the Nisei were more assimilated than the Issei. Thus, with each succeeding generation, acculturation to the American model becomes more widespread. Yet, according to Kitano and Daniels (1988), personality tests reflect scores that indicate that the Sansei generation shows more self-restraint, self-denial, submission, and deference to elders and those in authority than is found among majority individuals. This study shows that many Sansei still identify with their Japanese ancestry and take pride in traditional cultural values. However, there are those who believe that the Sansei may have acculturated or Americanized themselves to the point where it is impossible to permit effective ethnic recovery.

Many Sansei have lost their ethnicity in establishing their self-identity. Many first- and second-generation Japanese-Americans would say that the Sansei have adapted to the values of the majority culture by being more independent. Yet while they have moved away from the value of family dependence, they prefer the value of indirect confrontation over direct confrontation. By preferring to be called Japanese-Americans, the Sanseis have maintained a symbolic ethnicity, according to Gann (1979).

The Sansei generation participates in majority cultural activities with freedom and with fewer ethnic social controls than were found among the Issei or Nisei generations. The Sansei know little of Japanese cultural traditions and language. They participate less in Japanese events and art forms. They frequently marry out of the Japanese-American ethnic group.

Role of Japanese-American Women

Japanese-American women are among the more highly acculturated Asians. Their intermarriage rate among Asian subgroups is the highest in the United States. This indicates a permeable boundary existing between Japanese-Americans and the majority culture.

Role of Japanese-American Men

Japanese-American men today are freer of old obligations. They are in the mainstream of business and academic life due to their high regard for and achievement in higher education. They are accepting a more egalitarian role in their families—enjoying play with their children, for example—in ways that they never would have in the traditional home. They intermarry without concern.

SELECTED JAPANESE-AMERICAN TRADITIONAL FAMILY VALUES

Japanese-Americans place significant value on family and community responsibility. This means carrying out obligations and showing respect for those in authority, those who are elderly, and other family members. According to Roland (1984, 1988), the familial self of the Asian contrasts sharply with the highly individual self of the American. The familial self includes the rights, responsibilities, obligations, and loyalty to one's family and ethnic group.

Context refers to the collection of social and cultural conditions that surround and influence the life of an individual, a family, an organization, or a community. According to Hall (1966, 1983), the Japanese-American lives in a high-context culture as opposed to a low-context culture. For example, the Japanese pay much attention to the surrounding circumstances or context of an event. An example would be interpersonal communication, where phrasing, tone, gesture, posture, social status, history, and social setting are all crucial to the meaning of a message. In contrast, Euro-Americans, according to Hall, typically exist in the medium- to low-context culture and their identity is rooted in the individual rather than the family. In short, Japanese-Americans may see and hear nuances in events others seldom perceive because they are so very alert to context.

Culturally meaningful behavior and standards are difficult to address in a rapidly acculturating ethnic group. Because Japanese-Americans are socialized to pay close attention to the surrounding context, traditional values of importance are often obscured by the demands of the mainstream culture.

A central theme of the Japanese and Japanese-American culture is for people to be in harmony with their environment. Harmony is especially noticeable in Japanese art and gardens and this concept extends to being in harmony with one's internal psychology and one's social relations.

JAPANESE-AMERICAN FAMILIES AND THE EDUCATIONAL SYSTEM

Japanese-Americans have accepted the American view that education is the key to success, and that it will ensure a good life. For example, results of a 1992 study comparing parental involvement of three generations of Japanese-Americans, the Issei, Nisei, and Sansei, show that the ensuing generations of Japanese-Americans become more and more active and directly involved in the education of their children. The researchers concluded that this evolutionary development was highly related to language communication and familiarity with the dominant culture (Shoho, 1992). Parents want their children to succeed in school. All evidence points to the fact that most Japanese-American students work hard in their studies and their work and succeed at very high rates.

JAPANESE-AMERICAN FAMILIES AND THE HEALTH CARE SYSTEM

The Japanese-American population in Hawaii has one of the longest life expectancies of any large population subgroup in the United States as well as the world (Curb, Reed, Miller, and Yano, 1990). The average Japanese-American lives approximately six years longer than the average Caucasian. Their good health may be related to diet or lifestyle. With regard to health care, Japanese women, especially the elderly, prefer female doctors. Japanese-Americans are typically served well by the health care system because of their economic affluence.

JAPANESE-AMERICAN FAMILIES AND THE GOVERNMENTAL SYSTEM

Most Japanese-Americans, like other Americans, were totally bewildered by the bombing of Pearl Harbor and felt totally alienated from that act of aggression. Yet they were herded into concentration camps at the onset of World War II. As citizens of the United States, they were totally denied due process of law as required by the Fourteenth Amendment to the U.S. Constitution. Not one case of espionage was ever found among the 120,000 people interned (Daniels, 1981).

Today, there are a few Japanese-American members of Congress. It is difficult to generalize about party affiliations for most of the Japanese-Americans. There seems to be an even split among Democrats and Republicans, with generous monetary contributions going to both major parties. Senator Daniel Inouye from Hawaii, a wounded World War II veteran, has served in the Senate for many terms.

JAPANESE-AMERICAN FAMILIES AND THE ECONOMIC SYSTEM

Asian-Americans were called a model minority in 1982; America's super-minority in 1986; and, in 1987, a television program presented a special on Asian-American achievements and successes. Asian-Americans have been held up as role models and are compared with and encouraged to compete against other ethnic minority groups. Ignored are the many important variables that overshadow these glowing accounts. For example, reported higher family income among Asian-Americans is often reflective of more wage earners present in a family, rather than higher income per worker (Cabezas and Kawaguchi, 1988). In 1988, the United States Equal Employment Opportunity Commission revealed discrimination patterns of low employment for Asians in all occupations in private industry, with the exception of service work. According to Langberg and Farley (1985), Asian-Americans still experience some degree of discrimination and segregation in society, due to differences in racial and cultural background, despite high levels of education and economic achievement.

According to Jiobu (1988), it is clear that Japanese-Americans are beginning to assimilate socioeconomically and structurally. There are families who symbolically and consciously keep their Japanese cultural heritage and at the same time socialize their children to live in the culture of the dominant society. These are not people trapped as marginal, but people who have made choices to be dual-cultured. As the Japanese-American group succeeds, it can increasingly afford to maintain this duality.

Therefore, what may seem to be contradictory behavior to an outsider is really an expression of an adjustment to the perceived context. For example, when a majority person is invited to dinner, the dinner table appears similar to any other household, in terms of food, tableware, manners, conversation, and so forth. If, however, a Japanese-American person comes as a dinner guest, most likely there will be more ethnic foods served, the dishes and tableware may be very different, and sometimes one may even sit on the floor at a low table to eat dinner. Noticeable are the conversation style and figures of speech reflecting the cultural heritage.

Depending upon the household and the conscious maintenance of one's ethnicity, a Japanese-American may seem completely acculturated to the dominant society. However, the identities of Japanese-Americans often bear witness to the Japanese cultural heritage.

VIETNAMESE-AMERICAN FAMILIES

The end of the Vietnam War brought many Vietnamese individuals and families to the U.S. as refugees. Many of the early refugees were those who had helped the U.S. during the war and were then assisted in leaving Vietnam to save their lives. From 1975 to 1992, more than 856,500 Southeast Asians sought refuge in the United States. Most of the refugees were Vietnamese seeking asylum and fleeing from persecution. Those who could prove they were in danger because they had aided Americans in the war effort were airlifted out of the country. Those who were able to leave the country were allowed into the United States by way of a third country only upon showing proof of relatives living in the U.S. Subsequently, it became more and more difficult for the Vietnamese to immigrate into the U.S.

The first 1975 Vietnamese refugees have adjusted quite well to the United States. They arrived with higher educational levels and more exposure to Western culture as compared to later immigrants. Many recent refugees spent considerable time at sea or years in political prisons.

Amerasians.   Amerasians are children of Asian mothers and U.S. servicemen conceived in Vietnam during the Vietnam War. Most have experienced years of rejection by the Vietnamese people and many were totally unacknowledged by their American fathers. Amerasians were not allowed admittance into the U.S. before 1982 because of their illegitimate status. In Vietnam, due to the stigma attached to marrying an American serviceman, many mothers destroyed marriage licenses and birth certificates which would have given proof of their association with Americans. In the U.S., many Amerasians suffered because of their mixed race, especially those whose fathers were African-Americans. As mentioned earlier, most fathers did not claim their children.

In 1982, the Amerasian Immigration Act allowed only the children of U.S. servicemen into the United States. However, most Amerasians with any family were unwilling to leave them behind. Orphans and abandoned children generally had no monetary means of cutting through the enormous amount of red tape necessary to leave Vietnam. In 1982, of the total number of refugees admitted to the United States, 50.1 percent were 19 years old or younger (Office of Refugee Resettlement, 1982).

In 1987, Congress passed the Amerasian Homecoming Act, allowing relatives to accompany Amerasian "children" who are now adults. These families have strengths and weaknesses similar to other Vietnamese families who have lived here more than ten years. The Amerasians are 80 percent illiterate upon arrival in the U.S.

In spite of their high numbers, refugee youth have not been studied and there is a void in hard data and knowledge that also affects services for these young people and their families.

THE ECOLOGY OF VIETNAMESE-AMERICAN FAMILIES

The total number of Vietnamese-Americans living in the U.S. in 1990 was 614,547. This is an increase of 135 percent since 1980 (LEAP, 1993). The largest Vietnamese populations are found in Orange County, California, followed in order by Los Angeles, California; San Jose, California; Houston, Texas; Washington, DC; and San Diego, California.

The Vietnamese-American community is divided economically with half earning more than $38,205. The median household income in the U.S. is $35,000. There are 23.7 percent of Vietnamese-American families living in poverty (the U.S. poverty rate is 13.2 percent). The recent Vietnamese immigrant families experience a higher level of poverty and are four times as likely to receive welfare assistance (LEAP, 1993).

Family Structure

Most of the Vietnamese immigrants came from rural areas of Vietnam that contain several ethnic minority groups, each with their own language and cultural practices. There are several religions; however, Buddhism is the most prominent.

The Vietnamese family consists of parents, siblings, and all relatives. The family is considered more important than the individual. The individual owes loyalty to the family before all else and holds the family interest above personal interest (Brown, 1982).

The family is highly structured. There is a hierarchy of priorities with parental ties being most paramount. The family is the caretaker of its members' physical, social, and emotional well-being. Family members care for their families first and community second. The concept of "strangers" intervening does not exist in Vietnamese culture. There is great reluctance to admit problems to strangers. Well-intentioned interventions by helping professionals, for example, may be serious insults to the Vietnamese, who, out of politeness, will not reveal their feelings about the situation.

Vietnamese Male Roles.   A son's first obligation is to his parents, followed by obligations to his siblings. These are permanent expectations between parents, children, and siblings (Dillard, 1987).

The oldest male is the head of the family and has absolute power and responsibility for the care of other family members. Children live with their families until they marry, and care for their parents when they age. After the death of the oldest male, the oldest son becomes head of the family.

Vietnamese Female Roles.   A woman is expected to obey her father when single and her husband after she is married. When she is widowed, she is expected to live with her eldest son and accept his authority.

The Vietnamese woman's marital status seems to have a significant bearing on her adjustment to U.S. life. Older Vietnamese women without spouses demonstrate more serious psychiatric and social problems than their married counterparts.

Cultural Values.   The differences between the Vietnamese culture and the mainstream U.S. culture have been points of confusion and clashes for immigrants. Most noticeable and strongly observed are the behaviors of "saving face" versus frank expression, interdependence versus independence, quiet reserve versus openness, and authoritarian male hierarchical control versus individual freedom and egalitarian choice.

VIETNAMESE-AMERICAN FAMILIES AND THE EDUCATIONAL SYSTEM

According to Dillard (1987), the major stressors for Vietnamese refugee youths are (1) moving to a different community and school; (2) having difficulty with the English language; and (3) communicating with teachers and peers in school and social settings. Most refugee youths are not prepared to function in American schools where students are expected to take an active role. A number of academic and behavioral problems have been noted among some of the undereducated, the unaccompanied minors, and the Amerasians. Amerasian girls generally fare better in school than male Amerasians. It has been reported that Amerasian girls view their new education as a true luxury.

Vietnamese youths face incredible challenges and obstacles as they adapt at home, at school, and in the community. Many youths are faced with loneliness and social isolation. Yet there are cases of Vietnamese students attaining Valedictorian status in their high school classes and succeeding in college. Their drive and hard work pay off when they take advantage of opportunities offered.

VIETNAMESE-AMERICAN FAMILIES AND THE HEALTH CARE SYSTEM

Recent Vietnamese refugees typically have serious health problems. Many carry infections such as tuberculosis, hepatitis, parasites, and other infections that result in chronic nutritional deficiencies. Many have suffered malnutrition and starvation, along with excessive stress, resulting in stunted growth, delayed puberty, and other syndromes (Carlin and Sokoloff, 1985).

Some Amerasians develop psychological problems from coping with their mixed race. Identity problems seem to be more complex for Black Amerasians than others (Biagini, 1989).

Older people tend to acculturate more slowly than the younger generation; therefore, they tend to be more isolated from the mainstream of society as well as from their own family members. Most of the elderly Vietnamese are unable to speak English. Most cannot drive a car and spend most of their time at home alone. The older they are, the more depressed they are. Some have experienced extreme forms of violence, but shame keeps the elderly from discussing the past. Symptoms of Post Traumatic Stress Disorder, such as avoidance, hyperactive startle reactions, emotional numbness, intrusive thoughts, and nightmares have been noted in those who have sought psychiatric treatment (Carlin, 1986).

VIETNAMESE-AMERICANS AND THE GOVERNMENTAL SYSTEM

The picture of Vietnamese refugees and their relationship to the U.S. government is still coming into focus. Vietnamese refugees were not sufficiently supported when U.S. programs and policies settled Vietnamese families throughout the United States, precluding their gaining emotional support from other Vietnamese families, like most immigrant groups. Researchers believe that social support networks are the single most important factor in the adequate adjustment of the Vietnamese to the United States. Also, the shifting of health and nutritional responsibilities from federal to state governments made services either inadequate or inaccessible.

ROLES FOR HELPING PROFESSIONALS

Helping professionals of many kinds will find themselves interacting with Asian-Americans. The more recent Asian-American citizens need assistance in many of our governmental and community programs. Securing the assistance of language interpreters will be a first priority if you are not fluent in their languages. Seeking in-depth information about how to overcome some of the cultural issues that make serving this community difficult will be another priority. You will find subtle cultural variations that make each subgroup unique. Knowing the differences will help you bridge the gap in your role.

CONCLUSIONS

On the surface, Asian-Americans as a whole appear highly successful. The stereotype of the "model minority" disguises a complex community of controversies and a tug of war between traditional Asian practices and assimilation into the majority culture. In the Asian-American community, family pride and loyalty, academic achievement, hard work, and pressure to succeed have high priorities. Asian-Americans occupy a unique position in the United States. They are not considered a part of the majority, nor are they recognized as a minority in certain circumstances. They are like the shaded gray area between black and white, often the invisible citizen.

A review of demographic trends depicts an acceleration towards diversity. There are many Asian-American refugees and immigrants who are falling under the poverty line and are dropping out of the educational system. At the other end of the distribution, there are generations of Asian-Americans who have invested in education and the American promise and are highly successful.

STUDY QUESTIONS

1. List ten countries that many Asian-Americans call their ancestral homes.
2. List 10 complete sentences giving historical facts about the early Asian-American immigrants from their earliest days.
3. List the relative percentages of the U.S. population represented by Asian-Americans. What do these data tell you?
4. Two distinct groups of Asian-Americans were identified for extensive discussion. List these two groups and their identifying characteristics.
5. List the typical family structure found in the countries of Asia discussed in the chapter.
6. What religions were listed as contributing to the cultural values of Asians?
7. What is happening with respect to children of recent immigrants who enter American schools?
8. What data were offered to show Asian-Americans' success in the educational system?
9. List facts in complete sentences that show Asian-Americans' participation in the economic system.
10. There are names for each generation of Japanese-Americans living in the United States. List these names and give definitions.
11. How did U.S. government treatment of Japanese-Americans living in Hawaii differ from treatment of those living in the U.S. mainland during World War II?
12. List ten facts in complete sentences that show how Japanese-Americans have been acculturated.
13. Give 10 sentences that show Japanese-Americans' success with the educational system.
14. List 10 facts regarding Vietnamese immigration to the U.S.
15. List 10 facts presented about Amerasians.
16. List 10 ways that a helping professional might assist Vietnamese-Americans.

APPLICATIONS

1. Are Asian-Americans a "model minority"? Write a two-page essay giving at least five reasons why you do or do not support this characterization.
2. By claiming that Asian-Americans are a model minority, society can use them as an example to challenge other minority groups. Who benefits from the perpetuation of this stereotype? Write a two-page report.
3. Do you believe that Asian-Americans are over-represented in colleges in the U.S.? Research this idea further and give your opinion in a two-page report.

4. Discuss your opinion regarding the number of immigrants from Asia entering the U.S. in a two-page essay.

5. Some feel that Asian-Americans do not fully integrate into the majority culture as well as other immigrants because they are slow to adapt to the English language and they hold on to their cultural distinctions. How do you feel? Do some library research and write a two-page essay on what you learn.

6. A large portion of elderly Asian people experience stress and anomie in the United States. What are some suggestions to alleviate these problems? Write a one- or two-page essay.

7. State your own ethnic culture in a half-page report giving evidence. Comparing your culture and the Asian one, what are some of the common needs and goals expressed in different terms by the Asian culture? Write a two-page essay.

8. Some authorities treat cultural differences as though they do not exist. Others believe that putting differences squarely on the table is the best way to clear the air between individuals and groups. Write a one- or two-page essay defending one of the views.

REFERENCES

Biagini, J. (1989). *Issues of mental health and social adjustment for Southeast Asian refugees.* Upper Great Lakes Multifunctional Resource Center.

Broom, L., and Kitsuse, J. (1956). *The managed casualty.* Los Angeles, CA: University of California Press.

Brown, G. (1988). Issues in the resettlement of Indochinese refugees. *Social Casework, 63,* 155–159.

Cabezas, A., and Kawaguchi, G. (1988). Empirical evidence for continuing Asian American income inequity: The human capital model and labor market segmentation. In G. Y. Okihiro, et al. (Eds.), *Reflections on shattered windows: Promises and prospects for Asian American studies* (pp. 148, 154). Pullman, WA: Washington State University Press.

Carlin, J., and Sokoloff, B. (1985). Mental health treatment issues for Southeast Asian refugee children. In T. Owan (Ed.), *Southeast Asian mental health: Treatment, prevention services, training, and research.* Washington, D.C.: National Institute of Mental Health.

Chan, S. (1991). *Asian Americans: An interpretive history.* Boston, MA: Twayne Publishers.

Chung, D. (1992). Asian cultural commonalities: A comparison with mainstream American culture. In S. M. Furuto, et al. (Eds.), *Social work practice with Asian Americans* (pp. 27–44). Beverly Hills, CA: Sage Publications.

Curb, J., Reed, D., Miller, F., and Yano, K. (1990, September). Health status and life style in elderly Japanese men with a long life expectancy. *Journal of Gerontology, 45*(5), 206–11.

Daniels, R. (1981). *Concentration camps: Japanese Americans and World War II*. New York, NY: Holt, Rinehart and Winston.

Dillard, J. (1987). *Multicultural counseling: Toward ethnic and cultural relevance in human encounters*. Chicago: Nelson-Hall.

Gall, Susan, and Gall, Timothy. (Eds.). (1993). *Statistical record of Asian Americans*. Detroit, MI: Gale Research, Inc.

Gann, H. (1979, January). Symbolic ethnicity: The future of ethnic groups and cultures in America. *Ethnic and Racial Studies*, 1–20.

Hall, E. T. (1966). *The hidden dimension*. Garden City, NY: Doubleday.

Hall, E. T. (1980). *The silent language*. Garden City, NY: Doubleday.

Hall, E. T. (1983). *The dance of life*. Garden City, NY: Doubleday.

Hsia, J. and Nakanishi, M. (1989, November/December). The demographics of diversity: Asian Americans in higher education. *Change, 21*, 20–27.

Hu, A. (1988). Asian Americans: A model minority or double minority. *Amerasia, 15*(1), 243–257.

Ichioka, Y. (1988). *The Issei: The world of the first generation Japanese immigrants, 1885–1924*. New York, NY: Free Press.

Jiobu, R. (1988). *Ethnicity and assimilation*. Albany, NY: State University of New York Press.

Kitano, H. (1988). The Japanese American family. In C. Mindel, R. Habenstein, and R. Wright, Jr. (Eds.), *Ethnic families in America* (pp. 258–299). New York, NY: Elsevier.

Kitano, H., and Daniels, R. (1988). *Asian Americans: Emerging minorities*. New York, NY: Prentice-Hall.

Krenner, P., and Sabin, C. (1985). Indochinese immigrant children: Problems in psychiatric diagnosis. *Journal of the American Academy of Child Psychiatry, 24*, 453–458.

Lai, H., Lim, G., and Yung, J. (1981). *Island poetry and history of Chinese Immigrants on Angel Island, 1910–1940*. San Francisco, CA: Chinese Historical Society.

Langberg, M., and Farley, R. (1985). Residential segregation of Asian Americans in 1980. *Sociology and Social Research, 70*, 71–75.

LEAP. (1993). *The State of Asian Pacific America: A Public Policy Report, Policy Issues to the Year 2020*. LEAP Asian Pacific American Public Policy Institute, Los Angeles, California.

Leong, F., and Hayes, T. (1990, December). Occupational stereotyping of Asian Americans. *The Career Development Quarterly, 39*, 143–153.

Marden, C., Meyer, G., and Engel, M. (1992). *Minorities in American society.* New York, NY: HarperCollins, Publishers.

Mei, J. (1984). Socioeconomic origins of emigration: Guangdong to California, 1850–1882. In L. Cheng & E. Bonachich (Eds.), *Labor immigration under capitalism: Asian workers in the United States before World War II* (pp. 219–247). Berkeley, CA: University of California Press.

Nakanishi, D. (1989, November/December). A quota on excellence. *Change, 21,* 39–47.

Office of Refugee Resettlement. (1982, May). Monthly Data Report.

Office of Refugee Resettlement. (1984, July 6). Amerasian problems and issues [Memorandum].

Ogawa, D. (Ed.). (1978). *Kodomo no tame ni: For the sake of the children.* Honolulu, HI: University of Hawaii Press.

O'Hare, William, and Felt, Judy. (1991, February). *Asian Americans: America's fastest growing minority group.* Washington, DC: Population Reference Bureau, Inc.

Roland, A. (1984). The self in India and America: Toward a psychoanalysis of social and cultural contexts. In V. Kavolis (Ed.), *Design of selfhood* (pp. 170–194). London: Associated University Press.

Roland, A. (1988). *In search of self in India and Japan: Toward a cross cultural psychology.* Princeton, NJ: Princeton University Press.

Shoho, Alan. (1992, April). *An historical comparison of parental involvement of three generations of Japanese Americans (Issei, Nisei, and Sansei) in the education of their children.* Paper presented at the Annual Meeting of the American Educational Research Association, San Francisco, CA.

Strong, E. (1934). *The second generation Japanese problem.* Stanford, CA: Stanford University Press.

Suzuki, L., and Yamashiro, C. (1980). *A study of the attitude of third generation Japanese Americans in Hawaii and the mainland.* Master's Thesis, University of California at Los Angeles.

Takaki, R. (1989). *Strangers from a different shore: A history of Asian Americans.* Waltham, MA: Little, Brown and Co.

Takaki, R. (1993). *A different mirror.* Boston, MA: Little, Brown and Co.

True, Reiko. (1990). Psychotherapeutic issues with Asian American women. *Sex Roles, 22*(⅞), pp. 477–486.

Tsui, P., and Schultz, G. (1985). Failure of rapport: Why psychotherapeutic engagement fails in the treatment of Asian clients. *American Journal of Orthopsychiatry, 55*(4), 561–569.

U.S. Bureau of the Census. (1990). Money, income and poverty status in the U.S., 1989. (*Current Population Reports,* Series P-60, No. 168.) Washington, DC: Government Printing Office.

U.S. Bureau of the Census. (1990). Population estimates by age, sex, race and ethnic origin: 1980–1988. (*Current Population Reports,* Series P-25, No. 1045.) Washington, DC: Government Printing Office.

U.S. Bureau of the Census. (1991, June 12). Census bureau releases 1990 census counts on specific racial groups [Press release].

U.S. Department of Justice. (1964–1980). Immigration and Naturalization Service (1984). Washington, DC: Government Printing Office.

Yanagisako, S. (1985). *Transforming the past.* Stanford, CA: Stanford University Press.

CHAPTER 7

Arab-American Families

Key Concepts

◆ Muslim

◆ Koran

◆ Patrilineal

Be proud of being an American, but also be proud that your fathers and mothers came from a land upon which God laid His precious hand and raised His messengers.

— Kahlil Gibran (1883–1931)

Most immigrants are proud to be Americans, as Gibran suggests, yet fondly remember their homelands. This chapter will introduce you to Arab-Americans. It comes as a surprise to many that there are about 2.5 million Arab-Americans in the United States. Many Americans have recently become aware of how little they know about the Middle Eastern peoples. The Arab world has been grossly neglected in the education of most Americans. As helping professionals, you may have occasions to work with Arab-American families.

WHO ARE THE ARAB-AMERICANS?

Arab-Americans have lived in the United States for over a century and a half. Immigrants from Arab countries come from various regions of the Arab world—from the Atlantic coast of northern Africa in the west to the Arabian Sea in the east and from the Mediterranean Sea in the north to Central Africa in the south. Within this vast region, various linguistic, religious, and ethnic groups live together, sharing some common bonds of history and tradition.

Though representing different Arab countries and ecological regions, many Arabs see themselves as one nation. The League of Arab States was founded in 1945. Today there are 22 member states that identify themselves as Arab nations. The Arabic language is the common link between those who are by birth Syrians, Saudi Arabians, Egyptians, or Berbers. Although Islam is the dominant religion, there are various others (Ahmed and Gray, 1988).

Generally, Arabs prefer to be defined as those who consider themselves members of the Arab Nation and who enjoy a common heritage, language, culture, and destiny. There is a difference between "The Arab World" and the term "Middle East." For example, Turkey, Afghanistan, and Iran may be considered Muslim and part of the Middle East, but are not part of the Arab world.

Most of the early Arab immigrants to the United States (1875–1940) were Christians from the Syrian province of the Ottoman Empire (Turkey) (Naff, 1983). Many were single men from villages in the Mt. Lebanon region who immigrated for economic reasons. Like many other immigrant groups, Arabs tended to congregate in urban areas of the United States, such as Detroit, Michigan, and New York City. They sent home money and their stories of success.

Back home in the Middle East, news of economic success in America spread quickly and brought other small businessmen, skilled laborers, and craftsmen, many of whom also became economically successful and returned home prosperous (Naff, 1983). Success was a dream families had for their sons. It was customary for family resources to be pooled to help the young immigrant. Thus the Arab came to the United States with strong family support and the desire to work hard to earn money.

The first mosque was built in the United States in 1919, in Highland Park, Michigan. By 1959, it was estimated that only one Arab-American in eighteen was Muslim. In the 1960s, the small Arab-American community passed the half million mark without any recognition as a contributing ethnic group to the history of the United States. American children were studying Algebra without any knowledge of its Arab origin.

In the 1970s there was a new wave of Arab immigrants, mostly Lebanese, Palestinians, and Iraqis, who came because of political upheavals in their regions. Though economics was still an important factor in more recent Arab immigration, other social factors, such as political unrest, professional opportunities, and opportunities for their children and family, often influenced decisions to leave their homelands.

Today, there is a mingling of the old and the new immigrants. There are many first-generation Arab immigrants in the United States who are learning Western ways while retaining many of the characteristics of families in their homeland. Other Arab-Americans have been exposed to Western education and values, and have had an understanding of Western culture and language prior to their decision to make the United States their homeland.

THE ECOLOGY OF ARAB-AMERICAN FAMILIES

Given the regional and ethnic diversity in any one Arab nation, it is difficult to construct an Arab family profile. Our description of Arab-Americans represents a generalization and may not be characteristic of any one individual family. Just as the definition of an American may vary from individual to individual, there are factors such as religion, education, economic conditions, ethnic subgroups, and generational degrees of acculturation that affect individual and family values.

Arab-American Families and the Religious System

In Detroit, Michigan, there are approximately 200,000 Arab-American residents (Ahmed and Gray, 1988). Within this population, the four major nationality groups represented are the Lebanese/Syrian, Palestinian, Yemeni, and Iraqi-Chaldean. The typical religious affiliations of the Lebanese and Syrians are Greek or Syrian Orthodox, Maronite and Melkite Eastern Rite Catholics, or Sunni or Shia Muslims. The Palestinians are typically affiliated with Greek Orthodox, Roman Catholic, Protestant, or, more often, Sunni Muslim religions. The Yemeni Muslims are Shafei and Zeidi. The Iraqi/Chaldean are generally Eastern Rite Catholics or Muslims. Only a few but important teachings of the Islam religion will be presented because it is impossible to cover all religious aspects in the space available in this chapter.

According to Islamic tradition, *Allah,* or God, revealed to Muhammad through the angel Gabriel a series of revelations that became the basis of a new faith, *Islam*. Those who acknowledge Muhammad as the last prophet and submit to God's will are called *Muslims*. Muslims acknowledge a great reverence toward the Biblical prophets Adam, Noah, Abraham, Moses, and Jesus, for all helped to bring the world of God to man during their lifetimes. Islamic acts of devotion are based on the Five Pillars of Islam. These five pillars are faith, prayer, fasting, pilgrimage, and alms giving. Islam is more than a religion to Arabs; it is a way of life, physically, spiritually, morally, socially, legally, and politically.

Islam differs from country to country; for example, the practices in Oman differ from those in Iran. In Iran, Islamic women are required to have their heads covered, while in Kuwait, women do not necessarily cover their heads.

According to the *Encyclopaedia Britannica* and the *Encyclopedia Americana,* Muslims, Jews, and many others in Spain and elsewhere were persecuted and even burned at the stake for heresies during the Inquisition in the thirteenth and fourteenth centuries. Many were forced to convert to Catholicism to save their lives. Over the centuries, religious intolerance on the parts of many groups, that is, a refusal to permit diversity in peaceful dialog, has led to many persecutions and many delays in societal progress.

According to Sheikh Zayed, religious advisor to ABA dhabi's ruler, Islam is a continuation of the Judeo-Christian ethic. Many commonalities link the three religions of Islam, Christianity, and Judaism (Lorenz, 1993).

Some Arab-Americans are Arab Christians whose roots lie with the heritage of Eastern Christianity and the culture of the Arabic Middle East. It is often difficult to understand the experience of this complicated group, specifically those with Syrian and Lebanese origins. They are divided into two major religious bodies, Catholic and Eastern Orthodox, and two nationalities, Syrian and Lebanese. There is considerable cultural mixing because for generations marriage rates with partners outside the group have been very high, even exceeding 80 percent in the 1980s (Philip and Kayal, 1983). Intermarriage accelerates the process of acculturation and eases or erases the lines between groups.

Because of recent Arab-Israeli conflicts, contemporary Syrian-Lebanese Americans have been forced to examine their history, their ethnic identity, and their relationship with other Arab-Americans and the Arab world. It is left to each family to decide what Arab cultural features to retain and which features to accept from the American culture.

Arab-American Family Structure

The structure of the Arab family is usually described as patrilineal, patrilocal, patriarchal, and extended. In *patrilineal* families, descent is traced only through the male heirs, and loyalty of all family members is directed toward the father's family (see Figure 7–1). *Patrilocal* means that a newly married couple moves into the house or compound of the husband's family. *Patriarchal* refers to the father's complete authority over other family members. The Arab *extended* family refers to all male heirs and their families over the generations.

In the homelands of the ancestors of most Arab-Americans, the traditional Arab family is patrilineal, thus shaping the structure of the extended family to include the father, grandfather, father's brother's families and sisters, as well as grandparents on the father's side, his brothers and sisters and his brothers' sons and daughters. Also, his sons and his sons' children as well

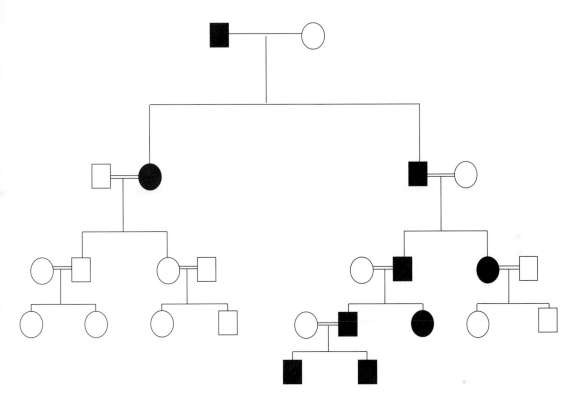

Although a child is related to both mother's and father's side of the family, the official family membership or family name is passed on only through the male descent (shaded).

Symbols represent:

◻ Male

○ Female

═ Marriage

│ Descent/offspring

Figure 7–1.   *The Patrilineal Family System*

as his daughters will be in his patrilineage (Aswad, 1988). This means certain individual rights are inherited only through a child's father.

A child from birth belongs to the father's group and this group never changes. The father's group is responsible to the child, and the child is answerable to them for all behavior. A woman will always be a part of her father's group from birth. However, her children will be a part of the husband's patrilineage. In traditional groups, the actual responsibility for life and death decisions of an individual belongs to the patrilineal group (Aswad, 1987). This is a powerful unit for political and economic success.

Female Roles and Responsibilities

Arab women, also, have rights and privileges. There are clear Islamic teachings that spell out the roles of women and their rights and duties in the patrilineage. When women marry, they retain their father's name and seldom adopt their husband's name. Father and brothers are expected to assume protection over girls and women. Close relationships are often formed between brothers and sisters. Under Islam, women may also inherit property; however, the majority of the holdings usually remain in the control of the patrilineage or male heirs.

Given the above characteristics of Arab families, some of the problems that develop after immigrating into the United States might be due to role changes and reversals as individuals acculturate at different rates.

Due to cultural differences in role expectations, female Arabs who come to the United States or Arab-American families who socialize daughters here often confront many problems. The family's name and honor are very important in Arab families. In the structure of the Arab society, family honor is intricately woven with loyalty to religion, sect, and community. For Arab-American females, the issues of co-education in public schools, equal education, manner of dress, driving a car, voting in elections, opportunities for leadership roles, and working alongside males other than relatives can be interpreted as shaming the family honor. The fear of shame may tend to restrain the female from accepting the ways of the majority culture and from accepting new family values.

Living in a new culture places a difficult burden on Arab mothers, for it is primarily the duty of the mother to socialize children in ways that maintain the respect and honor of the family and the family's name. For example, because the honor or dishonor of an individual reflects on the entire extended family, it is important in the traditional patrilineal lineage that women remain virgins until marriage, with the breaking of the hymen being a test of virginity on the marriage bed. This practice is being seriously challenged by some Americanized Arab young women as it is in some other groups. Therefore, to protect the family's name and honor, many traditional Arab-American parents allow, even encourage, their daughters to marry at an early age, rather than risk pregnancy and resulting shame and dishonor to the family. Early marriage, however, limits the young women's opportunities to pursue higher education. Challenges to the legal marriage age in many states may also follow.

Many Arab women in their native countries lived cloistered with extended family members behind compound walls, whereas in the United States, Arab-American women generally live in single-family homes or apartment units. Arab women typically enjoy close ties with other women, creating networks for helping each other, visiting each other, assisting with child care, sharing food, and emotionally supporting each other. In their home countries, Arab women primarily functioned in the private or domestic sphere while men dominated the public sphere (Aswad, 1988).

Stereotypes are found in many Western descriptions of the Arab woman, who often is not as powerless as suggested. It is not uncommon for a woman to support another married woman from another lineage or within the same family group. An Arab woman may resort to influencing her male kinsmen and/or spouse to exert pressure on another man if he mistreats his wife or daughter.

Often overlooked are the Koran's pronouncements on the subject of all women. The *Koran* is considered the holy book of Islam. Infanticide is prohibited. *Monogamy* is prescribed as a rule and *polygamy* only as an exception to be contracted in certain abnormal circumstances. The Koran outlines legal structures by which women could protest injustice and ill treatment, institute divorce in certain situations, and sue if their inheritance (half a man's share) was denied them. The Koran gave women the right to inherit property for the first time, granted them inalienable rights to their own inherited wealth, their personal jewelry, and their own earnings (Fernea & Bezirgan, 1977). Amiruddin (1939) emphasized that the prophet Muhammad raised women from the lowest social position to one of equality with men in most matters, and removed from women the stigma of responsibility for original sin and the fall of man, supporting legal and social reforms to improve the condition of women. However, there is a great variance between the protections for women commanded in the Koran and what is currently practiced in Muslim societies. Disregard of Islamic precepts is partly blamed for the low position of women in Muslim societies today.

Many modern Arab-American women pursue a career. The Koran states that a woman is entitled to keep her earnings. As more Arab-American women become more acculturated in Western ways, more educated, and more interested in finding work outside the home, family change, family stress, and family struggles occur (Aswad, 1988). One of the most profound impacts on the Arab family today is the emancipation of women through education and the growing freedom of women to move outside the home into the community (Berger, 1962).

Elders: Respect, Power and Prestige

Prestige and power are attached to age, and especially to Arab grandparents. The grandfather is the undisputed head of the household or clan and everyone submits to his authority. He passes on the oral traditions of the Arab culture, using parables for the moral guidance and character development of younger generations.

The grandmother is also very powerful in her role as mediator for the grandchildren. She often intercedes on behalf of her grandchildren when she views the child's father (her son) as being too harsh. Respect for the elderly is clearly demonstrated.

Children and Youths

Children are viewed as "the wealth of the Arabs." Therefore, the best marriages are ones that produce many children. For most traditional Arabs, a son is preferred as the first-born child. Arab women may be blamed when they give birth to girls, even though it is the male sperm that carries the chromosome for determining the sex of the fetus. However, female babies are also pampered and cherished, especially if they follow a male child. All infants and children are indulged. They are fed at the slightest sign of restlessness or hunger. An Arab child enjoys touch, play, security, and a sense of belonging to a group.

Children are always considered a part of the family. This value is displayed by the custom of addressing a child by a title that describes the child's relationship to the speaker rather than by a given name. The paternal uncles are of particular importance. For example, in the event of a father's death, the traditional practice is for the father's brother to assume all of the responsibilities in rearing his brother's children and supporting his widow.

Names are chosen from religious, historical, natural phenomenon, personality traits, or occupational categories only after much deliberation and consultation. Given names are often identified with the prophets or people in the holy books, the Koran and Bible. Children are not named after a parent or any living relative unless an aging grandparent or relative makes a request.

The father's role becomes increasingly important as children mature. Although the father is the final authority and chief disciplinarian of children, he is usually warm and tender towards his young children. However, parents are seldom ever viewed as children's friends (Shabbas, 1979). There is clear status and power distinction between the younger and older generations. Children are expected to show respect for all Arab elders.

As family values have been influenced by "American ways," some traditional practices have gone by the wayside. However, in some families, values related to childhood and the role of the child in the family are undergoing very slow change (Shabbas, 1988).

As children mature, and with each successive generation, struggles between parents and youth concerning acculturation have become more prevalent. Many youths who defy traditional views are seen as trying to dominate their parents. More traditional parents feel that the American culture allows and promotes an excessive amount of freedom for youngsters and worry about the consequences for their children.

Arab families that arrived recently in the U.S. see younger third or fourth generation Arab-Americans exhibiting new values and behaviors learned in the American culture. Many parents attribute this change to the educational system. Their fear is that these new values and mores will lead to less self-control, criminal behaviors, drug and alcohol use, out-of-wedlock babies, family violence, decline of the work ethic, and less economic security in the younger generations.

However, accommodation and change are characteristic of adult Arabs, as well as the younger generations. Educated urban Arabs are moving away from the traditional patterns of raising their children exactly as they themselves were raised. Children from Arab countries are seeking to express their individuality, something unheard of in the past. Some Arab parents are beginning to relax their control. Daughters are allowed more freedom in their choice of a husband. In certain subgroups, inter-ethnic marriages are not viewed as a major crisis.

ARAB-AMERICAN VALUES

Arab-Americans feel it is important that all children learn a social code or system of the right etiquette. The code prescribes correct behavioral patterns expected of well-behaved children, including the following: obey parents, respect elders, be polite in the presence of elders, and demonstrate generosity, cooperativeness, humility, and helpfulness toward others. Arab-Americans expect the family to instill these values by interweaving them into their everyday life and interactions with family members, friends, peers, and people in authority.

Many proverbs taught in the Arab culture reproach those who lie, gossip, quarrel, or say unkind words to others. Other proverbs express values of honesty, cooperation, hard work, and common sense. The family is responsible for teaching religious and moral attributes.

The most desired and cherished values of Arab-Americans are these: communal cohesion, honor, endurance, and grace of words and fluency of expression.

Communal Cohesion

Communal cohesion exists at different levels of complexity and is fluid in its boundaries. Loyalty to the group is paramount and disloyalty has at times led to the law of retribution. The extent of the group varies and can reach across the patrilineage to encompass the many Arab Nations.

Honor

Honor and respect are interchangeable to the Arab. Honor is displayed in behavioral terms, particularly in one's attitudes toward others, whether old or young, male or female, weak or strong. To be honorable refers to that "which strengthens the group and serves its interests. Shameful behavior is that which tends to disrupt, endanger, impair or weaken the social aggregate" (Patai, 1983, p. 90). In an effort to avoid loss of face, Arabs will often hide troubles from those close to them.

Endurance

Harsh ecological conditions of most Arab regions and the adaptation long ago to a Nomadic lifestyle exacted stamina and strength of will from individuals. The virtues of forethought and self-control contribute to the sustaining principle of physical and moral endurance, resulting in the hard-working attitudes of many recent immigrants.

Grace of Words and Fluency of Expression

A great appreciation of literary expression, spoken or written, is found among Arabic people. Portrayals of experiences and emotions are laced with grace and embellishments. What counts is not the logic of the argument, but the grace of the words and the fluency of the expression (Abd al-Auhir al Jurjani, 1972).

ARAB-AMERICAN FAMILIES AND THE EDUCATIONAL SYSTEM

Arab-American children are taught to respect teachers and to take advantage of the formal educational system. However, in some Arab communities, for example in the Detroit area of Michigan, Arab-American organizations are concerned about the low educational standards of the local school system and the subsequent low educational attainment by Middle Eastern youths.

The public educational system reports that Arab youngsters encounter problems in school. The problems seem to result from a lack of proficiency in the English language. This lack impedes Arab-American children in adapting to and succeeding in their new educational system. Consequently, many Arab-Americans, disappointed with the public school system, have organized and financed private schools enrolling large numbers of their children.

A fact often overlooked is that most American educators have little or no experience or prior exposure to the regions of the Middle East. Conflicts in these regions are recounted daily on television news reports and in major U.S. newspapers, usually conveying a negative image of Arab-Americans.

Often excluded from the textbooks used in the United States are many contributions of the Arab world. Some examples are:

1. Arabic words that have become common in our culture, such as ginger, coffee, sugar, syrup, sherbet, cotton, sesame, spinach, lemon, saffron, and oranges;
2. Sciences founded in the Middle East, such as astronomy, algebra, chemistry, and technology;
3. Medical discoveries such as anesthesia, disinfectants, and the vaccination for smallpox;
4. The word check, introduced by American banks, which comes from the Arabic word, *sakk;* and
5. Grafting and fertilizing, introduced in the agricultural industry.

Stereotypes and discrimination encountered in the peer culture contribute to the difficulties experienced by Arab-American youths. Representations of Arabs in the media are often negative. Arab-Americans may have difficulty establishing relationships with other Arabs. These troubles are heightened during periods of conflict in the Middle East. Anti-Arab sentiments among some Americans create conditions which make life difficult for many younger Arab-Americans. Fortunately, a large number of Arab-American scholars are appearing on university campuses. Their scholarship should help inform people of Arab-Americans' needs as well as provide positive models of Arab-Americans to college students.

ARAB-AMERICAN FAMILIES AND THE HEALTH CARE SYSTEM

According to Bernado (1981), St. Jude's Hospital in Memphis, Tennessee, famous for its treatment of leukemia-stricken children, was built by Danny Thomas, an Arab-American actor and celebrity, to give thanks to America. ALSAC, previously known as the American Lebanese Syrian Associated Club and now an acronym for Aiding Leukemia Stricken American Children, is a nonprofit charitable organization devoted to fund raising for the Memphis St. Jude's Hospital.

In cases of mental health issues, it is important to realize that the Arab individual from birth is socialized to be a member of a group. Members of a group or extended family are responsible for each other and will assist in any intended intervention directed at an individual member of the group. It is unrealistic to expect Arab-Americans to solve problems by themselves.

ARAB-AMERICAN FAMILIES AND THE GOVERNMENT SYSTEM

Arab-Americans have lived in the United States for over a century and a half. The Arab presence has been largely inconspicuous in American written history. Few school children learn anything at all about Arab-Americans. The relatively small size of the Arabic immigration, and the scattering of immigrants across the country, as well as their political quiescence, may offer some explanations for omissions. Some Americans took note when the Arab states curtailed oil production and oil prices rose, or when shipments of oil didn't reach the United States. Up until that point, many Americans perceived Arabs as picturesque, penniless nomads seeking water for their herds (Leuchtenburg, 1977). This image, particularly promoted by the film industry, included the nomad, the camel, the mosque, the desert, the palm tree, and the water hole.

Today, as the size of the Arab-American populace expands and gains economic parity, the younger generation of Arab-Americans has begun to take a more active and visible role in politics. For example, former Senate majority leader George Mitchell is a prominent Arab-American, having been a federal judge before he was elected to the Senate. However, Arab-Americans are more likely to win elective office in towns where their families have been prominent and where their ethnic origins play little or no part in their political success (Naff, 1983). Many Arab-Americans feel that future generations should avoid assimilation to the extent of becoming invisible.

ARAB-AMERICAN FAMILIES AND THE ECONOMIC SYSTEM

A standard stereotype of those from the Arab world is that they are sharp traders or businessmen. This view may arise simply because many emigrants from Arab lands have become people of commerce in many countries they emigrated to. Small businesses are often organized on a kin and ethnic basis (Zenner, 1982).

There is a generation gap between the established Arab-Americans and the newcomers. Members of the established Arab-American communities are largely urban dwellers taking active roles in business and commerce. The newcomers experience problems of economic inactivity centered around their lack of necessary experiences, skills, and education. One of the greatest problems many newcomers face is difficulty in learning the English language. For some, language is the greatest obstacle to adapting to and succeeding in the new American culture.

HELPING PROFESSIONALS AND ARAB AMERICANS

Arab-Americans are eager about entry into American life. Most want to learn English quickly. They accept assistance and guidance that let them help themselves. Many who enter the U.S. have family here. Because the Arab-American male holds the dominant role in the family, it may be necessary to approach him in order to help a child or a woman. Both the spoken and written Arabic are unknown to most Americans. Learning some key Arabic phrases may be useful in developing friendships and rapport. It is especially important to realize how many misconceptions arise because of language differences; therefore, you may need specialized language help to avoid conversational misunderstandings.

CONCLUSIONS

Though immigration records for Arab-Americans are inadequate, it is estimated that 2.5 million Americans claim their heritage as some place in the Arab World. Early Arab immigrants and the majority of second and third generation Arab-Americans were Lebanese Christians. In recent times, the number of Arab-Americans speaking Arabic who consider themselves Muslims has been on the rise.

Many Americans today maintain negative stereotypes of Arab-Americans. Textbooks covering history, geography, and social sciences offer inadequate and biased information on Middle Eastern peoples and countries (Suleiman, 1988). Many teachers are unaware of the omissions and biases and so a true picture of the culture is never conveyed.

According to the *Washington Report on Middle East Affairs* (1993), years of educational outreach by American Arabs have recently been undermined by the terrorist actions of a few. A number of prominent political and law enforcement officials, including President Clinton, former New York Governor Mario Cuomo, and the Director of the FBI, have recently stressed that the Muslim community as a whole should not be made a scapegoat in the wake of a few terrorist acts (Noakes, 1993).

Arab-American organizations immediately condemned the 1993 attack on Manhattan's World Trade Center. In a plea to the general public to avoid blaming the entire Arab community, the American Arab Anti-Discrimination Committee said, "It is a horrendous act; there is no place in America for this kind of senseless violence" (Willford, 1993). Just as all majority citizens are not blamed for a crime committed by a member of their racial group, Arab-Americans as a group should not be blamed for such acts.

The number of immigrants from Arab lands has been closely related to political unrest in several Middle Eastern countries. War and bloodshed in their own countries compel many Arabs to emigrate elsewhere in order to seek a safer life for themselves and their families.

With the historic signing of the Palestine-Israeli Accords in September of 1993, it was hoped that one of the world's hot spots had been defused. The Accords outlined a process for reconciling longstanding differences between the Israelis and Palestinians, getting each to acknowledge that both parties have a right to live in the region peacefully, productively, and with human dignity.

Watch closely as the future of this region of the world unfolds. Your work with families in your own Arab-American community will be profoundly affected by progress or lack of progress toward more harmonious relations.

STUDY QUESTIONS

1. Write down the countries that Arab-Americans consider their ancestral homes.
2. The approximate population of Arab-Americans today is _____.
3. Name the organization that united the Arab states. When was it founded?
4. What religion was most typical of America's first Arab immigrants? Today's immigrants?
5. When and where was the first mosque built in the U.S.?
6. Define: Koran, Islam, Allah, Muhammad, and mosque.
7. What was the Inquisition? How does it relate to the Arabs?

8. Define: patrilineal, patrilocal, and patriarchal as related to the Arab family structure.
9. Describe male and female roles in Arab culture.
10. Describe roles of the Arab elderly and children.
11. Discuss each of the four categories of Arab-American values.
12. List contributions to American life that originated in the Arab world.
13. List several prominent Arab-Americans.

APPLICATIONS

1. Read background material on various Arab countries in your encyclopedia. List countries that are predominantly Arab, predominantly Muslim, and predominantly both. Which are considered Middle Eastern?
2. Review five articles in a daily newspaper or a news magazine depicting an event in the Middle East or an event about Arab-Americans.
    (a) Describe each article briefly and record the citation;
    (b) State whether you feel the coverage is fair from the Arab-American viewpoint. Discuss in a two-page essay.
3. Perform a word association using the word Arabs. Write down the stereotypes that come to mind. Discuss whether your words are positive, negative, or neutral. Decide whether they are words you would like to be said about yourself. Write a one-page report.
4. Interview two Arab-Americans and ask them about their family history. (Remember, some may have been here for generations.) Ask: How long have you or your ancestors lived in the U.S.? What were the circumstances of their immigration? Did they know English when they came? How did they fare in their first months after immigration? Write a report of what you learn.
5. Read about Islam in an encyclopedia. Compare it with your own religion or some other religion in your community. Write a one-page summary of what you learn.

REFERENCES

Abd al-Auhir al Jurjani. (1972). *The secrets of eloquence.* Cairo, Egypt: Maktabat al-Qahirah.

Abraham, S., and Abraham, N. (Eds.). (1983). *Arabs in the new world.* Detroit, MI: Wayne State University, Center for Urban Studies.

Ahmed, Ismael, and Gray, Nancy. (Eds.). (1988). *The Arab American family: A resource manual for human service providers.* Ypsilanti, MI: Eastern Michigan University, Children's Bureau, Administration on Children, Youth and Families, Office of Human Development Services, Discretionary Funds Program.

Amiruddin, B. (1939). Woman's status in Islam: A Moslem view. *Muslim World, 28,* 153–163.

Aswad, Barbara. (1988). Strengths of the Arab family for mental health considerations and therapy. In Ismael Ahmed and Nancy Gray (Eds.), *The Arab-American family: A resource manual for human service providers.* Ypsilanti, MI: Eastern Michigan University.

Berger, M. (1962). *The Arab world today.* Garden City, NY: Doubleday.

Bernado, Stephanie. (1981). *The ethnic almanac.* Garden City, NY: Doubleday.

Fernea, E., and Bezirgan, B. (1977). *Middle Eastern Muslim women speak.* Austin, TX: University of Texas Press.

Leuchtenburg, W. (1977). The American perception of the Arab world. In G. Atiyeh (Ed.), *Arabs and the American culture* (pp. 15–25). Washington, DC: American Enterprise Institute for Public Policy Research.

Lorenz, A. (1993, April/May). National Press Club presents award to Palestinian journalist. *Washington Report on Middle East Affairs, 11*(9), p. 14.

Naff, Alixa. (1983). Arabs in America: A historical overview. In S. Abraham and N. Abraham (Eds.), *Arabs in the new world* (pp. 8–29). Detroit, MI: Wayne State University, Center for Urban Studies.

Naff, Alixa. (1985). *Becoming American.* Carbondale and Edwardsville, IL: Southern Illinois University Press.

Noakes, G. (1993, April/May). San Francisco spy ring, "The tip of the iceberg." *Washington Report on Middle East Affairs, 11*(9), 19–20.

Patai, R. (1983) *The Arab mind.* New York, NY: Charles Scribner's Sons.

Philip, M., and Kayal, J. (1983). The Syrian-Lebanese in America: A study in religion and assimilation. In S. Abraham and N. Abraham (Eds.), *Arabs in the new world.* Detroit, MI: Wayne State University, Center for Urban Studies.

Shabbas, Audrey. (1979, May/June). The child in the Arab family. *The Link.* New York, NY: Americans for Middle East Understanding.

Suleiman, Michael. (1988). *The Arabs in the mind of America.* Brattleboro, VT: Amana Books.

Willford, C. (1993, April/May). Arab American activism. *Washington Report on Middle East Affairs, 11*(9), 73–74.

Zenner, W. (1982, October). Arabic-speaking immigrants in North America as middleman minorities. *Ethnic and Racial Studies, 5*(4), 457–477.

CHAPTER 8

Native American Indian Families

Key Concepts

◆ Native Peoples
◆ American Indian Citizenship Act
◆ Matriarchal and Patriarchal Tribes
◆ Reservation Act
◆ Acculturation

I am tired of talk that comes to nothing. It makes my heart sick when I remember all good words and all the broken promises. There has been too much talking by men who had no right to talk. If the white man wants to live in peace with the Indians he can live in peace. Treat all men alike. Give them all the same law. Give them all an even chance to live and grow. . . .

— Chief Joseph, 1889, Nez Perce

This quote by Chief Joseph could well be a 1990s statement of Indian values.

As helping professionals, you will eventually be called upon to serve our very first Americans—the Native Americans. While you might have been introduced to this group as a school child, as a helping professional you will need to learn much more to adequately serve Native American families. In addition to the likelihood that you may serve Native Americans, there is the greater likelihood that some of your classmates will be Native Americans. After you have studied the chapter, you will have more appreciation of Native American Indians and the values that typically influence their lives. You need to take this chapter as a point of departure in your learning, rather than as a complete picture.

WHO ARE THE NATIVE AMERICAN INDIANS?

Native American Indians draw upon the fabric of their heritage to journey through the future. Indians are a nation of people who proudly claim that 46 percent of their population, about 1.4 million to 1.8 million, still live on identi-

fied Indian areas. These areas include recognized Indian reservations, tribal trust lands, Alaskan villages, and historic designated areas such as found in Oklahoma (U.S. Congress, Office of Technology Assessment Report, 1986, p. 4). The Native American population in any area may range from one tribal member living off the reservation, to approximately 175,000 living on the Navajo Nation's reservation, which is the largest in the United States (Bureau of Indian Affairs, 1985). The term North American Native People refers to all Indians, Alaska Natives, Aleuts, Eskimos, and Metis, or mixed bloods. In this chapter, the terms Native American Indians or American Indians will be used interchangeably to represent the Indian Nations. When referring to specific individuals or groups, tribal designations, such as Blackfeet, Cherokee, or Navajo, are used.

Native American Indians are many different people. There are approximately 300 federally recognized American Indian groups and probably another 100 "nonrecognized" tribes (Porter, 1983). There are 200 distinct tribal languages spoken today (Leap, 1981, pp. 271–280). Although the experiences with non-Indians have helped to create a pan-Indian or unified identity, each tribe developed its own language, customs and beliefs. Each has had its own history of experiences that led to various strategies for dealing with the rapid changes in their traditional lifestyles. For a Native American Indian, one's tribe (nation) is where one's primary ethnic identity lies.

Historical Background

North American Indians are the descendants of the only ethnic group that did not immigrate into North America in the last five hundred years. They were here long before settlers came from Europe and other parts of the world, but, ironically, only became U.S. citizens under the American Indian Citizenship Act of Congress in 1924. Some groups, like the Iroquois, have argued that they are not citizens of the United States since their nation existed in America prior to the formation of the United States government. Rather, they are citizens of their own nations.

Compounding identification matters was the Wheeler-Howard Act of 1934, which set up tribal corporations on Indian lands. Political power conflicts conveniently became the rationalization for The Indian Reorganization Act of 1934, allowing Indians to self-govern and self-direct their nations. As legal and politically sovereign nations, their self-determination as expressed in self-governance has been present at least since the first treaties were signed. The Act upholds the understanding that tribes are like states and local governments. Treaties promised Native American Indians constitutional sovereignty. However, it was only in 1970, during President Nixon's term in office, that this sovereignty for Native American Indian Nations finally became a reality in legislating Indian affairs.

According to social policy specialists, it was President Nixon's message to Congress on July 8, 1970, that led to respect for Indian participation and control concerning policies and programs that affect Indian life. Nixon argued that a trust relationship between the government and Indians should be guided by egalitarian principles and the keeping of the treaties signed (Gross, 1989). Even today, debates on issues related to Indian sovereignty rage in the halls of Congress and in corporate offices across the country.

Congress and Native American Indians still grapple over issues of self-determination and self-government. Many tribes are now demanding recognition of their rights as guaranteed through treaties over time with the United States Government. For example, some tribes are involved in legal battles over fishing and hunting rights; some are seeking payment and restoration of stolen land. Some Native American Indians are reestablishing traditional religious ceremonies as a source of strength and way of life. Indians are also forming their own schools to balance the knowledge of modern survival with the knowledge of Native Indian culture and philosophy (Reyhner, 1994). For additional information on past and present issues facing the Native American Indians, see the book *The State of Native America,* edited by M. Annette Jaimes (1992), listed in the References at the end of the chapter.

Demographic Information

Today a majority of Native American Indian families live on a median income that is about 40 percent of the national average of $20,025. In 1952, Congress passed the Relocation Act, which was designed to assimilate Indians into the mainstream population by promises of training and jobs if they moved to the cities. Given the high unemployment rates found on or near reservations, it is not surprising that more than 67,500 heads of households were relocated through this direct employment program (U.S. Bureau of the Census, Subject

Report: American Indians, 1970). Today, a majority of Indians are found in and around major urban cities. O'Connell (1987) found a 33.5 percent unemployment rate for Indians living on and adjacent to reservations in the 28 states containing the highest North American Indian population. Indian reservations typically have limited job opportunities for adolescents and adults.

There have been many Native American Indian cultural groups, with no one culture dominating. As American Indians increase their numbers, the birth rate has exceeded that of the general U.S. population and all minorities since 1955. The birth rate for all North American Indians was 28.0 per 1,000 persons as compared to 15.6 per 1,000 for all ethnic groups (U.S. Department of Health and Human Services, 1991). Many Native American Indians consider themselves members of a tribe, rather than individuals in a family or community.

THE ECOLOGY OF NATIVE AMERICAN INDIAN FAMILIES

The ecology includes the people, the natural environments, and the social-cultural adaptations to the environment. There are as many variations of family ecological systems as there are Indian families. The many required roles of individuals differ among the many tribes that exist. However, the importance of the family, their cultural heritage and tribal customs permeate the modern-day thinking of American Indians.

Family Structures

Historically, there was a wide diversity of family structures among Native Americans. However, through time, this diversity has diminished.

Some tribes are structured along matriarchal lines, such as the Navajo of the Southwest, where women govern, control, and have the most power in the family. Traditional Navajos practice *matrilineal* descent where the lineage or descent is traced through the woman's line. It is *matrilocal,* with the bride and groom moving in with the bride's mother's family.

The typical Native American Indian woman sees her destiny as a reflection of her tribe, her people. Her role is as diverse as the tribal cultures. In some tribes she is devalued; in others she wields considerable power. In some tribes she is a familial clan adjunct; in others she is virtually as autonomous as her psychological makeup and economic circumstances permit. A Native American woman has distinct personality traits that are unlike Western ideals or roles for women.

In *patriarchal* tribes, men are powerful and are the primary decision-makers. They exercise the governing roles in the family as well as in the clan and the tribe. In patriarchal tribes, women's roles are related to the care of the children and to functioning at the core of the family.

Family Practices

Native American Indians have always had diverse family practices. Practices vary regarding bride price, bride service, and dowry; arranged marriage, inter-family exchange marriage, and adoptive marriage; bride abduction and elopement; cross-cousin and parallel-cousin marriage; monogamy, polygyny, and polyandry; patriarchy and matriarchy; divorce, temporary marriage, and trial marriage; wife lending and spouse exchange; patrilineal, matrilineal, and bilateral inheritance and descent (John, 1988, p. 326). Assimilation and acculturation have reduced the diversity that once existed in Native American Indian family structures and practices.

If there is any common model of the Native American family, it is the extended family model. The Indian extended family is generally highly valued, although this form is not universally practiced by Native American Indians.

Red Horse, et al. (1978) offer a typology of three distinct family patterns existing among Native Americans today. They are the traditional, bi-cultural, and pan-traditional. These family patterns are a continuum based on the degree of acculturation felt and expressed by these families.

Acculturation refers to the degree of adaptation one group makes to the majority culture. Differences arise based on language used in the household, religious practices, value systems, and the kind of recreational and cultural activities the family participates in and with whom. Despite these degrees of difference in acculturation, there remain some common bonds between the three groups regarding family structures, relational bonding, and preferences in recreational and cultural activities.

Extended Families

The complex ecological web of family relationships extends to the clan, the tribe, and the Native American Indian Society. The web also extends over time and between generations. There is a collective mutual support system or inter-generational and intertribal interdependence that provides and nurtures an atmosphere of strong kinship bonds and affection. The many forced relocations and outside threats from non-Indians over many generations have aided and contributed to the solidarity of the Native American Indian people.

Members of the extended family network play important roles in facilitating the well-being of individuals within the community and the tribe. Extended family members are important teachers for transmitting traditional ways and values. Older generations of grandparents, great aunts, and great uncles are often as important as parents in serving as teachers and models for the children (Red Horse, et al., 1978).

The extended family form varies in different ecological settings. Family structures are different in small reservation communities, in interstate extended families, in urban areas, and in large metropolitan areas (John, 1988).

Under some circumstances family structures include kin and non-kin. According to Guillemin (1975, p. 142), an important dimension of who constitutes an Indian family includes the face-to-face interactions that are so important to Native American Indian families. Interactions convey far more meaning than letters or phone calls (John, 1988, p. 330).

A high family value is based on interdependence, which leads immediately to identification and sharing of resources, both human and material. A commonly held belief and practice among Native Americans is the value of "what is mine is also yours." Extended families have their own rules, norms, values, and traditions governing how they help and care for their members. Understanding the extended family requires an in-depth immersion into their cultural context and careful observations over a period of time.

Elders

The elders are the safekeepers of tribal stories and songs. Forming an indispensable part of the community, the elders share and pass on to each new generation the tribal oral traditions (Ryan, 1980). The tradition of passing information orally from one generation to the next is typical of all tribes.

Elders defend the values of the family through deeds as well as through words and thoughts. This respect and integration of the young and the elderly explain why Native American Indians have withstood assaults from outside professionals or officials who, with their differing values, have often had little sensitivity to Native American ways. Elders represent a pattern of family strength in the cultural fabric by assuming responsibilities and obligations to pass down orally one's traditions and history to future generations—also creating interpersonal bonding in the process. Interdependence of the elderly with the Indian extended family keeps the elderly permanently in the mainstream of family life and not in retirement. Native American Indians are taught that their life force carries the spirits of their ancestors and that this tradition is passed down through the generations by the elders (Red Horse, 1980). One benefit of the Indian tradition is the interaction and integration of the young and the old.

Children and Youths

Children are universally viewed as beloved gifts of life. Indians believe that each child is born with unique characteristics that help to determine his or her place in the tribe. This respect for the individual's autonomy begins at birth. It is exemplified by a traditional practice of observing the newborn over a period of time to determine what is an appropriate given name for the child as determined by the child's specific characteristics and surrounding circumstances. Depending on the traditional structure of the family, naming the child may take months after birth to ensure that a proper name is given at the naming ceremony.

From the time of birth, Native American Indian infants are reared in a cultural milieu valuing aspects of autonomy and interdependence. For example, a child is nurtured in a community where members exhibit community tolerance. Tolerance and respect for individuals are expected of the community. A cultural value of individual autonomy is practiced by rearing children in an environment where they are free to explore, to make decisions, and to make choices from a very young age. Children learn by experiencing the natural consequences of their decisions and choices. This is expressed as follows by a Pueblo grandmother of eleven boys and girls:

> *When you go to our children,*
> *try to become a friendly tree that*
> *they will want to sit near.*
> *Enjoy them. Forget yourself.*
> *If we all could only forget ourselves*
> *a bit more—then our children*
> *would feel free to be a bit more themselves.*
> *Sometimes we get too close to our*
> *children; we scare them with—*
> *with ourselves. They can't become themselves.*
> *It is them we should try to know.*
> *(Coles, 1977)*

The Native American Indian style of parenting that values autonomy and interdependence is contrary to the non-Indian view of child rearing and has often resulted in civil litigation against the Native American Indian family and community. This cultural misunderstanding has resulted in children becoming victims of power plays. Many non-Indian family service providers, due to lack of cultural understanding and wrongful expectations, react callously to Native American childrearing practices. It is important for every helping professional to learn to recognize and appreciate the special cultural strengths of the Native American child.

When there is a cultural match between Indian families and the surrounding community, children mature with a deep sense of cultural identity. In contrast, where families and the surrounding community lack the cohesive forces of cultural similarities, children experience psychological stresses that could impede their socio-psychological development as they move into other social systems outside of their families. For example, Boyce and Boyce (1983) found a higher incidence of mental health clinic visits for Indian youths among those families who were poorly matched with the surrounding community.

Native American Indian Values

Cultural values shape the Native American Indian's way of thinking, perceiving, acting, and speaking. Traditional values are subject to change and there

Native American Indian	Majority Society
Group emphasis/collectivism	Individualism
Process living	Goal oriented
Here and now orientation	Future orientation
Nonemphasis on time	Emphasis on time
Elders are revered	Youths are revered
Cooperation	Competition
Harmony with nature	Conquest and control of nature
Sharing/giving	Hoarding/saving
Nonaggressive	Aggressive
Silent or soft spoken	Noisy or brash
Respect for other's religion	Contempt for other's religion
Aestheticism	Materialism
Permissive/self choice	Coercive/other directed
Shame	Guilt
Natural resources belong to all	Natural resources belong to individuals
Egalitarian	Class conscious
Inner harmony	Outside appearance
Individuals serve others	Individuals serve self
Interdependent	Independent

Figure 8–1.   *Contrasting Cultural Values*

are various expressions of cultural values or beliefs. Each person appropriates various values in an individualistic way. However, Figure 8–1 provides examples of contrasting values between Indian cultures and majority cultures.

The Native American Indians judge things and people according to what is inside their being. They firmly believe in the importance of seeing inside things instead of outward appearances. In searching for a world invisible to others, American Indians believe that a good person can give good advice which flows from courage and wisdom. In contrast, they feel that majority people judge according to outward appearances, by individual achievement, or by material possessions.

According to Native Americans, all things, inanimate and animate, are related and are holy or sacred, possessing power. Relatedness, unity, or oneness is often expressed by the circle, a symbol of wholeness. Being in harmony with nature and other people is important. Sensitivity to others and a desire to get along with others have often been misinterpreted as apathy or low self-esteem.

The Indian way of life is detailed, practical, and concerned with the immediate. These traits are uniquely expressed in distinct family units of each of the tribes. Each family nourishes certain basic values that form distinct personalities, engendering generosity to other human beings and respect for individual rights. These characteristics are mediated through emotional restraint, tolerance, and even humorous relationships.

CULTURAL EXPRESSIONS OF VALUES

Indians have various ways of expressing their values, noted in the following four traits:

Traits of Self-Reliance.   American Indians are often hesitant to ask and receive help from non-Indians. Personal freedom is based on making personal decisions that are not imposed or coerced.

Traits of Non-Interference.   Many Native Americans consider interference in other people's lives a sign of disrespect, a threat, or an insult. There is a strong belief that people learn from their own mistakes and decisions. Native American Indians do not interfere and do not want to be interfered with.

Traits of Non-Confrontation.   Native American people prefer not to confront those with whom they disagree. If possible, they will avoid people who are confrontational.

Traits of Respect for Elders.   Traditionally, American Indians have revered the elders in the society. They may defer to an older majority person whom they trust even though they disagree with the person.

Understanding these traits as you become involved in the dynamics of interpersonal relations is important. Many professionals and officials who interact with Native Americans don't recognize the importance of these cultural values and traits. Misunderstandings and frustrations are likely to occur as a result. It is important for a helping professional to learn about and to become sensitive to these traits.

NATIVE AMERICAN INDIANS AND THE EDUCATIONAL SYSTEM

In 1812, a Cherokee named Sequoyah invented a phonetic syllabary notation system for the Cherokee language. This accomplishment was an extraordinary achievement and unprecedented in world history. Within three years all Cherokees could read and write their own language, and by 1828 the tribe had its own newspaper, a written constitution, and a code of laws (Parrillo, 1985).

Parrillo (1985) emphasized the fact that the first public education for Indians was developed by Native American Indians and not introduced by others.

In the early 1900s, most schooling for Indians took place within tribal communities. Later, the majority were in public boarding schools run by religious missions and the Bureau of Indian Affairs (BIA). The approach to education was strict conformity to Anglo culture. Students were punished for speaking native languages, dressing as an Indian, or identifying with anything resembling the Indian culture. Public and private boarding schools were used by the federal government as a channel for forced assimilation and acculturation.

By 1970, according to the U.S. Census, approximately 141,000 Native American Indian children were attending public schools; 52,000 in BIA schools and 11,000 in mission schools.

In 1980, 57 percent of Native American males and 54 percent of Native American females were high school graduates. School enrollments varied greatly among reservations, with the highest enrollments (95 percent) among the Pima and Papago reservations in Arizona (Feagin, 1989).

According to the National Center for Educational Statistics (1989), Native American Indian and Native Alaskan students have a dropout rate of 35.5 percent, approximately twice the national average and the highest dropout rate of any United States ethnic or racial group (Reyhner, 1994).

As Indian youths attend school with other Americans, difficulties often arise for many reasons. Many youths speak an Indian language as a first language. They practice an Indian religion with a loving respect for nature and have a sense of tribal spirituality (Hungry Wolf and Hungry Wolf, 1987). Strong cultural traditions often inhibit the Indian youngster from being direct, verbal, or assertive. These different cultural characteristics may result in an Indian child being misperceived and misunderstood at school and elsewhere.

Indian youths usually spend six or seven hours daily in an institutional setting of overtly different values and perplexingly subtle and ambiguous cultural expectations. Here they are expected to perform according to conventional majority culture and associated educational standards. One dilemma for Indian youth is how to balance the majority's cultural expectations of individual achievement and success with the Indian beliefs of cooperative interdependence, sharing, and working together. Often this becomes discouraging and results in a very uncomfortable existence for Indian young people.

Indian children's discomfort is recognized by those critical of Columbus Day celebrations in our schools and communities. From an Indian point of view, the following questions may arise concerning the arrival of Columbus to the Americas in 1492:

If you stand in an American Indian's shoes or moccasins, would you be happy to celebrate the European adventurer who started the invasion that killed your people, stole your land, and herded you off to reservations? Would you celebrate an event leading to the death of many of your people and still today leaving Indian survivors among the poorest economically in this land, with poor health and poor housing, and still portrayed as being obstacles to Western civilization and the westward expansion?

Every year Indian children are confronted with the Columbus Day celebration. The emotional support needed from others to circumvent the possible feelings of self blame and anger may not be available in a typical school system, community, or family. Also, with an increased movement to urban areas, Indian families have become isolated from their extended families and communities. By leaving the reservations in search of jobs, the supportive network of the extended family is disrupted. Thus, the psychological well-being of many youth often suffers. Many Indian parents remember having experienced similar school stresses. With the continuing pressures of discrimination and impoverishment throughout adulthood, many Indian parents have developed an attitude of overwhelming hopelessness (LaFromboise and Graff Low, 1989).

A study done in Oklahoma reported that successful Native American Indian students attending college were those who were more likely to conform to the standards and style of the majority educational institutions. In other words, they had become totally acculturated or had learned to balance both cultural systems. However, another Oklahoma study found that suicide rates among young Indian males were increasing and were highest among those who were the most assimilated within the white culture (Feagin, 1989). In certain environments, Native American Indian youths who succeed in school are berated by their peers for acting like whites and looking down on their own people.

However, other research studies show that Indian students who came from the most traditional homes, spoke their native language, and participated in traditional religious and social activities did not feel that the majority school curriculum was inappropriate for their studies. Perhaps a strong sense of cultural identity can be an advantage in school for some youths.

Problems faced by Native American Indian youths may be those of cultural discontinuity as well as those associated with other ecological issues, such as large schools in urban areas, passive teaching methods, economic necessity of finding jobs, long-distance commutes to school from reservations, alcoholism, teen pregnancy, insensitive teachers, and boredom with school curriculum.

NATIVE AMERICAN INDIAN FAMILIES AND THE HEALTH CARE SYSTEM

The roots of Native American Indian health care practitioners are as ancient as the ceremonies attached to medical care and belief systems. Practitioners were called by many names, such as shaman, healer, or the more Westernized medicine man. Armed with an extensive pharmacopoeia and faith, they strove to maintain and promote the physical and mental well-being of individuals. These successful Native American Indian medicine men used over 200 drugs and medicines that were later included in official pharmaceutical manuals. With the arrival of the Europeans, ancient Indian medical heritage and tradition were severely challenged (Washburn, 1970).

Contact with Europeans brought disaster to the Native American population. Through direct and indirect introduction of viruses and bacteria, diseases such as smallpox, measles, bubonic plague, cholera, typhoid, pleurisy, scarlet fever, diphtheria, mumps, whooping cough, colds, venereal diseases, and probably typhus, decimated the population (Dobyns, 1983). Catastrophes of epidemic and pandemic outbreaks ravaged the Native American Indian communities that had not been exposed to these pathogens and had no immunity to ward them off.

In order to protect American soldiers who were serving in military outposts on the frontier from these infectious diseases, the War Department became involved in the administration of medical services to Indians. Later, the responsibility for Indian health was transferred to the newly created Bureau of Indian Affairs under the Department of Interior. Then, in 1954, health care was transferred to the Department of Health, Education, and Welfare, under the direction of the Surgeon General (Mail, 1978). Presently, the Department of Health and Human Services is responsible for monitoring Indian health concerns.

The Indian Health Services have records of Indian medical problems occurring since 1955. The top ten causes of death for Native American Indians were accidents, disease of the heart, malignant neoplasms, cirrhosis of the liver, cerebrovascular disease, influenza and pneumonia, diseases of infancy, diabetes mellitus, homicide, and suicide (U.S. Public Health Service, 1974). In recent years, however, chronic disease and mental health problems, including alcoholism, have become the major health problems among Indian people.

In order to alleviate the shortage of medical personnel in Indian areas, Indian paraprofessionals have been trained to provide a range of primary health care functions. These workers serve to alleviate the language gaps and help reach out to culturally distinct people, especially those living in remote areas of Indian reservations.

Most urban Indian programs, many of which have their origins in volunteer services, are predominantly staffed by Indians. The urban programs attract the skilled Indian professionals away from the rural reservations, adding to the shortage of professionals on the reservations.

Increasingly, Native American Indians are becoming trained and are taking responsibility for the health care of their people. Modern medical knowledge and expectations are becoming more widespread even as recognition of the value of some traditional Indian medical practices increases. Modern Indian students who are participating in the health care services are seeing value in both traditional and modern medicine and are providing better health care services to Indian people.

In areas of mental health, the individual's environment and social context must be incorporated. Each Native American tribal culture has its own definition of appropriate behaviors which must be taken into account. For example, Dell (1980) reported, "The Hopi feel that a child's repetitive negative or 'bad' behaviors have a cumulative effect and the accumulation of these behaviors leads to eventual change." A Hopi parent might, therefore, accept, even welcome, the repetition of negative behaviors as a sign of imminent change. A non-Hopi therapist might conclude that the parents appear to be reinforcing poor behavior with their continual optimism and refusal to intervene. A non-Hopi therapist's intervention aimed to eliminate these reinforcing behaviors would strike at the very core of Hopi philosophy (LaFromboise and Graff Low, 1989).

Some traditional interventions have been used effectively, such as the purification and prevention "Sweat Lodge" ceremonies. Participation consists of fasting, praying, and offerings throughout serial purification sessions, referred to as "rounds." Ceremonies last for hours while participants make offerings for health and balance in life (Manson, Walker, and Kivlahan, 1987). Tribal practices, such as "four circles" or "talking circle," are reported to work well with Native American youngsters needing professional assistance. These are their versions of rap or discussion groups.

Tribal healers are valued as the keepers of the tribe. Healers working with American Indian therapy centers have helped in deciphering traditional values that come into conflict with the values of the dominant culture (Trimble, 1981).

Despite modernization and policies of assimilation, Indian cultural beliefs and practices continue. Today, Native American Indian medicine has incorporated some traditional Indian beliefs and healing practices into conventional medical treatment. Systems serving the needs of Native American Indians must become aware of the details of these various beliefs and practices.

NATIVE AMERICAN INDIAN FAMILIES AND THE GOVERNMENT SYSTEM

The Iroquois Nation, made up of the Cayuga, Mohawk, Oneida, Onondaga, and Seneca peoples, united in a League of Nations in 1570. A sixth tribe, the Tuscarora, was added in 1722. This League had a pronounced influence upon the provisions of the Articles of Confederation, the forerunner to the U.S. Constitution, when Benjamin Franklin drafted the Federation of States. The League's democratic processes served as the model for the colonists to emulate and include in the constitutional practices of representative government (Farb, 1968, p. 128).

In 1830, the Indian Removal Bill passed Congress and became law. All Indians living east of the Mississippi were to be expelled from their homeland. The U.S. government embarked on a policy of containment as a means of controlling the American Indians and encouraging settlers to move in.

One of the ugliest periods in American history began in October 1838, when army troops hunted, herded, and marched the Cherokee Indians westward to Oklahoman territory from South Carolina along what has since been named the Trail of Tears. Ten to twenty Indians died each day from exposure, hunger, illness, and other miseries. Over a third of the Cherokees died on the way to the Indian Territory, which is now Oklahoma.

Between 1850 and 1880, most of the approximately 300 existing Native American Indian reservations were established. These were areas set aside in various states segregating the Native American Indians. The results were devastating, with military force being used to constrain these proud and independent people. One method used to accomplish assimilation was to force the Native American Indian to depend upon the government for food, rations, and supplies.

In 1933, under President Franklin D. Roosevelt's administration, the assimilation policy was shifted to one of pluralism. *Pluralism* meant that the Native American Indians could maintain autonomy as an ethnic group and participate in the development of their culture.

NATIVE AMERICAN INDIAN FAMILIES AND THE ECONOMIC SYSTEM

Traditionally, in the Native American Indian family, property of economic value was owned by the extended family and the tribe. Property and resources were shared in common. "The country was made without lines of demarcation, and it is no man's business to divide it," claimed Chief Joseph of the Nez Perces. No member went without necessities if the rest of the tribe had resources. However, sometimes individuals owned personal items like songs, crests, and ornaments. This was a value favoring cooperative economics.

The world owes an economic and culinary debt to early Native Americans. Over half of the present world's food crops originally came from Native American Indian agriculture, for example, potatoes, corn, squash, beans, and pumpkins. In many tribes women contributed to the economy through agricultural activities such as growing and processing various agricultural products. In certain areas, fishing, hunting, and gathering food from wild plants were practiced by the tribes.

Jobs are linked to available resources. Adequate resources for productive employment were often lacking on Indian reservations. The problems of poverty and overpopulation on reservations were not examined seriously until 1952. At that time, the Bureau of Indian Affairs offered some 40,000 individuals financial aid to relocate to urban areas. Most of the Native Americans who chose to relocate found unskilled and semi-skilled jobs. However, the program was not particularly successful because more than a quarter of the people left the cities to return to the reservations where there was still a severe lack of jobs. This program was abandoned after 1960.

Today, over 627,000 Native Americans live in cities such as Los Angeles, Chicago, Boston, Dallas, Denver, Detroit, and Minneapolis. Lack of adequate job-related skills and education contributes to the poverty conditions many Indians face living in the cities.

Among all ethnic minorities in the United States, Native American Indians have the lowest median income and the highest unemployment rate. At this time, the median income for Native American Indians is about 48 percent of the national median.

Unemployment on reservations, ranging from 45 to 80 percent, remains a serious problem for the Native American. Why is this the case when some reservations are so rich in natural resources? For example, the 53 million acres of twenty-two Western tribes contain the nation's richest reserves of natural gas, oil, coal, and uranium (Parrillo, 1985). Native American Indians generally hold a spiritual reverence for the land, creating a reluctance to exploit resources, and these riches are part of Mother Earth. Corporations and governmental institutions, gaining access to the natural resources of Native American Indian land, sometimes victimize and subordinate the Native American Indian.

Economic Development on Reservations

There is much political controversy surrounding economic development on the reservations today. Examples of economic developments include:

Tribe	Industries
Eastern Band of Cherokees	Own largest mirror company in U.S.
White Mountain Apaches	One of the largest ski resorts
Navajos	Leased rights for mining uranium
Passamaquoddies of Maine	Cement company & blueberry farm
Ojibway, Seminole, & others	Large scale bingo and casino
Lummis	Fish farming industry

Economic progress and development have exacted a price in eroding the cultural heritage of tribal nations. For many Native American Indians, the more prosperous they become, the more difficult it is to preserve their Indian heritage. Some welcome many aspects of the cultural change, while others struggle to retain many traditions of the Native American Indian culture and still be a part of the larger U.S. society. Respect for individual preferences is essential as difficult choices are made.

CONCLUSIONS

Native American Indian traditions provide some holistic, humanistic, and existential principles that can benefit our contemporary technological society. The democratic federal principles on which the United States were founded draw upon the League of the Iroquois Confederacy. Strong relationships among tribal members have led to a resiliency that has helped withstand assaults over the decades. As a result of a strong feeling of identification with one's family, group, or tribe, informal supportive family kinship networks provide for affection and support.

Many popular foods we consume today are contributions of the Native American agricultural skills and practices. Many states, cities, counties, lakes, rivers, and mountains bear Native American names. Youth groups, such as the Boy Scouts, Girl Scouts, Campfire Girls, and YMCA Guides, include in their programs many Indian practices and lore, arts and crafts, and outdoor living skills.

Ecologists today are beginning to understand the importance of Native American Indian traditions respecting nature and the circle of life. All power comes from the earth, the sky, and the water. Understanding and working with diverse peoples is crucial if we are to move towards fruitful strategies leading to the good life for all peoples on the planet Earth.

> They had an ancient, lost reverence for earth and its web of life. They had what the world has lost. The world must have it back . . . lest it die. . . .
> (Collier, 1947, p. 15)

STUDY QUESTIONS

1. How many federally recognized Indian groups are there? How many languages?
2. America is over 200 years old. In what year were Indians officially made U.S. citizens?
3. President Nixon in 1970 changed the Indians' status by what principle?
4. Indians prefer to be considered (1) individual, (2) tribe, or (3) community?
5. Name and describe the typical Native American family structure. Use the special words that describe the type of structure.
6. There are a number of family practices that Indians observe. Name five of these practices.
7. Describe at least five salient characteristics of the Indian extended family.
8. Tell what Indian elders do to maintain their contact with their family.
9. Describe the Indian philosophy of child rearing.
10. List at least 10 values of Indians and the contrasting values of the majority society they conflict with.
11. List four major cultural expressions of values and the behaviors of Indians related to these traits.
12. List the different ways that Indian youngsters have been educated over the years. What are some typical educational problems of Indian children and youth?
13. Outline some of the health care issues that the Indians have been confronted with over history.

14. What are present day health care practices that appear to be improving health care among American Indians?
15. State at least five major federal government decisions that have affected Native Americans for years.
16. List the numerous ways that Indians have contributed to both the culinary and economic wealth of the world.

APPLICATIONS

1. Make a list of things your early teachers taught you about Indians. (a) Discuss these teachings, bringing up points you have learned in this chapter or elsewhere. Write a one- or two-page report.
2. Perform a word association task by listing the first 20 words that come to mind when someone mentions Indians. (a) Write an essay on the facts and fallacies included on your list. (b) Write a paragraph on how such stereotypes must feel to Indian youth your age.
3. Discuss with three people their recollections about celebrating Columbus Day as children. What do they recall? What is the problem, if any, with Columbus Day celebrations? Write a one-page report.
4. Native Americans request that artifacts from museums be restored to the Indian territory they came from. Discuss your personal attitude toward this requirement in a one-page essay.
5. Write a thoughtful essay of one or two pages on what must be learned before serving Native Americans as a professional in your chosen career.

REFERENCES

Beal, M. (1963). *I will fight no more forever: Chief Joseph and the Nez Perce war*. Seattle, WA: University of Washington Press.

Boyce, W., and Boyce, J. (1983). Acculturation and changes in health among Navajo school students. *Social Sciences and Medicine, 17,* 219–226.

Bureau of Indian Affairs. (1985, January). *Indian service population and labor force estimates*. Washington, DC: U.S. Government Printing Office.

Coles, R. (1977). Eskimos, Chicanos, Indians. *Children in Crisis, 4,* 62. Boston, MA: Little, Brown and Co.

Collier, J. (1947). *The Indians of the Americas*. New York, NY: W. W. Norton.

Dell, P. F. (1980). The Hopi family therapist and the Aristotelian parents. *Journal of Marital and Family Therapy, 6,* 123–130.

Dobyns, Henry F. (1983). *Their numbers become thinned: Native American population dynamics in eastern North America*. Knoxville, TN: University of Tennessee Press.

Farb, Peter. (1968). *Man's rise to civilization as shown by the Indians of North America from primeval times to the coming of the industrial state.* New York, NY: E. P. Dutton.

Feagin, Joe R. (1989). *Racial and ethnic relations.* Englewood Cliffs, NJ: Prentice-Hall.

Gross, E. R. (1989). *Contemporary federal policy toward American Indians.* New York, NY: Greenwood Press.

Guillemin, J. (1975). *Urban renegades: The cultural strategy of American Indians.* New York, NY: Columbia University Press.

Hungry Wolf, A., and Hungry Wolf, B. (1987). *Children of the sun.* New York, NY: Morrow.

Jaimes, M. A. (Ed.). (1992). *The state of native America.* Boston, MA: South End Press.

John, Robert. (1988). The native American family. In C. H. Mindel, R. W. Habenstein, and R. Wright (Eds.), *Ethnic families in America* (pp. 325–363). New York, NY: Elsevier Science Publishing Co.

LaFromboise, T. D., and Graff Low, K. (1989). American Indian children and adolescents. In J. T. Gibbs, L. N. Huang and Associates (Eds.), *Children of color.* San Francisco, CA: Jossey-Bass.

Leap, W. L. (1981). American Indian language maintenance. *Annual Review of Anthropology, 10,* 271–280.

Mail, Patricia D. (1978, March). Hippocrates was a medicine man: The health care of Native Americans in the twentieth century. *Annuals, AAPSS,* 436.

Manson, S. M., Walker, R. D., and Kivlahan, D. R. (1987). Psychiatric assessment and treatment of American Indians and Alaska natives. *Hospital and Community Psychiatry, 38,* 65–173.

Marden, C. F., Meyer, G., and Engel, M. H. (1992). *Minorities in American society.* New York, NY: HarperCollins Publishers.

Martin, W. E. (1991). Career development and American Indians living on reservations: Cross-cultural factors to consider. *The Career Development Quarterly, 39,* 273–283.

O'Connell, J. (1987). *A study of the special problems and needs of American Indian children both on and off the reservation.* Washington, DC.: U.S. Department of Education, Office of Special Education and Rehabilitative Services.

Parrillo, Vincent N. (1985). *Strangers to these shores: Race and ethnic relations in the United States.* New York, NY: John Wiley & Sons.

Porter, Frank W., III. (Ed.). (1983). *Nonrecognized American Indian tribes: An historical and legal perspective.* Paper of the McNickle Center for the Study of the American Indian, No. 7. Chicago, IL: Newberry Library.

Red Horse, John G. (1980). American Indian elders: Unifiers of Indian families. *Social Casework,* 61.

Red Horse, J., Lewis, R. G., Feit, M., and Decker, J. (1978). Family behavior of urban American Indians. *Social Casework, 59*, 67–72.

Redoy, Marlita. (Ed.). (1993). *Statistical record of native North Americans 1993*. Detroit, MI: Gale Research Inc.

Reyhner, J. (1994). American Indians out of school: A review of school-based causes and solutions. In R. C. Monk (Ed.), *Taking sides*. Sluice Dock, Guilford, CT: The Duskin Publishing Group, Inc.

Ryan, R. A. (1980). Strengths of the American Indian family: State of the art. In F. Hoffman (Ed.), *The American Indian family: Strengths and stresses* (pp. 25–43). Isleta, NM: American Indian Social Research and Development Associates.

Trimble, J. E. (1981). Value differentials and their importance in counseling American Indians. In P. Pedersen, J. Draguns, W. Lonner, and J. Trimble (Eds.), *Counseling across cultures* (pp. 203–226). Honolulu, HI: University Press of Hawaii.

USA Today. (1992, November and December). Primary source: Washington, DC: U.S. Census Bureau.

U.S. Bureau of the Census. (1970). *American Indian 1970*. Washington, DC: U.S. Government Printing Office.

U.S. Bureau of the Census. (1991). *1990 Census of the Population, Preliminary Report*. Washington, DC: U.S. Government Printing Office.

U.S. Congress, Office of Technology Assessment. (1986). *Indian Health Care* (OTA-H290). Washington, DC: U.S. Government Printing Office.

U.S. Public Health Service. (1974). *Indian Health Trends and Services*, (DHEW Publication No. IISA 74-12, 009, p. 32). Washington, DC: U.S. Government Printing Office.

Vogel, V. (1970). *American Indian medicine*. Norman, OK: University of Oklahoma Press.

Vogel, V. (1972). Indian ways with farming and wild foods. In Bernard Fontana (Ed.), *Look to the mountain top* (pp. 61–66). San Jose, CA: H. M. Gousha Col.

Washburn, W. (1970). *The Indian in America*. Norman, OK: University of Oklahoma Press.

FURTHER READING

Allen, Paula Gunn. (1987). *The sacred hoop: Recovering the feminine in American Indian traditions*. Boston, MA: Beacon Press.

Deloria, Vine, Jr. (1988). *Custer died for your sins: An Indian manifesto*. Norman, OK: University of Oklahoma Press.

Farb, Peter. (1968). *Man's rise to civilization*. New York, NY: E. P. Dutton.

Klein, Barry T. (Ed.). (1992). *Reference Encyclopedia of the American Indian* (6th Ed.). West Nyack, NY: Todd Publications.

OTHER BOOKS

Caduto, Michael J., and Bruchec, Joseph. (1988). *Keepers of the earth, Native American stories and environmental activities for children.* Golden, CO: Fulcrum Inc.

Slapin, Beverly, and Seale, Doris. (Eds.). (1991). *Through Indian eyes: The native experience in books for children.* Berkeley, CA: Oyate.

MEDIA RESOURCES

More Than Bows and Arrows. (1992). Color, 60 min. Insight Media, 121 West 85th St., New York, NY 10024.

Native American Cultures. (1992). 60 min. Insight Media, 121 West 85th St., New York, NY 10024.

Navajo Moon. Color, 28 min. Films for the Humanities & Sciences, P.O. Box 2053, Princeton, NJ 08543–2053.

CHAPTER 9

Amish-American Families

Key Concepts

◆ The Plain People
◆ Anabaptists
◆ Ordnung
◆ Shunning

Little children you should seek
Rather to be good than wise:
For the thoughts you do not speak
Shine out in your cheeks and eyes.

— Hostetler & Huntington (1971)

Religion can be a major variable related to an ethnic minority's status. The values and behaviors of some religious groups differentiate them from the larger society and set them apart as a unique subgroup. The Amish will be discussed as an example of a religious minority. If you are interested in other religious groups, the framework used in this textbook may be helpful in your study of families of a particular group. As a professional working with religious minority families, it is important to learn enough about the group to be effective.

WHO ARE THE AMISH?

Equal access to power is foreign to the Amish people's definition of self and community. They want only to have the right to practice their beliefs without persecution. The Amish have chosen and maintained a way of life that disregards notions of political power, as usually understood by the dominant American society. They are an example of an ecological subgroup that has maintained a semi-closed boundary between themselves and the majority culture, having very limited transactions with the larger society.

Historical Background

The Amish have, at times, been identified by phrases such as People of the Preservation, the Plain People, Horse and Buggy Amish, House Amish, or Old

Order Amish. In Switzerland in 1693, the followers of Jakob Amman split from the Swiss Anabaptists. Amman's followers immigrated to America in the eighteenth century.

The Amish who immigrated to America found opportunity for free land an attractive inducement for their families and their way of life. They could farm and live next to each other as neighbors and form their tight-knit religious community. The Amish and their descendants who remained in Europe rather than immigrate to America reunited with the main body of European Mennonites or gave up their Amish identity. Many suffered extreme religious persecution. Subsequently, all Amish settlements in Europe died out (Hostetler, 1968).

Being pacifists, the Amish resisted military service in Europe as well as the United States. The Amish, Mennonites, Church of the Brethren, and other "Plain People" share doctrines of nonresistance or pacifism, adult baptism, and separation from the world. The degree of separateness of the Amish church from the world is defined differently by each of the Plain People religious groups. The strictest of this group is the Old Order Amish.

During the last half of the nineteenth century, the American Amish group again divided due to differences in religious views. The name Old Order Amish came into usage to distinguish the group that retained the old traditions from other groups of Amish who became assimilated by varying degrees into the American mainstream. The more assimilated individuals often joined the Mennonite Church (Scott, 1988). All of the Plain People share values or ideals of plainness, simplicity, mutuality, visible identities, and nonviolence or pacifism.

Settlements differ on issues of conformity and on the norms of religious practice. There are many variations of the Old Order Amish and the differences are based on the rules of the church called the Ordnung. At the conservative end of the continuum are the Old Order Amish while at the progressive end are the "Beachy" Amish who own and drive automobiles, use electricity, tractors, and other labor-saving technologies. Many of the differences among Amish groups are unnoticeable to outsiders. Groups of like-minded Amish tend to live in a community or church district.

Amish church districts that are in fellowship with one another are rather homogeneous in character. These fellowships interpret the Ordnung similarly. There are at least seven different Old Order Amish affiliations that are not in fellowship with one another. Therefore, one church district may belong to the conservative group, while across the state another community of Amish may belong to the more progressive branch (Huntington, 1988).

The Old Order Amish families adapted and survived in small rural folk societies in the U.S. Redfield's (1947) definition of a folk society includes the Amish who formed a small, isolated, traditional, simple, and homogeneous settlement. In these settlements, personal and emotional relationships, and tradition and customs are highly valued. Practical experience and knowledge are more important than formal education, science, or abstractions. Change is avoided and uncomfortable. The Amish have an attitude of "We-ness" or the Gemeinschaft-like community overshadowing the "I-ness." Amish traditions and customs are patterned with symbolic meanings and ingrained in everyday behaviors.

For example, at the dinner table, the Amish father sits at one end of the table with his sons on one side and daughters on the other side next to the mother. Another example is the avoidance of saying "thank you" after someone helps another with a task because the helping behavior is expected.

Religion is diffused throughout everyday living, from playing and singing, to harvesting and planting. All of life is an act of living out their Christian faith. Influences from outside the Amish community, like voting or television, are deplored and resisted.

Though surrounded by a rapidly changing American society, the Amish community has largely maintained its customs, and has remained relatively unchanged. The practice of *meidung,* or shunning, pressures individuals and families to follow the Ordnung, the rules of the Church. Shunning is the practice of banning an individual from ceremonial and social participation within the community. It prohibits any interaction or transaction between the individual and others, for example through eating, sleeping, buying, or selling. Shunning is used to control the behavior of the erring members who seem to be moving toward the attractions of the outer society. According to Huntington (1988), shunning is used to help the erring member realize the gravity of their sin and the need to return to the rules of the church. Shunning has helped to insulate the Amish culture from infusions and assaults by the larger society.

Demographic Information

The Amish is a growing church with an increasing membership. In 1905, the Amish population numbered approximately 8,200; in 1980, there were approximately 92,000 members. Since they do not proselytize, high birth rates (about seven children per family), as well as a determination to keep their grown children and families within the Amish community, help to perpetuate this unique subculture. Amish household size may vary from a married couple with no children to one with 15 children.

THE ECOLOGY OF OLD ORDER AMISH FAMILIES

Old Order Amish communities are mostly rural and are known for their distinctiveness, smallness, homogeneity, and self-sufficiency. These small communities are scattered predominantly throughout the rural Midwest. Nearly 75 percent of the Amish population resides in Pennsylvania, Ohio and Indiana. Other states with Amish communities include: Missouri, Wisconsin, Iowa, Illinois, Michigan, New York, Delaware, Tennessee, Minnesota, Kentucky, Maryland, Mississippi, Kansas, Oklahoma, Virginia, and Florida (Huntington, 1988). Amish communities are also found in Canada, Mexico, and Central and South America, with many settling in these countries in order to continue the farming occupations of their ancestors.

Agricultural Enterprises

Each Amish settlement usually contains small businessmen, such as blacksmiths, harness makers, carpenters, buggy makers, and plumbers, who help form a self-sufficient community. These small businessmen support the farmers who are the backbone of the community and who may farm without the use of modern machinery. Some reports say they produce at least as much per acre as their non-Amish neighbors who use mechanized equipment (Ruth, 1985).

According to Toffler (1970), the Amish have been protected from the encroachment of technology, a wasteful mentality, and the excessive stimulation of individuals.

The Old Order Amish prohibit the use of automobiles, telephones, and electricity. They also have strict dress codes, forbid rubber-tired tractors, central heating, and cameras (Huntington, 1988).

Obedience to Amish Codes of Behavior

Amish clothing has changed little over the centuries. There are a number of subtle differences in dress among the groups, such as the width of the strings or ribbons on the women's caps, the use of pins rather than buttons, or the type of cloth that is used for clothing. To the Amish, clothing is a form of communication. There is disdain for the flashy and quick-changing fads of the outside society.

Differences in dress among Amish groups are usually not discernible to outsiders and, therefore, appear as uniformity. To outsiders, this uniformity seems to be a contradiction, since the Amish supposedly resist conformity but abide by community standards of dress and behavior.

Buggies, a major source of transportation, offer another example of strict obedience seen among the various Amish groups. They have buggies of varying colors representing degrees of conservatism, with black for liberal, yellow for middle conservative, and white indicating the most conservative. An owner of a white buggy reveals that he follows traditions of an earlier period when undyed cloth was considered most proper.

Language

In their homes, the Old Order Amish read the German Bible and speak a German dialect called Pennsylvania Dutch. Their practices, values, and beliefs include strict rules of behavior which strongly emphasize the importance of the family and the cohesion of the Amish community.

Community Organization

An Amish settlement typically consists of a church district led by a Bishop, two ministers, and a deacon, and contains 25 to 35 nuclear families that join together with a network of communing church districts (Huntington, 1988). The size of the community is mainly determined by the density or number of people in the community. Worship services are held in homes or barns. When the community becomes too large, the district divides.

There is typically no single, visible boundary that sets off the Amish community or district. However, the ideological boundary is formed by traditional believers who follow the Ordnung or rules of the church district. Within these districts people are "in fellowship" with one another. All Amish members can recite the unwritten Ordnung of their particular church district.

Amish Family Structure

The family is the basic unit in Amish society. Rearing children is the most important function of a family. According to Amish beliefs, parents are accountable to God for their children's spiritual welfare. Fathers and mothers are always expected to be united in disciplining the children. Parents are responsible and obligated to nurture their children by standing united in teaching, guiding, loving, and admonishing them. Parents constantly strive to be good role models for their children. Typically, Amish families are large, with an average of seven children. Women have a long reproductive period with no indications that contraceptives are used.

An Amish man's occupation is only important in providing the basic economic necessities of living, and is in no way given the same status or importance as jobs held by the larger society. The husband is the head of the household. Amish women do not work outside the home. The husband is expected to be considerate of his wife emotionally, physically, and spiritually. A wife's commitment is first to God and then to her husband. Despite being a patriarchal family, the wife's position in the Amish culture can best be explained by her position in church, where she has an equal vote, but not an equal voice (Huntington, 1988). A wife is expected to support her husband in all relationships with others, including the children, grandparents, and neighbors. In an economy where self-sufficiency is desired, women are responsible for home production. The Old Order Amish are monogamous and divorce is prohibited.

Amish Life Stages

The Amish individual passes through six stages from birth to death. Each of these stages requires different responsibilities and obligations. While these stage labels are typical of many cultural groups, each represents important behavioral dimensions among the Amish.

Infancy.   This stage covers the period from birth until the child learns to walk. Infants are always welcomed by families and the community. The Amish believe that babies are without sin and can do no wrong. The first two years of life are filled with indulgence and love, whether the baby is a girl or a boy. No strict feeding schedule is followed. If the baby cries, caretakers believe the baby is in need of comfort or food, not discipline. Mothers, fathers, brothers, sisters, uncles, aunts, cousins, and members of the community all share in a similar style of permissive child rearing. Amish babies are rarely left alone. They are held during waking hours, bathed on their mother's lap, and even sleep in the parents' bed. On outings, babies are barely conspicuous, as the Amish do not want outsiders to notice them. The Amish do not like outsiders to care for their children (Hostetler and Huntington, 1971).

Preschool Children.   This stage covers the period from walking until entrance into school. After the second year, discipline becomes important and Amish children are taught to respect the authority of the parents. Parents are deeply concerned about their children and are responsible for teaching them the "right way." The "right way" translates into the Amish religious way, which includes learning to care for anyone younger and less able and sharing and helping others. Parents insulate children by separating themselves and their children from the moral and physical dangers of the outside world.

During the preschool years, children learn that work is perceived as helping others and is a part of one's responsibility. Tasks are done without being thanked; a job well done is reward in and of itself. Both boys and girls accompany their father around the farm and help their mother with household chores. Young children are expected to be useful, but are chastised for asking too many questions.

School Children.   This is the period when children attend public or Amish schools. They are often referred to as "scholars." Children attend Amish schools between the ages of six and 15. While parents are primarily responsible for teaching attitudes and values to their children, teachers are from the Amish community and play an important supplemental role as a socializing agent in the lives of youths. Children are taught the importance of being concerned for other people. They are rewarded for developing responsibility, appreciating work, and practicing the right attitudes of humility, forgiveness, admission of error, and sympathy.

Although most of the scholars help wherever they are needed, most of the time boys work with their fathers and girls with their mothers. They are taught to make things with their hands. For example, girls learn to cook, bake, sew, and make things for their playhouses. Boys build toys and birdhouses, as well as feed the livestock and poultry.

Young Adult.   This is the stage where those who have completed their eight years of schooling can now do a full day's work. They are often between 14 to 16 years of age and engaged in the social life of their peers. The young person is no longer in elementary school and is vulnerable to the influences of the outside world. Amish adolescents who attend a public high school often experience great anxiety due to conflicting cultural norms and values. Such anxieties may last for a lifetime. The Amish believe that schooling beyond the elementary years hampers successful integration into adult Amish roles and ways helpful to living in an Amish community. In states requiring education until age 16, the Amish school their youths at home.

The Amish believe that the peer group is much more influential than the parents, or church. Therefore, Amish parents strongly hope that the adolescent will have Amish peers for friends and not the "English," as they call those of the majority culture. They fear that if adolescents associate with the "English," they will eventually leave the Amish community for the outside world. Yet, even if young persons break many of the rules and venture into the outside world, belonging to Amish peer groups almost guarantees their return to the values of the Amish culture. Amish parents often ignore the minor transgressions of youth, such as owning a radio or attending a movie. The Amish adolescent is allowed a little more freedom at this point in life to test the boundaries of the cultural ecosystem.

At about age 16, courting usually begins to take place. Informal Sunday evening singing get-togethers are common in the Amish community. Along with socializing and singing, dates are arranged. Other social gatherings where young adults can meet include barn raisings, corn huskings, weddings, and other work-related activities. Secrecy pervades the entire courtship period.

Adulthood.   Baptism signifies religious adulthood; however, it is marriage and the birth of a baby that bring about social adulthood. While marriage itself proclaims social adulthood, full adulthood comes with the birth of the first child (Huntington, 1988).

An Amish man or woman must marry another person of the Amish faith, either from one's own district or from another affiliation that is in "fellowship." Should a young adult choose to marry someone from the majority culture, excommunication and shunning result. Most men marry between the ages of 22 to 24, while females usually marry a year or more younger.

The Amish wedding ceremony differs from settlement to settlement. For example, most Amish marriages in Lancaster, Pennsylvania, occur in November, December, January, and rarely in February. Farm work, religious beliefs, and traditions all help determine when a wedding will take place. The preferred day for weddings is Thursday, with Tuesday the second choice (Scott, 1988). In other Amish communities, weddings are held in almost any season except during the summer, when preservation of food at a wedding feast is a problem due to lack of refrigeration.

The role of parents of the bride and groom differs greatly from one Amish community to another. In Lancaster, Pennsylvania, for example, the parents of the bride have special privileges and are not responsible for planning any part of the wedding. In other communities, the parents of the bride are responsible for managing the food preparation for all guests. The customs and traditions of the wedding ceremony and those followed after the marriage usually differ from one Amish group to another (Scott, 1988).

First cousin marriages are taboo; and, although second cousin marriages are discouraged, they do occur. One must take into account that the Amish of early times recorded only surnames. They have married within their group for generations. Thus, many of the people may be closely related genetically.

The Amish adult is responsible for maintaining and transferring the Amish way of life to the next generation. Adults are guardians who protect and watch over the boundaries of their culture, preventing children from assimilation and acculturation into the outside world. In order to maintain their boundaries from intrusions, families try to remain economically self-sufficient. They do not participate in the social security system. They help one another and accept no outside aid, welfare, or insurance. The Amish community takes care of its ill. They largely prefer not to take part in the political system by voting or serving on juries. However, if they feel threatened by systems that infringe on traditional Amish rights and beliefs, they will actively protest their case to the government. One instance was when the Amish fought to keep their traditional educational system for their youths.

The Elderly.   The Amish elderly generally retire after their youngest child has married and started a family. They move from the big house to the grandfather house.

Amish socialization patterns provide for the individual throughout the natural stages of human life. The age for retirement in the dominant society holds no meaning within Amish communities. Retirement for men and women is voluntary and often influenced by the combination of their health and the need to relinquish farmland to their children, usually the youngest child to earn a living. Grandparents usually retire gradually, helping their married children on certain occasions or when they have specific needs.

The Amish elderly patriarch indicates his retirement by moving into the "grandfather house," which is usually an adjacent farm dwelling or one near the edge of the community. The elderly Amish live close to their children and grandchildren and do not enter homes for the aged. Grandfather continues to have his own horse and buggy, which still plays an important part in his life. The elderly still have many obligations, such as attending funerals and visiting the sick (Hostetler and Huntington, 1971). Freed from most of their normal farm and household tasks, they are able to do good deeds for relatives, neighbors, the community, and the world.

Prestige and respect accompany old age. The elderly serve as ties to the past and to the old ways of living. Knowledge of how things were done is transmitted by the older people as they readily give advice to the younger generation. Grandfather is an important source of information on farm management problems. Grandmother is an expert on children and helpful with child rearing concerns. The elderly have a strong sense of belonging in a society that finds the elderly an important asset in maintaining traditional ways. According to Hostetler and Huntington (1971), the elderly Amish look back at their lives with satisfaction.

The elderly usually die with dignity at home, surrounded by friends and relatives. At their death, the family is relieved of all household tasks and farm chores. Members of the community take over all funeral arrangements. The family members meditate and pray. Friends call to see their deceased friend and talk to the bereaved family sitting by the bier. Mourners stay up all night for a wake. Following the burial, mourners return to the house of the deceased to share a meal together. All roles and relationships return to normal with the sharing of a meal on this third day after the death. Age-old customs dictate the rituals to follow after a death (Hostetler and Huntington, 1971).

THE AMISH AND THE EDUCATIONAL SYSTEM

Historically, the relationship between the Amish and the public school system has been tumultuous. The Amish believe that the public school may be suitable for children who want to be a part of the world, but not for training their children in humility and the simple way of life. The Amish have increasingly built and managed their own elementary schools. In 1925, the American Amish had one school, in 1950, there were 16 schools, in 1970, over 300 schools, and in 1990, many more. In the past, the strong Amish belief in remaining separate from the world has meant spending time in jail to support their conviction of separate schools for their children.

Amish elementary schools are integrated into the whole of the Amish agricultural community, including planting and harvesting. Teachers, who usually have only an eighth-grade education, support and reinforce the Amish family's values and way of life. A qualified Amish teacher is not a state-certified teacher, but one with "God given" abilities to be a good role model and teacher. A person is approached by the Amish parents to teach in their schools and not vice versa.

Children in school learn that cooperating is more important than competing with one another. Their willingness to help one another and to work at difficult tasks is encouraged. Most knowledge is taught through traditional memorization and drill.

The Amish Vocational School

Vocational schools are for children 14 to 16 years of age. The teaching methods vary with the teacher and the children's age. However, the primary emphasis is combining technical skills with a job role. The students and teachers meet at least once a week; most of the curriculum covers home projects. Helping with chores on the farm and with housekeeping tasks allows the young people to work with others in the family as well as with others in the community. Amish young people obtain satisfaction from manual work.

Few Amish young people enter the public high school. If a young person goes to a high school outside the Amish community, it is almost certain he or she will not remain Amish.

THE AMISH AND THE RELIGIOUS SYSTEM

Here in America, the Amish people have maintained their unique fundamental Christian religion for over 250 years. At first glance, religion is thought to be the stronghold for maintaining their stability. However, religion is also an area of vulnerability. Like a two-edged sword, religion is a realm in which other Christians have similar knowledge and background, and, therefore, are able to communicate with the Amish. Communication with outsiders creates the possibility of a more permeable cultural boundary (Huntington, 1988).

Religious services are held every other Sunday in the home of one of the members. Food is prepared on Friday at the host family house by neighbor women. After the preaching service on Sunday, a meal is shared by everyone. Activities and behaviors are steeped in tradition and symbolism. For example, men and women are seated on opposite sides of the room in which the service is held. Everyone, including infants, attends.

The Amish practice only adult baptism. Therefore, once a year there is an adult baptism service held for young adults who wish to join the Amish Christian faith. This baptism commits the adult to the responsibilities and obligations of keeping the Ordnung of this church community. Upon taking the vow, one becomes a complete adult in full fellowship, and, if called, is expected to be willing to serve as a minister in the church community. Only males become ministers and they serve for life.

The maintenance and continuance of the Amish church community are structured by the Ordnung. Each district has its own Ordnung with its various rules and regulations. In order to maintain the Ordnung, shunning or *mei-dung* and excommunication or banning are practiced.

Shunning is enforced on someone who breaks the rules. The individual is considered an outcast and is avoided economically, socially, physically, and religiously by the entire community. One cannot even eat at the same table with the shunned person until the individual repents publicly.

Excommunication is more severe than shunning. Members who have broken their vows and will not mend their ways are excommunicated from the church community. No further communication or transactions are allowed between the Amish and the excommunicated. For example, an Amish who marries a non-Amish, an outsider, is excommunicated.

THE AMISH AND THE HEALTH CARE SYSTEM

Amish families have many children. Fortunately, they have good medical care. This is attributed to their relatively high standard of living (Huntington, 1988). The Amish find nothing in the Bible that prohibits them from seeking modern medical care, immunizations, or blood transfusions.

The Amish have a system of beliefs and practices that relate to health and illness. Most of these practices come from everyday experiences. When scientific concepts of health care conflict with their traditional folk medicine, stress for the individual or family results. Illness that is not cured by professionals is treated with traditional folk remedies that are usually considered benign (Helman, 1990).

THE AMISH AND THE GOVERNMENTAL SYSTEM

The relationship between the Amish and the national, state, and local governments has not always been cordial. According to Locke (1992), the Amish have been forced into many legal battles with the U.S. government. The open practice of their religious beliefs has been repeatedly threatened. For example, because of their strong pacifist beliefs, they have often been treated as traitors during times of war; they have fought against compulsory high school education for their adolescents; and they have fought against paying social security because they do not take any aid from the government. The Amish practice political separatism and have had to confront issues that conflict with their beliefs in the courts. However, rather than defend themselves in court, a non-Amish group, the National Committee for Amish Religious Freedom, defends their cases.

THE AMISH AND THE ECONOMIC SYSTEM

The Amish tend to be self-sufficient as an economic unit. They are mostly small farmers or small businessmen. The Amish live simply and cheaply by making most of their clothing, building most of their houses and barns, maintaining their own equipment, planting vegetable gardens, raising pigs, cows, chickens, and horses, gathering honey and maple syrup, and selling homemade quilts, bread, and other small items (Locke, 1992).

THE ROLE OF HELPING PROFESSIONALS

As helping professionals, your interaction with the Old Order Amish will likely be limited, aside from a few encounters in offices or stores. It will be important that you learn some of the particular characteristics of the Amish community in order to give them the respect they deserve and appreciate the difficulties they face in interacting outside their home community. Your study of the Amish could be a model for studying any other religious group, helping you to be sensitive to their values, goals, and practices. We encourage you to make this kind of study of your own faith. Are you curious about what you might discover?

CONCLUSIONS

It is often difficult for the Amish to resist pressures from the majority community, especially if larger economic rewards are needed when families remain large and the youth do not leave home to make a living elsewhere. When small businessmen of the church community, such as carpenters and plumbers, need specialized equipment, they often need to communicate directly with outside institutions. Also, the Amish people who work in small outside factories to make ends meet are differentially treated under the Ordnung. Allowing for differential treatment encourages outside influences that slowly erode the basic foundation of the church community.

A serious problem is the shortage of available farm land for the Amish children. Amish families expect their children to settle nearby and wish for parents to help raise their grandchildren. Diversified family farming is followed in order to promote self-sufficiency and help insure a good Amish life. The Amish provided an experiment concerning a more sustainable agricultural system needed to help protect the global ecosystem and keep it free of pesticides and herbicides.

As farm land in the U.S. became scarce, some Amish families emigrated to other countries in search of agricultural land. Some have gone to South and Central America. Some have felt the need to relocate and compromise to become economically more viable, adapting somewhat to conditions in a rapidly changing society to survive economically.

STUDY QUESTIONS

1. List some names that refer to the Amish.
2. After reading about the Amish people's history, make a list of important facts. Where are Amish communities in the U.S.? Elsewhere?
3. Ordnung, shunning, and banning are names of three practices followed by the Amish. Define these terms.
4. Make a list of demographic characteristics of the Amish people.
5. Make a list of characteristics of the Amish farmers' operations.
6. Make a list of characteristics of the Amish home and family.
7. List characteristics of each life stage of the Amish.
8. Describe a typical Amish child in the educational system.
9. Describe how a typical Amish family practices its religion.
10. Describe the health care for a typical Amish family.
11. Describe the typical Amish family's interaction with the government system.

APPLICATIONS

1. Describe in a one-page essay any experience you have had with Amish people either directly or indirectly. List any questions you had following these experiences.
2. Consider your own or another religion; use the same headings used in the chapter and write a two-page essay describing the families of that religion.
   (a) Describe how a helping professional might interact with those of the religion you are analyzing.
3. Write a one-page essay on the strengths of the Amish family.
4. Write a two-page essay on how you would prepare to be a professional in a community where you might encounter Amish people.
5. Write a one-page essay on how you would show respect to those who are Amish or of another religion.
6. Select two or three Amish values and write a two-page essay on how your own values are alike or different from theirs.
7. Study the Amish child rearing practices, then write a two-page essay on how the child rearing practices of your home community are alike or different.
8. Write a one-page essay on how communication could be developed or maintained with Amish members of a community.
9. Perform a word association using the word Amish. Write down all the concepts that come to mind. Write an essay regarding these stereotypes and discuss it with your classmates.
10. What are the strengths of the Amish community? How do you think these communities have managed to remain stable for so many years?

REFERENCES

Helman, C. G. (1990). *Culture, health and illness: An introduction to health professionals*. London: Wright.

Hostetler, J. A. (1968). *Amish society*. Baltimore, MD: Johns Hopkins Press.

Hostetler, J. A., & Huntington, G. E. (1971). *Children in Amish society*. New York, NY: Holt, Rinehart and Winston, Inc.

Huntington, G. E. (1988). The Amish family. In Charles H. Mindel, Robert W. Habenstein, & Roosevelt Wright, Jr. (Eds.), *Ethnic families in America*. New York, NY: Elsevier Science Publishing Co.

Locke, Don C. (1992). *Increasing multicultural understanding: A comprehensive model*. Newbury Park, CA: Sage Publications, Inc.

Parrillo, V. N. (1985). *Strangers to these shores*. New York, NY: John Wiley & Sons.

Redfield, R. (1947, January). The folk society. *American Journal of Sociology*, pp. 292–308.

Ruth, J. (1985). *A quiet and peaceable life*. Intercourse, PA: Good Books.

Scott, S. (1988). *The Amish wedding and other special occasions of the old order communities*. Intercourse, PA: Good Books.

Toffler, Alvin. (1970). *Future shock*. New York, NY: Random House.

MEDIA RESOURCES

Ruth, John R. (Producer) and Hostetler, John A. (Consultant). *The Amish: A People of Preservation*. 25- or 53-minute 16mm film. Encyclopedia Britannica, 425 North Michigan Avenue, Chicago, Illinois 60611.

PART III

Lifestyle Variations Among United States Families

CHAPTER 10

Single Teenage Parent Families

Key Concepts

◆ Never-married parents
◆ Feminization of poverty
◆ Parenting alliance
◆ Institutional racism

Unwed mothers, at that time, were a specific group; they fell somewhere between criminals and patients and, like criminals and patients, they were prescribed an exact and fortifying treatment; they were made to disappear.

— Solinger, (1992) (Description of maternity homes of 1958)

Single-parent families have existed throughout the history of the United States. These have included never-married single parents, single parents who are divorced, and widows or widowers who are single parents. It is clear from our social history that people have very different opinions and value judgments about the strength or the appropriateness of single-parent families as environments in which to raise children. Single-parent families consist of at least one child with a parent. Due to the interest and concern for this family form and the extent of the literature on the topic, the entire chapter will focus on never-married single teenage parents. Chapter 11 will focus on divorced single-parent families.

SOCIETAL CONCERN AND DEBATE

Between 1970 and 1988, the number of single parents with children under 18 living in the home more than doubled, from 3.8 million to 9.4 million (Bureau of the Census, 1989). Societal feelings of responsibility toward the nurturance of children have fueled a public debate about how children and families are endangered by the increasing number of single-parent families. In much of this debate, there is a confusion over our public and private interests and responsibilities. Since the socialization of children is an important function of families,

much of the debate has centered around whether single-parent families can appropriately nurture and rear children to productive adulthood. Politicians and citizens, without professional knowledge of human development or family life, have frequently engaged in debates about the negative impact of single-parent families, based on economics or moral standards. Alarmists and critics of the single-parent family frequently claim to have the interests of children and optimal human development at heart, but their arguments and suggestions for policies often appear uninformed, short-sighted, or judgmental.

If we study the single-parent family, we notice that this category is not so simply described. Social class, race or ethnic background, and previous family history are all important influences on the structure, prevalence, and success of single-parent families. In actuality, when we categorize a family as a "single-parent family," the only thing we know about the family is that there is at least one child present and there is no current legal marriage involving the child's biological custodial parent. Since 88 percent of children living in single-parent families live with their mothers, the discussion is usually about mothers and children (National Commission on Children, 1993).

If we want to understand how to support single-parent families, we need to look closely at the circumstances of sub-groups of these families, and then even more closely at individual families themselves. It is useful to look at single-parent families by studying separately never-married single parents, divorced single parents, and widows or widowers with children. What we find are limited similarities; the structure of the family is a single parent with a child or children, but there is a great deal of diversity in resources and practices within these families. These differences can be seen in the division of labor or responsibilities, in the relationships to other supportive systems, and in the specific parenting styles and patterns. As much as possible, the influence of social class will be discussed with each of the sub-types of single-parent families. Social class is a designation of the social and economic variables that tend to create life patterns and influence opportunity and outcome for family members. Ordinarily, family social class is determined by a combination of factors, such as education, income, and job classification of the adults in the family.

NEVER-MARRIED PARENTS

Parents who have never married are increasing in number relative to divorced parents (see Figure 10–1). In the latter part of the twentieth century, we've seen an increase in two primary groups of never-married parents: the largest group is young adolescents, while the smaller group is older professional women nearing the end of their childbearing years who finally decide to fulfill a maternal desire. The two groups differ in many respects.

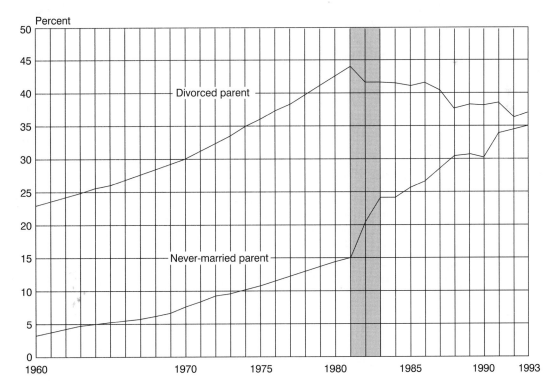

Figure 10–1.   *Children of Single Parents, by Marital Status of Parent: 1960–1993*

Source: Saluter, Arlene F. (1994). U.S. Bureau of the Census.

The other major group of single parents is composed largely of persons of color who have never married. They may have a series of monogamous hetero-sexual relationships, or one enduring primary relationship, which never results in legalized marriage.

Any discussion of never-married parents in the United States quickly focuses on the young teenage parent. There are strong feelings of concern for successful child outcomes in families headed by young, never-married teenage mothers. Income, education, maturity, and support are in short supply for this type of family. Given this vulnerability, it is natural that there should be much public debate about the large increase in single adolescent parents in the 1970s, 1980s, and 1990s. Dramatic increases in the number of teenage preg-nancies and the changing patterns regarding marriage, abortion, and adoption have fueled this discussion.

TRENDS IN NUMBERS

The largest number of births in the United States since 1962 occurred in 1990. A slight downward trend occurred in 1991 and 1992. Every year from 1986 to 1990, there was an increase in births to teenage mothers, largely due to the higher birth rate and earlier pregnancies of Hispanic and African-American women. Births to young never-married mothers were not uniformly distrib-uted across ethnic groups. In 1987, black teenagers represented 14 percent of the adolescent population, but contributed 28 percent of all the adolescent births, and 47 percent of births to unmarried females (Strober and Dornbush, 1988). By 1990, 67 percent of African-American babies were born to unmarried women, compared to 37 percent of Hispanic babies born to single mothers, and 20 percent of white babies born to single mothers (Ventura and Martin, 1993).

Increase in Adolescent Parents

While these data alone are alarming, there are some particular details of these trends that cause concern. In almost seventy years, from 1917 to 1983, the birth rate for adolescent women declined slightly, but by the late 1950s, the post-World War II baby boom had increased the total population of teenagers. During this same period, older females reduced their birth rate, so that of those babies born during this post-war period, an increasingly larger percent were born to teenage mothers (Solinger, 1992). Family life professionals were concerned that the largest rise in the birth rate in the late 1980s was occurring in the under 15 age group. Practically all of these births to very young adoles-cents were to African-Americans (Williams, 1991). Researchers have substanti-ated that young adolescents who become sexually active wait an average of one year before using some form of birth control. Older teenagers are more likely to use birth control earlier and to use more effective birth control methods (Allen-Meares, 1989).

Increase in Fecundity

Historians note that one important reason for the rise in births to teenagers is the gradual increase in the general health and fecundity (or capability of having children) of young women. While in 1870 only 13 percent of 17-year-olds were fecund, by 1992, 94 percent of American girls were. Between 1940 and 1968 alone, the proportion of fecund fifteen-year-old girls in the United States increased by 31 percent (Coontz, 1992).

Differential Birth Rates

Differential birth rates contributed to the increasing alarm about births to unmarried women. While in 1950, African-Americans represented 75 percent of all minority groups in the United States, by 1990 they represented less than half. Non-Hispanic white women give birth to an average of 1.9 children in their lifetimes and African-American women average 2.5 children. Hispanic women's birth rates range from a low of 1.5 children for Cuban-Americans to 3.2 for Mexican-Americans. Asian birth rates range from 1.1 for Japanese-Americans to 3.2 for Hawaiians. American Indians and Alaska Natives show a birth rate of 2.7 percent (Haub, 1993). In the years between 1970 and 1988, as shown in Figure 10–2, the percentage of single-parent families has increased.

By the year 2025, minorities will account for almost half of all United States children. Since childbearing is differentiated across the ethnic groups and teenage births occur more frequently among Hawaiians, African-Americans, Hispanics (except for Cubans) and Native Americans, the predictions of increased proportions of children born to young never-married women raise some concerns (Schorr, 1988). As shown in Figure 10–3, by 1995 the United States' Hispanic population was younger in age than the general population. Some ethnic groups, such as Mexican-Americans and other Hispanics, continue to give birth well into their late childbearing years, while black and Native American women tend to begin having children early but complete their families while relatively young. These different birth patterns tend to predict different life courses and problems for a single mother whose first child is born in the mother's adolescence.

Changes in Marriage Patterns

The story of adolescent births in the United States is compelling because the unwed mother represents a contrast to the traditional model of two-parent families. It is generally acknowledged that, following World War II, the United States promoted a return to the traditional pattern of a nuclear family, with one spouse working. Many women who had worked in the defense industry or in other jobs to support the military were encouraged to leave the workplace and return home. A patriarchal family model was emulated, and early marriages increased. By the late 1950s, almost 50 percent of all women were mar-

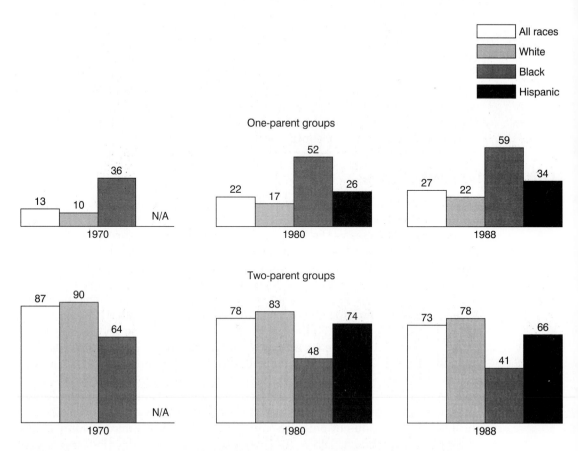

Figure 10–2.   *The Proportion of Single-Parent Families Has More Than Doubled Since 1970 (Figures shown in percent)*

Source: Single Parents and Their Children. U.S. Bureau of the Census, S.B. 3–89.

ried by age twenty (Coontz, 1992; Wojtkiewicz, 1993). Births rose to a high of 25.3 per 1,000 women of child-bearing age in 1957. The birth rate for third children doubled between 1940 and 1960, and for fourth children, it tripled (Coontz, 1992).

The post-war early marriage rate produced a record number of births. These "baby-boom" children grew to adolescence in the late 1950s and early 1960s and had a remarkably visible influence on society. Simultaneously, the vigorous pursuit of civil rights legislation refueled a backlash of conservative concern about the procreative practices of minorities. At the same time, many inner-city neighborhoods saw an influx of ethnic minorities seeking urban employment in areas with inadequate infrastructure to sustain successful communities.

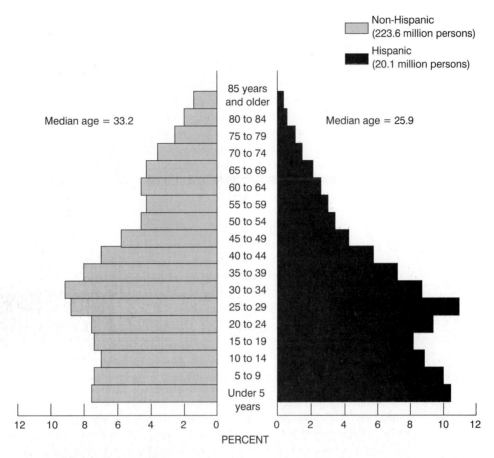

Figure 10-3. *The Hispanic Population is much younger than the Non-Hispanic Population*
Source: Hispanics in the United States. U.S. Bureau of the Census, S.B. 4–90.

Changes in Adoption Practices

Another change in behavior of never-married mothers that attracted concern related to decisions about keeping children or giving them up for adoption. In the 1950s and 1960s, 90 percent of all adoptions were of children born to unmarried mothers (Solinger, 1992). White pregnant adolescents in particular were encouraged to give their children up for adoption. Many white pregnant adolescents were labeled mentally disturbed and described as angry at their fathers and seeking revenge against their parents. A psychological diagnosis that included a mental disturbance enabled a white adolescent with economic means to receive a therapeutic abortion. If this option was not possible or not desired by the family, a frequent pattern was to have the white adolescent "disappear" on a trip or on a scholarship for a period of time until the birth and adoption had been completed. Stories of black market baby mills and pressures to be "cleansed" or "retrained" in homes for unwed mothers are documented in a number of studies of this period (Solinger, 1992). The description that opens this chapter is part of that picture.

During this same time it was much less likely that black adolescents sought abortions. With a tradition of strong, independent women being forced by social and economic circumstances to rear children alone, adolescent pregnancy was not viewed as negatively in the African-American community. It was more likely that extended family members in the African-American community would assist an adolescent parent and frequently play vital roles in the rearing of the children. During the 1970s, economic restructuring in the United States brought severe job dislocation to many African-American males. Black median family income was only 56 percent of white median family income from 1979 through 1987 (U.S. Bureau of the Census, 1990).

Since poverty reduces the resources available to establish independent households, black adolescents were less apt to marry. In 1960, almost one-third of all 18- to 19-year-old African-American women were married. By 1984, less than 3 percent were married (Saluter, 1989). In 1950, 78 percent of black family households consisted of married couples. By 1991, only 48 percent included married couples.

Political Criticism of African-American Patterns

A particularly difficult period of social history was marked by the 1958 introduction of House Bill 479 by David H. Glass, a Mississippi State Representative (Solinger, 1992). The purpose of this legislation was to pass regulations requiring the sterilization of African-American women, particularly adolescent mothers. The legislation was not passed, but it illustrated an active struggle with racism in the march toward civil rights legislation.

In 1965, the landmark Moynihan Report on the family was published. The impact of this report has been described as eliminating a balanced scholarship about adolescent parenthood and African-American families for at least twenty years. Moynihan was the Assistant Secretary of Labor to President Lyndon Johnson (1963–1968), and his description of the African-American family as a matriarchal system marked by poverty, joblessness, and illegitimacy in a tangle of pathology had sharp political overtones. The report suggested that the strains on the African-American family were due largely to the inadequacy of the black male to exhibit the necessary responsibility, discipline, and diligence to support a family. A strong theme of poverty was stressed, with an inadequate exploration of the power of racism to limit opportunities for the African-American family. In response, governmental policymakers began an era of institutional racism by advocating work programs for African-American women and aggressive child support enforcement against black men. In the resultant political debate between liberals and conservatives, a redemptive romanticized picture of African-American families as resilient, creative, religious, and nurturant to all children was present. Neither view contributed to balanced social or government policies.

From 1980 to 1992, the focus of government policy was to reduce aid to dependent individuals and families and to urge self-control and the delay of sexual activity. Not until the publishing of the landmark work, *The Truly Disadvantaged: The Inner-city, the Underclass and Public Policy,* by W. J. Wilson (1987), did the debate begin to return to a clear understanding of the effects of poverty and social class on birth rates and family patterns. Wilson sounded an elegant alarm that the real problems of African-American families were not cultural but economic. The modernization of the industrial sector had reduced the need for low-skilled jobs, and citizens with less access to education could not compete. The affluent and middle-class urban dwellers had all fled to the suburbs, and the remaining infrastructure was inadequate to inspire or recruit low-income youth to stay in school, or adult workers to enter retraining or vocational transition programs.

Wilson and other social scientists claimed that the social problems being blamed on the inadequate family structures of African-Americans and other minorities were the results of the power of poverty and economic dislocation, and were enough to ruin hope in any ethnic group. In addition, economists noted that a delay in marriage and in establishing independent households reflected insufficient incomes to cover the expenses involved.

One of the ironies of the alarm about minority single parents rests on the confusion generated by data. While the birth rate of unmarried African-American women fell by 13 percent between 1970 and 1992, the birth rate of married African-American women fell by 38 percent, and the marriage rate of African-American women fell by 50 percent. Thus, the proportion of black children born to single parents has grown. During the same period, the percent of unmarried white women giving birth rose by 27 percent (Coontz, 1992).

SOCIO-CULTURAL FOUNDATIONS

Responses to never-married single parents illustrate great conflicts in American society. Discussions frequently include moral and economic issues. Discussions about the never-married single-parent family often revolve around early sexual activity, responsible parenthood, healthy parent-child bonds, the father's role, and the economic and career possibilities for the mother and child. In the 1970s, the link between marriage and sexual activity was severed, and pregnant adolescents did not see marriage as an imperative. Owing to the differential access to abortions, which still continues, white adolescents were more likely to obtain abortions than were African-American adolescents and other minorities.

Adolescent mothers may see parenthood as a way to express maturity and become more responsible. These values of responsibility and affectionate relationships with children may also reflect a sense of despair or frustration in establishing nurturing relationships with a partner. For African-American women, finding an eligible male who is employed and can be a responsible partner has been increasingly difficult. By 1987, women of marriageable age in the African-American community had less than a 50 percent chance of finding a partner who was not in jail, on drugs, or unemployed (Wilson, 1987). Many critics of the welfare system claim that single parenting and the African-American custom of extended kinship and joint parenting have been facilitated by benefits from the Aid to Families with Dependent Children (AFDC) program.

Among all women, the influence of the women's movement and the tendency to redefine marriage as a companion relationship, rather than primarily a procreative relationship, have opened options and created alternative practices. If men and women see marriage as largely an arrangement to ensure the birth and nurturance of children, then a devotion to children includes the positive valuing of marriage. If marriage is viewed as an adult relationship which must be satisfying to both partners and create an economically independent unit, then society as a whole suffers from the inability of young people to establish satisfying, economically sustainable marriages.

ECONOMIC STATUS

One of the most alarming characteristics of never-married parents is their economic vulnerability. However, the economic status of all young families has become discouraging in the latter part of the twentieth century. The poverty rate of single-mother-headed families in 1981 was 47 percent (Wilson, 1987). By 1992, 66 percent of America's poor children lived in two-parent families. Nearly 75 percent of American children growing up in single-parent families will experience poverty during their first ten years, but 52 percent of *total years* of childhood poverty occur while the children are in two-parent homes (National Commission on Children, 1993).

Many unmarried adolescent mothers rely on Aid to Families with Dependent Children (AFDC). In contrast to Social Security and widow's benefits, and some alimony or child support awards, AFDC had no cost-of-living adjustments for many years. Many adolescent mothers lived with their own mothers as subfamily groups. Prior to 1982, the U.S. census did not identify these adolescent mothers as family heads. In 1989, about 20 percent of single parents lived within someone else's household (Bureau of the Census, 1992). Since the paternity of their children is often not declared and child support enforcement has been lax, only 20 percent of unmarried mothers receive awarded child support (National Commission on Children, 1993).

The social status of unmarried mothers tends to be lower than mothers who are married, divorced, or widowed. However, ethnic and social class patterns around status vary. In some communities where there are few jobs and little hope for a career, one of the only ways for young women to acquire status is to become a mother. While the larger environment may view this young woman as of a lower status, within her own family or neighborhood she may acquire value, status, and pride. Examples of life stories of young women who report this effect are told by Williams in *Black Teenaged Mothers: Pregnancy and Childrearing from Their Perspective* (1991).

CHANGING ROLES OF FEMALES

Among single-parent families, the vast majority of unwed or never-married parents with custody of children are females. The power of the women's movement, the trend toward a companionate marriage, and the controversy over abortion have led many pregnant teens to carry their pregnancies to term, and more single teens to keep their infants. In addition, tremendous controversy over providing sex education in public schools and private and public agencies has resulted in fewer adolescents possessing accurate information and procreative health services.

In the precarious world of poverty, it is frequently the mother-child system that provides the only stability or centeredness for a household. Frequently, grandmothers or aunts are important supports for teenage mothers and children, especially in the African-American community (McAdoo and McAdoo, 1985). Some adolescent parents report an enhancement of their status to that of a companion with their mother or grandmother once they have given birth. Adolescent mothers who rely heavily on their mothers and grandmothers for child care and support may resent the involvement of the older generations in the discipline and care of their children. In her intensive study of black adolescent mothers, Williams (1991) reports the interest of some young mothers in moving away from their maternal home and establishing their own households to achieve independent power. With former teenage mothers becoming grandmothers at age 30, many current teenage mothers are supported more by their babies' great-grandmothers, now in their late forties or early fifties, than by their own mothers. These grandmothers may be 30 years old and disdain the age stereotype involved in that role. They prefer to be classified as young, not old, and remain free to socialize away from home. Variations in cross-generational family models are described by Apfel and Seitz (1991).

CHANGING ROLES OF MALES

Young men who have fathered children in their adolescence or with an adolescent female frequently have precarious relationships with the mothers of their children. In Moynihan's 1965 report, African-American males were compared with African-American females and were found to be worse off in education and employment. Opportunities for service jobs at minimum wage have been more often open to minority females than to males. The inability to obtain employment and persist in educational pursuits has decreased the power of many adolescent fathers. Vulnerable in the areas of education and employment, many of these young men are not able to maintain stable relationships with mothers of their children. A University of Chicago study reported that, in 1990, employed black men in the inner city were 22 times more likely to marry the mother of their children than were unemployed fathers (Coontz, 1992).

The Guttmacher Institute has claimed that 25 percent of females who became mothers in adolescence were impregnated by males in their twenties whom the young mothers perceived as authority figures (McAdoo, 1988). Some Guttmacher studies show the fathers being older, as old as in their fifties, making many professionals recognize the possibility of incest and rape. These findings help question the young-love-one-mistake notion that is a popular reason given for adolescent pregnancy.

In a dramatic 1986 television program, video journalist Bill Moyers showed young adolescent males whose only way to exhibit power was to father children for whom they showed little subsequent economic responsibility (Moyers, 1986). In contrast, a number of social service programs have observed that 80 percent of birth fathers visit their new children during the hospital stay of the mother and child. In one study, when approached by a social service agency and invited to claim paternity, 50 percent of these young men did so (Children's Defense Fund, 1987). This legal declaration is accompanied by financial obligations that are sometimes difficult to fulfill. The Budget Reconciliation Act of 1993 requires all states to offer simple processes for in-hospital voluntary declaration of paternity around the time of the child's birth. Once paternity is established, support orders can be issued (Children's Defense Fund Reports, 1993).

In her study of adolescent mothers, Williams (1991) reports the frequent phenomenon of failure to report the father's name, because the public policy demands for child support payment are beyond the young man's ability to pay. Although she may withhold this official information, the young mother may still enjoy visits and a variety of services and goods purchased by the father. Family life educators who have organized programs for adolescent parents frequently comment on the frustration and despair of adolescent fathers who wish to be more actively and responsibly involved in their children's lives but cannot identify a legal public role without incriminating themselves.

SOCIALIZATION OF CHILDREN

The 1990 census documented 65 percent of children of black single mothers as poor, compared with only 18 percent of children of black married parents (U.S. Bureau of the Census, 1993). Children of never-married parents are vulnerable to the effects of poverty and the low educational level of their parents. Children of single mothers are significantly more at risk for learning problems, for being left back, and for dropping out. The literature on school dropouts and maternity rates indicates that young women who are one to two years behind grade level are at risk for early childbearing. Particularly, if the young woman is delayed in school, her motivation and ability to return to school are lower after pregnancy. A young woman who was at grade level when she became a mother is much more likely to pursue education, and obtain eventual employment.

Of more direct concern for the children of young never-married women are parenting skills. Some studies have reported that adolescent parents are apt to provide for the physical care of their children without understanding their need for stimulation and individualized nurturance. Newberger (1977) developed a model of four levels of parental understanding based on Kohlberg's stages of moral development. Some family life professionals have used this model to observe adolescent parents. These levels are: egotistical, conventional, subjective and analytic. The *egotistical* parental understanding tends to be self-centered and fails to take the individual needs of the child into consideration. A parent with a *conventional* understanding of the role tends to see strict "good boy/bad boy" or normative rules for correct behavior. With *subjective* or individualistic understanding of parenting, the parent tries to understand the child's point of view, and finally, the *analytic* understanding of parenthood involves a mutual understanding of both the parent's and child's needs and some ability to negotiate the meeting of those individual needs.

In Williams's (1991) observation of thirty adolescent unmarried mothers, only two exhibited the more immature egotistical parenting style. The group ranged in age from 15 to 19 and exhibited all levels of parenting understanding. Williams noted that adolescent mothers who showed an analytic understanding of parenting also were more independent and goal-oriented about their own lives. Such mothers more frequently attended school or vocational programs, and supported themselves and their children. This same interaction between the mother's self-development and parenting skills was documented in early programs, such as the St. Paul's Mechanical Arts High School-based program, which indicated that the greatest development in parental skills was seen when the young women's own educational and vocational needs were supported (Schorr, 1988).

ROLE OF GRANDPARENTS AND OTHERS

Many adolescent unmarried mothers live in households containing three or four generations. Their own parents, aunts, uncles, or grandparents are important to the rearing of their children, and the provision of child care and economic support. Because the children often reside with the mother, it is frequently the maternal relatives who are immediately most supportive. However, there are ample descriptions in the literature of paternal grandparents and other relatives who encourage a positive relationship with the child, and indeed provide support and nurturance.

ECOLOGICAL FACTORS

Never-married single parents and their children are vulnerable family units that need support from a number of community systems. However, much of the needed support is due to the effects of inflation and the lack of income for all young families, not simply the status of single-parent families.

Demographics

According to the 1990 census, 20 percent of all children lived in single-parent families. The 1991 census report showed that 37 percent of these children lived in families with divorced parents and 60 percent with never-married parents. In addition, the census reported a number of households classified as three generational. These households obviously included a number of unmarried young parents. In 1990, of 1 million babies born, one third were born to women under twenty years of age (National Commission on Children, 1993).

There are reported differences in the frequency of unmarried parents by ethnic group. According to a 1993 Bureau of the Census study, within the African-American community, 58.4 percent of children were reported as living with single parents; half of these parents had never married. Within the white community, 20.2 percent were living with single parents and 30.1 percent of Hispanic children were living with single parents (see Figure 10–4). The birth *rate* data tell a more specific story. Births to never-married women cross economic groups; 66 percent of African-American babies and 32 percent of white babies were born to unmarried women with an annual income of less than $10,000. The figures are 32 percent and 8 percent for families with incomes ranging from $25,000 to $30,000, and 22 percent and 3 percent for families with incomes over $75,000. In 1991, 66 percent of all children living with unmarried mothers were poor (U.S. Bureau of the Census, 1992).

Aesthetics

Though few examples of literature and music are aimed at unmarried parent families, there is a strong theme of maternal nurturance and strength in many other art forms. From visual arts such as Mary Cassatt's romanticized paintings of mothers and children in the Impressionist period to folk songs about strong mountain women and powerful biographies of women trapped by circumstances in single motherhood, there is a theme of independence and strength. The popular 1991 novel, *Waiting to Exhale* (McMillan, 1991), portrays the strength, creativity and frustration of four black single women. While some of this material is anti-male, or in the category of the "wounded women" genre, a great deal of it is uplifting and strengthening with messages of hope and love.

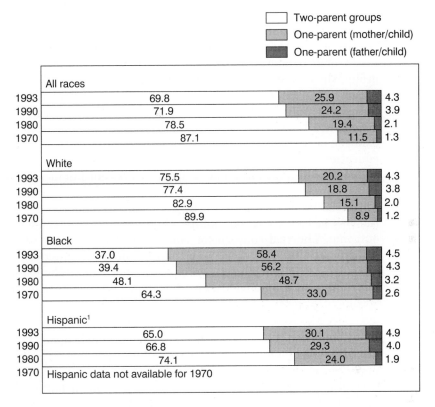

Figure 10–4.   *Composition of Family Groups with Children, by Race and Hispanic Origin: 1970–1993*

[1]Hispanic may be of any race.

Note: Family groups comprise family households and subfamilies.

Source: Rawlings, Steve W. *Household Family Characteristics: March 1993.* U.S. Bureau of the Census, P20–477, Washington, DC: U.S. Government Printing Office.

Education

There are negative consequences for education of both parents and children in the families of never-married parents. Early childbearing for a single woman frequently interferes with education. Indeed, until the 1960s, pregnant females were expected to drop out of school. Early pregnancy is the single most important reason that females leave high school before graduation. Finally, schools began making classes available for pregnant students and for young mothers, including classes on caring for infants.

Statistics from the National Commission on Children (1993) show that young adults ranging in age from 18 to 23 with basic educational skills in the bottom fifth of distribution in comparison to their peers are nine times as likely as those in the top half to bear a child before marriage.

In a study of adolescent mothers done by Furstenberg et al. (1987), there was a high incidence of eventual return to education. For 80 percent of the group, the outcome for these adolescent mothers, twenty years after the birth of their first children, was fairly positive and independent. This successful group generally returned to school or obtained a General Education Diploma (GED) and became self-supporting. However, in contrast to the mothers, the children of this sample tended to show difficulties with school achievement and educational goal-setting. Children in single-parent families are twice as likely to drop out of school as children from two-parent families, score lower on standardized tests, and receive lower grades in school (National Commission on Children, 1993). Being raised by a single parent is frequently cited as one of the risk factors for school failure. However, one risk alone does not determine outcome. The real concern for education of never-married parents and their children is that they are too often *also* poor, unemployed, underemployed, uninsured, and living in dangerous neighborhoods. The combination of these factors is seen most obviously in poor school performance or dropping out.

Religion

Within this population there are no clear unifying religious themes, but a variety of studies give some reflection on the influence of religion. Some young never-married women who become pregnant indicate that their religious values eliminate abortion as a viable option. Yet, about half of the pregnancies of teens are terminated by abortion, even among teens whose religious affiliation opposes abortion. Other young women report that religion enabled them to find ways to support their children without a partner and to bring structure and hope to their lives.

Particularly because of the romanticized image of the African-American extended, resilient, religious family, which emerged in contrast to Moynihan's (1965) report, it is interesting to note a lack of assertive response from African-American churches to support unmarried parents. Recent efforts to enhance the development of young urban men, and to include single parents in the church community, are viewed very positively in a variety of high-stress, low-income neighborhoods. One remarkable reflection in Williams' (1991) study of adolescent African-American parents is the absence or irrelevance of the church community in their urban lives. For many of those young mothers, the neighborhood exhibited a striking lack of social or religious groups or activities to nurture them during adolescence or provide support for them in single parenthood.

The Health Care System and Teenagers

Professionals in the health care and medical systems are concerned about preteens, teenagers, and their sexual practices and pregnancies. For over 20 years, many programs have been designed to prevent pre-teen and teen pregnancies. Pregnancies have been reported at ages as young as nine, with the rate of pregnancies in pre-teens increasing rapidly. Professionals are finding evidence of incest and rape in some of these pregnancies. Some fathers of teenagers' babies are reported by the girls to be in their fifties. In addition, men are reported to be seeking younger girls for sex (prostitution), both here and abroad, in hopes of avoiding infection with AIDS (Acquired Immune Deficiency Syndrome). However, some infected men will be transmitting the virus to the girls. Such reports show that teen pregnancy is not always simply the pictured romantic interlude between two classmates, caught in a passionate moment without contraceptives.

Adequate education concerning reproductive health, family planning, abortion and adoption options, and prenatal health care needs to be part of health care programs for teenagers. Many teens are neither advised by nor cared for by any health professional during their teen years. It is common for teens to be unaware of where the nearest health services are located and how to access them, especially if parental knowledge of pregnancy is a concern. Such conditions give substance to arguments for in-school clinics. Contraceptives must be understood by and be available to young girls who refuse to maintain their virginity. The archaic notion of protecting the girls from information on sexuality, birth control, and methods and supplies for family planning may lead to girls' pregnancy, illness, and death. Boys also need this information if they are going to fulfill their responsibility for preventing pregnancy, infection with the AIDS virus, and other sexually transmitted diseases. In the age of equality for women, the double standard must end, wherein boys blame the girls and accept no legal or financial responsibility for pregnancies, babies, and the spread of disease.

A strong family planning component for any pre-teen and teen parenting program is an imperative. Certainly, preventing a second pregnancy should be a required goal of parenting programs designed by teens, parents, and school authorities, if there is to be hope of responsible parenthood and a good life for mothers and babies. This would allow a teenager to pursue high school and solve one critical problem in those high schools where about 10 percent of teenage girls are pregnant.

Medical authorities are very concerned about girls with immature bodies giving birth. Giving birth at young ages contributes to high maternal mortality rates and high infant mortality rates—especially for low birthweight babies. Many experts, for a variety of reasons, strongly discourage girls from getting pregnant until they are beyond their teen years. Early prenatal care is a major concern for prevention of many serious problems for mothers and infants. Early measurements of the birth canal, proper nutrition for the mother, and regular monitoring can produce healthier babies and mothers. Physicians in public hospitals report in many cases the moment of entering the delivery room being the first time the girl and the physician have met. After such a delivery, the mother goes home almost immediately, generally due to the lack of hospital insurance.

Many teens are smokers, too, adding another negative factor in the prognosis for their babies. Compared to nonsmokers, mothers who smoke have more low birthweight babies. Low birth weights create significant problems for babies. Alcohol consumption can contribute to *fetal alcohol syndrome* (FAS), a form of mental retardation—a lifetime burden to the family and society. Drugs of many types can damage the fetus with serious outcomes. These facts give school authorities compelling reasons to include complete health information in their school services and curricula.

Teachers and school health care workers are often unperceptive about a girl's pregnant condition. Some girls have played basketball into the later months; others gave birth in the restroom. The lack of any class that prepares adolescents for parenthood is commonplace. Though such classes are offered by some school systems, the classes are seldom selected by all students, or even by those who are pregnant at the time and attending school.

The health of the never-married single-parent family is dependent on access to medical services (including insurance, Medicaid, and transportation), an understanding of the importance of preventive health measures and the motivation to use them. Access to health care is reported as one of the factors that discourage marriage, because medical benefits given to teen mothers by the Medicaid Program are lost upon marriage. The National Commission on Children (1993) gave this example: an AFDC recipient who marries a man with an income of $15,000 plus benefits actually loses real income and benefits after the marriage. Therefore, it is more economically astute to remain unmarried and keep welfare benefits.

The Budget Reconciliation Act of 1993 required all states to put laws and procedures in place by April 1, 1994, and to remove barriers that keep children from obtaining health insurance coverage through an absent parent's health insurance. States that must enact new legislation to implement this mandate are allowed later effective dates.

When the never-married parent is a young adolescent, health officials are generally concerned about the adequacy of American teenaged diets during pregnancy. A frequent problem in the adolescent population is a diet low in calcium, iron and the B vitamins. Since diet is one area where economics and personal values and goals play a major role, access to programs such as the Women, Infants and Children (WIC) program of the Department of Agriculture and food stamp programs can assist young mothers in balancing their diets.

All professionals and persons concerned about the pregnant and parenting adolescent need to be concerned about adolescents' attitudes toward diet and weight gain. Professionals who have worked with pregnant adolescents report heightened concern about loss of a slim figure and a dramatic change in self-image. Frequently, such females try to reduce their food intake to slow down an inevitable physiological change.

Another reason for inadequate health care during pregnancy relates to the lack of emotional acceptance of the pregnancy and poor planning for a successful birth on the part of the young mother. Frequently, young females do not admit to pregnancy or seek assistance until some point in the second trimester. Since significant fetal development occurs in the first trimester, a compromise in the mother's diet and a delay in adequate prenatal care concerns health professionals.

There is disagreement on the physiological stress on the body created by an early pregnancy for a healthy adolescent. Physiological principles of species survival suggest that the health of the pregnant mother will be compromised to ensure that nutrients for development are absorbed by the developing fetus. The adolescent mother may not feel as healthy or energetic as she would on a more adequate diet, and, therefore, her ability to plan and prepare for the birth may be compromised.

The family size of a never-married single-parent family shows variation by social class and ethnic group. Frequently, since the young, never-married mother may be living in an extended family, the household size may include several adult relatives and their children. A public criticism of young unmarried mothers is that many of them initiated pregnancy and birth to enhance their own independence and create an income. Studies increasingly discount this argument as simplistic and inaccurate (Coontz, 1992). Young unmarried women who have their first child before the age of nineteen frequently show a motivation to limit the size of their own family, but their ability to act on this goal is strongly influenced by the size of their family of origin, their access to contraceptive information and contraceptives, and their own educational and vocational goals.

In a longitudinal study done by Furstenberg et al. (1987), the education of the adolescent's parents, the adolescent's educational goals, and an understanding of and access to effective family planning techniques strongly influenced family life outcome. Most of the questions about access to health care are mediated directly by income. Inevitably, younger unmarried heads of households have access to Medicaid, which can enhance health care. It is more often the underemployed, minimum wage-earning unmarried parent who does not have access to health care for the family. Of the 37 million Americans who did not have insurance in 1992, 85 percent of them lived in families with at least one working adult (White House Domestic Policy Council, 1993). Young parents frequently find employment in part-time jobs that offer no benefits.

Economic Factors

The erosion of real income for all families is an American crisis; for families with young children it is especially alarming. In 1991, the average income for a white family with two parents working was $46,629. If only the husband worked in a two-parent family, the family income was $33,961. If only the wife worked, the family income was $26,151. A single white working mother's average income was only $13,012 (National Commission on Children, 1993).

Forty-five percent of all female-headed households were poor in 1991; among African-American female-led households, 50 percent were poor. Since 1965, the poverty rate for American families headed by single parents has remained at a plateau of a little less than 50 percent (National Commission on Children, 1991). When one looks at the adolescent single-parent headed household, the figures are even more dramatic. Starting one's family before there has been adequate time to develop education or an employment record to enhance income creates risks for families.

From 1973 to 1990, young families with children lost significant economic ground. Adjusting for inflation, families with children and a head of household younger than 30 lost 44 percent in real income. For young black families with children, the loss was 70 percent, and median income decreased from $13,860 to $4,030 in real dollars. For a single woman head of household under 30 years of age with children, the 1990 median annual income was $1,878 or 20 percent of the poverty level (National Commission on Children, 1993)!

For the young parent, frequent frustrations are centered around the provision of child care for any employment. Numerous analyses have shown that for the young unmarried parent, remaining on AFDC with access to Medicaid is a much sounder management decision than attempting to enter the job market at minimum wage with few benefits and little bargaining power. Social critics charge the welfare system with providing benefits that are too low to lift a family out of poverty (National Commission on Children, 1993). In 1991, only 60 percent of children in poverty received AFDC benefits. As one looks at the economic resources of the never-married female headed household, there are dramatic challenges to all systems in society to assist in nurturing both adults and children.

Housing

Housing for the young, unmarried family is frequently communal or three-generation housing including other adult family members or friends (see Table 10–1). As long as a major part of the family's resources are provided by a parent and grandparent generation, the family can receive some protection, but attempting to establish a separate household for very young single parents is problematic. Only since 1983 have these single parent "subfamilies" living with their parents been reported as separate families by the U.S. Bureau of the Census. Prior to 1983, the mother was coded as a child and her own child was coded as a relative of the household head. When the Bureau of the Census made this reporting change, the number of single-parent families approximately doubled in one year (Mulroy, 1988)! Communal living enhances the resource base for the nurturance of family members. In 1991, according to the U.S. Bureau of the Census, 5 percent of children under 18 lived in a household with their grandparents. This represents 3.2 million children, a 40 percent increase from 1980 (U.S. Bureau of the Census, 1992).

The question of housing cuts deeply to the question of culturally preferred patterns for family life. American dominant culture patterns suggest

Table 10–1. *Grandchildren of the Householder, by Presence of Parents, Race, and Hispanic Origin: 1993, 1980 and 1970*

[Numbers in thousands]

Living arrangement	1993				1980 Census	1970 Census
	Total	White	Black	Hispanic*		
Total children under 18 years	66,893	53,075	10,660	7,776	63,369	69,276
Grandchild of householder	3,368	1,947	1,290	460	2,306	2,214
Percent of all children under 18 years	5.0	3.7	12.1	5.9	3.6	3.2
With both parents present	475	395	56	107	310	363
With mother only present	1,647	904	683	218	922	817
With father only present	229	163	52	29	86	78
With neither parent present	1,017	485	499	105	988	957
Percent	100.0	100.0	100.0	100.0	100.0	100.0
With both parents present	14.1	20.3	4.3	23.3	13.4	16.4
With mother only present	48.9	46.4	52.9	47.4	40.0	36.9
With father only present	6.8	8.4	4.0	6.3	3.7	3.5
With neither parent present	30.2	24.9	38.7	22.8	42.8	43.2

*Persons of Hispanic origin may be of any race.

Source: U.S. Bureau of the Census, 1970 Census of Population, PC(2)-4B, *Persons by Family Characteristics*, Table 1, and 1980 Census of Population, PC80-2-4B, Table 1. Excludes inmates of institutions.

that a nuclear family separate household is preferable for all families. A government policy that gave housing preference to individual family units is illustrated by the fact that in 1985, direct governmental support for low-income housing was 13.9 billion dollars. The same year, federal support for home ownership was four times that amount, or 53.9 billion dollars. While families with incomes of more than $50,000 represented only 20 percent of the households, they received 52.2 percent of the federal government's housing subsidies. Such subsidies include a variety of mortgage assistance programs not available to many young families (Mulroy, 1988).

According to the Department of Housing and Urban Development (HUD), female heads of households occupy over 49 percent of "problem-ridden" residences. Sixty-seven percent of female heads of household with minor children have housing problems. During the Reagan presidency, affordable housing programs suffered a 75 percent cutback in public investment. Families headed by a single mother were the largest growing segment of the homeless population in the United States between 1985 and 1990. A national 29-city survey of homeless families in 1987 found that two-thirds were headed by single parents (Mulroy, 1988).

Housing Designs

In a policy study, authors Strober and Dornbush (1988) point out a need for housing designs that more clearly support current family relationship patterns and structures. New housing designs might include more appropriately planned communal space, such as laundry facilities, gardens, parks, and recreational areas with small units for parent/child families to maintain some privacy. Convertible space that might be used for a variety of family structures is especially needed. As we have seen, a number of cultures prefer and plan for households that include more than two generations and a variety of extended family relationships.

Currently, many single-parent families live in old housing which is expensive because of high utility costs from inefficient energy use and the presence of health dangers such as lead-based paint, asbestos, inadequate ventilation, and degenerating structural features.

GOVERNMENTAL POLICIES AND AGENCIES

There is probably no type of family on which governmental policies have had such a dramatic impact as the never-married single-parent family. A confusion of aims and contrasts between punitive and supportive policies has marked the period from World War II through 1990. A general concern for the vulnerability of the single-parent family led to the establishment of the AFDC program. In addition, the establishment of the Medicaid health care program has been aimed particularly at vulnerable young families. A variety of other programs, such as federal food stamps, public or subsidized housing, WIC (Women, Infants, and Children food program), and Head Start, also respond to the needs of the vulnerable young family frequently headed by a single parent.

While the intent of a number of these policies was to provide support for young families, the policies were frequently flawed in implementation or in design. Thus, separate application and authorization offices were frequently created for each separate governmental program. Young families frequently had to go to a number of different offices to apply for benefits, and regulations were frequently discouraging to family stability. In addition, from 1980 to 1992, decreases in funding made them unavailable for many families who were previously eligible.

Public schools often expelled unmarried high school students from attendance, or provided them with a home-bound special education service. This meant that the young mother was immediately cut off from active involvement with other young people pursuing education, and from the support and positive resources of many aspects of the educational system.

Some single young mothers were encouraged to establish separate households in order to receive additional benefits. While this may be initially attractive to the young person, it essentially cuts them off from their family of origin and from easy access to extended family members for assistance in child care and other services. In 1993, the National Commission on Children charged the welfare system with discouraging employment, family formation and stability. The AFDC program does not allow for cost-of-living adjustments, and states are permitted to establish their own award levels for eligible clients.

The policies of the 1980s and 1990s included a concerted effort to require young mothers to enter education or job training which frequently led to minimum wage work. The goal was to give girls some goals for their lives as well as skills. This meant that at the conclusion of education or training, a young mother would first qualify for a minimum wage job that frequently carried no medical or other benefits. The actual reduction in real income made this a punitive governmental policy that reduced the incentive toward education and employment. As stated in the Final Report of the National Commission on Children, "the unfortunate reality is that for millions of American families, work simply does not pay" (National Commission on Children, 1993).

In a 1993 West Virginia study of governmental programs impacting young families, six separate federal agencies and 199 programs were identified as potentially supportive to young vulnerable families (West Virginia Cabinet on Children and Families, 1993). However, the administrative duplication and confusion to clients often result in inefficient systems and fewer families served than are eligible. In the early part of the Clinton administration, an intense interest in integrated service plans in states, particularly Indiana and West Virginia, was a positive response to this concern about the poor use of resources. An integrated service plan would enable a state to empower local communities to make interagency service plans which would create efficiencies of administration and prioritize the spending of money for the most important needs in the local community. Much of this work grew out of general interest in reinventing government.

KINSHIP NETWORKS AND INTERACTIONS

Among strong and well functioning never-married single-parent families, the importance of extended friends and families cannot be overestimated. Young mothers frequently report that they survived the adjustment to parenthood only because of grandparent and other extended family members' support.

A clear message of the celebration of parenthood is given by many of these young families. In fact, in Williams' (1991) interview study of young African-American mothers, almost all of the subjects reported not wanting pregnancies but being delighted with birth and babies. They indicated a positive socialization towards parenthood and a delight in the parent-child bonding. Many young unmarried mothers describe the importance of the affection received from their children and celebrate the joy of parenting. This desire to receive affection from a child has historically been of concern to some social service professionals. In extreme, this relationship is labeled a "role reversal" in that a young parent may be seeking love, affection and stability from a child. A family system that demands loyalty, affection, and stability from a child can jeopardize the stability and development of both child and mother, especially when the child is unable to fulfill these needs.

If we are concerned about the stability and development of the young single-parent family, we need to encourage the support and services provided to both children and adults by their kinship network. As Furstenberg et al. (1987) argue, the presence of extended family support to adolescent parents enhanced the development of their children in the preschool years. This support in the family environment probably has no public service substitute.

CHANGE AND ADAPTATION

The major societal concerns about never-married single-parent headed families relate to the vulnerability of youth. The feminization of poverty is illustrated by the fact that a female-headed household is six times more likely to live below the poverty line than a two-parent family. Furthermore, of never-married mothers who receive welfare benefits, almost 40 percent remain on public assistance for ten years or longer. Among whites, daughters of single parents are 53 percent more likely to marry as teenagers, 164 percent more likely to have a premarital birth and 92 percent more likely to be divorced. Sixty percent of single white mothers and 80 percent of single black mothers receive no support from fathers of their children, according to a study done in the late 1980s (Children's Defense Fund, 1987).

The twenty-year longitudinal study of mothers who became parents in adolescence done by Furstenberg et al. (1987) makes several clear statements about the resiliency of the human spirit. Approximately two thirds of the mothers, twenty years later, were maintaining economic independence and had achieved a sense of economic stability that was comfortable. Through a variety of personal challenges, they had acquired education, limited their subsequent childbearing, and gained self-confidence. Two areas of long-term struggle and adaptation are noteworthy. The children born to these adolescent parents struggled for their own academic achievement and balance during their early years. One interpretation would be that, while adults can assimilate lessons and reverse the negative effects of earlier life events, their ability to simultaneously protect and guide their children may be compromised.

A second finding of the Furstenberg et al. (1987) study is that females who became parents in adolescence had discouraging subsequent relationships with males. The majority of the women in the study had a series of conflictive and time-limited relationships with men who did not become sources of stability in their lives. One wonders how much their attitudes help shape the acceptance of male partners or their ability to negotiate a stable relationship. Williams' (1991) teenaged mothers were generally not interested in marriage, and preferred to be independent even when men asked to be economic and legal partners.

In a life dominated by poverty and uncertain economic security, it is difficult to form enduring unions between adults who are not able to bring successful employment to the marriage. Many family life scholars have suggested that an appropriate adaptation to these circumstances is to strengthen the parent/child bonds and increase the informal family networking that helps co-parent children in the extended family network.

One particularly difficult issue in the adaptation of single-parent families is the supervision of the young adolescent and the repetition of the early single-parent pattern in the next generation. Youth workers frequently describe the lack of positive role models and social organizations within neighborhoods high in poverty and unemployment. Without significant and powerful bonded relationships with churches and youth-serving organizations, it is difficult to find adequate supervision and alternative activities to premature sexual experimentation. Williams' (1991) young teenage mothers reported almost universally a lack of attention or supervision from the parent generation in their late elementary and early junior high years. Half of them had working mothers who didn't arrive home until hours after public school was dismissed.

The Guttmacher Institute studies have reported that the most frequent environment in which a young adolescent becomes pregnant is in her own home with no adult supervision (McAdoo and McAdoo, 1985). This lack of supervision may be due to government policies that encourage a single parent to acquire her own household separate from her family of origin. The positive image of the independent household may obscure the need for supervision which is more likely to be available in an extended family household.

In addition, teenage mothers frequently report their own parents' ambivalence upon discovering their daughters' pregnancy. While many in the grandparent generation desire education and economic success for their children, they also wish to convey to their young people their delight in parenting and their commitment to rearing children. There is a tendency to encourage their pregnant unmarried daughter to bear and keep the baby as a validation of the grandparents' own earlier choices. In a community with few avenues for declaring accomplishments and strengths, becoming pregnant, bearing a child, and accepting parental responsibilities are often among the few roles open to young females.

In contrast to a 1950s attitude of alarm and a deterministic elimination of options for the adolescent, unmarried female, today's options are more numerous and seem to be initially supportive of parenthood. Some political analysts suggest that this amounts to a tacit approval of unmarried parenting, and a removal of societal controls on personal, self-indulgent destructive behaviors. The never-married single-parent family is most often headed by a female, in poverty and out of the mainstream of education. Whether or not the development of children and parents continues in a positive direction depends deeply upon the ability of professionals in many systems to support them and their informal networks with appropriate service.

SERVING SINGLE TEENAGE PARENT FAMILIES

One important consideration in serving the never-married single-parent family is to understand the variation by social class and ethnic group that is represented by these families. In addition, it is extremely important to distinguish between programs in support of child and youth development in these families, and programs to support the adults. A number of programs contain elements that blame the children, or discriminate against them in the provision of services based on a moral judgment of their parents' behavior. Repeatedly, research has illustrated that the most successful programs in assisting single-parent families in further development of their own skills, and those of their children, rest on services that respect the needs of each generation.

According to Lizabeth Schorr (1988), social scientists and service providers already know what elements make for positive programs in support of vulnerable young families. The needs are for funding, service organizations, and positive professional attitudes and roles. Schorr relates that programs that are responsive to these families have the following characteristics:

1. They are flexible. They have rules that can be adjusted or changed as necessitated by the need to serve families.
2. They are comprehensive. They provide services for education, employment, child care, health, etc. all in one agency or in close proximity and in a cooperative framework.
3. They are respectful of individual family needs and they create trust and partnerships between families and professionals.
4. They are adaptable, resilient, and able to change services and create new linkages among new service providers.

5. They stress that children are nested in families and family preservation is a strong goal.

These five qualities are very similar to the principles for empowering families presented in Chapter 3. They demand that each of us use our own powers of observation and criticism to increase the effectiveness of programs with which we work.

Furstenberg et al. (1987) make an important point about professionals who work with young never-married parents. Frequently these service relationships are time limited, such as prenatal health care or preschool services. Professionals in such settings do not benefit from the opportunity to see these young parents over time and observe their continued development. Biases and limited information about the strengths of these families may limit these professionals' effectiveness in offering appropriate services.

Family life professionals encourage researchers and service providers to ask families directly about the meaning of events or resources in their lives. Frequently professionals view families from their own experience and fail to understand messages from families themselves. Scarr (1989) commented that each of us is "biased by the human tendency to seek facts which are congruent with our own previous beliefs." Dilworth-Anderson, Burton, and Turner (1993) comment that there is no value-free work, particularly with other human beings. Marital relationships, parenting relationships, gender and family relationships are all viewed through our own perceptions of what we think is important, what we ask about, and what we are interested in.

First Meeting

When first meeting a single-parent family, all we know about that family is that there is a parent and a child, and there is no current, legal marriage. We do not know how many "fictive kin" are associated with this family and are providing on-going service and support. Fictive kin are defined as non-blood kin who, in relationships, define themselves as part of the family. This is a very strong pattern in Native American cultures and clear examples of this are seen in African-American communities.

With regard to a single mother and child, we do not know how many significant males are providing enduring and supportive models to the child. We do not know how many neighborhood acquaintances assist in providing transportation, clothing, and food as needed for this family. We do not know if the parent has an affectionate and on-going relationship with the child's other biological parent. In short, we have much to learn!

Our basic goals should be to create an atmosphere of inclusiveness for other significant adults in the child's life and parent's life, and assist the parent in acquiring resources to meet their needs. Depending on the role we play with this family, such as a teacher, social worker, health practitioner, or juvenile justice professional, we need to look carefully at our own biases toward this family type. We need to assume diversity within this family type and reinforce every possible strength.

Establishing Partnerships

If a family enters a program you supervise, you need to indicate the program's objectives, engage the family members in a discussion of their own objectives, and negotiate where possible for shared objectives.

You should assume there are serious economic and time constraints on the part of the single parent, and make certain that your requests do not place an undue burden on the parent that could drive that parent away. For the child or youth you are serving, you need to provide maximum stability, opportunities to bond with positive role models, and opportunities to participate in meaningful decisions about their activities or goals.

Professionals should find ways to encourage single parents to learn from each other and to provide supportive networks in group meetings, telephone trees, social activities, and informal meetings. The positive results of the Head Start Parent Advisory Councils are well known to professionals working in that program. The opportunity that Head Start parents have to participate in decision-making for their child, to join in a community effort at supporting educational programs, and to learn skills as decision-makers has provided many parents with an initiation into job training, education and more economic independence.

Compassionate Observations

Observations of the child or youth and their single parent need to be made compassionately and with an understanding of the personality characteristics of the child and the parent. Evidence that a child or youth is extremely compliant and supportive to the parent may indicate that a great deal of meaning for that child is vested in being a partner and support to the parent. Within limits this is a positive strength for that child. The parent may need assistance and encouragement to engage in adult activities, to enhance strengths, and to find other adult relationships which are reinforcing and supportive.

In a balanced view, however, new adult relationships, such as a new romantic partner or new, close friends, can limit the power of a child who was a strong partner to a single parent. Helping the child find friends and motivating experiences for his or her own development is an important part of our ability to serve this family effectively. A child or youth who has had major family responsibilities can be encouraged to relax and enjoy learning, and to take leadership positions in other appropriate group settings.

Seeking Information

In gathering information about the family, we should be clear about the reasons for needing that information and be respectful of the family's need to withhold information. Thus, questions such as "how do you handle this in your family," or "what do you want for your son or daughter," enable you to obtain information to help you form a strong partnership with the parents.

Encouraging a single parent to bring friends and family members to events in your agency or school is extremely family-supportive. Many parents assume only the legal parents of the child can participate in a school or agency event. Encourage children and youth to talk about who is important to them, and encourage parents to bring these people who are part of the child's on-going life. Setting up barriers between a school or agency and the family simply encourages a child to show family loyalty by rejecting an organization's activities or services.

Make certain that you can provide information on other opportunities such as organizations that are supportive of single parents; churches, synagogues, and other religious groups that have single-parent activities or programs; cooperatives that share child care, clothing, or exchange services; transportation systems, and a variety of free public services. Professionals working with young single-parent families frequently indicate that the parents may not know about available parks, libraries, youth-serving agencies, or may not feel they are eligible to use these services. A supportive family activity can be to gather a group of parents and attend some activity in a community agency.

Include Legal and Biological Parents

When offering parenting classes or education, be certain to include both the biological parent or legal guardian and other significant members of the child's household. Stress the sharing and participation aspects of parent groups. Ask the parents what challenges they would like to discuss. One of the most important things to teach all parents is to appreciate the particular temperament and strengths of their own children. Help them understand how patterns of authoritative parenting can be respectful and supportive of a child's growth. Authoritative parenting is described by Baumrind (1967) as a parenting role that sets clear consistent limits, but provides reasons for these rules. In addition, the authoritative parent provides the child with negotiating and decision-making power appropriate to that child's development.

Young parents often need assistance in practicing skills such as how to read aloud to their child, how to question a child actively while watching TV, how to enjoy play with their child, and how to set appropriate limits. Professionals who work with homeless families observe that many parents cannot engage in cooperative play with their own children until they, as adults, have had a protected time to enjoy the toys or activities themselves before interacting with their children. Such observations reflect the more limited experiences and economic means of many young parents. Professionals serving these young families are in key positions to develop partnerships with parents. After parents gain experience and confidence, they will be able to seek services from the various helping agencies.

CONCLUSIONS

Professionals serving the never-married single-parent family need to learn about the variation among these families, understand their own biases, and institute changes in language, practices, and service that empower the parent and nurture the child. When these families are in the early stages of development, what they learn about the sensitivity and skills of professionals can influence progress for many years.

Professionals can help increase their sensitivity by understanding that some parents often lack time and money. Encouraging linkages between parents in similar circumstances helps develop supporting groups. Exchanging information about services and opportunities can assist development. Encouraging agencies or services to collaborate in providing information, joint training, or educational events would be helpful to families.

Including additional significant adults related to the family in conferences and celebrations around your agency's services is an important acknowledgment of the variety of relationships that nurture both children and adults. Any educational or social services plan for an individual child or family should develop partnerships between professionals and families, and other people parents describe as significant and meaningful to their development.

It is important to be respectful of the anger and frustration of a single-parent family. Many societal messages are critical and much public debate concentrates on "what to do" about single parents. In order for children and adults in these families to make progress toward their goals, it is important for them to use their energy to appreciate their own uniqueness and obtain developmentally supportive services. Professionals who are respected and trusted can become helpful partners as these families work hard toward their goals. In many cases, these families feel that the mainstream social institutions have denied their need for attention, supervision, education, and support. As the twenty-first century approaches, the problems facing this group of families must be solved.

STUDY QUESTIONS

1. State in 10 complete sentences the facts presented concerning the never-married teenage parent family.
2. State the explanation for the increase in the number of teenage pregnancies.
3. State the authors' explanation for the change in age of fecundity.
4. State the authors' explanation for the phenomenon of teen pregnancy being related to changes in marriage patterns.
5. State the authors' analysis related to changes in adoption practices.
6. State the positions of political figures on the matter of teen childbirth.

7. As you study the chapter, notice the economic factors that appear to be involved in the phenomenon of teenage families. Make a comprehensive list of the statements you find.

8. List male roles in relation to teen pregnancy.

9. List female roles and teen pregnancy from a three- or four-generation view.

10. Under the main ecological heading find and list two factors from each of the systems discussed.

11. List the governmental agencies involved in the matter of teenage pregnancy as discussed under various topics in the chapter.

APPLICATIONS

1. Assign a class member to make an appointment with the Office of Social Services to apply for Aid to Families with Dependent Children. Form a committee to help the student prepare for this appointment by identifying documents to take, questions to ask, observations to make, etc. After the student has completed this appointment, ask him or her to report to the committee and have the committee prepare a report to give to the class on this experience. Part of the class report should include recommendations for changes in policies or practices at the local office. In addition, students should brainstorm about ways that volunteers (such as students themselves) might assist in making the service more effective.

2. Assign a class member or members to review advertisements in the local newspaper or the yellow pages to identify groups that offer programs for single parents. Call the organizers of the programs and inquire about the age requirement for attendance, the cost, the objectives of the program, and any qualifying characteristics such as divorced, never married, etc. Report to the class on the availability of these support groups and educational programs. Include an impression of whether the never-married parent is welcome and served well in your community.

3. Make an appointment to talk with the Medicaid Prenatal Clinic Supervisor or health practitioner who provides the majority of care to unwed adolescent mothers in your community. Ask the clinic director about the need for additional services or volunteers. If possible, observe a clinic setting and interview a client about their satisfaction with services in the community.

4. Contact a local Home Economics teacher, Family Life teacher, or Family Sociology teacher at a Junior or Senior High School. Inquire as to whether a Family Studies class or Marriage class includes information on the unmarried parent. Volunteer to present a program for the class, including a presentation by a young, unmarried parent. Contact the

local Medicaid Prenatal clinic, the WIC clinic, or high school Guidance Counselors for the name of an appropriate young mother who would be willing to talk with other students about her experiences.

5. Attend an organized meeting of a young mothers' support group, if permission is given by the group organizer or chairperson. Be respectful and observant and indicate to the members that you would like to understand more about the ways they are supportive to each other and what some of their goals are for their children. Talk with the group's organizer about the variation and special qualities of members in the group.

6. Contact the Children and Youth committee chair in your state legislature. Find out whether or not there is an ongoing review for legislative proposals that impact the young family. Follow a piece of legislation through the process of committee hearings to presentation, or interview members of the legislature about how current state legislation impacts young, unmarried parents.

7. Interview a member of the state Health and Human Services Department about the department's policy toward young, unmarried parents. Inquire about the integration of services between their department and others, and ask for a list of the three most important needs of the young, unmarried parent in your state.

8. Make an appointment with the principal of a local high school in your community to talk about services available to unmarried students in your school district. Inquire about medical services, family planning information, parenting education, self-study or alternative forms of education, GED classes, vocational training, child care, transportation, etc.

9. Make an appointment with the manager of a local public housing family site to talk about services available to unmarried parents. If possible, visit an apartment and tour the facility. Look for evidence of parent support groups, safe play areas for children, parent education opportunities, and ties with the wider community.

REFERENCES

Allen-Meares, Paula. (1989). Adolescent sexuality and premature parenting: Role of the black church in prevention. *Journal of Social Work and Human Sexuality, 8*(1), 133–142.

Apfel, N. H., and Seitz, V. (1991). Four models of adolescent mother-grandmother relationships in black inner-city families. *Family Relations, 40,* 421–429.

Barnes, Annie S. (1987). *Single parents in black America.* Bristol, IN: Wyndham Hall Press.

Baumrind, D. (1967). Child-care practices anteceding three patterns of preschool behavior. *Genetic Psychology Monographs, 75,* 43–88.

Booth, Alan, and Amato, Paul. (1992). Divorce, residential change and stress. *Journal of Divorce and Remarriage, 18*(1–2), 205–214.

Brenner, A. (1984). *Helping children cope with stress.* Lexington, MA: D. C. Heath.

Brooks-Gunn, J., and Furstenberg, F. F., Jr. (1986). The children of adolescent mothers: Physical, academic and psychological outcomes. *Developmental Review, 6,* 224–251.

Buehler, Cheryl, and Legg, B. H. (1993). Mothers' receipt of social support and their psychological well-being following marital separation. *Journal of Family Issues, 14*(1), 21–38.

Children's Defense Fund. (1987). *Declining earnings of young men: Their relation to poverty, teenaged pregnancy and family formation.* Washington, DC: CDF Adolescent Pregnancy Prevention Clearinghouse.

Children's Defense Fund. (1993). *New child support requirements.* CDF Reports 14, 12–13. Washington, DC: CDF Adolescent Pregnancy Prevention Clearinghouse.

Coontz, Stephanie. (1992). *The way we never were.* New York, NY: Basic Books.

Dilworth-Anderson, P., Burton, L. M., and Turner, W. L. (1993). The importance of values in the study of culturally diverse families. *Family Relations, 42*(3), 243–248.

Duran-Aydintug, C. (1993). Relationships with former in-laws: Normative guidelines and actual behavior. *Journal of Divorce and Remarriage, 19*(3–9), 69–82.

Furstenberg, Frank F., Jr., Brooks-Gunn, J., and Morgan, S. Phillip. (1987). *Adolescent mothers in later life.* Cambridge, MA: Cambridge University Press.

Gigy, L., and Kelly, J. B. (1992). Reasons for divorce: Perspectives of divorcing men and women. *Journal of Divorce and Remarriage, 18*(1–2), 169–187.

Haub, C. (1993). Births per U.S. women? *Population Today, 21*(9), 6–10. Washington, DC: Population Reference Bureau.

Ingrassia, H. (1993, August 30). Endangered family. *Newsweek,* pp. 17–29.

McAdoo, H. (1980). Black mothers and the extended family support network. In Rodgers-Rose (Ed.), *The black woman.* Beverly Hills, CA: Sage Publications.

McAdoo, H. R., and McAdoo, J. L. (1985). *Black children: Social, educational, and parental environments.* Beverly Hills, CA: Sage Publications.

McMillan, Terry. (1991). *Waiting to exhale.* New York, NY: Viking Press.

Moynihan, Daniel Patrick. (1965). *The Negro family: The case for action.* Washington, DC: Office of Policy Planning and Research, U.S. Department of Labor.

Moynihan, Daniel Patrick. (1986). *Family and nation: The Godkin lectures.* New York, NY: Harcourt, Brace, Jovanovich.

Mulroy, Elizabeth A. (Ed.). (1988). *Women as single parents.* Dover, MA: Auburn House Publishing Co.

National Commission on Children. (1991). *Beyond rhetoric: A new American agenda for children and families.* Washington, DC: U.S. Government Printing Office.

National Commission on Children. (1993). *Just the facts.* Washington, DC: U.S. Government Printing Office.

Nelson, Kristine, and Landsmen, Miriam J. (1992). *Alternative models of family preservation: Family based services in context.* Springfield, IL: Charles C. Thomas.

Newberger, C. M. (1977). *Parental conceptions of children and child rearing: A structural developmental analysis.* Doctoral dissertation, Harvard University.

O'Hare, W. P. (1993). Diversity trend: More minorities looking less alike. *Population Today, 21*(4), 1–4. Washington, DC: Population Reference Bureau.

Olson, David H. (Ed.). (1988). *Family prospectives in child and youth services.* New York, NY: Haworth Press.

Polakow, Valerie. (1993). *Lives on the edge: Single mothers and their children in the other America.* Chicago, IL: University of Chicago Press.

Rawlings, Steve W. (1994). *Household and family characteristics: March 1993.* U.S. Bureau of the Census, Series P20–477. Washington, DC: U.S. Government Printing Office.

Saluter, Arlene F. (1989). Changes in American family life. *U.S. Bureau of the Census Current Population Reports, Special Studies* (P–23). U.S. Government Printing Office.

Saluter, Arlene F. (1994). *Marital status and living arrangements: March 1993.* U.S. Bureau of the Census, Series P20–478. Washington, DC: U.S. Government Printing Office.

Scarr, Sandra. (1989). *Caring for children: Challenge to America.* Hillsdale, NJ: L. Erlbaum Associates.

Scarr, Sandra. (1989, April). *Transracial adoption.* Discussion at the Biennial Meeting of the Society for Research in Child Development, Kansas City, MO.

Schorr, L. B. (1988). *Within our reach: Breaking the cycle of disadvantage.* New York, NY: Anchor Press.

Solinger, Rickie. (1992). *Wake-up little Susie: Single pregnancy and race before Roe v. Wade.* New York, NY: Routledge.

Strober, M. H., and Dornbush, S. M. (1988). Public policy alternatives. In S. M. Dornbush and M. H. Strober (Eds.), *Feminism, children and the new families* (pp. 327–357). New York, NY: Guilford Press.

U.S. Bureau of the Census. (1990). *The Black population in the United States: March 1988* (Series P20–442). Washington, DC: U.S. Government Printing Office.

U.S. Bureau of the Census. (1990). *How we are changing* (Series 9–23, No. 170). Washington, DC: U.S. Government Printing Office.

U.S. Bureau of the Census. (1992). *Poverty in the United States.* Washington, DC: U.S. Government Printing Office.

U.S. Bureau of the Census. (1992). Family life today and how it has changed. *Statistical Briefs* (No. 92–13). Washington, DC: U.S. Government Printing Office.

U.S. Bureau of the Census. (1993). *Black Americans: A profile* (SB 1993-2). Washington, DC: U.S. Government Printing Office.

Ventura, S., and Martin, J. (1993, February 25). *Advance report of natality statistics, 1990* (Vol. 41, No. 9 Supplement). Washington, DC: National Center for Health Statistics.

Wells, Kathleen, and Biegel, David E. (Eds.). (1991). *Family preservation services: Research and evaluation.* Newbury Park, CA: Sage Publications, Inc.

West Virginia Cabinet on Children and Families. (1993). *A West Virginia proposal for using consolidated state and local plans for services to children, youth and families.* Draft Document.

White House Domestic Policy Council. (1993). *Health security: The President's report to the American people.* Washington, DC: U.S. Government Printing Office.

Williams, Constance Willard. (1991). *Black teen-aged mothers: Pregnancy and childrearing from their perspective.* Lexington, MA: Lexington Books.

Wilson, W. J. (1987). *The truly disadvantaged: The inner city, the underclass, and public policy.* Chicago, IL: University of Chicago Press.

Wojtkiewicz, Robert A. (1993). Household change and racial inequality in economic well-being, 1960–1980. *Journal of Family History, 18*(3), 249–264.

MEDIA RESOURCES

Kids Raising Kids. (45 minutes.) Charleston, WV: Cambridge Educational.

Moyers, W. (1986). The vanishing family: Crisis in black America. *CBS Special Reports.*

Teen Parent TV News. (28 minutes.) Los Angeles, CA: Churchill Media.

Who's Supporting the Kids? U.S. Bureau of the Census (SB/91-18). Washington, DC: Government Printing Office.

OTHER BOOKS

Robinson, B., and Barrett, R. (1988). *Teenage fathers*. Lexington, MA: Lexington Books.

ORGANIZATIONS

Single Parent Resource Center. 1165 Broadway, Room 504, New York, NY 10001.

Sisterhood of Black Single Mothers. 1360 Fulton St., Suite 423, Brooklyn, NY 11216. (718) 638-0413.

CHAPTER 11

Divorced Single-Parent Families

Key Concepts

◆ Legal Issues
◆ Division of Property
◆ Grieving Period
◆ No-fault Divorce
◆ Bifocal Family
◆ Binuclear Family

The time in my life when I felt most supported and had the strongest group of good friends was during the years in which I was a divorced parent.

— Professional remarried parent

Most of us have experienced one of our closest friends or neighbors announce that she or he is getting a divorce. Like many, you may admit that you didn't realize that their problems were "that bad." With fifty percent of present-day marriages heading for the divorce courts, divorce is a phenomenon that occurs in many families. More than half of divorces involve children. Thus, divorce complicates life for many children and youth.

Every newly singled parent has many adjustments and decisions to make while carrying on with the business of rearing their families. These families, whose situation is vastly different from those never-married single parents discussed in the previous chapter, will frequently be seen by helping professionals.

Most Americans have an unrealistic understanding of the variation and incidence of divorced single-parent families. By definition, this group experiences major changes in household structure. These changes often attract attention from many family members and friends, especially during the initial adjustment period. When a family social group changes, this movement ripples through many different relationships in the environment.

HISTORICAL BACKGROUND

The divorced single-parent family represents an alarming situation to many citizens for both relationship and economic reasons. In the earlier part of American history, the most frequent cause of family disruption was the death of a parent. In fact, not until 1900 were there even any legal grounds and procedures for divorce in the United States. As medical care and diagnostic services improved, fewer parents died during their children's early years. By 1974, divorce eclipsed death as the leading cause of disruption of family life. Divorce causes a relationship loss for which many people have only the model of death, or a complete separation, for guidance. As our experiences with divorce have accumulated, it is clear that the economic strength of the family is often dramatically changed after divorce, and relationships become more complex and ambiguous.

No-Fault Divorce

In 1970, California led a reform of legislation with a new "no-fault" divorce statute that eliminated the necessity of blame and fault in the legal proceedings. This change has also had profound impact on the financial settlements between the divorcing parties. Prior to 1970, the "victim" or injured party in a divorce usually received compensation through a financial settlement. Once no-fault divorce, with its assumptions of rationality and partnership, became the norm, the couple's assets were often divided equally, with unanticipated consequences.

PROPERTY SETTLEMENT

When family property is equally divided following divorce, one spouse may be disadvantaged. This occurs because of the way marital property may be defined and distributed, and because of differing standards for awarding alimony and child support. Some divorce scholars believe that if one spouse has not been employed outside the home, or has a much lower earning capacity than the other, then that person is entitled to some of the ex-spouse's earning power. This recommendation reflects the understanding that both partners have, in fact, invested in and created the family asset, that is, the earning capacity of one of the spouses.

Alimony is a protection for the divorced spouse who has not been employed in the marketplace and is still responsible for family assets and obligations under no-fault divorce law. However, divorce awards since 1970 have tended to reduce or eliminate alimony awards from most settlements, or dramatically decrease them to short-term "transitional" awards. This is a particularly difficult situation for the older housewife coming out of a long traditional marriage and possessing minimal skills for employment.

CHILDREN'S EXPERIENCE IN DIVORCE

Child support has similarly not been awarded at adequate levels to maintain child care, housing, food, and clothing. The Children's Defense Fund reported in 1992 that none of the 50 states provided a high enough allotment in Aid to Families with Dependent Children (AFDC) payments to keep families out of poverty. Low awards, plus the fact that only about 50 percent of divorced fathers pay their child support, mean that many children in divorced parent households enter the ranks of poverty. As shown in Table 11–1 there are dramatic losses in family income and increases in poverty following divorce.

During the 1950s, only 11 percent of all children experienced the divorce of their parents by the age of eighteen. Beginning in the mid-1960s, a rapid increase in the divorce rate culminated in the highest rate of 23 divorces per 1,000 marriages in 1979. In 1991, there were 21 divorces per 1,000 marriages. In most states the marriage and divorce statistics have narrowed so that the number of marriages per year is practically equal to the number of divorces per year. By the late 1980s, demographers predicted that half of all American marriages would end in divorce.

Thirty-one percent of children now living in two-parent families will see their parents divorced prior to their eighteenth birthday. Of children living in

Table 11–1. *Economic Status of Children under 15 Years Old, Four months Before and Four Months After Parental Separation*

Measurement of well-being	Before	After
Average monthly per capita income	$549	$436
Average monthly family income*	$2,435	$1,543
Average monthly household income*	$2,461	$1,546
Income/needs ratio*	2.4	1.8
Percent whose mother worked full-time, all weeks	33	41
Percent whose mother did not work at all	43	31
Percent reporting weekly hours worked	60	72
Average weekly hours of those with hours	34	37
Percent in poverty	19	36
Percent receiving child support	16	44
Percent receiving AFDC	9	18
Percent receiving food stamps	10	27

*The income/needs ratio is a ratio of family income to the poverty threshold. An income/needs ratio below 1.0 denotes a standard of living below the poverty level. Household income aggregates income of all persons residing with the child in a given month. Family income excludes income from persons unrelated to the child.

Source: *The Economics of Family Disruption.* U.S. Bureau of the Census, SB 91–10. Washington, DC: U.S. Government Printing Office.

step-families, one half of them will see a divorce in that marriage prior to their eighteenth birthday. Differences in ethnic group experiences with divorce are obvious from the data. The number of African-American children who cope with divorce is lower than Hispanic or white children because the African-American marriage rate is lower. In the 1990s, the typical single African-American mother was never married, while the typical single white mother was a divorcee. Since 1960, about two thirds of the increase in white single-parent households was due to divorce. By 1991, 70 percent of white children residing with a single parent lived with a divorced or separated single parent (National Commission on Children, 1993).

As the demographics of the United States change, with immigration and differential birth rates, the number of children among ethnic minorities is climbing rapidly. Only since 1990 has the National Center for Health Statistics recorded births based on the mother's race and ethnicity. Prior to that time, there was confusion in the reporting of the child's ethnic group, depending on the mother's choice, or on information filled out on different records. Of the 4.2 million children born in the United States in 1990, 2.6 million were non-Hispanic white. Approximately 662,000 were non-Hispanic black, 600,000 were Hispanic, 142,000 were Asian or Pacific Islander, and less than 40,000 were Native American (Haub, 1993). These statistics point to differences in the percentage of ethnic and racial minorities today in the United States as compared to a decade ago.

Because divorce is more often experienced in the white community, and because children are more likely to be born into marriages in the white community, most divorced mothers are white. Eighty percent of all divorced men remarry, but they marry a combination of previously married and never married women. On an average, women who remarry spend approximately six years as single parents (Coontz, 1992). Considering six years as one-third of a child's youth, from birth to eighteen years of age, many children spend a significant portion of their childhood in a single-parent home even though their parents may remarry.

SOCIO-CULTURAL FOUNDATIONS

When parents divorce, the resulting separate households often experience great contrasts in resources and support from social systems. One of the most visible public debates about divorce is the assessment of whether a divorce enhances the development of any of the family members. Critics of divorce argue on moral, religious, and developmental grounds that children deserve and need sustained relationships in a unit that socializes them consistently throughout their childhood. In addition, they argue that the transitions into divorce and the likelihood of remarriage or cohabitation of the parents mean that different values are communicated to children at different times in their development. Most child developmentalists agree that consistency and security of structure are important foundations for healthy development. While 20 percent of divorces occur because of spousal violence or extreme marital conflict, an increasing number are due to dissatisfaction with the economic and relationship aspects of marriage (Fine, 1993). Obtaining accurate data on the amount of physical and emotional abuse that often precedes divorce is very difficult. A number of partners will separate but never divorce due to religious or cultural values surrounding divorce, in spite of emotional abuse.

Divorce has been made more feasible by the increasing economic opportunities for women, the encouragement of personal evaluation of the companion values of the marriage relationship, and the availability of birth control measures. While 15 percent of divorces are initiated when one of the partners pursues another relationship, many divorces occur because of disengagement and dissatisfaction in the emotional exchange of marriage (Gigy and Kelly, 1992). The desire to have a marriage partner fulfill companion, friend, and sexual roles, as well as economic and reproductive ones, has caused more adults to feel dissatisfied with marriage and thus leave more readily.

With the prevalence of divorce in the United States, many parents are in the process of evaluating the merits of continuing or dissolving a marriage. As Whitehead (1993) comments, frequently the advantages for adults in the family may be in contrast to or in conflict with the advantages to the children. Overall, those values that encourage divorce are usually values of independence, self actualization, and reduction of conflict.

Status

In general, the status of divorced parents has strong economic and moral interpretations. Among some elements of society, divorce represents a failed relationship, and a divorced person's status is lowered immediately. In other situations, a divorced person's status is directly related to the economic and employment status of each of the partners. At the personal level, divorced persons often comment about the loss of social support and stature. Much conflict surrounds the selection of enduring adult relationships after a divorce. Fear that divorce could happen to them as well often arises among friends of the divorced. Rands reported that approximately 40 percent of an individual's social support system disappears after a separation or divorce (Buehler and Legg, 1993).

Gender Differences

One important influence on changes in status reported by divorced persons involves gender. Since approximately 90 percent of the divorced persons who retain custody of the children are female, and only 10 percent are male, there are important differences among divorced parents' custody experiences (DeMaris and Greif, 1992). Many of these differences relate specifically to the role and status that females, in contrast to males, have in this society. One study showed that women with custody experience a 73 percent drop in their standard of living in the year following a divorce. In contrast, the same study found men showing a 42 percent increase in standard of living a year after a divorce (Gottleib, Gottleib, and Slavin, 1988). Since the standard of living has clear status implications, men and women often find themselves with very different levels of status after divorce.

Racial Differences

There are also important status differences by race after divorce. Zinn (1992) reports that much poverty is the result of already poor two-parent households breaking up with inadequate resources to create two households.

Three quarters of whites who become poor after divorce were not in that category prior to divorce. In contrast, of the African-Americans who were poor after a divorce transition, two thirds had been poor before. These data are important to keep in mind, because divorce scholars are concerned that policy makers believe divorce and single-parent households are to blame for poverty, rather than understanding the importance of social class and race in determining economic status for all families.

Increased Choices in Families

Most people understand that part of the rise in the divorce rate is due to increasing freedom and choice available to females in the United States. Availability of contraceptives, smaller families, influence of the women's movement, examples of friends, siblings and parents who have divorced, and the increasing employment of women create more independence, freedom, and choice. Moreover, as we have seen in the previous section, the economic realities of many communities have often deterred women from entering or remaining in a marriage that offers little economic security. Researchers document that the higher a woman's income, the more apt she is to seek divorce as a solution to an unsatisfactory marriage.

Impact of Divorce on Daughters

The divorce literature is also very clear about the differential impact of divorce on girls in contrast to boys. Since most children are in the custody of their mothers, and family research often describes the complementary role that mothers and fathers play in family interaction, it should be no surprise that children who live in the custody of their mothers react differently by gender.

Research findings suggest that children living with the same-sex parent are happier and more socially competent than those living with the opposite-sex parent. It is likely that girls living with divorced mothers see their mother as a model of greater independence and self-determination. However, there is also a description of the "sleeper effect" by age in the adjustment of some girls.

Some studies indicate that preadolescent girls seem to adapt fairly well to divorce, but during adolescence show higher levels of struggle in relationships with the opposite sex and anger toward fathers. Given the frequent decrease in the economic means of mothers, many daughters observe specific ways their mothers respond to this challenge. Some mothers are able to sustain their standard of living by substituting activities at lower cost, and by bargaining and exchanging goods and services with their friends. These mothers are seen by their daughters as creative and independent.

Mothers who feel more victimized and less able to cope with the loss of income give their children a different message. Women, more than men, are often described as the "kin keepers," or are responsible for maintaining supportive ties with more extended family members. Women are, therefore, sometimes more able than men to maintain helpful relationships with grandparents or with ex-in-laws because they were responsible for maintaining these relationships during the marriage (Duran-Aydintug, 1993).

Another gender effect in divorce relates to the fact that 75 percent of divorces are initiated by females (Wallerstein and Kelly, 1980). Since an important part of post-divorce adjustment relates to whether or not the individual was the "surprised spouse," it is likely that fewer women suffer from anger and confusion over why the divorce occurred. However, one of the clearest gender differences after divorce remains the differential level of economic resources.

In a no-fault divorce, a woman may request custody of the children and leave the material objects to the husband. When material possessions are difficult to divide, such as the joint ownership in a home, a family business, or a farm, the maintenance of the family resources is sometimes dependent on keeping the property together. Most often the husband is in charge of property, and property judgments have frequently favored males. However, settlements that consider both spouses' investment in the man's career, or the employment skills of the woman, are frequently more equitable, with the woman receiving enough of a settlement to maintain the family. In Figure 11–1, data from a study by the Census Bureau show that only 58 percent of women alone with children were awarded child support from the absent father. Of those awarded, only half received the full amount. As seen in Table 11–2, marital history, race and education all affected the receiving of child support.

Increased Choices for Males

Changing roles for boys, men, husbands and fathers are emerging also. In the post-divorce single-parent family, the father is usually the parent who lives apart from the children. While joint custody actions have increased, a great

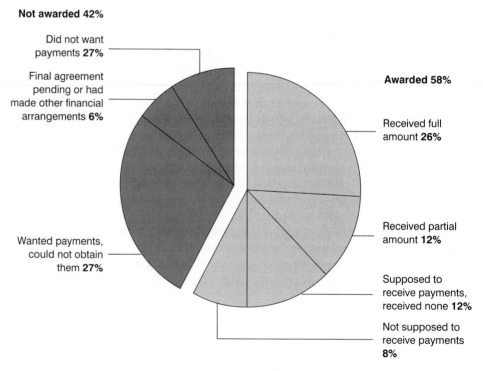

Not awarded 42%

Did not want payments **27%**

Final agreement pending or had made other financial arrangements **6%**

Wanted payments, could not obtain them **27%**

Awarded 58%

Received full amount **26%**

Received partial amount **12%**

Supposed to receive payments, received none **12%**

Not supposed to receive payments **8%**

Figure 11–1. *Child Support Award Status of Women with Children from an Absent Father: Spring 1990*

Source: *Who's Supporting the Kids?* U.S. Bureau of the Census, SB 91–18. Washington, DC: U.S. Government Printing Office.

Table 11–2. *Mean Dollar Amount of Child Support Received in 1989 by Women Aged 15 and Over Who Received Payments, By Selected Demographic Characteristics*

All women receiving payments	$2,995
Divorced and separated	$3,268
Never married	$1,888
White	$3,132
Black	$2,263
Hispanic origin	$2,965
Four or more years of college	$4,850
High school diploma (or some college)	$2,900
No high school diploma	$1,754
Below poverty line	$1,889
Above poverty line	$3,304

Source: *Who's Supporting the Kids?* U.S. Bureau of the Census, SB 91–18. Washington, DC: U.S. Government Printing Office.

deal of this custody is not physical joint custody. In other words, the divorce decree names both parents as equally responsible for decisions regarding the children, but the residence of the children is basically with only one parent. Donnelly and Finkelhor (1993) report, in their review of divorce judgments, that a range of 2 to 16 percent of divorces includes some kind of joint custody. Most children still remain in the custody of their mothers following divorce. As income and education level of the divorcing partners increase, joint custody levels also increase.

Fathers are most often in the position of paying some form of child support and of arranging a visitation schedule with their children. Fathers frequently report their distress and confusion about arranging activities for these visits. A feeling of being irrelevant to their child's life or only providing recreation and meals out in restaurants is distressing to men who wish to play a more fully involved parenting role.

The literature suggests that fathers who were involved in all aspects of parenting prior to the divorce are more apt to have sole or joint custody of the children and are more apt to more fully share or cooperate with the ex-spouse in raising the children. When divorced parents view each other as equal partners, they can create a parenting partnership with communication and decision-making that is respectful of each other and supportive of their children. Fathers who visit their children on a regular schedule and are involved in decisions about their lives are more apt to be paying child support regularly.

Studies show that children who rarely see their fathers often show psychological patterns that are neither healthy nor helpful for optimal development. They may imagine or fantasize about the positive characteristics of a hero-father they rarely see; or they may show deep and continuing anger toward all males and fail to find satisfactory ways to enter into and maintain positive relationships with males.

Much of the research completed prior to 1975 on the effects of divorce on children was flawed by the assumption that the absence of the father was the most important characteristic of a divorced family with children in the custody of the mother. This is a very simplistic interpretation of real family life. Many children whose mothers are not married or remarried have on-going, close relationships with friends, uncles, grandfathers, and other significant males. In addition, social class considerations, particularly income and education, play profound roles in how the family prospers and develops. In most cases, race, education, and social class are more powerful determinants in predicting outcomes for children than the presence or absence of a male in the home.

Impact of Divorce on Sons

The divorce literature shows repeatedly that divorce has a different impact on boys than girls. This appears logical, considering that boys are most apt to be in the custody of their mothers. While sons appear to be more vulnerable than daughters to the family disruption, this seems to occur only immediately following the divorce. Frequently, divorced mothers report that their sons are more argumentative, angry, and exhibit acting out behaviors. These boys may be demanding that their mothers exert more authority and create structures that were previously established and maintained by the father in the home. Family life scholars believe that children and youth learn their appropriate gender roles from a family that includes both mothers and fathers. This theory of social roles suggests that, without a father in the household, the male child may become disorganized and potentially angry. Likewise, a girl in a home without a mother may respond similarly. Thus, appropriate adult gender roles may be easier to learn for the same-sex child. This role model argument is frequently made in reference to high levels of male unemployment and female-headed households in the African-American community (Ingrassia, 1993).

Boys may exhibit deep anger toward a mother they blame for separating them from their fathers. Boys show problems in adjusting to divorce from preschool through adolescence. In Wallerstein and Kelly's (1980) well-known study of divorce, the fifteen-year follow-up study showed that two thirds of the children had not heard or seen their fathers in the previous year. With such a pattern of differential access to mothers and fathers after divorce, it is logical that boys are impacted differently than girls.

SOCIALIZATION OF CHILDREN

The post-divorce family moves through a process of adjustment to the changing circumstances of their family life. While estimates vary, some scholars indicate that one-third to one-half of divorced American parents engage in a prolonged and often unsolvable legal dispute over details of custody, child support, visitation and so forth (Kramer and Washo, 1993). During this process, the goals of socialization for the children may be less important than confrontational goals for adults. Donnelly and Finkelhor (1993) report that many joint custody awards are actually bitter agreements following a prolonged or antici-pated battle over custody. If joint custody is awarded in a highly conflicted situ-ation, it very rarely works. Joint custody demands more time, negotiation, and discussion between parents than does sole custody. Parents with a high degree of conflict are known to negotiate inadequately and exhibit behaviors that cause fear and anxiety among their children.

When there are dramatic pre- and post-divorce differences in life circum-stances of the children and the parent with custody, socialization goals for everyone must include stability and comfort in the new situation. Children's positive adjustment to divorce is closely related to the lack of conflict in their parents' negotiations and to the stability of their current family life. If they remain in the same home, school and/or neighborhood, with access to familiar friends, teachers and extended family members, children's adjustment is more positive. If parental conflict is high, the children change residences, dramatic differences in economic support occur, and the custodial parent is highly dis-tressed, then children will logically display behavior that represents their own conflict, anger and fear.

The research of Heatherington, Cox and Cox (1985) and Wallerstein and Kelly (1980) documents a developmental process of adjustment to a divorce that takes approximately 24 months, when some stability and resolution of the major life changes and conflicts are likely to occur. In a process that surprises both divorcing partners and friends, there is often a period of some stability one year after divorce and then increasing conflict and distress at about 18 months after divorce. This process may reflect an initial ability to handle or cope with crisis, followed by the gradual realization that there are dramatic grief processes that must be completed as the family struggles for a new defini-tion of functioning.

These grief processes include the loss of the idealized harmonious mar-riage, the change in available resources, the disruption of familiar patterns, and the loneliness of changing social roles with friends and other adults. Many divorced persons deal competently with the immediate demands of finding new housing or creating new family schedules, only to find themselves overwhelmed with anger at their losses and filled with guilt over failures. This guilt and anger are frequently increased by society's criticism of the divorced family.

Two-Family Model

Ahrons and Rogers (1987) suggest that one of the most positive ways to view the divorced family is as a bifocal family, or binuclear family. These terms sug-gest that the child now has two homes, and the family consists of two major centers, whereas previously the family was described as nuclear, or having only one center, or nucleus.

One of the crucial tasks of this bifocal family is to decide whether it is an adult-centered or a child-centered group. While neither extreme is appropriate for long-term functioning, a number of divorce experts have suggested that much of the law surrounding divorce is linked to the property and legal rights of parents, and not in the best interests of the child.

"Best Interests of the Child" Doctrine

The courts claim to use a doctrine of "best interests of the child," in relation to divorce judgments. There is sharp disagreement between mental health professionals and legal professionals on the meaning of the best interest of the child. Some argue that the "best interest" doctrine is still used to protect the interests of the father, who is defined as the head of the family and is more often responsible for family property and resources. In addition, some judges have deliberately awarded child custody to fathers with the rationale that this would keep more children off public welfare. Since fathers typically have higher incomes, they were given custody in order to reduce the need for public tax dollars to support a new single-parent family.

A great deal of support from helping professionals may be needed for many fathers seeking to establish sole custody or significant on-going coparenting responsibility for their children. Scholars who have studied custody and visitation arrangements report that children have a more realistic understanding of their parents' lives when given longer periods of time with the noncustodial parent, instead of just weekends.

When visits with the non-custodial parent are long enough, the parent and child settle into the normal events of that parent's life. If the child stays during vacation for an entire month or summer, the child is more apt to understand life beyond an entertainment focus. Most child development and family life specialists agree that longer periods offer a more realistic model for life roles and family behaviors. In addition, the literature is clear that children adjust more positively to divorce when they have on-going stable relationships with both parents.

Role of Grandparents and Others

In the divorced family, the grandparents, uncles, aunts and ex-in-laws are important connections for the stability and adjustment of family members. Grandparents in particular have traditionally represented ancestry and unconditional love and support for children. Since 1986, every state in the United States has passed a statute enabling grandparents to petition the courts for the right to visit their grandchildren. These petitions are frequently brought when there is a conflictive divorce and the grandparents are denied access to their grandchildren. The courts use certain guides related to on-going stability and family relationships prior to divorce in responding to these petitions. Thus, if the grandparents have established significant relationships with the children, or even provided a household for the children during the divorce process, the court is more likely to award them visitation rights (Parnell and Bagbee, 1993).

Some researchers have documented that informal relationships within post-divorce families often include regular time spent with ex-in-laws and parents of the other spouse. It is interesting to note that many divorced parents report that they are often urged by friends and the general public to make a "clean break" or disconnect themselves from all relatives of an ex-spouse. It appears that individual parents use their own personal values and experience as a guide. Those who have had positive relationships with their ex-spouse's relatives often continue to maintain them.

Friendly Communications

Johnson (1988) reports that in a sample of middle-class divorced parents, one-third of the spouses maintained positive on-going relationships with the "ex-relatives." Divorced spouses who maintain a relationship that is amicable over their parenting responsibilities find that their children are more positive and better adjusted. This is a particularly challenging task for divorced families.

Communication between parents concerning responsibilities for the children needs to take priority over all other family topics. In most families, many things are discussed simultaneously. Discussions about the children's relationships often include references to adult relationships. Friendship and cooperation with an ex-spouse do not necessarily include consultation and the sharing of news about other parts of one's life.

Communicating effectively is a learning process for parents involved in divorce. Frequently, grandparents or extended family members can help with this process by maintaining their relationships with the children, and reassuring them about the connections of the on-going family traditions.

ECOLOGICAL FACTORS

The environment of the divorced parent changes quite radically following separation and divorce.

Demographics

American families have experienced a dramatic increase in the divorce rate in recent decades. In 1990, 24.1 percent of all children lived in single-parent families. This translates into thirteen million children, with more than half of all African-American children, one third of Hispanics and one fifth of white children living in single-parent families. During the 1980s, only four states, Connecticut, Nebraska, New Hampshire and Rhode Island, saw a decline in the percentage of children living in single-parent families. In 1990, only 90 percent of children living in the United States were living with their parent or parents. Seven percent were living with other relatives, and two percent were living outside the family (Center for the Study of Social Policy, 1993).

One of the reasons for concern about the impact of the divorce experience on children is that we are experiencing a lower percentage of children as a part of the total United States population. Every child's optimal development is important to the country as a whole. In 1970, children constituted 34.3 percent of the entire United States population. By the year 2000, it is projected that they will constitute only 24.5 percent of the total population.

In the 1950s, for every person of retirement age who was receiving Social Security benefits, there were sixteen people employed in the work force contributing to the system. By 1990, there were only three employed workers for every person in their retirement years. Figure 11–2 shows the dramatic difference in the support ratio of children and the elderly projected from 1980 to 2050.

Experts predict that one half of all marriages and 56 percent of all remarriages in the 1990s will end in divorce. Before they turn 18, one half of all children living in stepfamilies will see their parents divorce again, and 80 percent

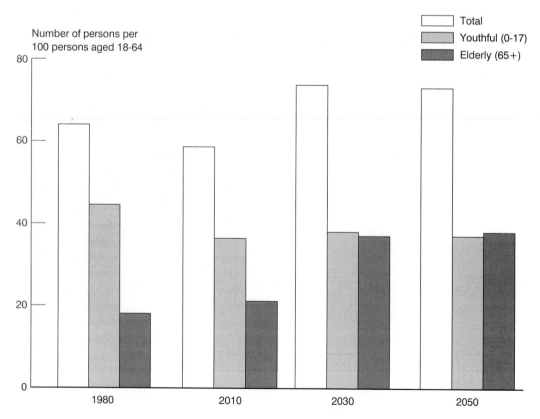

Figure 11–2. *Support Ratios of Children and the Elderly: 1980–2050*

Source: *Age Structure of the U.S. Population in the 21st Century.* U.S. Bureau of the Census, SB 1–86. Washington, DC: U.S. Government Printing Office.

will see their divorced fathers remarry. When these changes in family structure limit opportunities for optimal development of children and parents, our national human capital resource declines (Mulroy, 1988).

Aesthetics

For years, divorce was not talked about, even in families where it occurred. Thus, literature and music about divorce are relatively new phenomena. Most of the literature or music that relates to divorce is autobiographical, and portrays divorce as a crisis or life transition. The Country and Western song popular in the 1970s, "D-I-V-O-R-C-E," is an example of a folk cultural portrayal of an experience that is increasingly common. As talk show hosts and comedians have included references to divorce in their routines, the increasing universal experience with divorce has been emphasized. There are whole new categories of self-help literature for both women and men following divorce.

In addition, there are now excellent books for children that give a child's view of divorce from preschool through adolescence. Some outstanding examples of these books include those written exclusively by children such as *The Kids' Book About Divorce* (Rofes, 1982) written by children in a Boston private school classroom, and the video tape "Tender Places," whose author is a thirteen-year-old boy who experienced divorce. (See References and Media Resources at the end of the chapter.) One of the important functions of these personal stories is to help people deal with the cognitive and emotional transitions of the divorce process. For many persons, the tasks associated with divorce are new and stressful. The arts provide universal ideas and perspectives that can be particularly supportive.

Education and Re-education

The interaction between education and divorce is complex. Re-entering the educational process is extremely important for many women experiencing dependency and economic limitation after divorce. Programs such as Displaced Homemaker categories within the Jobs Transition Program Act (JTPA), or the jobs programs for mothers of dependent children, reflect a nationally recognized need to assist people who have been inadequately prepared to enter today's employment market.

How Divorce Impacts Children's Education

The impact of divorce on children's educational goals and achievements is even more complex. There are clear variations depending on income and parent education level. Children in middle- and upper-class families are more likely to continue their education. Researchers have documented a concern on the part of teachers that family disorganization results in children being less successful in school. Children typically have less access to parents' support in completing homework assignments or their encouragement of academic excellence. Earlier studies associated these negative effects with the absence of a father in the home (Brown and Fox, 1979; and Hepworth, Ryder and Dreyer, 1984).

More recent studies on the impact of divorce have shown that the child's ability, the academic aspirations of the child and the family, and the ethnic group membership are more powerful than family structure in influencing academic achievement. Since children spend a great deal of their waking hours in school, and are observed by a variety of people in that environment, it is likely that their fears and insecurities concerning the divorce may be exhibited in behavior in the school setting.

In Wallerstein and Kelly's (1980) follow-up work with children of divorce, two thirds of the original sample of children continued to be successful in academic achievement. In addition, one half of the children who originally reacted negatively to the divorce process (one-third of the whole sample) had achieved some new sense of balance and academic success. The authors indicate that a number of these originally distressed children were not fulfilling their academic abilities or promise. In addition, funding for higher education for children with divorced parents was problematic, even though this group of families was from middle- and upper-middle social classes.

Educational opportunity for young people is increasingly related to access to economic resources. In states where divorced parents are obligated to pay child support only through age eighteen, often no arrangements have been made for college costs. Many parents are finding it difficult to bear the costs associated with college attendance. For families who are extremely impoverished following divorce, concerns for minimum income and shelter often take priority over spending for education or health.

The structure and schedules of schools make cooperation difficult for parents without custody who want to stay involved in parenting their children. Notices about meetings or conferences are frequently sent to only one parent who must then convey invitations to the non-custodial parent. One study of Ohio schools (Austin, 1993) found that the majority of school districts did not collect any information on noncustodial parents, and in almost half of the districts, noncustodial parents were excluded from the educational process.

Preschool and school officials sometimes find themselves conferring with parents separately, especially when divorce processes have been marred by conflict. Divorced parents may be struggling to agree on basic issues relating to their child's development, and cannot concentrate on school achievement.

Impact of Religion

Like never-married single parents, many divorced parents find support rather than adverse judgments of their actions in religion. Many pastors, priests, and rabbis are called upon to provide support and counseling to parents considering divorce. A number of these professionals, through schooling, have enhanced their own skills at understanding and facilitating decision-making around a potential divorce. Religious organizations that have provided support groups for single parents experiencing divorce find that these groups effectively lead to gains for both adults and children. For many divorced people, religion highlights deep conflicts arising from a perceived failure of their own personal choices to demonstrate the ideals of their faith.

Health Care Impacts

Family-planning information is available to divorced parents if they have the knowledge and economic resources to take advantage of this service. Fifty percent of divorced individuals say that a new sexual partner in the first six months following divorce was significant in healing the relationship wounds of the divorce. This finding suggests that many divorced persons are sexually active, and family planning can be an important resource for them.

A serious health problem for divorced parents is access to medical insurance and services for the children and the custodial parent. While divorce decrees often include the requirement that medical insurance coverage be provided to the children on an on-going basis, the custodial parent sometimes is left vulnerable. Access to routine preventive health care is particularly a problem for many women who have not worked previously and whose income is sharply reduced following divorce. The 1993 Budget Reconciliation Act required procedures to be established in all states by April 1, 1994, to remove barriers preventing children from obtaining health insurance coverage through their non-custodial parents' insurance (Children's Defense Fund Reports, 1993).

The mental health literature documents that major transitions like divorce impact a person's physical and mental health. Typically, an increase in stomach and digestive ailments, headaches, a susceptibility to upper respiratory infections and intestinal infections, lowered energy, and depression are all physical manifestations of the interaction of life events and health. Both adults and children may be exposed to new health risks, particularly if families change their residence. Studies report that 38 percent of children and their divorced mothers change their residence within the first year following divorce (Booth and Amato, 1992).

Economic Impacts

A husband's level of income and stability at work are among the strongest variables associated with higher marriage stability. This suggests that economic stability lessens the likelihood of divorce. Women who are divorced are particularly vulnerable to lowered economic resources. The proportion of female-headed families in poverty has remained stable at 45 percent for the past twenty years. In contrast, poverty among two-parent families has varied with changes in the economy (National Commission on Children, 1993).

Only one custodial mother in four receives the full amount of court-ordered child support, and one in four with a court-ordered child support award in place receives no support. The tremendous variation in the awarding and collecting of child support and alimony following divorce has created confusion and inequity in the economic condition of the divorced family unit. A national trend has been to require the recording of the social security number of a divorced partner with child support obligations. Such record-keeping would facilitate an integrated nation-wide regulatory system of enforcement.

The Family Support Act of 1988 (P.L. 100-485) required states to begin wage withholding for all child-support orders issued after January 1, 1994. States may use the state child support enforcement agency for collecting and distributing payments even if the family would not otherwise be served by that agency. States are also permitted to establish a separate mechanism for wage withholding.

Many professionals believed the introduction of joint custody in no-fault divorce processes was one possible way to enhance the legal obligation and on-going relationship between the parents and children so that economic support would continue. However, given the level of conflict surrounding many divorces, and the skill needed to negotiate decisions between people living in different houses, joint custody has not proved to be as beneficial as once thought. In fact, some professionals have re-labeled "no fault divorce" laws as "no responsibility" laws (Coontz, 1992).

Laws to Reduce Economic Impact

Public Law 9838-387, passed in 1984, required that all states establish standards to determine support awards for divorced spouses and children. Sixty-one percent of non-custodial fathers are ordered to pay support, but there is great variation in the enforcement of that support (Fine and Fine, 1992). The Family Support Act of 1988 required that the parents' social security numbers be listed on birth certificates of all children whenever this information was available to enhance the ability of states to collect child support payments. Child support enforcement units in state Departments of Social Services have the responsibility to collect awarded support for families who are receiving Aid to Families with Dependent Children (AFDC), but there is great variation in their resources to complete this task.

Strong advocacy for a federal law to provide the mechanism for the Internal Revenue Service to collect child support payments that are in arrears influenced language in the 1993 Budget Reconciliation Bill. At the present time, the jurisdiction for child support awards still resides with the court in the state that awarded the divorce. Parents frequently relocate after divorce, and obtaining legal assistance to enforce child support payments from another jurisdiction becomes too costly for most families to consider. Since 80 percent of divorced fathers remarry, there are also competing demands on the remarried father's income and resources.

Family law specialists are in conflict about whether priority should be given to supporting the children of the previous or the present marriage. Some are disdainful of men who create family after family without supporting them.

Numerous studies indicate that non-custodial parents often provide economic resources for their stepchildren with whom they reside before providing economic resources to their biological children not in their custody. These decisions obviously reflect current relationship pressures in new marriages. The topic of child support and the economic viability of divorced parents illustrates the male-oriented bias of many courts. Legal precedents that were designed largely to protect adult property rights are often inappropriate for making decisions related to dependent children and adults in divorced families.

Housing Impacts

Following a divorce, the father typically leaves the family home and establishes a new place of residence. Many mothers who retain ownership of homes after the divorce process find the expenses and upkeep unrealistic on their current income. This often results in family homes being sold and the mother and children moving to a smaller residence. This process takes considerable time during which the psychological sense of loss for children and mothers has to be dealt with.

The disposition of the family home is probably second only to custody questions in raising conflict around divorce. For the children, a house often means continuity and stability in their lives. This is one area where the rights and interests of the adults can be in sharp conflict with those of the children. For the divorcing partners, the house may represent conflict and old memories they wish to leave behind.

When there has been an extreme amount of conflict in the marriage and home, the home might represent the visual stage for these memories also. Many families do not own a home, and the divorce process leaves them dependent on public funding. Public housing sites include many mothers and children of divorce.

Another social phenomenon is the number of divorced families that have returned to their own families of origin. Middle-aged parents are finding their children returning home with grandchildren. While these arrangements can be successful, they require skilled negotiation about property rights, boundary issues between the generations, and the amount of economic and supervision assistance the grandparents can provide. Grandparents frequently are asked to provide vital resources for the young family's survival at a time when they have to deal with their distress and grief over their children's divorce. In cultures where extended family patterns are frequent and valued by the community, this transition may be easier. In never-married single-parent families, the pattern frequently consists of the young parent giving birth and parenting while continuing to reside in the parental home.

Government Policies and Agencies

All divorced families have experienced interaction with the courts. Indeed, owing to the rise in divorce and other family-related matters, currently 50 percent of all court cases relate to some aspect of family law (Fine, 1993). The fact that courts have historically been adversarial environments has led many states to institute enhanced responsibility for family courts, or encourage the processes of family mediation to maintain the marriage or to provide help with the divorce process.

Many divorced families are also involved with the Department of Social Services through a variety of assistance programs, particularly the Aid to Families with Dependent Children (AFDC) program. As an outgrowth of these services, families interact with the Child Support Enforcement Division and Medicaid personnel. Family and child advocates bemoan the fact that many services for vulnerable children and families have been ineffective because they are housed in so many different agencies at both the state and federal levels. Significant issues needing research, public discussion, and decisions include providing for the rights of the child, reasonable child support, effective systems for changing custody arrangements, and revisions of regulations surrounding acceptable custodial arrangements for a child.

Grandparents who raise their grandchildren because of divorce, death, or instability on the part of the child's parents frequently have a difficult time receiving any public assistance because the children do not legally belong to them. Miller (1993) comments that policies affecting adoption, custody, and the provision of benefits to children should be judged by their power to reduce the damaging effects of poverty on healthy child development. Parents frequently continue to claim AFDC benefits in order to receive Medicaid assistance. Yet the income in such programs is so low that parents cannot save money or acquire resources to help move them beyond the poverty level.

The federal government's policy of allowing states to establish reimbursement formulas for public assistance programs means that tremendous inconsistencies exist between states and from program to program within the state. More thorough understanding of how such policies continue to trap young divorced families into poverty could help improve futures for these families.

KINSHIP NETWORKS AND INTERACTIONS

Kinship networks are extremely important to all families and to the divorced family in particular. Divorced parents often return to live with their own parents, at least for a period of time. Due to economic impacts, the young divorced family is particularly dependent on the support of their friends and kin networks. In addition, as shown in Figure 11–3, two-parent families who are poor are more than twice as likely to divorce as families who have not experienced poverty.

In 1990, sixty-six percent of single mothers were reported in the work force, with one in eight employed mothers working more than 40 hours a week. Many of the children of these mothers are cared for by friends and family while the mothers work. Seven million children under the age of thirteen

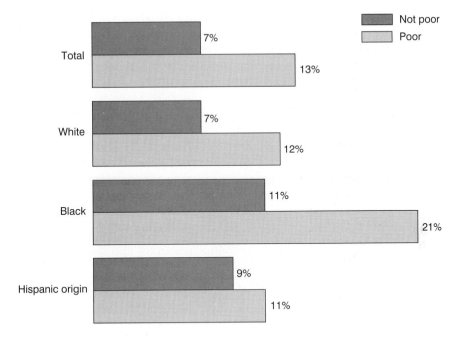

Figure 11–3. *Percent of Two-Parent Families That Discontinued Within Two Years: Mid-1980s*

Source: *When Families Break Up.* U.S. Bureau of the Census, SB 92–12. Washington, DC: U.S. Government Printing Office.

were cared for by a relative other than a parent in 1990 (U.S. Bureau of the Census, 1992). Many of these arrangements for care are relatively informal and vulnerable to the demands of competing influences on relatives' lives. The ability of a network of friends and family to exchange services and provide emotional and material support is extremely vital.

Family interactions around the celebration of holidays often become conflictual. When divorce has divided a household, it is often the extended family that has a difficult time adjusting to the reduced access to children in the family. The extended family will often not change its patterns to adjust to the reality of one divorced couple in the family network. This means that divorced parents often feel conflict and a lack of support around the times of the year when their earlier family memories may have been very positive and cohesive.

CHANGE AND ADAPTATION

A family group going through a divorce must change and adapt. Divorced families experience difficult times, particularly for 12 to 18 months following the separation. By 24 to 30 months, most divorced couples and their children have achieved some new level of stability (Heatherington, Cox and Cox, 1985). During this period of time a significant number of major developmental tasks must be accomplished. While a divorce is often identified by the legal date or document in the court system, in actuality the divorce is a process that takes place over an extended period of time.

Stages of Divorce

Those who provide support activities and education concerning divorce recognize four stages of divorce that can be described as follows:

1. *A psychological/emotional divorce.* This stage is often initiated by one party and may be felt for an extended period of time before it is verbalized and acted upon.
2. *A physical divorce or separation.* This stage may be linked to the availability of economic resources and usually means that one parent moves out of the family's home.
3. *A legal divorce.* This stage is often prolonged until the parties have the economic resources or the will to complete a legal divorce. In addition, there may be a legal separation document that precedes an actual divorce.
4. *A social divorce.* In this final stage, people declare that ties to certain social groups or friends are changed or severed and new social relationships are established.

A person can obtain a legal divorce and a physical divorce and never complete the psychological/emotional or the social divorces. Some people accomplish the stages in a different order. Some may never work through all stages. Some may need professional assistance in completing the processes.

Parenting Alliances

The literature on parenting through the divorce process includes many examples of parents struggling to assert a parenting alliance that allows the divorced parents to cooperate in decisions relating to their children. Whether or not they hold joint custody, both parents usually have an enduring interest in the development of their children.

When there is a high amount of conflict, a great deal of adult energy may go into maintaining the adult conflict rather than establishing new and stable regimes for themselves and the children in separate households. Some of these struggles result essentially in parallel parenting, or two separate households that deal with the child in separate ways with little negotiation or sharing of information between them.

Children can usually learn to adjust to new situations. They do adjust to differences between home and school, or between their parents' household and other extended family members' households. However, one can ask, what "adjustment" is appropriate or ideal for optimal development? Some agreement on values and reinforcement of achievement goals for children would seem appropriate for divorced parents. Children can grow to understand that both parents have the children's interests in mind and are cooperating for their good.

New Patterns

Single mothers, who typically must become more assertive in disciplining their children, may find the discipline task difficult. Depressed or exhausted by the divorce process, parents sometimes do not exert enough energy and resources to create new stable patterns for the children. For divorced parents with custody, learning how to manage on a reduced level of resources with increased demands on their time and energy is extremely important.

Establishing new adult relationships is critical, yet single mothers often have fewer adult relationships just when they need them the most. Research on emotional stress suggests that social support is extremely important to buffer the effects of stress. With few new friends, a divorced mother often seeks social support from her family. Role reversal, which happens when a parent relies too heavily on the children for emotional and social support, is sometimes a result of this period of stress.

As divorced parents initiate their own social relationships, they must develop new roles. The divorce literature suggests that only 15 percent of divorced adults marry a person with whom they had a pre-divorce extramarital relationship. Many of these new, post-divorce adult relationships will be with new partners. Balancing the need for adult exploration of relationships with the children's need for stability is an important function for all family members. Most divorced parents remarry, but statistics show that rates of divorce in a second marriage are a bit higher than in a first marriage. Given these realities, children who have experienced one divorce are likely to experience additional relationship beginnings and endings in the future.

SERVING DIVORCED SINGLE-PARENT FAMILIES

Professionals serving these families should be aware that divorce, as a process of transition, continues over a number of months. The process involves loss, grief, and endings. These are processes that the American culture has usually not dealt with comfortably. Frequently our work with these families requires assisting them in separating child needs from adult needs. Divorce-transition adults frequently tell their divorce stories to anyone who will listen, in order to gain clarification for themselves or to seek alliances. When meeting with parents and discussing issues relating to their children, the focus should be on the child's development and how to maintain the child's safety, stability, and optimal development. Professionals working with such families should try to meet with both divorced parents together, if that is reasonable. When it is not possible, it is necessary for professionals to set separate times to work with each of the parents, assuming the non-custodial parent is available locally.

In consideration of children's needs, ground rules are needed, such as not allowing one parent to talk disparagingly about the other parent in front of the child. Also, the child needs to be encouraged to talk freely about and maintain psychological and emotional connections with both parents.

In schools and youth-serving agencies, there should be available literature and media resources that talk about the process of divorce, and describe people with a variety of family structures. Children whose parents have experienced divorce need to be kept in as stable a classroom situation as possible and close to staff members who can be empathetic and supportive. Reducing the number of changes children have to cope with is important.

Allowing children an opportunity to discuss questions or frustrations is extremely important. School-based groups for children and youth who have experienced divorce provide helpful outlets for children. Showing unexpected insight, children frequently indicate that their parents are so absorbed in grief and transition processes that the fears and anxieties of children are ignored. Children who are quiet, helpful, and positive during the divorce process can be feeling just as stressed and grief-stricken as those who are acting out and confronting authority. Kurkowski, Gordon and Arbuthnot (1993) found that a technique as simple as having high school students complete a questionnaire about their feelings of being caught "in the middle" between two parents and sharing the group results in a letter to all households produced significant improvements in parent/youth communication.

Serving these families should always take into account reduced income and reduced time for family members to participate in education or leisure/social events. Ideas for low-cost activities to participate in with children, combining several objectives in one family activity, can promote family effectiveness and economy.

Professionals need to understand their own attitudes when working with families of divorce and be careful not to convey unhelpful attitudes to families (Gray, 1985). Referring to a family as broken, separated, unsuccessful, or "in trouble" reinforces negative images and expectations concerning this difficult transition. Children can be expected to feel distressed and to show some changes in their behavior while they adjust. Arranging a school or social setting where children feel comfortable will enable them to speak about and overcome this behavior. Professionals serving such children should expect changes, be supportive, and give the child assurances and structure rather than confront the parent with the child's anxieties. Two years may be required for new sound relationships to become stabilized within a family. For young children particularly, two years can be a very long time.

Staff Training

Finding ways to understand the normal transitions of divorce, and becoming aware of how to be supportive, are important professional skills. Developing a good list of resources for use by staff and parents is helpful. Referring children or parents to agencies that have individuals skilled in divorce transitions and counseling can be another positive act. Parents who have had earlier experiences with divorce can be a helpful resource. You can encourage newly divorced parents to seek out single-parent support groups as well as support groups for children. Introducing parents to others who might be sources of support and friendship is another helpful step.

Independence and isolation of the nuclear family form in America is still alive and well in some families. Coontz (1992) comments that a general Anglo-American notion that dependence is immature and weak interferes with the social support and inter-dependence that is so helpful in divorce transitions. Understanding the importance of sharing resources and needs with other families can be an important professional goal as you work with many families of divorce. As a professional, you need to help families of divorce understand the importance of networking and cooperating with other families or groups.

When families come from an ethnic group or culture that is supportive, there will be good support for the divorce adjustment process. However, some religious and ethnic groups are not supportive of the divorce process, even though they are supportive of extended family relationships. Because of their personal choices, divorced parents then may feel an acute loss of approval and bondedness within the religious and ethnic setting. Finding other people who can be supportive and linking them with divorced families is certainly a needed service you can provide.

New Celebrations

Encouraging these families to establish new rituals, festivals, and celebrations is another important aspect of your professional work. Because extended family networks often compete for attention during traditional holiday times, divorced families may need to initiate other events that become special to their family. For example, if children visit the non-custodial parent on weekends, a Sunday night homecoming ritual or a Monday evening family time may assist children in starting new patterns that will work well within the new family structure.

CONCLUSIONS

Families experiencing divorce need professional support during this important period of transition. The specific circumstances of individual families will be different, but there are important actions you can take concerning divorced and separated families. You need to be sensitive to the loss of economic resources and the complexities of establishing new households. Children need stability, reassurance, and permission to communicate their concerns. Adults need supportive connections with other families and assistance in creating appropriate new patterns in a two-household family.

STUDY QUESTIONS

1. Define the terms alimony and no-fault divorce.
2. Review the statistics and state which U.S. group has the greatest number of divorces. Explain.
3. State gender differences regarding economic outcome for each gender following divorce.
4. What do studies show as factors contributing to more divorces?
5. Define the terms joint custody, legal joint custody, and physical joint custody.
6. State what studies show to be the impact of divorce on sons.
7. State what studies show to be the impact of divorce on daughters.
8. What is a typical time requirement for the divorce process to be completed and stability to come in a family?
9. What is the "best interest of the child" doctrine?
10. What typically occurs with regard to property rights in a divorce?

APPLICATIONS

1. Compare and contrast a pedifocal family with a patrifocal family.
2. Discuss why father-absence research is inadequate in understanding the divorce process.
3. Compare and contrast parallel parenting with parenting alliances.
4. Study and describe the positive and negative aspects of children residing, after divorce, in the custody of their mother. What does it affect, and how?
5. What systems are most significant in impacting the feelings and success of divorced families?
6. Make a list of guidelines for helping professionals to use in working with divorced parents.
7. Write a three-page essay giving advice to a friend of your own gender about how to proceed once a decision is made to divorce.

REFERENCES

Ahrons, C. R., and Rodgers, R. H. (1987). *Divorced families: A multidisciplinary view.* New York, NY: Norton.

Booth, Alan, and Amato, Paul. (1992). Divorce, residential change and stress. *Journal of Divorce and Remarriage, 18*(1–2), 169–187.

Brenner, A. (1993). *Helping children cope with stress.* Lexington, MA: D.C. Heath.

Brief educational intervention for divorced parents. (1993).

Brown, P., and Fox, H. (1979). Sex differences in divorce. In F. S. Gonsberg and V. Franks (Eds.), *Gender disordered behavior: Sex differences in psychopathology.* New York, NY: Brunner/Nagel.

Buehler, Cheryl, and Legg, B. H. (1993). Mothers' receipt of social support and their psychological well-being following marital separation. *Journal of Family Issues, 14*(1), 21–38.

Children's Defense Fund. (1987). *Declining earnings of young men: Their relation to poverty, teenaged pregnancy and family formation.* Washington, D.C.: CDF Adolescent Pregnancy Prevention Clearinghouse.

Children's Defense Fund. (1992). No more "working poor" families. *CDF Reports, 14*(2), 8–9.

Children's Defense Fund. (1993). Child poverty hits record level. *CDF Reports, 14*(12), 11.

Compher, John Victor. (1989). *Family-centered practice: The interactional dance beyond the family system.* New York, NY: Plenum Publishing.

Coontz, Stephanie. (1992). *The way we never were.* New York, NY: Basic Books.

DeMaris, A., and Greif, G. L. (1992). The relationship between family structure and parent-child relationship problems in single father households. *Journal of Divorce and Remarriage, 18*(1–2), 55–57.

Dickenson, G. E., and Lemming, M. R. (1990). *Understanding families: Diversity, continuity and change.* Boston, MA: Allyn and Bacon.

Donnelly, D., and Finkelhor, D. (1993). Who has joint custody? Class differences in the determination of custody arrangements. *Family Relations, 42*(1), 57–61.

Duran-Aydintug, C. (1993). Relationships with former in-laws: Normative guidelines and actual behavior. *Journal of Divorce and Remarriage, 19*(3–9), 69–82.

Family Support Act of 1988. (1988, Oct. 13, PL 100-485). *United States Statistics at Large, 102,* 2343–2428.

Fine, Mark A. (1993). Current approaches to understanding family diversity: An overview of a special issue. *Family Relations, 42*(3), 235–237.

Fine, M. A., and Fine, D. R. (1992). Recent changes in law affecting stepfamilies: Suggestions for legal reform. *Family Relations, 42,* 334–340.

Gigy, L., and Kelly, J. B. (1992). Reasons for divorce: Perspectives of divorcing men and women. *Journal of Divorce and Remarriage, 18*(1–2), 169–187.

Gottlieb, Dorothy Weiss, Gottlieb, Inez Bellow, and Slavin, Marjorie A. (1988). *What to do when your son or daughter divorces.* New York, NY: Bantam Books.

Gray, Mary McPhail, and Coleman, Marilyn. (1985). Separation through divorce: Supportive professional practices. *Child Care Quarterly, 14*(4), 248–261.

Haub, Carl. (1993). Births per U.S. woman? *Population Today, 2*(9), 6–7.

Heatherington, E. M., Cox, M., and Cox, R. (1985). Long-term effects on divorce and remarriage on the adjustment of children. *Journal of American Academy of Child Psychiatry, 24,* 518–530.

Hepworth, J., Ryder, R. G., and Dreyer, A. S. (1984). The effects of parental loss on the formation of intimate relationships. *Journal of Marital and Family Therapy, 10,* 73–82.

Ingrassia, Michelle. (1993, August 30). Endangered family. *Newsweek,* pp. 17–29.

Johnson, Colleen Leahy. (1988). *Ex-families: Grandparents, parents, and children adjust to divorce.* New Brunswick, NJ: Rutgers University Press.

Kids count data book: State profiles of child well-being. (1993). Washington, DC: Center for the Study of Social Policy.

Kinney, Jill, Haapala, David, and Booth, Charlotte. (1991). *Keeping families together: The home builder's model.* New York, NY: Aldine DeGruyter.

Kramer, L., and Washo, C. A. (1993). Evaluation of a court-mandated prevention program for divorcing parents: The children first program. *Family Relations, 41,* 224–229.

Kurkowski, Kevin P., Gordon, Donald A., and Arbuthnot, Jack. (1993). Children caught in the middle: A brief educational intervention for divorced parents. *Journal of Divorce and Remarriage, 20*(3/4), 139–152.

Levy-Schiff, R. (1982). The effects of father absence on young children in mother-headed families. *Child Development, 53*(5), 1400–1405.

Miller, G. (1993). The psychological best interests of the child. *Journal of Divorce and Remarriage, 19*(1–2), 21–39.

Mulroy, E. A. (Ed). (1988). *Women as single parents.* Dover, MA: Auburn House Publishing Co.

National Commission on Children. (1993). *Just the facts.* Washington, DC: U.S. Government Printing Office.

Parnell, M., and Bagbee, B. H. (1993). Grandparents' rights: Implications for family specialists. *Family Relations, 42*(2), 173–179.

Rofes, Eric. (Ed.). (1982). *The kids' book about divorce.* New York, NY: Vintage Books.

Shaffer, D., and Lyons, C. (1986). *How do I tell the children?* New York, NY: Newmarket Press.

U.S. Bureau of the Census. (1989). *The black population in the United States: A chartbook.* Series P-20, No. 442. Washington, DC: U.S. Government Printing Office.

U.S. Bureau of the Census. (1992). Family life today . . . and how it has changed. *U.S. Bureau of the Census Statistical Briefs* (pp. 92–13). Washington, DC: U.S. Government Printing Office.

Wallerstein, J. S., and Kelly, J. (1980). *Surviving the breakup: How children and parents cope with divorce.* New York, NY: Basic Books.

Whitehead, Barbara Defoe. (1993, April). Dan Quayle was right. *The Atlantic Monthly, 271*(4), 47–84.

Zinn, Maxine Baca. (1992). Family, race and poverty in the eighties. In Barrie Thorne (Ed.), *Rethinking the family.* Boston, MA: NYU Press.

MEDIA RESOURCES

Dad's House, Mom's House. (1986). (33 min.) National Film Board of Canada, New York, NY.

Dear Distant Dad. (23 min.) Vision Video, Inc., Worcester, PA.

A Kid's Guide to Family Changes. (40 min.) Learning Tree Publishing, Inc., Englewood, CO.

Do Children Also Divorce? (1988). (28 min.) Filmmaker's Library, New York, NY.

Tender Places. (1988). (25 min.) MTI Film and Video. Group W Television Sales, Deerfield, IL.

ORGANIZATIONS

International Association for Widowed People. P.O. Box 3564, Springfield, IL. (217) 787-0886.

The Joint Custody Association. 10606 Wilkins Ave., Los Angeles, CA 90024. (213) 475-5352.

National Council on Family Relations. 1910 West County Rd. B, Suite 147, St. Paul, MN 55113. (612) 633-6933.

PACE (Parents and Children's Equality). 1816 Florida Ave., Palm Harbor, FL 34683. (813) 787-3875.

Parents Without Partners, Inc. 8807 Colesville Rd., Silver Springs, MD 20910. 1-800-638-807.

OTHER BOOKS FOR ADULTS

Bieninfeld, Florence. (1987). *Helping your child succeed after divorce.* Claremont, CA: Hente House.

Covington, J. (1982). *Confessions of a single father.* New York, NY: Pilgrim Press.

Kamerman, Sheila B., and Kohn, Alfred J. (1988). *Mothers alone: strategies for a time of change.* Dove, MA: Auburn House.

Pruett, Kyle. (1987). *The nurturing father: Journey toward the complete man.* New York, NY: Warner Books.

Ware, C. (1982). *Sharing parenthood after divorce: An enlightened custody guide for mother, father and the kids.* New York, NY: Viking Press.

Wayman, Anne. (1981). *Successful single parenting: A practical guide.* Meadowbrook, NY: Simon and Schuster.

BOOKS FOR CHILDREN COPING WITH DIVORCE

Dolmetsch, Paul, and Shil, Alexa. (Eds.). *The kids book about single parent families.* Garden City, NY: Doubleday.

Fleming, Alice M. (1985). *Welcome to Grossville.* New York, NY: Charles Scribner's Sons.

Giraid, Linda Walvoord. (1987). *At Daddy's on Saturdays.* Niles, IL: Albert Whitman.

Jones, Adrienne. (1983). *A matter of spunk.* New York, NY: Harper and Row.

Watson, Jane Weaver, Swetzer, Robert E., and Hirschberg, J. Cotter. (1988). *Sometimes a family has to split up: A read aloud book for parents and children.* New York, NY: Crown Publishers.

CHAPTER 12

Stepfamilies

Key Concepts

◆ Binuclear Families
◆ Custodial Parent
◆ Remarried Family

Today's stepfamily consists of you, me, your kids, my kids, our kids, your ex's, my ex's, even our ex's new mates, and all the kin of these various folks. Step-families give a new meaning to the concept of complex family relationships.

— A variation of a definition of stepfamilies, by Delia Ephron (1986)

As helping professionals, it is important to understand the reality of life in stepfamilies. Scholars report that stepfamilies that fare well see this new and distinct family form as a challenge for each member if it is to succeed. Behaviors carried over from early marriages must be discarded. New forms of communication must be planned. Outside support from kin, friends, and professionals must be utilized. In spite of the organizational complexity, research shows that, on the average, a higher level of satisfaction occurs between second-marriage partners than between first-marriage partners.

COMPLEX STRUCTURE OF STEPFAMILIES

A stepfamily is a complex form of social organization with tremendous variation in structure. Stepfamilies may appear to many to be like traditional two-parent families. However, by creating a *genogram,* a detailed organizational chart, one can see the complexity of significant relationships that predate the current remarriage. Glick (1989) defines a *remarried* family as consisting of a husband, wife, and children and at least one or both of the spouses being in their second or subsequent marriage. Further, a *stepfamily* is created when one remarried spouse has at least one biological child under age 18 who was born during a prior marriage or relationship. Stepfamilies include both divorced and widowed parents, and parents who were previously cohabiting with another partner. The primary focus of this chapter will be on stepfamilies formed following divorce.

Members of stepfamilies are sensitive to judgments of the wider culture, and, therefore, have been reluctant to participate in research. Some simply deny that they are any different than first-marriage families and this myth often gets in the way of solving some of the problems they face. Over the years, America has experienced a public debate about the strength and stability of families. Because there have been so many negative inferences surrounding stepfamilies, their reluctance to reveal their innermost workings is understandable. Stepfamilies are newly committed to marriage; however, partners often carry feelings of failure from their first marriages, and worry about their ability to develop better relationships in their new family.

As helping professionals, it is important to understand the reality of life in stepfamilies. Scholars report that most conflicts in stepfamilies result from the inappropriate application of traditional parent-child roles in the new circumstances. With knowledge, professionals can facilitate the planning of realistic services to give stepfamilies the support they need.

HISTORICAL BACKGROUND

Stepfamilies emerge from a combination of out-of-wedlock births, a high divorce rate and a commitment to marriage. In Table 12–1, a 1991 survey showed the changing patterns of parent marital status in the United States. The increasing number of children born out of wedlock means that stepfamilies may increasingly involve partners for whom the new marriage is the first legally sanctioned union. Americans continue to believe in marriage, and want to start anew even after the loss of one family structure. Some social scientists

Table 12-1.   *Living Arrangements of Children Under 18 Years, by Race and Hispanic Origin: Summer 1991*

[Numbers in thousands]

Living arrangement	All races	White	Black	Hispanic origin[1]
Children under 18 years.	65,727	51,944	10,571	7,525
Living with—				
Two parents.	47,826	40,995	4,404	4,826
In a traditional nuclear family[2].	33,403	29,292	2,741	2,846
One parent	15,748	9,919	5,196	2,337
Mother only.	13,955	8,503	4,938	2,141
Father only	1,793	1,416	258	196
Grandparents only	1,099	469	570	100
Other.	689	385	262	110
Unknown[3]	365	175	138	152
Percent.	100.0	100.0	100.0	100.0
Living with—				
Two parents.	72.8	78.9	41.7	64.1
In a traditional nuclear family[2].	50.8	56.4	25.9	37.8
One parent	24.0	19.1	49.2	31.1
Mother only.	21.2	16.4	46.7	28.5
Father only	2.7	2.7	2.4	2.6
Grandparents only	1.7	0.9	5.4	1.3
Other.	1.0	0.7	2.5	1.5
Unknown[3]	0.6	0.3	1.3	2.0

[1]Persons of Hispanic origin may be of any race.

[2]Children in a traditional nuclear family live with both biological parents and, if siblings are present, with full brothers and sisters. No other household members are present.

[3]Data on living arrangements are missing for these children.

Source: Furukawa, Stacy. (1994). *The Diverse Living Arrangements of Children: Summer 1991.* U.S. Bureau of the Census, Series P70, No. 38. Washington, DC: U.S. Government Printing Office.

think it may be unrealistic for 95 percent of adults in our culture to sustain one marriage throughout their lives with a person they chose in the early years of their adult development. An increase in life expectancy means that adults have more years to spend in their husband-wife relationship. Learning brings different opportunities to people. Life events affect individuals differently, and the women's movement has helped redefine a satisfactory marriage as one that involves much more of a balance of power between partners.

In 1987, of 11 million remarried families in the United States, approximately half contained children under the age of 18. The remainder had no children from previous marriages, or the children were over 18. There are 4.3 million stepfamily households represented among these remarried families because these remarried couples *brought* to the new household children of previous marriages (Glick, 1991).

There are 35 million stepparents in America, and by the late 1980s, 1,300 stepfamilies were being formed every day. One out of every five children has a stepparent, and, by the late 1990s, more children will be living in second marriages or in single-parent families than in first marriages. In the last quarter of this century, the United States divorce rate has been the highest in the world. Since half of all divorces involve children, and sixty percent of divorced persons remarry, the number of stepfamilies is on the rise. In 1980, forty percent of all marriages in the United States were remarriages for at least one partner. This is in contrast to the early part of the century, when a child had a stepparent more often due to the death of a biological parent. By 1990, 60 percent of marriages were remarriages, more often due to divorce (Coontz, 1992).

One fact that is often ignored in discussing these data is that life expectancy has increased greatly since the early 1900s. This means that there are now many more years of marriage to negotiate and sustain successfully. In 1992, because of increased life expectancy, the average woman faced forty or more years of life after the children leave home, compared with only 10 to 15 years for women in the early 1900s (Coontz, 1992).

Economic strains in the United States as a whole in the latter part of the twentieth century have created stress on all families. The economic status of American families with children has declined steadily since 1970. Economic stress has been particularly difficult for young families in their prime child-rearing years. The median income for families headed by someone under the age of thirty fell by approximately one-third, or thirty-two percent in real dollar income from 1973 to 1990 (National Commission on Children, 1993). When divorced or widowed parents create a stepfamily, there are financial and relationship obligations to children of previous marriages. Economic strains and the challenge of new relationships demand significant learning and cooperation toward shared goals for stepfamily members.

Stepfamilies are found in a variety of ethnic and racial groups (see Table 12–2). Many stepfamilies value unity to the point that they deny their actual remarriage, and may discount their history of other marriages or relationships. Successful completion of all phases of a previous divorce or widowhood enhances the ability of a couple to enter and maintain the stepfamily successfully.

While adults usually make personally oriented decisions to remarry, these may conflict with the desires and needs of their children. Children often do not accept their biological parents' divorce and fantasize about their remarriage to each other, even when the relationship was filled with conflict. As long as the parents have not remarried, the children can fantasize that their parents will remarry and reconstruct the original family unit. Once one parent remarries a new partner this fantasy dies, resulting in grief for the children.

Table 12–2.   *Children Living with Two Parents by Their Biological, Step, Adoptive, and Foster Status, by Race and Hispanic Origin: Summer 1991.*

[Numbers in thousands]

Characteristics of parents	All races	White	Black	Hispanic origin[1]
Children living with two parents	47,826	40,995	4,404	4,826
Biological mother and father	40,553	35,002	3,576	4,129
Biological mother and stepfather	3,672	3,195	351	367
Biological father and stepmother	830	740	40	43
Adoptive mother and father[2]	582	387	103	42
Foster mother and father[3]	195	147	48	–
Other	1,994	1,524	286	245
Percent distribution	100.0	100.0	100.0	100.0
Biological mother and father	84.8	85.4	81.2	85.6
Biological mother and stepfather	7.7	7.8	8.0	7.6
Biological father and stepmother	1.7	1.8	0.9	0.9
Adoptive mother and father[2]	1.2	0.9	2.3	0.9
Foster mother and father[3]	–	–	1.1	–
Other	4.2	3.7	6.5	5.1

– Represents zero, or a number that rounds to zero.

[1]Persons of Hispanic origin may be of any race.

[2]Children living with one biological parent and one adoptive parent have been placed in a biological parent/stepparent category.

[3]Foster relationships only include official placements by a government agency or representative of a government agency.

Source: Furukawa, Stacy. (1994). *The Diverse Living Arrangements of Children: Summer 1991.* U.S. Bureau of the Census, Series P70, No. 38. Washington, DC: U.S. Government Printing Office.

SOCIO-CULTURAL FOUNDATIONS

One of the major tasks for every stepfamily is the establishment of a new family structure with practices and celebrations that are new and unique to its members. Valuing the lessons learned from previous family experiences can enhance adjustment in the new stepfamily, but everyone must understand that the new family system is now more complex. There are more relatives to communicate with and individual family members have responsibilities to members from earlier marriages. The amount of resources and attention given to the new stepfamily, in contrast to relationships with previous spouses or with the children's other biological parents, is a continual negotiation process for the stepfamily.

Families report the need to negotiate continually the amount of time and attention given to each of the family subsystems. If the new relationships are good, the tendency is not to deal with transitions and not to maintain relationships with parts of the previous extended family. Ahrons and Rodgers (1987) proposed the concept of the *binuclear* or two-household family, which honors the previous marriages plus the present marriage. Their concept may be helpful to many stepfamilies. In a binuclear family, there are two centers of activity or decision-making instead of one.

Early studies often reported conflict involving the stepfather and the children living at home. Recent studies suggest that this conflict depends on (1) the amount of time that has elapsed since the original divorce, (2) the length of time in the new stepfamily, and (3) the gender of the children. Bray and Berger (1990) found a relationship between the child's psychological adjustment and the amount of contact the child had with the noncustodial parent. For boys living in stepfamilies after two and one-half to seven years, and girls living in stepfamilies after six months to seven years, there was no relationship between adjustment, contact, or closeness with the noncustodial father. However, during the immediate first six months in the new stepfamily for girls, and during the first two and a half years for boys, positive and enhanced relations with the noncustodial father increased the children's adjustment.

These results show that considerable time is needed for transitional grieving and for gradual entering into relationships in a new stepfamily. Ganong and Coleman's (1993) research with stepfamilies showed that stepchildren were a bigger concern for stepparents than stepsiblings were for each other. The researchers suggest that, overall, stepsiblings may not have high expectations of each other and usually maintain a measure of distance and neutrality. In contrast, stepparents feel responsible and may expect more obedience, attention, and affection from stepchildren than is realistic. Numerous authors comment that the stepparent role is the least rewarding and the most rarely appreciated role in family life. "You can wait your entire life for a thank you!" commented one stepfather.

New Parenting Roles

The new relationship formed by the two spouses in the family creates a system separate from the children. While this is true of any marriage, in a first marriage the spousal relationship has time to develop and stabilize before there are children in the home. However, in a stepfamily, there are immediately subsystems within the stepfamily that demand loyalties that may interfere with stepfamily unity. For example, children usually have a strong relationship with the biological parent in a new stepfamily, and with their absent biological parent. While the spouses are actively working on their relationship patterns and strengths, and children are adjusting to new stepparents and possibly new stepsiblings, common sense and a sense of humor are extremely helpful.

In actuality, *everyone* is learning new roles. If one stepparent has not previously had children, that individual is learning the parenting role upon entering the family. For most adults, the only parenting role with which they are familiar is the biological parenting role, or the one they enjoyed with their own biological parents. It is rare for a stepparent to enter a family with an awareness of how a stepparenting role may differ from the biological parenting role. Adults frequently feel that being a good stepparent is like being a good biological parent. The reality is sometimes a startling lesson.

Children's Perspectives of New Roles

In helping children understand the new stepfamily system and adjust to life within it, parents need to be extremely sensitive. Depending on the child's age and gender, different reactions can be expected. A child who had been the oldest child in the family and then enters a stepfamily with older children may be particularly threatened. Likewise, the child who may have been the only girl, or the only boy, and now has a stepsibling of the same gender can find this threatening. On the other hand, as Coleman and Ganong (1990) point out, many times these relationships present positive opportunities for growth for the people involved.

Since these new relationships are variations from the nuclear family, they are often viewed negatively by society. While it is clear that confusion and ambiguity may result from the addition of relatives and extended family members, these relationships can also provide more opportunities for greater nurturance and create a resiliency of variation and strength in the family. A number of stepchildren report that acquiring a stepparent in addition to their biological parents provides them with another adult to look to for guidance and counsel within a positive framework.

Stepchildren have particularly reported delight in acquiring new sets of grandparents who are positive about meeting stepchildren and are able to interact with them as new friends and family members. One of the amusing and creative areas of stepfamily life occurs around the names or titles used to refer to different family members. Most researchers agree that children should be encouraged to select their own name for their stepparent or stepgrandparents, rather than having a name imposed by the newly married couple. The variety of names given stepparents indicate whimsical and ambivalent feelings from children. The awkwardness of phrases like "my ex-sister-in-law," or "my ex-husband's new wife," indicate the inadequacy of our current language for such increasingly common relationships.

New Relationship Models

An interesting article by Crosbie-Burnett and Lewis (1993) suggests that a useful model for stepfamily relationships can be found in African-American families that have developed the strength to cope with family strain and disruption caused by external cultural pressures. Aunts and uncles, or fictive kin, who are important parts of the family but are not necessarily blood or legal relatives, can be a very positive part of the new, nontraditional family form.

These researchers suggest that African-American families have created flexibility in relationships through involving other people in the coparenting of children. This is primarily due to economic strains and limited cultural opportunities that reinforce the need for extended kin to assist in child rearing and to give general family support. Coontz (1992) comments that in a society with a concern for private control over family issues, this general support for children and parents usually is not available.

STATUS CHANGES

Stepfamilies occur in all social classes. However, the strains caused by lower income tend to create more divorce and fewer remarriages among families with less stable and less adequate economic resources. In addition, a stepfamily may give members a different status than their previous social, economic, or moral status within a community, neighborhood, or extended family group. In general, combining two adults and their children in a new family enhances status because it reflects a commitment to a family form that externally appears traditional, and supports the societal values of marriage and commitment. In addition, the stepfamily represents the strong American belief in risk-taking for new ventures.

The maintenance of positive family status generally depends on how well a stepfamily deals with the complexity of relationships and economic demands that are placed on the new family. Within particular religious groups, while remarried partners may be welcomed, the actual standing of the new family frequently depends on that group's view of divorce and serial monogamy. Since most research scholars have found that successful stepfamilies maintain positive and cooperative relationships with previous partners and the children's biological parents, the complexity of these relationships may be difficult for some religious groups to accept and support.

Changing Roles in Families

The role of the mother in a stepfamily has special significance because of the general societal expectation that women are the "kin-keepers," or the family relationship enhancers. Women entering stepfamilies usually feel a heightened sense of responsibility to make relationships work. Einstein and Albert (1987) describe unrealistic expectations in stepfamilies, linked to the image of a happy, harmonious group that finds immediate success.

Impacts on Children

A stepmother's first meeting with the children of her new spouse is often difficult. Her positive, skilled, and loving overtures may not be reciprocated by the children. At a time in which the two adults are positive about entering into a new relationship, they are also simultaneously faced with the tasks of assisting children with grieving the loss of the previous marriage and helping them move into new relationships. Women often are responsible for managing the parallel and conflicting emotions of these two developmental tasks for the family.

The area of greatest conflict for stepfamilies is dealing with children residing with the current marriage partners. The second most common area of conflict concerns financial matters. Peterson and Nord (1990) report that, when women remarry, there is a reduction in child support from the former husband. Evidently, the ex-husband feels some loss of responsibility and access to his children, and begins to provide child support less consistently. While it is difficult to know all of the reasons for child support being reduced under these circumstances, it is probable that the mother is then put in the position of having to negotiate, protest, and seek child support from her ex-spouse in order to demonstrate her loyalty and commitment to her new spouse and their economic plans. Creating a positive relationship to handle negotiation about child rearing with an ex-spouse may be a very difficult task for some women, particularly if there was intense conflict in the previous relationship.

Sex Role Ambiguities and Sexual Abuse

Family crisis literature presents increasing evidence of rape and other forms of sexual harassment and abuse in stepfamily settings. Family life professionals warn about the potential for coercive sexual relations when adults and youth enter a new stepfamily without a history of well-defined, nurturing relationships. Counselors and therapists working with stepfamilies need to be alert to the potential of abusive relationships when remarriage creates family intimacy and ambiguously defined new roles. Since most states mandate the reporting of sexual and physical abuse, families working with a reputable professional sign an initial release indicating they understand this obligation. Other professionals serving stepfamilies may need information to alert them to this potential for abuse and to the reporting obligation.

For both children and adults in stepfamilies, new relationships create some ambiguity in roles. Cherlin (1992) suggests that the need to create new role relationships in stepfamilies is a new challenge. Visher and Visher (1980) comment that one of the challenges for the new stepfamily is the lessening of taboos against sexual relationships among people who are not blood relatives, such as between new stepsiblings, or between a stepparent and child. Since stepmarriages are more often formed between parents with children in late elementary and junior and senior high school, issues that involve sexual development and sexual behavior are a normal part of the developmental stage. The literature on sexual abuse suggests that wife- and child-battering more often occurs in families with inadequate income marked by "constant competition over who will be taken care of" (Kempe, 1980). The task of establishing new relationships and allocating scarce resources between competing needs can generate frustration and anger in stepfamilies. In addition, incestuous fathers and stepfathers tend to be socially isolated and have an overly private approach to the family (Rush, 1980). The demand for flexibility and responsiveness required in forming new stepfamilies may be unsettling for some men and successful negotiation of positive sexual roles may be difficult.

Historically, one of the important functions of marriage and family life has been to define and provide support for socially sanctioned sexual relationships. Thus, stepfamilies create new threats to the social order. It is not unusual for one stepparent to be significantly older than the other, or for the two spouses to have children of greatly differing ages. For example, a mother with preschool children may find it disconcerting or threatening to become the stepparent of a teenager. Children and youth in stepfamilies may be vulnerable to inappropriate sexual advances from new stepsiblings or a stepparent. The fact that both family members and professionals are often naive about the potential for sexual assault or abuse is evidence that many Americans are not yet able to foresee the potential problems of new family forms realistically (Johnson, 1980).

CHANGING ROLES FOR FEMALES

There have been few high quality studies done on stepfamily functioning and patterns. Maglin and Schneidewind (1989) suggested that the shortage of guidelines has resulted in women and girls in stepfamilies feeling very isolated and without guidance for creating satisfying roles within stepfamilies. Our culture's view of the stepmother still tends to be dominated by the stereotype of the wicked stepmother in fairy tales. Nevertheless, many family scholars recommend that "stepfamily" as a title acknowledges the complicated, rich structures of families. They recommend against using the term "blended," which, like the concept of America as a melting pot, suggests the disappearance of individual differences and the erasing of previous family history.

A stepmother who parents her spouse's children is often haunted by the image of the absent, perfect, biological mother, in contrast to the image of a wicked stepmother. Women tend to have strong impulses to protect the mother-child bond. Thus, stepmothers are often in the awkward position of forging new bonds with a stepchild while trying to help the child maintain bonds with that perfect biological mother.

The role of the new wife may be distressing to other women in the husband's life (such as the ex-wife) and may likely create complications among women in extended stepfamilies. Stepmothers acknowledge that their relationship with an ex-husband's new wife is often marked by conflicting emotions. Such emotions are natural even while they recognize that the new wife may be doing most of the parenting of her husband's children from his former marriage.

An additional complication of this task is that while the newly married mother with custody of her children wants to protect the bond and intimacy she has with her children, at the same time she must create a new bond with her spouse. This conflict appears stronger for women than for men placed in similar situations. The essays in Maglin and Schneidewind (1989) give eloquent voice to women's pain when they try to make the stepfamily into a successful first-marriage family.

Changing Roles for Males

Studies show that fathers who receive custody of their children upon divorce have typically taken active parenting roles prior to the divorce. In 20 percent of stepfamilies, the father's biological children reside, while in 80 percent of stepfamilies, the mother's children reside with the new married partners. The perception of satisfaction with a marriage varies according to which spouse's children are residing in the stepfamily's home. The biological parent of the residential children is more apt to see the marriage and family as satisfying and intimate than the stepparent in that same family.

Researchers have noted that all children react to the remarriage of their custodial parents. However, preadolescent boys in stepfamilies seem to adjust better over time than preadolescent girls in stepfather families. The studies suggest that boys have a more difficult adjustment than girls living in single-mother families. Thus, the entry of a stepfather into the family system appears to facilitate adolescent male development and stability. However, the literature also contains many stories of the stepfather's struggle to find an appropriate role to play with his stepchildren.

Replacing a biological father or imitating a biological parent is usually an inappropriate role. New stepfathers should be sensitive to their ambiguous or precarious authority over stepchildren. Since men and women often view males as heavy discipliners, it is tempting to encourage stepfathers to take on a strong authoritarian role. In most stepfamilies, the children are more accepting of discipline from their biological parent, even though this may change traditional gender role patterns.

Most successful stepfathers find that playing the role of an uncle provides clear structure and an affectionate relationship without trying to replicate or replace the biological father.

CHANGES AS CHILDREN AGE

Stepfamilies continuously adjust to new relationships over time; thus, physical custody arrangements are often different than legal custody arrangements. Ganong and Coleman (1993) have shown that some children in stepfamilies change their physical living arrangements without changing their legal status. Changing residence without changing legal status is particularly common in adolescence. When relationships with adolescent males have been full of conflict in a stepfamily, the son often moves out of the biological mother-stepfather household and back to his biological father's residence. Heatherington (1989) noted that, in her research, stepfathers frequently were rebuffed in their initial attempt to become involved with their stepchildren in a positive way. Without sustained, positive attempts and strong support from their spouse, stepfathers tended to retreat and disengage themselves from their stepchildren's lives. This finding probably reflects the tremendous commitment and creativity needed to forge new skills for parenting roles in the stepfamily and the few social supports for enhancing parenting skills among men.

While stepparents and biological parents should spend some time with the children as an entire family, each parent also needs to take some time to spend with each child individually. A number of men in stepfamilies report that they felt independence and pride in forging their own relationships with children individually. In first-marriage families, wives often mediate the relationships between husbands and children because fathers are inexperienced in interacting with children. If men have more private relationships with their children and stepchildren, then a greater range of expressiveness for fathers will develop.

SOCIALIZATION OF CHILDREN

Realistic goals in a stepfamily involve the establishment of new harmonious relationships between children and their stepsiblings, between the children and the new stepparents, and between the children and their biological parents.

Children may have less access to their biological parent and more conflict over the new relationships which were determined by adult choices. Particularly in stepfamilies, it is very apparent to children that much of their world is determined by adult decisions, and they often feel angry and resentful of these new realities. Socialization skills for children in a stepfamily often need to include conflict resolution or negotiation skills for situations in which competing loyalties cause stress for the child. Children in stepfamilies are very clear about their anger over being put into positions in which they are disappointing one parent or another.

Children's adjustments are facilitated when stepfamilies can create friendly parenting alliances with biological parents. When the stepfamily is formed fairly soon after a divorce, children's adjustment is more complex. Many issues may still remain that are not resolved from the previous marriage, and children need time to adjust to the reality of new and different roles. Frequently the choices or loyalties of children are different from those of the parents. Conflicts often surround momentous events for children, such as high school graduation or a marriage ceremony—especially issues like who should be present and what roles extended members should play. If possible, a wise family facilitates the children's choices at these times.

Positive adjustment to stepparents occurs when there is protected time for relationship building or maintenance for each child, with both the biological parents and the stepparents. The maintenance of an appropriate visitation schedule with the biological noncustodial parent can reassure the child, sustain those relationships, and provide the new stepparents the time alone for enhancing the new marital relationship.

ROLES OF GRANDPARENTS AND OTHERS

The role of grandparents and additional extended family members in stepfamilies can be similar to the support role played in divorced families (see Chapter 11). Positive relationships can facilitate the transition to the stepfamily and sooth conflicts and fears on the part of both generations. Family counselors and family life practitioners often comment on the need for the grandparent generation to have education and support as they assimilate new roles, facilitate relationships, and deal with their own feelings of loss. Kennedy and Kennedy (1993) report that those who most valued grandparent relationships in their research study were young adults from stepfamilies. Kennedy and Kennedy believe that grandparents maintain a sense of family heritage and history that is comforting to young adults who need roots from which to explore their own development and growth.

ECOLOGICAL FACTORS

A number of systems affect stepfamilies and they, in turn, affect the systems with which they interact. A number of the systems within the ecological system will be discussed.

Demographics

The number of stepfamilies in the United States is difficult to accurately determine, since the data are not all routinely reported. While it is believed that approximately forty million stepfamilies existed in the United States in 1990, these data do not include unmarried couples living together, and same-sex couples who define themselves as stepfamilies. Due to the lower marriage rate among African-Americans, the percentage of divorces among African-Americans is lower as is the percentage of remarriages. Crosbie-Burnett and Lewis (1993) compared white middle-class stepparents struggling with new kinship relationships to the complex relationships in the African-American community. Permeability of family boundaries, parallel parenting households, or parenting alliances that cross over biological or legal role definitions are some of the strengths of the African-American families that can be instructive to many stepfamilies.

Aesthetics

Much of our popular culture creates a romanticized myth of stepfamilies through such portrayals as "The Brady Bunch," a popular television program of the 1970s and 1980s; "Cheaper by the Dozen," the 1920s novel made into a 1950s movie; the 1970s movie, "Yours, Mine and Ours"; and recent television programs such as "My Two Dads," "Full House," "Getting By," "Step by Step," and "Hearts Afire." These examples provide an overly optimistic view of stepfamilies (Ganong and Coleman, 1986). Calling the stepfamily "reconstituted" or "blended" suggests that marital history can be ignored and that a new family form can emerge in some different blend. Such pictures belie the cultural struggle involved in the reality of stepfamilies.

Many transitions in a society are first portrayed in the humor and personal literature of the culture. This is certainly true for stepfamilies. Maglin's (1989) review of stepfamily fiction reveals that stories of stepfamilies often exonerate men and place heavy responsibility for a stepfamily's success on women. Maglin and Schneidewind's *Women and Stepfamilies: Voices of Anger and Love* portrays personal literature by stepmothers with intense emotion, humor, and celebration. Literature of this type will become more available in public markets as stepfamilies, and the need to explore positive variation, are accepted by more Americans. These authors suggest that democratic and cooperative relationships can make a special contribution to life in stepfamilies. The two authors advise that this success rests on women giving up an overly responsible "good mother" myth and replacing it with a picture of a "mature adult woman" who develops effective interactions with both women and men in the extended stepfamily.

Education

In general, stepfamilies show a higher level of education than families that are first marriages or single-parent families. This is partly because stepfamilies are often formed later in adults' lives, after more education has been acquired. The other contributing variable is that social class is generally correlated with a higher frequency of marriages. The divorce and remarriage rates, therefore, are somewhat higher among more highly educated persons.

One specific economic challenge in stepfamilies is the high cost of education for the children. Since only one in four divorced women receives the full court-ordered support for her children, and divorce decrees often do not include the costs of college education, many stepfamilies find their children's educational costs a heavy burden on the family. In addition to the lack of child support enforcement, there are problems that surround the legal responsibility of the stepparents to their stepchildren. The finding that divorced mothers receive lower child support in a new stepfamily may relate to the pattern of fathers paying for the expenses of the children in their new marriage. When a divorce and remarriage involve extreme conflict between the biological parents, consistent economic support for many child expenses, including postsecondary education, has often been problematic. Funds for college should be a point of negotiation in divorce settlements.

Religion

Most religious communities welcome stepfamilies. Indeed, a number of congregations have created special marriage ceremonies for stepfamilies that honor their family history and provide a role for the children in the wedding ceremony. Particularly because of the commitment involved in a religious remarriage ceremony, congregations are glad to assist in the stabilization of this family form.

For the stepfamily, marriage in a religious community may be both positive and negative. The positive effects are confirming of one's faith, and placing the new family within a supportive religious community. However, there can be a tendency for the newly married stepfamily to believe that using the symbols of the first-marriage religious community erases the real differences in the stepfamily. While one can easily light a symbolic candle in a marriage ceremony, establishing new rules for discipline, forging a widening array of new relationships, and accessing and distributing resources in a stepfamily are far more complex. The need for on-going support, faith, and creativity in the new stepfamily cannot be overemphasized.

Health Care

Access to health care and family planning in stepfamilies is correlated strongly with income, social class, and residence. While many children are born into stepfamilies, those data are not readily available. Couples need to be especially clear about their decision to have more children. Ages of both spouses can be a significant factor. The decision to have more children may be different if one parent has no previous children than if both are already parents. The total number of family members the two parents can support, both emotionally and financially, needs to be considered. At any rate, birth control should be used until relationships are clarified, just as in early marriages. The most difficult issues around health may involve who should provide on-going health care benefits for the children of previous marriages.

Economic Factors

Stepfamilies typically consist of both spouses being in the workforce, both parents having independently headed households before the marriage and having invested in careers. In addition, being a dual-career family probably relates to the high cost of raising children, to the possibility that one of the spouses has to maintain economic support for children from a previous marriage, and to long-range economic security. That is, once a spouse has experienced a marriage breakup or the death of a spouse, any economic independence achieved is very difficult to give up.

Housing is one of the important economic and relationship decisions for the stepfamily. It is usually not a good idea for the family to live in a residence that was formerly the residence of one of the marriage partners. This can cause territorial feelings for those people who resided in the house previously, or cause them to be protective of their space and to resent change and intrusion. On the other hand, literature on children's transition through divorce and remarriage stresses the importance of maintaining continuity and relationships for the children in neighborhoods and schools. Sometimes these two objectives can conflict, and the family must make tough decisions about how to establish a new home that is fair to everyone involved and gives them all a chance for new interpersonal relationships.

When economic realities or market conditions suggest the wisdom of remaining in one of the adults' current residences, remodeling, redecorating, or reassigning space to facilitate the new relationships needs to be considered. It is particularly important that children of late elementary and junior and senior high school age have private space away from the parents' space. Such designs are sometimes difficult to find except in higher-priced housing.

When a divorced or widowed woman with dependent children remarries, her financial status typically improves. However, a divorced man who remarries typically assumes more financial responsibility and often feels torn between the financial demands of the two families. Stepfamilies bring their financial history from earlier marriages into the new relationship. The new marriage has more complex relationships and, perhaps, more sources of income, so new patterns of handling money may be needed. Aside from spousal employment, support payments (and their inconsistency) and money and gifts from noncustodial parents and relatives are additional sources of income. The pattern of pooling all sources of income seems to increase the stability of the new marriage. However, it may be necessary to keep separate records of how money for child support is spent. Spouses may wish for a measure of financial independence, too.

Government Policies and Agencies

Stepfamilies have dealt with the court responsible for granting divorces, and many have dealt with the Department of Social Services enforcement division for child support, or Aid to Families with Dependent Children (AFDC). The lack of legal standing for a stepparent with regard to the stepchildren may cause concern.

Stepparents who are strongly committed to their new family frequently voice frustration and confusion over their legal responsibility for their stepchildren in matters of health care. Legal guardianship usually remains with the biological parents until they die or give up legal responsibility for their children.

In situations where the biological noncustodial parent agrees, stepparents can legally adopt their stepchildren. When a single, never-married parent marries, there are ambiguous interpretations of statutes surrounding the parental rights of the noncustodial biological parent. When a single person without children marries a person with children, the new stepparent may have especially favorable feelings toward adopting the stepchildren. These new family relationships point out the need to revise policies that are now outdated and inadequate.

In situations where children have lived for many years with a stepparent, and that remarriage ends in divorce, ambiguity about that stepparent's legal standing gives little support to the maintenance of relationships with the children.

Children report that when their parent and stepparent divorced, after establishing a caring relationship with a stepparent, they found no legal protection for that relationship. In addition, if a custodial biological parent dies prematurely, the children may be placed in the custody of the surviving noncustodial biological parent, even though they have been living happily with and were being nurtured by a stepparent who desires to continue that role. Grandparent relationships also are often severed by death or divorce.

FAMILY INTERACTIONS AND KINSHIP NETWORKS

Extended family interactions in divorce and remarriage can be either supportive or harmful. Stepfamilies create an increasing number of relationships, and there must be negotiations about the intensity of involvement, the scheduling, and decision-making power in extended family relationships. A new stepfamily needs to establish its own practices, but also honor the connections to meaningful relationships that were established prior to the marriage.

Patience and creativity on the part of the new family members are needed. Honesty and clear negotiation with extended family members are important. Stepparents frequently report that the extended family members provide helpful respite care for children or continuity of relationships while the newly married pair establish their own patterns and take time for nurturing their relationship.

Strength and satisfaction in the marital relationship are strong predictors of satisfaction and endurance of the first marriage, according to most family literature. However, within stepfamilies, the satisfaction with or the lack of conflict between stepparent and stepchildren is the most powerful determinant of family satisfaction and endurance. Therefore, it is important for extended family members to help stabilize and encourage positive stepparent-stepchild relationships and to provide support and nurturance for the new family. Understanding and flexibility can help maintain realistic and caring connections with the new stepfamily.

CHANGE AND ADAPTATION

The stepfamily that arises after divorce is a relatively new reality in American society, and many of our social and educational systems are not yet sensitive to the needs of this family type. Due to negative societal attitudes and inadequate information, many stepfamilies struggle alone with very complex challenges. The adaptations required in a stepfamily often challenge ideas about how resources should be shared, how children should be raised, and how families should function. Many adults entering stepfamilies have not had informed professional support in making their decision and planning for this new family form. Men in particular have been socialized to a more domineering role, allowing less flexibility in the family. A stepfather needs to create a new role with stepchildren and with other extended family members. Professionals working with stepfamilies find that over time the rules and relationships often change. Stepfamilies need to remain flexible and responsive to members' needs.

Just as divorce studies suggested that a period of 18 to 24 months following a divorce is necessary to reintegrate and balance the new family structure, stepfamilies also report a need to adjust and change over time. Stepfamilies with adolescent children seem to be particularly stressed by divided loyalties, challenges to family decisions, and the competing activities of peer groups. Noncustodial parents, trying to maintain healthy relationships with their adolescents, find that individual time with their children is increasingly difficult to arrange. Noncustodial parents usually find it necessary to travel to the community where their children reside in order to participate in school and community activities during their children's adolescent years. Similarly, stepfamilies find that attendance at school and community events quickly makes them confront the challenge of maintaining positive communication with ex-spouses—the children's biological parents.

Over time, many children in stepfamilies may change their residence, as conflict increases, or as the need for different resources becomes apparent. Adolescents nearing college age may move to the community of their other biological parent in order to qualify for residential status near an institution of higher education. Other young people may change their residence in order to be in a job market that provides more employment opportunities for a young person who is saving for college or other goals. Parents may find that much of their relationship has to be maintained by phone or letters.

New stepfamilies often find that extended family members are usually immediately positive and initiate invitations for the new family to join in. Following this initial enthusiasm, a comfortable pattern of inclusion and support must evolve. As children in stepfamilies mature, maintaining relationships with a variety of extended family members can be very positive. While conflicts may emerge between a stepparent and child, a supportive grandparent, aunt, or uncle may facilitate the maintenance of family bonds. Children benefit from the richness of all the relationships that support positive development, resulting in a stepfamily that works well together.

One of the most difficult periods of time for all stepfamilies comes when the family members recognize that life is complicated and that active negotiation skills are needed. The fantasized myths portrayed in literature, or imagined by two adults during the courting period, must be laid to rest before positive, realistic family patterns can be accepted. When harmony and effectiveness are not achieved automatically, a stepfamily can become discouraged at their lack of success. Professionals and other stepfamilies can be key supporters, providing humor, support, and realistic family plans.

SERVING STEPFAMILIES

Research and counseling literature give a number of helpful guidelines for professionals serving and supporting stepfamilies. Your attitudes and any discomfort over language barriers and topics related to these should be discussed with both parents and all children.

Inadequacy of Agency Forms

The forms used by social service agencies frequently do not provide adequate spaces or correct titles to account for all members of the household or family. Enrollment forms frequently only ask for parent names. Stepfamilies are then confused about whether they should list custodial parents, stepparents, or biological parents, or, for reasons of insurance or emergencies, only the person with the health care policy, etc. These examples illustrate the need to modernize our processes and procedures for gaining accurate information about families in order to serve them well. Including the names of persons important to the children and their relationships would aid educational discussions as well as decision-making sessions with professionals.

Support Groups

As children and youth enter stepfamilies, it is important to remember that their attitudes are likely to be different from those of the adults. While it is important to acknowledge and celebrate changes with children, in their school, youth group, social setting, church, or synagogue, one should be sensitive to the children's feelings about these changes. A public announcement about a new stepfamily may need to be accompanied by special private time with a professional in which the child or youth has a chance to express confusion, fears, and concerns about the new family form. Professionals serving these families should acknowledge children's feelings, helping them deal with these significant transitions. Encouraging children to provide drawings or photographs of everyone in their family and to talk about the new relationships are important parts of this process. Support groups among children and youth, led by a professional skilled in identifying the expected struggles of children in transition, are also helpful.

Family conferences, where decisions about children are made, should include all relevant adults involved with the children. Family nights or intergenerational programs should make families feel welcome to bring both the biological and stepparents to celebrate with the child. Children and youth are often not certain whether their new family form is acceptable in the wider community. Professionals, supportive of children, can initiate positive introductions and interactions among the group of parents and extended family members.

Ask the legal guardians directly about who the young child can be released to, and what information can be shared with other significant adults. School evaluation sessions, report cards, and news about neighborhood youth events can then be shared with both of the child's households.

The goal of your relationships with stepfamilies, as a professional, is to facilitate good family relationships and the child's growth and development in the new family. Literature and media pieces that include references to stepfamilies and information sources for stepfamilies will provide help and make this family form more visible and supported in the wider environment. A stepfamily is not just like a first-marriage family. Both biological and stepparents should be included in discussions about family issues.

Encouraging children and youth to invent new names and special rituals with new relatives will also help in their adjustment. New rules need to be developed for the specifics of each particular stepfamily. When a young person has been living with a single parent, the inclusion of the new stepparent in personal decisions or in household work discussions can be frustrating and awkward. Helping a stepparent and stepchild negotiate new rules with a third party can be an important function for a sensitive professional. Examples might include helping a child learn how to introduce a stepparent, or what family matters need to be discussed by both parents before a decision is made.

Attempts to make the stepfamily like a family from another era or structure are inappropriate. Organization in this new family requires intelligence, good humor, and creativity on everyone's part. Professionals can sometimes play key roles in providing new perspectives, approval, and acceptance of new family rituals and relationships. When children's entrance into a stepfamily results in a move away from friends, professionals can help with this transition. Youth organizations, for example scout troops, sometimes have farewell celebrations for the child. In addition, providing photographs for the children to take with them and some ways the children can keep in contact, either by phone or by letters, are important transition supports for their new life structure.

Many stepfamilies are unaware of the national and local support groups for stepfamilies. The Stepfamily Association of America and the Stepfamily Foundation, Inc. both have educational and advocacy information for members. Consult the names and addresses at the end of this chapter for information. All professionals who are in regular contact with families should also be members of these organizations in order to receive their materials. The latest accurate and positive information can then be shared with co-workers and clients.

CONCLUSIONS

The stepfamily is one form of families that will be increasing in the United States during the coming years. While there are social class differences in the numbers of stepfamilies, they increasingly involve people from all ethnic and cultural groups in the United States. Many families with similar structures are not considered stepfamilies. Cohabiting heterosexual adults or homosexual adults with their children from previous marriages often function as stepfamilies but are not counted as such. A number of adults in such relationships do not divorce and/or remarry due to religious, legal, or economic considerations. When public assistance, child support, or alimony terminates upon a parent's remarriage, some parents make the decision to forego legal marriage in order to maintain economic security. Such personal decisions reflect the inadequacy of family law, public policies, and society in dealing with new family forms.

A stepfamily involves relationships that are more complex than first marriages, even though many stepfamilies pretend they are just like first-marriage families. The legal system in the U.S. has largely neglected stepfamilies and our social systems are not prepared to understand and support these relationships.

For stepfamilies to succeed, it is important to understand the diversity and complexity of new roles. Dealing honestly and openly with the differences in each of the family members' perspectives and needs is important. While the divorce rate is somewhat higher among stepfamilies than first-marriage families, adults seem generally satisfied with their second choices. Relationships with the children in stepfamilies is a significant key to the success and stability of the marriage. Professionals who provide transition groups for stepchildren, and for children and parents together, are delivering an important service to these families.

Finally, stepfamilies provide opportunities to understand and recognize the joys and complexity of diverse families. Positive supportive messages from you, as a helping professional, will go a long way toward helping these families deal realistically with challenges. The myths of the wicked stepmother and the "blended" family group should disappear with recognition that successful stepfamilies are flexible, complex, and resilient positive family forms.

STUDY QUESTIONS

1. What are the negative implications of the terms "blended" families or "reconstituted" families?
2. Currently, how many first marriages in the United States end in divorce? How many remarriages end in divorce?
3. What three major trends have increased the number of stepfamilies in this country?
4. Why do some stepfamilies deny they are a remarried couple?

5. What are the most important predictors of a strong, enduring stepfamily?

6. Why is it recommended that a stepfamily move into a new home rather than remain in the present house of one of the partners?

7. Describe ideal roles for a stepfather and a stepmother.

8. List the positive and negative aspects of being in a stepfamily for children.

9. List ways the extended family members can show support for stepfamily members.

10. Why are some professionals concerned about incest or sexual abuse in stepfamilies?

11. Describe the typical stepfamily as far as custody and residence of children.

12. How do the tasks for children entering a new stepfamily differ from the tasks of their parents?

13. How does the media view of stepfamilies interfere with positive stepfamily adjustments?

APPLICATIONS

1. Investigate whether there are Stepfamily Association affiliate groups in your local community, and attend a meeting of this group. Report on the issues raised and on the various family forms represented.

2. Interview stepfamilies who are willing to talk about their current family structure. Make certain to complete a genogram of the family, which includes a chart of all the significant biological, legal and fictive kin relationships.

3. Obtain copies of the Stepfamily Association of America Newsletter and report on the central themes of articles.

4. Watch a popular, current television show that portrays a stepfamily. Make up a list of the challenges to discuss in class.

5. Reflect on the power and psychological implications of stepparents having no legal right or responsibilities towards their stepchildren. Interview a stepparent on this topic and write a one-page summary of his or her experiences and recommendations.

6. Design a family bonding ritual for a new stepmother with two biological children, and a stepfather with a biological son. Consider topics that should be included and activities to bond the new family form.

7. Design a family schedule for vacations and holidays for a stepfamily of five with two children in custody of the father and one child from the wife's previous marriage not in her custody.

8. Write a two-page essay on the implications of a new stepfamily being formed before the social and psychological divorces from the previous marriages have been completed.

9. Create a set of rules for establishing a family budget in a new step-family with children from two previous marriages and two working parents.
10. Write a one-page essay on the advantages of viewing a stepfamily from a *binuclear* view.
11. Obtain the school enrollment and the emergency forms from a local school district. Write a brief summary of whether they are appropriate for the relationships in a new stepfamily.

REFERENCES

Ahrons, C. R., and Rodgers, R. H. (1987). *Divorced families: A multidisciplinary view.* New York, NY: Norton.

Austin, James F. (1993). The impact of school policies on noncustodial parents. *Journal of Divorce and Remarriage, 20*(3/4), 153–170.

Bray, J. M., and Berger, S. H. (1990). Noncustodial father and paternal grandfather relationships in stepfamilies. *Family Relations, 39,* 414–419.

Buehler, Cheryl, and Legg, B. H. (1993). Mothers' receipt of social support and their psychological well-being following marital separation. *Journal of Family Issues, 14*(1), 21–38.

Cherlin, A. J. (1992). *Marriage, divorce and remarriage.* Cambridge, MA: Harvard University Press.

Coleman, M., and Ganong, L. (1990). Personal communication. Colombia, MO.

Coleman, M., and Ganong, L. (1990). Remarriage and stepfamily research in the 1980s: Increased interest in an old family form. *Journal of Marriage and the Family, 52,* 925–940.

Coontz, Stephanie. (1992). *The way we never were.* New York, NY: Basic Books.

Crosbie-Burnett, M., and Lewis, Edith A. (1993). Use of African American family structures and functioning to address the challenges of European American postdivorce families. *Family Relations, 42*(3), 243–246.

DeMaris, A., and Greif, G. L. (1992). The relationship between family structure and parent-child relationship problems in single father households. *Journal of Divorce and Remarriage, 18*(1–2), 55–77.

Donnelly, D., and Finkelhor, D. (1993). Who has joint custody? Class differences in the determination of custody arrangements. *Family Relations, 42*(1), 57–61.

Duran-Aydintug, C. (1993). Relationships with former in-laws: Normative guidelines and actual behavior. *Journal of Divorce and Remarriage, 19*(3–9), 69–82.

Einstein, Elizabeth, and Albert, Linda. (1986). *Strengthening stepfamilies.* Falls Church, VA: American Guidance.

Einstein, Elizabeth, and Albert, Linda. (1987). *Pitfalls and possibilities.* Ithaca, New York: The Step-Family Living Series.

Ephron, Delia. (1986). *Funny sauce: Us, the ex, the ex's new mate, the new mate's ex and the kids.* New York, NY: Viking Press.

Fine, M. A., and Fine, D. R. (1992). Recent changes in law affecting stepfamilies: Suggestions for legal reform. *Family Relations, 41,* 334–340.

Furukawa, Stacy. (1994). *The diverse living arrangements of children: Summer 1991.* U.S. Bureau of the Census, Series P70, No. 38. Washington, DC: U.S. Government Printing Office.

Ganong, L., and Coleman, M. (1986). A comparison of clinical and empirical literature on children in stepfamilies. *Journal of Marriage and the Family, 48,* 309–318.

Ganong, L., and Coleman, M. (1993). An exploratory study of step-sibling subsystems. *Journal of Divorce and Remarriage, 19*(3–4), 125–141.

Ganong, L., and Coleman, M. (1993). A meta-analytic comparison of the self-esteem and behavior problems of stepchildren to children in other family structures. *Journal of Divorce and Remarriage, 19*(3–4), 143–163.

Gigy, L., and Kelly, J. B. (1992). Reasons for divorce: Perspectives of divorcing men and women. *Journal of Divorce and Remarriage, 18*(1–2), 169–187.

Glick, P. C. (1989). Remarried families, stepfamilies and stepchildren: A brief demographic profile. *Family Relations, 38,* 24–27.

Glick, P. C. (1991). *Parents with young stepchildren and with adult stepchildren: A demographic profile.* Paper presented at the annual meeting of the Stepfamily Association of America, Lincoln, NE.

Gold, Joshua M., Bubenzer, Donald M., and West, John D. (1993). Differentiation from ex-spouses and step-family marital intimacy. *Journal of Divorce and Remarriage, 19*(3), 83–6.

Heatherington, E. M. (1989). Coping with family transitions: Winners, losers and survivors. *Child Development, 60,* 1–14.

Johnson, H. C. (1980). Working with stepfamilies: Principles of practice. *Journal of Social Work, 50,* 304–308.

Kempe, Harry C. (1980). Incest and other forms of sexual abuse. In Henry C. Kempe and Ray E. Helfer (Eds.), *The battered child* (pp. 41–53). Chicago, IL: University of Chicago Press.

Kennedy, Gregory E., and Kennedy, C. E. (1993). Grandparents: A special resource for children in step-families. *Journal of Divorce and Remarriage, 19*(3–4), 45–68.

Maglin, Nan Bauer. (1989). Reading stepfamily fiction. In Nan Bauer Maglin and Nancy Schneidewind (Eds.), *Women and stepfamilies: Voices of anger and love* (pp. 67–85). Philadelphia, PA: Temple University Press.

Maglin, Nan Bauer, and Schneidewind, Nancy. (Eds.). (1989). *Women and stepfamilies: Voices of anger and love.* Philadelphia: Temple University Press.

Miller, G. (1993). The psychological best interests of the child. *Journal of Divorce and Remarriage, 19*(1–2), 21–39.

Mulroy, Elizabeth A. (Ed.). (1988). *Women as single parents.* Dover, MA: Auburn House Publishing Co.

National Commission on Children. (1993). *Just the Facts.* Washington, DC: U.S. Government Printing Office.

Newman, B., Skopin, A. R., and McKerry, P. C. (1993). Influences on the quality of stepfather-adolescent relationships: Views of both family members. *Journal of Divorce and Remarriage, 19*(3–4), 181–196.

Peterson, J. L., and Nord, C. W. (1990). The regular receipt of child support: A multistep process. *Journal of Marriage and the Family, 52,* 539–551.

Ramsey, S. H. (1986). Stepparent support of stepchildren: The changing legal context and the need for empirical policy research. *Family Relations, 35,* 363–369.

Rush, Florence. (1980). *The best kept secret: Sexual abuse of children.* Englewood Cliffs, NJ: Prentice-Hall.

Visher, E. B., and Visher, J. S. (1980). Stepfamilies are different. *Journal of Family Therapy, 7,* 9–18.

Wallerstein, J. S., and Kelly, J. (1980). *Surviving the breakup: How children and parents cope with divorce.* New York, NY: Basic Books.

Whitehead, Barbara Dafoe. (1993, April 4). Dan Quayle was right. *The Atlantic Monthly,* p. 271.

Zinn, Maxine Baca. (1992). Family, race and poverty in the eighties. In Barrie Thorne (Ed.), *Rethinking the family* (pp. 71–90). Boston, MA: NYU Press.

FURTHER READING

Burns, Cherie. (1985). *Stepmotherhood: How to survive without feeling frustrated, left out or abused.* New York, NY: Harper & Row.

Thayer, Nancy. (1981). *Stepping.* London: Sphere Books.

Wolkoff, Judith. (1982). *Happily ever after . . . almost.* New York: Dell.

Visher, E., and Visher, S. S. (1988). *Old loyalties, new ties.* New York, NY: Brunner Nagel.

ORGANIZATIONS

The Stepfamily Association of America. 602 East Joppa Rd., Baltimore, MD 21204. (301) 823-7570.

Stepfamily Foundation, Inc. 333 West End Ave., New York, NY 10023.

CHAPTER 13

Families with Challenged Members

Key Concepts

◆ Early Intervention Program
◆ Individual Service Plan
◆ Least Restrictive Environment
◆ Partnering
◆ Individualized Family Service Plan

Kids often stare at her and ask what's wrong with her. I don't mind, because I tell them how being different makes her special. But when she's older, will she have any friends?

Will other kids' curiosity turn into taunting? It really hits me at the playground that Laura will never be normal. All the other kids are running and climbing and she needs my help. The oddity is that she has a great time while I get depressed.

— Father of a child with special needs

Families with members who are physically, emotionally, or cognitively challenged are a population that needs support and flexible educational and social service systems. These families as a group do not represent a specific structure, social class, or ethnicity. Rather, challenged members are found in families of single parents, stepparents, communal cohabiting, homosexual partners and across all ethnic groups. Obviously both children and adults can have special challenges, but this chapter will focus largely on families with challenged children. Successful nurturing of a challenged child places unique demands on the family, no matter what its structure. Many parents of children with special needs talk about the dramatic change in their lives after the clear diagnosis of a disability in their child.

PARTNERING WITH PARENTS

Parents need the partnering with professionals embodied in the new concept of service for families with a disabled or challenged member. According to Hudgens et al. (1989), chronic illness and disabling conditions are "powerful forces

that often control the structure, actions, and reactions of family members. They can affect sweeping changes in family roles, realign subsystems within the family, and isolate family members from each other and outside influences" (p. 68). Many professionals say this group "does not discriminate. You can join at any time." Disabilities often develop from accidents resulting from the actions of someone else, creating a life-long challenge.

The powerful influence that a specifically challenged family member can have on the rest of the system has been described by many social workers, educators and researchers. The family members have to cope with problems that usually don't exist for children without disabilities. There are questions about appropriate child care, finances for special services, and practical problems of relationship building and family care roles. There are also fundamental questions about how much independence a child can achieve, what kind of support these children will need to cope with certain challenges, and what the future holds.

Families face a lifetime of concern for a disabled child. As noted in the opening vignette, parents have strong reactions of grief, depression, and fear as they struggle with meeting their child's needs. Dramatic changes in laws and in the models of services for persons with disabilities have opened up many possibilities for children and their families. However, many challenged children live in communities, neighborhoods, and families that may not know about the availability of or fully take advantage of benefits from recently enhanced services. As professionals serving families, you need to know how to partner with these families, and how to make certain that they receive information about all services for which they are eligible. This information must be provided in ways that enable the family to participate fully in decision-making about services to their child.

The new model of an Individualized Family Service Plan (IFSP), provided for in the 1986 federal law, Education of the Handicapped Amendments (P.L. 99-457), is a clear statement of a service philosophy toward persons with disabilities. However, at the same time that this new philosophy provides better partnerships between systems for the provision of services, the economic strains in the United States have caused resentment and conflict over the cost and appropriateness of a variety of services. Professionals who serve families with challenged members need skills in understanding advocacy, in interpreting public laws, and in coping with the realities of public opinion and public criticism of special services for children with disabilities. Helping those with disabilities become personally independent and economically self-sufficient are important goals for the country.

HISTORICAL BACKGROUND

Significant progress in advocacy and legislation for persons with disabilities was achieved in the U.S. during the 1970s and 1980s. This progress came on the heels of a general societal concern supporting advocacy for women and minorities, leading to some achievements in the civil rights arena. There are now clear statements in public law reinforcing the commitment to inclusiveness in education and social services and to involving families as partners in creating appropriate services for their family members. It is important to recognize that this new method of working with families is a departure from earlier periods in our history. If you review models of services for persons with disabilities in the late 1800s and early 1900s, treatment could be labeled as benign neglect. In other words, families were left to take care of their own members. If the child or young person did not readily fit into services or education provided to other children and youth, the family was expected to create needed services on their own. For persons with extreme disabilities, there were references to abandonment or to accidents that appeared deliberate or the result of neglect. Public institutions were at best custodial, and, at worst, physically and psychologically abusive.

Segregation

Families struggled alone with challenged members well into the twentieth century. Change came slowly as a result of aggressive actions on the part of a few social reformers and the publication of works such as Ward's (1946) *The Snake Pit*. As part of these reform efforts, family members and their advocates began increasingly to understand that the provision of services for persons with disabilities would not be made available unless family members themselves, who were most knowledgeable about the realities, became aggressive and eloquent spokespersons. Their actions resulted in an increasing number of special services that today would be labeled "segregated service." During this period of time, there was an attempt to provide education and social services, but always segregated or separated from other children and youth who were receiving public education and social services. There was little thought that these children could become economically self-sufficient or included in the whole community.

Mainstreaming

As families and advocates continued to protest and educate the broader public and the policymakers, significant federal legislation introduced an era of integrated services, bringing with it the term "mainstreaming." In 1975, the Education for All Handicapped Children's Act (Public Law 94-142) was passed, mandating that all states must provide a free and appropriate education for all children. A key provision of the law was the development of an Individualized Educational Plan (IEP) for each child and a commitment to serve the child in the "least restrictive environment." Under this philosophy of service, children were placed with their age peers in "mainstream" educational services. For example, children who were "learning disabled" spent time in a resource room with a specially trained teacher only for those subjects most directly impacted by the learning disability. At other times they participated in classes and social interaction with their age peers.

This era of "mainstreaming," or integrated services, had both positive and negative results. In a very positive sense, more children were allowed access to a variety of services and experiences in their education. Their lives were enhanced by these opportunities and they became more visible in the community. On the other hand, the federal law, which mandates these services, creates an imperative for school districts to provide appropriate services for children with special needs even when they are financially unable to do so. Some children with disabilities require extensive and sophisticated teaching and support in mainstream environments. When teachers have not been adequately prepared in pre-service or in-service training, they cannot provide appropriate education for children with disabilities and at the same time adequately teach all students in the classroom. Public Law 94-142 has implications for teacher education. Many colleges and universities are still enhancing their curricula to respond to these demands. Teachers who were trained before the pre-service curriculum prepared them for students with disabilities needed special in-service opportunities and on-going consultation.

Partnerships

The latest era of service models for children with disabilities could be labeled a partnership, that is, a family-based model for education and services, linking the entire family and the professional. While Public Law 94-142 of 1975 required that parents be present at the Individualized Educational Plan (IEP) meetings and sign off on plans, there was still strong emphasis on the parent as a recipient of professional recommendations. Subsequently, three relevant public laws have been passed.

Federal Legislation

The first was Public Law 99-457 of 1986. Part H of this act added to the Education of the Handicapped Act. This new act, known as the "Early Intervention Act," requires states to establish comprehensive multidisciplinary systems for early intervention services to infants and toddlers. With this act, schools became responsible for providing appropriate educational services for challenged children and youth from birth through age twenty-five.

In 1991, Public Law 102-52 gave states the option of taking two additional years to develop a system for serving all eligible children in their state. In October of 1991, Public Law 102-119 reauthorized the early intervention part of the Education of the Handicapped Act and strengthened its family partnership provisions. These last three laws are known as IDEA, or the Individuals with Disabilities Education Act. The purposes of these laws are:

1. To enhance the development of infants and toddlers and minimize potential developmental delay.
2. To reduce the need for Special Education classes once these infants and toddlers reach school age.
3. To increase the likelihood that individuals with disabilities will lead productive lives.
4. To enhance the capacity of families to meet their infants' and toddlers' needs.
5. To increase agencies' and service providers' capacity to identify, evaluate and meet the needs of minority, low-income, inner-city, rural, and other under-represented populations with special services.

Interagency Councils

In order to meet these goals, each state is responsible for developing comprehensive, coordinated, multidisciplinary, interagency programs for infants, toddlers, and their families. In addition, they are to coordinate the payment for these services from federal, state, local, and private sources of funding, and to improve and enhance existing services for intervention. An important requirement is that the State Interagency Coordinating Council, which oversees Early Intervention Services, must include a state education representative with enough authority to engage in policy planning and implementation. This protects children and families from having to advocate individually for the implementation of the plan agreed upon in the interagency, interdisciplinary team meeting.

Family Participation

This legislation, protecting family interests and mandating early intervention with regard to infants and toddlers, exemplifies society's new understanding of the importance of early development and partnerships with parents. One of the most important requirements of Public Law 102-119 is that of informed parental consent. Before any services are provided, the child and the family must receive an explanation of the recommendations. The family does not have to accept all services offered, but only those agreed to as appropriate by the family. In the new law, the Individualized Educational Plan was changed to the Individualized Family Service Plan (IFSP). The IFSP is the state's legally binding commitment to providing services to the family. Another important part of Public Law 102-119 is the requirement that states plan a smooth transition for the child from the Early Intervention Program into a handicapped preschool children's program by age three.

SOCIO-CULTURAL FOUNDATIONS

Children with disabilities exist across all social classes and racial and cultural groups. Since there are so many different types of disabilities, and so many individuals with multiple disabilities, describing these families as one group is not appropriate. As professionals serving these families, you need to understand how individual children with special challenges place demands on families and how the families organize themselves to respond.

Public litigation to protect the rights of and services to persons with disabilities over the last quarter of the twentieth century reflects a general compassion toward vulnerable children and families. Also reflected is a sense of equal justice and the recognition that public education and social and health services should be more universally available. Indeed, some claim the true test of a humane culture is the effectiveness of services to its most vulnerable citizens.

Providing appropriate nurturance and challenge to persons with disabilities represents a value placed on individual development, achievement, and independence. However, these values, which reflect a respect for individual lives and a shared responsibility for development, conflict with economic concerns about limited resources and the need to prioritize where resources are spent. Many families with children who have disabilities talk about the constant demand in caring for their children to the best of their ability, and the need to be effective and aggressive advocates for appropriate services from school districts, health professionals, social service agencies, and other community systems.

While the roles of both caretaker and advocate are not unique to families with children who have disabilities, a number of researchers and service providers describe the intense sense of stress and grief and anger that these families experience (Mullins, 1987; Singer and Irvin, 1989). Beavers (1989) wrote about the need for families to grieve over the loss of the "perfect" child, and learn to deal realistically with the challenges their child presents. This parental task is not unique to parents of children with disabilities because most parents reveal the struggle to accept their child's individual characteristics as different from the child they imagined before birth or adoption. Yet parents who have a child with disabilities may have to give up certain goals for their child. Grief and frustration are attached to the loss of companionship, vigorous athletic achievements, and economic and social success that they imagined for their child. There is also a high rate of abandonment by fathers in families with a challenged child.

DELAYED AND AMBIGUOUS DIAGNOSES

There are also special struggles for families with children whose disabilities are not recognized immediately at birth. Disabilities, which are apparent only gradually or occur after a later trauma or accident, present different challenges to families. A slow process of questioning, fear, and anxiety can be destructive to a parent's sense of pride and competence. In addition, disabilities that are believed to be caused by parental behaviors, such as fetal alcohol syndrome (FAS), present a different struggle for families and society, ranging from compassion for the child to anger against the family.

Helping professionals, service providers, and policymakers are often uncomfortable with the amount of ambiguity that surrounds the etiology of disabilities. About half of challenged children show disabilities with unknown causes. In a society that values the scientific pursuit of knowledge, this lack of information frustrates and angers some people. There are clear challenges to the sufficiency of resources and ingenuity.

Appropriate Environment

Many families with disabled children describe their own value conflicts around the appropriate environments for their children. If their children are given segregated education and services, they may be with like peers and have the protection and support of specially trained professionals. On the other hand, their world and stimulation are more limited, and the family's ability to gain support from the wider community is limited as well. If these children are included by society in all their activities, then more children and adults are educated about the realistic range of human development. However, individual children with disabilities may be discriminated against, misunderstood, abused, or not provided with optimal services.

These decisions about appropriate environments for education and care are complex because of the interaction of physical, cognitive, and socio-emotional abilities. Because inclusive environments provide less protection and more stimulation, a critical understanding of a child's socio-emotional strengths should be made before any service is implemented. Every team that is developing an Individualized Education Plan or Individual Family Service Plan should consider the specific characteristics of the child, the family, and the potential placement environments. Many parents express their frustration by indicating a simple wish for their child to be accepted. However, there is ample evidence from research that merely including a child with disabilities in an environment with other children does not guarantee acceptance and a positive outcome. In fact, according to Derman-Sparks (1989), "Contact by itself does not necessarily reduce non-disabled children's misconceptions or fears. It may even intensify them unless adults take active steps to promote children's learning about each other." Many parents of children with disabilities relate that their most difficult struggle with values is to assist their child with independence, appropriate to his or her situation. This is particularly an issue in adolescence, with questions about appropriate living environments, economic independence, and the possibility of procreation or sexual relationships with partners.

Status

Because of prejudice and a lack of experience in the wider culture, an individual with a disability is often seen as less valuable in an economic and social sense. A specifically challenged child represents new service demands on the family and the community. A challenged adult can be seen as a drain on resources without any possibility of recouping these losses. As more disabled adults are mainstreamed into the work force, these views may change.

Among families and professionals serving children with disabilities, there are continuing debates about the process of diagnostic labeling. Categorical diagnostic labels, such as "learning disabled," access state and federal special services. However, these labels can create lifelong categories of difference, and increased vulnerability to prejudice and misunderstanding. Most professionals agree that we all need assistance in using appropriate language when referring to disabilities and when including challenged individuals in various environments.

Since the federal statute requiring inclusion and appropriate planning for people with disabilities was passed in 1975, our social service system contains professionals who have experience with inclusion requirements. These professionals are engaged in a major task of reorganizing the services of our educational, health, and social systems. Most families with challenged children report that they continually educate others who have no experience in responding to or appropriately interacting with children who have disabilities.

Changing Roles of Females

Typically, a family that includes a child with disabilities creates a care challenge for the mother, who often is most responsible for the caretaking and interaction with professionals. James May (1991) reports that one result of these practices is that fathers are frequently excluded and professionals have little experience dealing with the total family. Most often mothers are put in the position of interpreting information to their spouses or other family members when they inadequately understand it themselves and/or are deeply distressed over its meaning for their family.

It is often mothers who have been instrumental in creating parent support groups and in reaching out to other parents of children with disabilities. Early advocacy for persons with mental retardation was largely initiated by mothers. Many women reported personal gains in their self-confidence after advocating aggressively for the needs of their children. Sisters of children with disabilities are in a unique position in most families. Females are usually encouraged toward nurturing tasks. Sisters of persons with disabilities report a great deal of responsibility and involvement with their challenged siblings. For some females, this can be a positive, growth-enhancing process. For others, it can cause anger and interfere with their own need for individualized parenting and nurturance. Since approximately two-thirds of children with disabilities are male, a societal pattern of females caring for males is reinforced.

Changing Roles of Males

A number of researchers have begun advocating strongly for fathers to be more actively involved in planning for their challenged children. They urge educators and social agencies to hold planning conferences in the early morning or late afternoon hours to facilitate participation by all family members without conflicting with work schedules. In addition, they encourage phone conferences or evening or weekend conferences, so that fathers might be more involved. Professionals who have led groups for fathers of children with disabilities note very positive support and sharing between the men occurring (Pruett, 1989). Professionals working with fathers often relate that it is difficult to help them express their feelings about their children with disabilities and to communicate effectively with their spouses. With support from professionals, fathers can gain more control over their lives by coming to terms with their grief, finding emotional support from other men, and learning appropriate father/child interaction patterns.

Family life research suggests that men play the parenting role differently than women. Therefore, it is important that men have a chance to talk with other fathers about appropriate patterns and activities. Professionals find that discussion groups with fathers are most successful if leadership is shared by fathers, if time is provided for emotional sharing and support, and if time is provided for active skill development in which fathers and their children interact together. Having special father and child potluck suppers or outings with their children can reinforce skills and feelings of competence among fathers.

The higher proportion of males among persons with disabilities means that fathers more often grieve about the loss in potential development for sons instead of daughters. There is increasing evidence that fathers who are more fully engaged with their children are happier with themselves, show fewer signs of stress-related illnesses, and have wives who are more satisfied with their marriage. There is also evidence that fathers tend to set a tone for the whole family's attitudes toward children with disabilities (Frye et al., 1989). Therefore, understanding the father's perspective and role in the family is crucial to gaining successful help in support of a child's development.

Research comparing mothers and fathers of all children shows that mothers often become more skilled than fathers at parenting because they assume the caretaker responsibility more actively and accumulate more experience in interpreting their children's needs. This difference is heightened among parents of children with disabilities. A man who already feels somewhat intimidated about his parenting skills may feel extremely sensitive about his inability to participate fully in parenting a child who is specially challenged.

Socialization Goals for Children

All parents must reconcile an image of a mythical, high-achieving child with a realistic picture of their child's present abilities and future possibilities. For parents of children with disabilities, this is particularly difficult. The more effectively families, educators, and service providers work together, the more positive the child's development. Research has shown that, the earlier the intervention, the more areas of the child's development can be successfully enhanced.

The Early Intervention Programs (EIP) encourage partnerships between parents and professionals. Planning individualized interventions for infants and toddlers can help parents see the power of their teaching and nurturance of their child. Parents need professional partnerships to help them in making decisions about the timing of intervention. Many professionals do not want to discourage parents from trying to give their child optimal advantages, but they also do not want parents to have an unrealistic picture of their child's potential. Parents frequently struggle with the need to be realistic as they obtain information about their children.

Family members need to talk about the amount and variety of resources available to provide for a child with disabilities. With the advent of Individualized Family Service Plans (IFSP) under the federal law, more families are provided with respite care, or day care, that facilitates their own involvement in the workforce or in a wider social community. The parent of a child with disabilities can become extremely hesitant about seeking assistance from friends, families, or professionals. This federal law assists a family in feeling comfortable with their right to create plans both for the child and the family. These laws have provided dramatic changes for families. Now a quiet weekend for two or a break from caretaking for the rest of the family is not only possible, but actively supported.

Family life literature substantiates that the divorce rate is higher among couples who have children with disabilities. Since all stress in a family can affect the strength and viability of a marriage, this outcome is not unexpected. However, recent research has also suggested that divorce is more likely to occur if the disability is extremely severe and if it occurs relatively early in the couple's life *(The Wall Street Journal,* Sept. 27, 1993). Many professionals comment that a family that has successfully parented a child without disabilities has more confidence and strength when dealing with a challenged child born later. Maturity and experience contribute to parenting skills and provide a better understanding of children.

The Role of Grandparents and Others

Families with children who have disabilities often experience demands on time and caretaking far beyond the demands other families experience. Grandparents may be important partners in dealing with these demands if they live nearby and are able to be supportive. Some parents report that grandparents exhibit more patience with the special learning challenges of their grandchildren. Of course, grandparents who are frail or lack concentration may have a difficult time with the physical care demands of some children. Most grandparents can probably learn to be supportive of the children's parents by encouraging them to seek information and take time for themselves, especially if they have a disabled child.

A special note should be made of the grandparents' role in supporting their adult children's choices after learning the results of the genetic diagnostic tests called *amniocentesis* and *chorionic villi sampling.* As America has seen an increase in childbearing among older women, physicians usually recommend that these families take advantage of diagnostic tests. The possibility of birth defects and genetic anomalies increases with the age of the parents, especially the mother. More families are informed about potential risks and seek the additional information available through medical technology. Families opting for abortion following diagnostic results often do so without the knowledge of other people to avoid value-laden judgments. However, support for this decision could come from numerous different sources.

Grandparents often report that one of the most difficult realities to deal with is their grief concerning the limitations on accomplishments of seriously disabled grandchildren. Grandparents who discuss these concerns with others are better able to come to terms with the realities of the support the family needs. The support and approval of the grandparenting generation are important to the stability and strength of families with challenged children.

Grandparents as Substitute Parents

Of the 5 percent of all children in the United States reported to be living with their grandparents in 1991, 28 percent had neither parent present in the household (U.S. Census Bureau, 1992). Their parents were often unavailable due to incarceration, desertion, death, or problems with substance abuse. For parenting grandparents, the conflict between supporting the grandchildren and reconciling the disappearance or failure of their own adult children is a major task. Luckily, a number of support groups for these grandparents are being developed, and the media increasingly provides information about these new family challenges.

Substance abuse by the parents may have impacted the children. They may exhibit challenges caused by such abuse during their gestation. These challenges require interdisciplinary Individualized Family Service Plans (IFSP) which bring many service systems of the community together. At the same time, special consideration must be given to possible limitations on economic and legal resources of the family system. Grandparents involved in these systems need special support and strength.

ECOLOGICAL FACTORS

Ecological factors facing challenged children include the incidence and severity of disabilities in relation to the adequacy of the human-built infrastructures to respond. Disabilities cross social classes. Many of the demands for appropriate services that face professionals working with these families are influenced by both societal and individual family resources and the severity and type of disability (Chilman et al., 1988).

Demographics

Disabilities are caused by both genetic and environmental events. A large number of diseases or disorders can be detected by genetic tests done prior to conception. While the medical community is increasing its sophistication in diagnosis and genetic counseling, many of the rare, genetically inherited traits that cause disabilities occur at such an infrequent rate that most families are not prepared for the birth of a child with a genetic disability. Approximately 50 percent of disabilities that cause mental retardation are of unknown cause. Furthermore, we are increasingly becoming aware of disabilities that result from the complex interaction of genetics with the environment.

Incidence of Disabilities in Children

The total incidence of disabilities in the United States population is generally quoted as between 10 to 12 percent, depending on the definition of disabilities.

When additional categories, such as culturally disadvantaged, are added to this group, then percentages up to 50 percent are sometimes quoted.

The most conservative estimate of the percentage of children with disabilities in the United States is reflected in Table 13–1 (National Information Center for Children and Youth with Disabilities, 1991) with categories in descending order of incidence.

Impacts on Families

Different types of challenges can impact families in different ways, depending on how they affect the child's development. Disabilities that are visually apparent to the public, such as Down's syndrome, blindness, hyperactivity, and those concerning mobility and orthopedics, give an immediate message to onlookers. Many parents comment on how weary they become of the stares and insensitive questions from strangers when they appear with their children in public. Other parents have adjusted to these questions and see them as opportunities for public education and for making a statement about the rights and capabilities of children with disabilities.

Other challenges, such as learning disabilities or emotional disturbances, are not so quickly evident. Parents of these children might not get immediate questions or curious looks. However, when their children exhibit the behaviors associated with a disability, people are surprised and sometimes alarmed. Parents of children with mental retardation often comment that because their child looks physically normal, people expect them to act similar to their age peers. An "inappropriate" behavior is met with impatience, surprise, and sometimes even anger.

One of the most difficult realities for families with challenged children is that many parenting tasks demand thought and planning. In most families, parenting is interwoven with daily life events and reflects total values, experi-

Table 13–1   *Estimated Percentage of Disabilities in Children Ages 5–18*

Disability	Percentage
Learning	4.73
Speech and language	2.5 – 4.0
Mental retardation	1.7
Visually impaired	1.2
Emotionally impaired	.8
Physically and health impaired	.5
Severe	.14
Autism	.05 – .15
Total	11.62 – 13.22

Source: National Information Center for Children and Youth with Disabilities, 1991. Washington, DC.

ences, and skills of the parents. Disabilities usually demand a deliberate team effort in analyzing how to teach certain skills, or how to encourage the development of skills in children and youth. A parenting role that requires deliberate teaching sessions or engineered activities with specific rewards for behavior that is considered difficult for children to learn, is a new and demanding role for parents, requiring a great deal of education as well as support.

A child's ability to learn impacts school achievement and lifelong potential. Impairment in communication and in social-emotional skills exacts a heavy toll on the family. Parenting is a demanding and complex task, and many parents comment on the love and affection they receive from their children as a primary motivator and support for this role. When children are depressed, extremely disturbed, and unable to express positive emotions, parents find it difficult to maintain the energy needed to provide loving, supportive, and learning environments for their children.

A Deficit Model

Parents of children with disabilities sometimes feel all their time is spent emphasizing the deficits of their child instead of their strengths. That is, a parent may forget that a blind child can run, play, sing, talk, and laugh—all strengths parents enjoy. Parents of children with disabilities often must interact frequently with diagnosticians who only focus on the child's disabilities. These professionals become extremely skilled at making suggestions concerning the deficits rather than the child's strengths.

Our entire service system is built on defining a child's deficit by etiology or behavior (review Table 13–1) which draws attention to what the child cannot do. Parents and family members would like to see a greater concentration on the child's learning and relationship strengths and more time spent reinforcing those qualities. Parents need to see the positive strengths of the child in order to have the fortitude to deal with the child's disability every day.

Family members also must cope with the stress of the unknown with their challenged children. Besides dealing with a stranger who does not understand why a child is behaving differently, projecting how a new medication might influence a child, or wondering what a child might achieve in the way of independence and economic self-sufficiency, there are many additional areas of ambiguity and uncertainty for parents of challenged children.

Studies on stress substantiate the fact that individuals who feel they have little control over their environment and their future become emotionally stressed. Knowing this, many diagnosticians attempt to give families very clear diagnostic projections or specific goals for their children. The deficit approach can help families become realistic, but it also can be negative as far as concentrating on limitations and discouraging a family from trying unique and creative ways to enhance the future for their challenged member. Helping professionals can assist both families and children in finding their strengths and emphasizing them.

Aesthetics

Most parents of children with disabilities admit that it is difficult for their friends and relatives in the wider community to appreciate and love their children because they do not look as attractive or act as vigorous as other children. As a society, the United States has a deep love affair with physical beauty and perfection. Learning to appreciate and understand the inner beauty and small increments of growth of children with disabilities is a constant struggle for their families. Many parents indicate that their disabled children have taught them beautiful lessons about caring, patience, and nurturance.

The parents of children with disabilities talk about their own strengths and the emergence of new humane traits in themselves through the experience of their parenting. The most eloquent statements about the special feelings and memories in parenting challenged children are found in books written by parents themselves, books such as Josh Greenfield's *A Child Called Noah* (1970), and Simon's *After the Tears* (1987). The reader sees a clear picture of the impact children with disabilities can have on families, and the coping strength that emerges in their families.

Education

The education of children with disabilities is supported by federal legislation. Our public education system, endeavoring to follow legislative mandates, made it increasingly apparent to both families and educators that teachers were ill-equipped to teach children with disabilities in the classrooms. Consequently, teacher preparation institutions needed to develop new specialized training and methods for teachers who would have children with disabilities in their classroom settings. The advocacy of families and professionals created federal laws which guarantee free and appropriate education to children with disabilities. This resulted in the growth of an extensive network of special education curriculum consultants, administrators, and support personnel. However, the federal statutes were largely unsupported by federal funds, creating an increased burden on already over-taxed public school budgets.

For families, the power of the most recent special educational legislation has been to support their role as decision-makers on the team that creates the Individualized Educational Plan (IEP). If an educational plan is to be successful, parents must understand and agree on its objectives, and have information on how their family activities may be supportive of school activities and vice versa. This education service philosophy is an extremely positive one for parents and other family members.

As research on the causes of various disabilities has proceeded, more accurate information is available to share with parents. In some cases, this is a welcome change from an era of "blame the parents" to an era of "partner with the parents." The case of autism is a very eloquent example.

Autistic behaviors include repetitive movements, alarm and concern about changes, avoidance of normal social interaction, and poor communication patterns. During the 1950s and 1960s, the reigning model for the developmental cause of autism was a psychoanalytic model. A cold and rejecting parenting style was blamed for the disability. Subsequent study and research clarified the predictable traits of this syndrome and revealed that the condition is more likely a neurological or brain disorder. In Public Law 101-476, the Individuals with Disabilities Education Act, autism was included as a separate disability category due to its complexity and the need for specialized training for effective intervention.

Inclusive Environments

The inclusion of children with disabilities in wider environments means that they will gain greater opportunities for stimulation and more normal experiences. For children with certain disabilities, this stimulation can be disorganizing and frustrating, and careful individual plans need to be made. Special education research has helped reveal how complex human learning is and how frequently children learn unexpected lessons from environments in which they participate. While direct and targeted training of certain educational skills can be planned in the classroom, a great deal of incidental learning occurs informally around communication, support and interaction, inclusion or rejection at play, and social problem solving. Observations of inclusive educational settings often reveal a much richer educational environment than educators normally describe. These environments can be both positive and negative and a team including parents, educators, and diagnosticians must make placement decisions appropriate for each individual child.

In the latter part of the twentieth century, educators in the United States were profoundly impacted by civil rights legislation and concerns about discrimination toward special education students. This discrimination was also seen in basic diagnostic assessments. During the 1970s it was documented that children from middle- or upper-class families were more likely to be diagnosed as learning disabled instead of mentally retarded. While this judgment may represent diagnostic bias on the part of professionals, it also reflects the complex interaction of genetics and environment in the development of any child. A child being raised in a highly stressed community with few resources may fail to develop as fully as a child with similar genetic potential, but with an enhanced family and community resource base.

Religion

Many families claim that their religious faith sustains them through difficult times of stress. Children with disabilities present special challenges to religious communities. Many religious communities provide religious education for children, such as Sunday Schools, but do not have specialized professionals who can appropriately support the inclusion of children with disabilities. Finding compassionate and skilled adults who are able to be inclusive can provide special support for a family. Members of a religious community may have the organizational structure to help recruit and train child care providers for families who need respite care from time to time.

Religious groups vary greatly in theology and in the formality of their structures. When theology suggests a deterministic view of human development, which states that a challenged child may represent a judgment against the family, parents may feel a strong sense of shame and guilt, or martyrdom in relation to the care of their child with disabilities. If the religious community helps parents build hope and positive goals for themselves and their children, then their religious faith represents a strength in their lives. Pastors, priests, rabbis, and other religious leaders can be powerful assistants in counseling and providing compassionate support as families make key decisions about the care and education of their special children. A religious leader may know of other families who have struggled with similar decisions and can bring families together to talk and share support.

In the informal social environment of a religious community, children with disabilities may have more choices of what activities they participate in and what groups they can join. If their religious community has inclusiveness as a strong value, then families with challenged children and the rest of the community can be more creative and positive about opportunities.

Health Care System

Children with disabilities often have special health requirements as well. If a child has a sensory impairment, such as blindness or deafness, or a specific mobility limitation or is confined to a wheelchair, then there are often costs associated with additional equipment and devices to encourage learning and independence. Some disabilities have long been recognized with special funding and services made available to the disabled and their families. Examples of these are the multiple services to the blind and services available through the Easter Seal Society.

Certain disabilities are likely to carry special health risks, such as Down's Syndrome. Children with Down's Syndrome are more susceptible to upper respiratory problems. This means that families must have access to regular preventive medical care, and all care providers must be sensitive to practices that enhance health.

The Americans with Disabilities Act of 1990 requires that all public institutions and places of employment make reasonable accommodations to include persons with disabilities in their environments. Adaptive aids and equipment, such as computers, head-sticks, clamps, modified cups and eating utensils, and communication boards, are all now included in equipment and adaptive technologies available to persons with disabilities. Specific health challenges requiring medication and careful monitoring of behavior, such as epilepsy, demand positive and open communication between parents, schools, and physicians in order to manage behavior successfully.

One special area for decision-making support from educators and the health community is family planning and procreative options for challenged children as they grow to maturity. Some parents limit the size of their families once they learn they have a child with a disability. Particularly when there is a genetic component to the disability, families may make use of genetics counseling. Some families report that they make decisions about future children based on clinical genetic information.

Many syndromes are rare and recessive, so that the probability of another child similarly affected may be very low. A number of families have reported feelings of guilt and despair after receiving specific information from genetics clinics. The feelings of helplessness and self-blame after bearing a child with a genetic disability can also be extremely stressful. Sensitive and compassionate support of parents is important at these times.

As children with disabilities grow to maturity, their parents and the health care professionals may assist with decisions about their active sexuality. An informed society must understand that all persons need and deserve a positive expression of their sexual selves. When persons with disabilities consider an active sexual life, the nature, severity and cause of their disability need to be considered. Some disabled persons have elected to refrain from becoming biological parents even when they are able, due to the specific characteristics of their disability. Others have made a choice to be biological parents or to parent others' children as a teacher or aide, or to adopt or provide foster care to children who need a family. Various options can be considered as realistic and compassionate discussion takes place between family members and health professionals.

Economic Factors

Since the passing of federal legislation providing free and appropriate education to children with disabilities, families have been continually advocating for assistance in respite care and other services to help their children with a variety of opportunities. The Vocational Rehabilitation Act and the Americans with Disabilities Act mandate the availability of devices and equipment necessary for the productive functioning of people with disabilities. Organizations like the National Rehabilitation Information Center provide information on parents' and families' rights, sources of funding, and information on how to obtain needed services and equipment. Many families need assistance in application procedures to obtain necessary equipment and resources for their family members.

Throughout a family's life, the special economic demands of having a child with a disability can vary. Initial needs for special equipment to position or support a child with limited mobility will change as the child grows. The Americans with Disabilities Act of 1992 is a landmark piece of legislation creating opportunities for education and employment to persons with disabilities. The act requires employers to make a "reasonable accommodation in their environment" for the employment of or the service to persons with specific disabilities. While this legislation has alarmed many small businesses, there are reasonable ways to provide accommodations so that the contributions and skills of persons with disabilities can be optimally used.

Families of persons with lifelong disabilities and limitations in income need to plan for lifelong support. The increasing availability of new techniques, group independent care situations, and home care services makes it possible for many challenged people to live independently. When a person with a disability qualifies for SSI benefits under the Social Security Administration, families need to plan what portion of their estate and family resources they wish to allocate to protect each member of the family.

A provocative column in *The Wall Street Journal* in October 1993 described the increasing effectiveness of advocacy for special needs students, and declared that this effectiveness had resulted in mandated programs which are increasingly expensive. In school districts where budgets have remained stable or are decreasing, the increasing costs of mandated special education programs create economic conflicts. In an era of economic difficulties, there may be increasing conflicts over programs for persons with disabilities. Are the disabled "entitled" to these programs, paid entirely by public monies, or should family resources also be utilized? One suggestion is that parents who have children with disabilities, who are financially able, should be required to pay a portion of the costs incurred in educating their disabled children. However, a large proportion of special education students come from low-income families, so requiring family payments will not dramatically affect the educational budgets at the local level.

One lesson learned from these economic shortages is that creative partnerships between schools and parents may help keep costs down. For example, if educators help parents understand that the schools do not have certain resources to provide optimal services for their children, parents might volunteer to help in special education programs, or generate money through fund raising and in-kind contributions. When there is a need for additional personnel to support the education of some challenged children, families, neighborhoods, or religious communities might help organize a system of volunteers to help recruit the needed human resources. Increased attention to children's needs is a positive result of creating more inclusiveness.

Housing

Families with children who have disabilities often have special housing needs. Housing needs vary according to the specific disability of the child, but often include special concerns about supervision, safety of the neighborhood, and convenience for the use of wheelchairs or other helping devices. For a child with limited mobility, living quarters that are not safe and accessible on one floor can cause tremendous physical strain on family members from lifting the disabled child, as well as the psychological strain of isolation for the child.

Sometimes the home can be made more appropriate for the child and family with some adaptations. These might include ramps into the house, the widening of doorways, or the construction of a wall or a higher fence to provide a protected play area. Many of these adaptations could be provided by volunteer labor in a community in response to needs that specialists or parents identify. Housing problems are especially acute for a low-income family needing to find affordable housing. In many cases, it may be important for educators and other health and educational service providers to advocate for families and assist in locating appropriate housing.

Government Policies and Agencies

Since the middle of the twentieth century, the federal government, and specifically public education, have assumed increasing responsibility for the education of disabled children and youth. Throughout this time, it has become clear that education must be a strong partner with health professionals and employment sectors in providing appropriate lifelong education, care, and jobs for persons with disabilities. Interagency councils, required by the early intervention federal statutes, have built important cooperative networks. However, there are still numerous examples of regulations making the coordination and communication between agencies difficult.

All professionals who serve families with challenged children need to become aware of regulations that need changing to facilitate coordination and communication. Each state department of education is responsible for creating a state plan that complies with federal mandates for serving disabled children and youth. Most state departments designate intermediate or local school districts as their representatives in working directly with families and children to create services. Since the school districts must both provide services and find the clients who need them, departments of education may be somewhat reluctant to be strong advocates for challenged children and their families.

Increasingly, volunteer agencies or organizations play an important role in helping educate families about rights for their child and in helping with "Child Find," a national program using mass communication to find children who need special services. Those who wish to learn more about services available in their area, or wish to advocate for a particular child or family, can obtain a copy of their state's plan to implement special education services from their state department of education in their state's capital. The plan should include conditions for the involvement of parents, a description of parents' rights, and a process whereby parents can appeal decisions of the team providing services for their family member.

FAMILY INTERACTIONS AND KINSHIP NETWORKS

Families who are able to purchase additional services in the form of child care, respite care, household assistance, and/or special transportation and equipment have an advantage over families with fewer economic resources. For these families, the ability to activate support from their extended family, neighborhood, and community is an important asset. Families with strong and supportive circles of relatives and friends who provide wisdom and an assertive management style are able to activate many resources for themselves and their children.

Families with challenged children relate that support groups that include other families with disabled children help them in making plans for pleasure and respite. Sometimes exchanging child care and supervision is possible; however, this is not realistic for some children with extreme disabilities. Highly specialized care may require a contracted Respite Care Service.

One special point that is important for all professionals to understand is that families of children with disabilities frequently need respite care and do not always adequately receive it. Caretakers need time away from their charges in order to remain strong and energetic. Strong feelings of martyrdom and guilt on the part of mothers can make it difficult for couples to have time alone to nurture their relationship.

Single parents of children with disabilities are particularly vulnerable to burnout and stress. Finding a group of friends that can be supportive can be especially helpful to single parents. The more severe the health risks, and/or the caretaking demands of a challenged person, the more difficult it is to obtain assistance in respite care. Parents who have become very skilled at providing health services and care for their child may have a difficult time learning to trust and leave their child with other caretakers. For this reason, it is important to encourage relationships with two or more respite care environments and encourage parent participation in local advocacy and support groups.

A particularly difficult topic for families with children who have disabilities is the issue of a family vacation. If families have the means to go on a vacation, they must face the question about whether they should leave their challenged family members in respite care, or take them along. For more freedom and independent action, respite care would be best. However, taking disabled children on family vacations can be a wonderful opportunity for many children. Balancing competing goals is needed. Parents may need supportive professionals to assist with realistic information and problem solving concerning this decision.

CHANGES AND ADAPTATIONS

The most significant change and adaptation for families with challenged children is the movement from a position of powerlessness and despair to one of an active problem solving and partnering role. This attitude often involves a change from accepting professional diagnostic advice *carte blanche* to seeking information and participating more fully in decisions about their children. A movement toward assertive involvement can be encouraged by recruiting other experienced parents to serve as mentors or advocates, and by attending diagnostic sessions and planning sessions with experienced parents. Gradually, parents learn to understand the limits of the system and the means for obtaining services and information from a variety of sources.

The second major change is to learn to adapt to the children's accomplishments and development over time. Caring for a child who has breathing difficulties as an infant is a much different proposition than handling the social frustration of a learning disabled teenager. As families learn, they generally develop habits to cope with parenting challenges. The amount of power and control they may wish to have over each child's life can affect the role they play with their challenged child. Most parents report that as their children approach adolescence and young adulthood, they face important changes for themselves as they allow their youngsters greater independence. Parents learn to trust community agencies to be more involved in the care and education of their children.

Disabilities exist along a continuum ranging from minimal impact, such as a well-controlled seizure disorder or a stuttering pattern, to a lifelong limitation of cognitive skill or mobility. Family development must depend on the hopes and resources, not only of the person with disabilities, but also that of the family and community. All of us need to understand that with increasing age comes the greater likelihood of having a disability. In 1992, the Bureau of the Census reported that 49 million noninstitutionalized Americans aged 15 and older had a disability. As shown in Figure 13–1, the older the individual, the greater the incidence of both disabilities and those disabilities being defined as severe.

For adults, disabilities are normally classified as functional disabilities, disabilities in activities of daily living (ADLs) or instrumental activities of daily living (IADLs). Functional disabilities include some compromise in the ability to lift, walk independently, read, hear, or speak. ADLs include freedom of mobility, bathing, dressing, toileting and eating. IADLs include independence in shopping or keeping appointments, doing housework and cooking, keeping financial records and using the telephone. It's easy to realize that, as America ages, more individuals will need assistance with regard to both ADLs and IADLs. In 1992, the Census Bureau reported that 34 million adults over 15 had a functional disability, 3.9 million persons required assistance with ADLs from another person, and 9 million persons needed assistance for IADLs (U.S. Bureau of the Census, 1994). These numbers represent challenges for the provision of new services and the need for creativity and cooperation in funding. Table 13–2 shows that the causes of disabilities in older people are different from those of youth. For youth under 15, these later life disabilities can be added to earlier diagnoses.

SERVING FAMILIES WITH CHALLENGED MEMBERS

Special educators are essential for serving families with children who have disabilities. In addition, many other teachers, health care workers, religious lead-

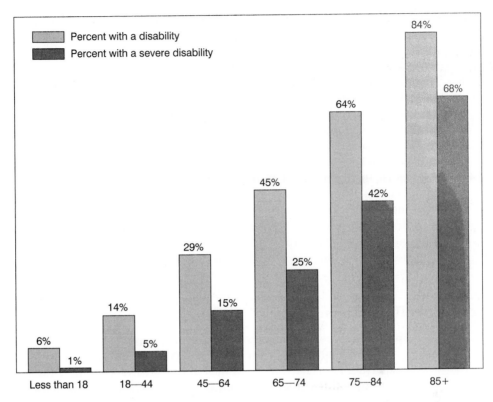

Figure 13–1. *Percent of Persons with a Disability and Percent with a Severe Disability, By Age Group: 1991–1992*

Source: U.S. Bureau of the Census.

Table 13–2. *Physical Conditions That Cause Disabilities*

Condition	Number with condition (millions)
Arthritis or rheumatism	7.2
Back or spine problems	5.7
Heart trouble	4.6
Lung or respiratory trouble	2.8
High blood pressure	2.2
Stiffness or deformity of extremity	2.0
Diabetes	1.6
Blindness or vision problems	1.5

Source: U.S. Bureau of the Census.

ers, youth workers, and family service providers will interact with these families. Your professional service may be in one of these key agencies.

Learn Relevant Laws

All professionals must understand the federal laws that outline services mandated for children and their families. These laws include specific requirements for education, access to services, vocational training, and independent living. Professionals need to obtain accurate information on the state plans and the agencies responsible for services in their area. For a professional expecting to work in this area, it is important to build trusting relationships with colleagues who can serve as consultants or provide information. There is an increasing emphasis on the importance of early intervention programs for children with disabilities. The inclusion of children in mainstream environments goes a long way toward enhancing children's development for lifelong independence. Also, the opportunities for understanding and growth of all children are enhanced.

Seek Specific Information

Many professionals have not had extensive experience in dealing with people who have disabilities. They need in-service training to learn more about specific disabilities. Persons with disabilities always state how important it is for others to be honest with them. Learn how to ask for information in a respectful and open manner. You might say, "I have never had an experience with someone who is blind. I will need information about how to be supportive and appropriate in my actions. Can we make an appointment to visit?"

Your goal is to become an informed partner with parents. If you are a teacher who is including a child with disabilities in your class, it will be important to see this new student in as many different settings as possible. Make a home visit. Go with the family on an outing so that you can see the practices the parents have developed to enhance their child's opportunities. Once you have seen the child in a variety of environments, you can be more creative in adapting your own environment to suit the child and family. In this way, you come to know both the child and the family. You can help assure that family rights are respected and that you are providing appropriate and accurate information for the other professionals in your service environment. Environments that include all children are richer in learning and creative opportunities than environments that provide only segregated services.

Clarify Professional Recommendations

As a professional working with a family, you need to talk with parents about their many interactions with a variety of professionals. Some interactions may be highly charged with tension, fear, and frustration on both sides. Helping a family continue to relate positively to professionals is an important part of your task. As you meet initially with families, give them an opportunity to talk about their relationship with other professionals to better understand developments that occurred prior to when you began working with the child.

Families frequently will share with professionals their frustration, confusion, or hostility about information provided by another group. Help parents articulate their questions so they may better understand information shared with them. To be supportive, you may need to accompany them to future appointments with specialists. However, avoid assuming responsibility for the family. Respectfully convey to other professionals when the family has been unable to use certain information and when it needs to be clarified.

Individualize Family Interaction

Ask family members what kinds of information or interactions have been most positive and supportive of their family goals. When you need to share information, you may find that a particular family prefers brief phone conversations about their child, while another family may need longer face-to-face visits. If you have difficulty contacting a parent, you might ask permission to communicate through letters. Sometimes at their request another trusted friend or extended family member becomes an information gatherer for them. In all of these communications it is important to convey the fact that you hope to develop an effective information network that can respond immediately to the questions or concerns of anyone in the service group.

Many professionals that families talk to have their own specific limited agenda because of their professional responsibility, experience, or training. For example, the mobility specialist talks to a family about devices to assist with mobility. After a number of these conferences, a family may feel that no one has asked them specifically about their family goals for their child. These goals may not be immediately accomplished in your environment, but, knowing the family's interests, you can adapt conditions in your environment and assist parents in finding other resources to accomplish other objectives. An important style for these interactions is to ask periodically, "How are we doing with your son or daughter?" This will enable the family to feel free to talk with you about things that are going well and things that they might wish to change.

Stress Human Values

One of the most important things you can convey when working with all families is that you see the child as a whole person. This means you recognize the child's temperament, personality, abilities, and the special unique characteristics that are beyond a specific disability. Every parent wants their child to be accepted in a compassionate, individualized way. Many of the interactions between professionals and families of children with disabilities focus only on the disability itself. In a comprehensive, Individualized Service Plan meeting, the planning group should first consider the child's needs as a human being. The specific detailed goals for skill development, say speech, should be discussed only after comprehensive goals are stated. Think about both the short-term goals as well as the long-term goals to demonstrate your commitment to your responsibilities.

Parents will feel comfortable in your environment if you develop a sustained relationship with them over time. If you have very limited interaction with a family, be clear about welcoming them, asking specific questions to discover their needs, goals, and values. Then, develop a plan that is responsive to their goals. Sustained interaction over time will allow you to visit from time to time and inquire about the entire balance of the family's life. You can learn whether they are taking time for total family enjoyment. Do the parents have time as a couple? As a single parent, does she or he have some time away from family responsibilities? In this ongoing relationship you can encourage parents' right to lead a balanced life with supports and enrichments for their own growth, which usually helps the child. Theirs is a lifetime job, so parental burnout must be prevented for the child's good.

Grief and Sorrow

Grief is expected when a family member is born disabled or becomes disabled. This grief process has received much attention from specialists. There are references to the importance of family acceptance and adjustment to the reality of a child's disability. However, this is very different from the resolution of grief after a death. The anger, frustration, and denial around the disability can provide the energy that families need from time to time for advocacy or assertiveness with professionals.

As professionals serving families, you need to learn to accept their intense emotions. There may be anger and accusations about missed opportunities for their child, or inappropriate diagnoses or suggestions from professionals. Grief and frustration can be expected as parents realize that their dreams for their child's future may not be fulfilled.

As a professional, you'll gain experience in being compassionate and quiet at times. Other times you'll learn to be forcefully articulate in helping parents identify a specific incident that triggered their anger. Helping parents express their pain and frustration takes skilled responsiveness on the part of professionals. You'll train for years to develop this skill. You need to feel comfortable saying things like: "You are really angry right now, and I know it will not be very productive for us to try to plan this today. Let's make an appointment for another time to deal with service plans."

Many parents of children with disabilities indicate that they find it very useful to talk about their needs with other families and with members of community organizations. Community members and service club leaders often help change policies or provide new services for families whose needs have not been recognized. Encouraging parents to join parent support organizations, such as the Association for Retarded Citizens of the United States (now known as The ARC), or the Learning Disabilities Association of America (LDA), can give them opportunities to help advocate for their family members. Organizations can help families practice language and strategies for effective community and societal changes.

Given the stresses that some challenged children place on a family and a marriage, the increase in the divorce rate is understandable. Knowing where and how to send parents for marriage help is an important skill. You may be in a position to counsel or support parents on the verge of a breakup, or those going through a divorce. Finding ways to continue the appropriate care and joint decision-making for the challenged child is important.

Some divorced parents report that one of the most positive things about the divorce is having some time alone and being relieved of the responsibility of the children when an ex-spouse takes care of them. Your goal is to help both parents deal with necessary decisions regarding their child with disabilities. Distraught parents have been known to disappear completely from the family.

Families may feel unable to cope with the multiple appointments and numerous professionals. Your role in helping parents clarify their own values, their goals for their children, and their most comfortable way of interacting with professionals can help them make wiser use of available resources. For example, a highly specialized pediatric neurologist can probably spend very little time with a family. However, if you assist the family in writing out questions, and help them in the interview, they will find the consultation with the specialist more meaningful and supportive of their family goals and values.

A final important goal in dealing with all families is to reinforce a sense of inclusiveness and a sense of justice. Human life presents many challenges for children and adults. To deny any of us the opportunity to see a full range of human characteristics is to render all of us less flexible, less creative, and less compassionate. Our work with families who have challenged children can provide us many opportunities for including them and others in a richer and more varied community.

CONCLUSIONS

Persons with disabilities are, first of all, human beings. Anyone can join this category at any time, through accident or illness. Their hopes, skills, abilities, creativity and motivation need to be nurtured. Many persons engaged in diversity education are aware of the African proverb "It takes a whole village to raise a child." This is particularly true of challenged children. Compassion and creativity are needed by all so that all children have a chance to give and receive from persons with a variety of characteristics. Long-term goals of self-sufficiency and economic sufficiency can be achieved for many individuals.

Many people have never interacted with disabled persons and may be frightened by the prospect. Your role will often be to facilitate positive, clear information and to help achieve creative problem solving. By the twenty-first century, all persons attending public schools will have learned important and specific lessons about valuing and facilitating the development of persons with disabilities.

STUDY QUESTIONS

1. Define the terms disability, challenged, and handicapped.
2. Write a paragraph describing what is meant by "least restrictive environment." Give examples of a two-year-old and a sixteen-year-old in such an environment.
3. Define segregated services, and contrast them with mainstream and inclusive services in a one-page essay.
4. Define Individualized Educational Plan. What legislation requires this IEP?
5. Define Individual Family Service Plan. What legislation requires this?
6. Describe four special education eras: privatization, segregation, mainstreaming, and partnerships.
7. Define etiology, ambiguity, and uncertainty around etiology.
8. Contrast the typical role of mothers with challenged children against the role of fathers with challenged children in a two-page discussion.
9. What is the total percentage of challenged children in the American population? What is the most common disability?
10. How will the percentages of challenged individuals change in the U.S. over the next 25 years?

APPLICATIONS

1. Make an appointment with a Special Education Administrator in a local school district. Discuss their current policy on inclusion and support to mainstream teachers for including persons with disabilities. If possible, obtain a copy of the policy, find out whether the district offers workshops for teachers, and arrange to observe an in-service meeting or workshop.
2. Call or visit your local Special Education office, and ask for a parent information packet. Review the forms that are provided to parents when an individualized educational planning meeting is held. Look over the parent approval forms and the outline for the educational plan. Evaluate the level of reading and education a parent needs to understand these forms and processes.

3. Attend a local chapter meeting of a Special Education Parent Support group. Listen to their program or interaction and if possible interview a couple of parents about the role this group plays in their lives and how valuable it is.

4. Interview a child/youth librarian at a local library on any books about children with disabilities. Ask to see resources on understanding children with disabilities, and other resources that may simply include pictures of disabled children as part of their illustrations. Write an evaluation of the lessons provided to children by these examples.

5. Make an appointment with the chair of the Curriculum and Instruction department at your university or college. Discuss how teachers are prepared for the inclusion of disabled children in the classroom. Ask how much of the program is devoted to special needs children, and what part of a pre-service, internship or student teaching assignment includes such children. Ask them about their long-term plan for increasing commitment and involvement.

6. Call a local Special Education administrator and inquire whether you may attend a meeting of a support group for young children with disabilities. At the meeting, ask the parents if they would help you understand what kinds of diagnostic and educational experiences have been most helpful for them. Tell them you are a professional-in-training, and you want to learn how to be more compassionate and appropriate in supporting family needs.

7. Find out if there is a lawyer in town who handles cases relating to advocacy and rights of children with disabilities. Make an appointment to discuss usual cases brought to his or her attention. Discuss whether they represent omissions in the law or in public communication and education.

8. Interview five students on campus about their personal experience with challenged children and youth. Develop a set of questions about the students' knowledge, impressions, attitudes and experience with challenged students. What can you conclude about the value of these experiences?

9. Arrange with the local administrators of the local special education program to observe children in an inclusive or mainstreamed setting, and children in a segregated or specialized setting. Describe the activities you observe as well as the advantages to the challenged students, the teacher, and the other students in the classroom. Describe the disadvantages for the same groups.

10. Call local special education administrators for information regarding respite care services. Where are they available? Call or visit an administrator of such a service. Describe the services provided, costs, and family experiences from the viewpoint of the agency.

11. Obtain the name of a family that has used a respite care service at least three times. Interview a member of the family by phone or in person. Why did the family decide to use this service? What are the advantages of this service to the family? What are the challenges?

12. Interview seniors in Teacher Education Programs about their experiences with challenged students. Summarize the courses each has had, and the internship or placement experiences with challenged students. Discuss whether they feel prepared to include challenged students in their classroom.

13. Locate the office at your college or university that handles information and support services for challenged university students. Interview a member of that office about the recruitment and advocacy services for the institution.

REFERENCES

Beavers, Jeanette. (1989). Physical and cognitive handicaps. In Lee Combrinck-Graham (Ed.), *Children in family contexts* (pp. 193–212). New York, NY: The Guilford Press.

Child Care Law Center. (1992). *Caring for children with special needs: The Americans with Disabilities Act and child care.* San Francisco, CA: Author.

Chilman, Catherine, Nunnally, Elam, and Fox, Fred. (Eds.). (1988). *Chronic illness and disability.* Newbury Park, CA: Sage Publications.

Couples with ill children more likely to split up. (1993, September 27). *The Wall Street Journal,* p. 14.

Derman-Sparks, L., and ABC Task Force. (1989). *Anti-bias curriculum: Tools for empowering young children.* Washington, DC: National Association for the Education of Young Children.

Frye, K. S., Greenburg, M. T., and Fewell, R. R. (1989). Stress and coping among parents of exceptional children: A multidimensional approach. *American Journal on Mental Retardation, 94,* 3.

Goldstein, J., Solnit, A., and Freud, A. (1979). *Beyond the best interests of the child.* New York, NY: The Free Press.

Greenfield, J. (1970). *A child called Noah.* New York, NY: Pocket Books.

Hudgens, L., Hobfall, S. E., and Lerman, M. (1989). Predicting receipt of social support: Longitudinal study of parents' reaction to their children's illness. *Health Psychology, 8,* 61–77.

May, James E. (1991). *Fathers of children with special needs: New horizons.* Bethesda, MD: Association for the Care of Children's Health.

Meisels, S. J., and Shonkoff, J. P. (Eds.). (1990). *Handbook of early childhood intervention.* Cambridge, MA: Cambridge University Press.

The Mental Health Law Project. (1992). *The Early Intervention Advocacy Network Notebook*. Washington, DC: Author.

Mullins, J. B. (1987). Authentic voices from parents of exceptional children. *Family Relations, 36,* 30–33.

Myer, D. J., and Vadasy, P. F. (1985). *Grandparent workshops: How to organize workshops for grandparents of children with handicaps*. Seattle, WA: University of Washington Press.

Myer, D. J., Vadasy, P. F., and Fewell, R. R. (1985). *Sibshops: A handbook for implementing workshops for siblings of children with special needs*. Seattle, WA: University of Washington Press.

National Center for Family-Centered Care. (1990). *What is family-centered care?* Bethesda, MD: Association for the Care of Children's Health.

National Information Center for Children and Youth with Disabilities. (1991). *Partners: A manual for family-centered respite care*. Washington, DC: Author.

Paley, Vivian Gussian. (1992). *You can't say you can't play*. Cambridge, MA: Harvard University Press.

Pruett, K. (1989). *The promise of fatherhood: Fathers in their relationships with infants, toddlers and service providers*. Plenary session presented at the National Center for Clinical Infant Programs, Sixth Biennial. National Training Institute, Washington, DC.

Public Law 94-142. Education for All Handicapped Children Act of 1975.

Public Law 99-457 of 1986, Part H. Education of the Handicapped Amendments.

Public Law 101–336. The Americans with Disabilities Act of 1990.

Public Law 101-476 of 1993. The Individuals with Disabilities Education Act (IDEA).

Public Law 102-119 of 1991. Amendments to the Individuals with Disabilities Education Act.

Roberts, R. (1990). *Developing culturally competent programs for children with special needs*. Washington, DC: Georgetown University Child Development Center.

Shelton, T., Jeppson, E., and Johnson, B. H. (1987). *Family-centered care for children with special health needs*. Washington, DC: Association for the Care of Children's Health.

Simons, R. (1987). *After the tears: Parents talk about raising a child with disabilities*. New York, NY: Harcourt Brace Jovanovich.

Singer, G. H. S. and Irvin, L. K. (Eds.). (1989). *Support for caregiving families: Enabling positive adaptation to disability*. Baltimore, MD: Paul H. Brookes.

Special ed's special costs. (1993, October 20). *The Wall Street Journal*, p. 10.

Trute, B., and Hauch, C. (1988). Social network attributes of families with positive adaptation to the birth of developmentally disabled child. *Canadian Journal of Community Mental Health, 7,* 5–16.

U.S. Bureau of the Census. (1994). Americans with Disabilities, (SB-94-1). Washington, DC: Government Printing Office.

Ward, Mary Jane. (1946). *The Snake Pit.* New York, NY: Gosset and Dunlap.

Wolfe, R. (1989). Partnerships beyond pretense: A challenge to moms and dads. *Family Research Coalition, 3,* 3.

FURTHER READING

Johnson, B. H., McConigel, M. J., and Kaufman, R. K. (Eds.). (1989). *Guidelines and recommended practices for the individualized family service plan.* Chapel Hill, NC: National Early Childhood Technical Assistance Systems.

Mayer, D. J., and Vadasy, P. F. (1986). *Grandparent workshops: How to organize workshops for grandparents of children with handicaps.* Seattle, WA: University of Washington Press.

Park, Clara. (1981). *The seige.* Boston, MA: Little, Brown and Co.

Randall-Davis, Z. (1989). *Strategies for working with culturally diverse communities and their clients.* Bethesda, MD: Association for the Care of Children's Health (ACCH).

Shelton, T., Jeppson, E., and Johnson, B. H. (1987). *Family-centered care for children with special health needs.* Washington, DC: Association for the Care of Children's Health.

Simons, R. (1987). *After the tears: Parents talk about raising a child with disabilities.* New York, NY: Harcourt Brace Jovanovich.

MEDIA RESOURCES

Drugs, alcohol and pregnancy: What you should know. (28 min). Human Relations Media, 175 Tompkins Ave., Pleasantville, NY 10570.

The sky's the limit. (10 min). Center for Persons with Disabilities, Utah State University, Logan, UT 84322-6855.

May, James (Producer). (1989). *Special kids, special dads.* ACCH, 16120 NE Eighth St., Bellevue, WA 98008.

ORGANIZATIONS

American Speech-Language-Hearing Association (ASHA). 10801 Rockville Pike, Rockville, MD 20852. 1-800-638-8255.
Professional association for communication disability areas.

The ARC (formerly the Association for Retarded Citizens of the United States). 500 East Border St., Suite 300, Arlington, Texas 76010. (817) 261-6003.
> The oldest and largest organization for advocacy and education about disabilities including retardation.

The Council for Exceptional Children (CEC). 1930 Association Dr., Reston, VA 22091-1589. (703) 620-3660.
> Umbrella organization of professionals with sub-groups for each area of disabilities.

Learning Disabilities Association of America (LDA). 4156 Library Road, Pittsburgh, PA 15234. (412) 341-1515.
> LDA provides general information on learning disabilities as well as advocacy.

National Center for Family-Centered Care. ACCH, 7910 Woodmont Ave., Suite 300, Battlesea, MD 20814. (301) 654-6599.
> Works to provide information to families and professionals to enhance care by families.

National Clearinghouse on Family Support and Children's Mental Health. Portland State University, P.O. Box 751, Portland, OR 97207-0751. 1-800-628-1696.
> Has directory of services for parents of children with behavioral and emotional disabilities.

National Information Center for Children and Youth with Disabilities (NICHCY). P.O. Box 1492, Washington, D.C. 20013. 1-800-999-5599.
> Has information and resources on all disability areas, legislation and advocacy.

Technical Assistance for Parent Programs (TAPP). Federation for Children With Special Needs, 312 Stuart St., Suite B 2-11, Boston, MA 02116. (617) 482-2915.
> National project that works to improve services to underserved and underrepresented groups of parents of children with disabilities.

CHAPTER 14

Other Family Forms

Key Concepts

◆ Chosen Families

◆ Grandparent Families

◆ Domestic Partnerships

◆ Same Sex Partners

◆ Privacy Rights

We are the people who consider all the various traditions and customs and question them. . . . We have a great responsibility here. The human race depends on us to do this. . . . We question . . . we bring changes. . . .

— Sherman (1992)

T he various chapters of this book have shown just how truly diverse people and family structures can be. Sherman's statement above reinforces the idea of questioning and looking rationally at every aspect of families. You have read, thought about, and discussed various family formats without any coercion to pick one of them for yourself. The goal of this book is to give you insight into your role as a helping professional working with diverse families. Every family structure has positive and negative aspects from your point of view. You will make decisions about your own personal family choice based on all the insights you accumulate and with rights to privacy.

The twenty-first century will likely bring forth improved health conditions that result in greater longevity for the world's people. The commitment to the spousal partnership in families will continue with increased life expectancy. The commitment of a spouse, partner, or companion who reciprocates with mutual and sustained support and affection over time takes on added meaning in the context of longevity. Loneliness for some humans is the worst of all existences. For many, living with a cherished person is the ideal happiness.

FAMILY DEFINITION REVISITED

As you have studied the diverse families highlighted in this book, you may now appreciate more our early definition of a family—a group of persons who share

common resources and a commitment to each other over time. This definition helps prevent a premature rush to judgment. While understanding a family format requires objectivity, it does not require you to adopt it personally. As helping professionals, you will succeed in your service if you reserve judgment and allow others to make sense of the human ecological system in which they reside and that serves their own needs.

One technique that may be useful for your clients is to create a time line—a picture calendar of sorts—that shows goals for each age period of an individual's life span and how various roles—schooling, family, career, recreation, travel, etc.—will overlap. A time line helps individuals develop long-range perspectives concerning present and future goals, desires, and decisions.

ECOLOGY OF CHOSEN FAMILIES

Human ecology helps us consider the various systems that affect humans, and how, through study, experiences, and growth of wisdom over time, systems have been developed and adapted to serve family and societal needs. Change and adaptation, part of any ecosystem, influence family formats over the centuries.

Throughout our history, there have been examples of families that involve more members and more complex relationships than those of a nuclear family. Many such families have been linked to strong ideological or religious structures.

Historical Background

Social experiments with family living arrangements and relationships have existed throughout American history. In the seventeenth and eighteenth centuries, religious communities such as the Mennonites, Shakers, and Quakers were formed, combining a group's labor and economic resources to create a community. In several of these communities, the position of children and regulations regarding their responsibilities were important topics for decision-making by the entire community.

An interesting example of this type of community was the Shaker community, organized by Sister Ann Lee in the latter part of the seventeenth century. The Shakers practiced celibacy. Any children in the community were brought to the community by their parents, or were taken into the community from orphanages, or from the wider community, with the intent of providing a home for children whose needs were not being met. While the Shakers were economically successful in their agrarian-based enterprises, eventually the practice of celibacy and the increasing pressures toward the individual freedom of relationships led to the collapse of the community in the early 1900s.

During the 1920s and 1930s, a variety of communities were created largely due to political and economic utopian ideas. The New York Oneida Community and West Virginia's Arthurdale Community (a planned community for out-of-work miners supported by Bernard Baruch and Eleanor Roosevelt to alleviate the poverty of the residents) were attempts to implement a socialist model of shared labor, resources, and responsibility. In the 1960s and 1970s, a resurgence of communal living coincided with the anti-war movement of the Vietnam War era. A return to a utopian communal design, with the nurturing of children as a high priority, was seen in many of these communities. Many of the residents were driven by an intensity to reform politics. Often the communities had limited economic resources and did not survive long. These efforts created experiences that challenged the nuclear family structure as a place to rear children, and probably made it easier for households in the 1980s and 1990s to consider alternative arrangements.

Economic System

As economic recessions depress real income, families facing economic crises feel the need for community support. The result has been the emergence of a variety of chosen family groups. In some cases, these family forms are three-generational families in which young parents, in their parenting years, return to their family of origin. Needed housing or child care may be provided by cooperating with others to gain support. In Table 14–1, a comparison of households between 1970 and 1993 shows an increase in children living with their grandparents with only one parent being present. The communal family may emerge without much prior planning. Three-generational communal families are similar to extended families.

Table 14–1. *Grandchildren of the Householder, by Presence of Parents, Race, and Hispanic Origin: 1993, 1980, and 1970*

[Numbers in thousands]

Living arrangement	1993				1980 Census	1970 Census
	Total	White	Black	Hispanic*		
Total children under 18 years	66,893	53,075	10,660	7,776	63,369	69,276
Grandchild of householder	3,368	1,947	1,290	460	2,306	2,214
Percent of all children under 18 years	5.0	3.7	12.1	5.9	3.6	3.2
With both parents present	475	395	56	107	310	363
With mother only present	1,647	904	683	218	922	817
With father only present	229	163	52	29	86	78
With neither parent present	1,017	485	499	105	988	957
Percent	100.0	100.0	100.0	100.0	100.0	100.0
With both parents present	14.1	20.3	4.3	23.3	13.4	16.4
With mother only present	48.9	46.4	52.9	47.4	40.0	36.9
With father only present	6.8	8.4	4.0	6.3	3.7	3.5
With neither parent present	30.2	24.9	38.7	22.8	42.8	43.2

*Persons of Hispanic origin may be of any race.

Source: U.S. Bureau of the Census, 1970 Census of Population, PC(2)-4B, *Persons by Family Characteristics*, Table 1, and 1980 Census of Population, PC80-2-4B, Table 1. Excludes inmates of institutions.

Grandparent families are often formed primarily due to health or economic reasons. Two or more young professional single parents may pool property and incomes to create a household and a supportive unit for rearing children. Several generations of adults may move into a joint household where they share space and other resources and responsibilities. In most of these households, the emphasis is on sharing economic resources and creating positive social environments. Intimate relationships, or paired relationships, may or may not be included. What these households represent is a practical response to the reality of reduced family income in the United States. According to the 1990 census, there were 23.7 million people living in non-family households. Eighty-four percent of these were persons living alone; the remaining sixteen percent probably represent a variety of homosexual couples and chosen families, such as several single parents and their children living together, or unmarried adults living together. One can estimate that approximately two million people lived in such households at the start of the 1990s (U.S. Bureau of the Census, 1992). The group home, providing semi-independent living for some mentally ill and disabled people, may have characteristics similar to those of a communal family.

SERVING CHOSEN FAMILIES

In serving children or youth from these households, professionals have a responsibility to ask for accurate membership in the household and make sure information is communicated to the appropriate person. Including all significant adults in the child's life during planning sessions or conferences, and making certain that the family feels accepted, are important parts of professional work. When a single parent lives in such a household, other family members can provide helpful resources. Acknowledging help, and welcoming all household members into conferences, meetings, and celebrations, are important to the trust and cooperative relationships you share with that family.

Because a communal household may have a somewhat fluid membership, information regarding changes in the household is needed by the professionals who are responsible for helping children and families. Facilitating communication will help reduce any concerns of the household members that they might be judged negatively. This initiative by professionals is especially important in serving adults who cohabitate outside legal marriages. In 1988, the Bureau of the Census reported that 38 percent of children in the United States who were living with one parent were living with a divorced parent, while 31 percent were living with a parent who had never married. The remaining parents were widowed or legally or informally separated. Chapters 10 and 11 particularly discuss the compelling economic and social pressures that have encouraged cohabitation. In our society, racism and poverty have often defined the mother-children unit as the only stable organization. Sexual and companionate needs may be met by a series of partners who cohabitate with these mothers over the years.

GAY AND LESBIAN FAMILIES

American views toward sexuality and family have undergone changes over the last few decades. Controversy over appropriate classifications and definitions of families and their right to resources and benefits through the employment system or government policies has fueled extensive debate. The families in this chapter represent variations that are either chosen by the adult members or felt to be inevitable by some partners. Different motivations for creating a family reflect the variation in human society. Part of society's debate and struggle to understand and support variation in families rests on people's comfort level with variation and inclusiveness, and national struggles with problems of economics, health, and gender relationships. In many ways, these discussions concern public and private rights and responsibilities.

When families function well, members are able to engage in productive and positive work in society, and to participate in critiquing and developing new, more just, productive, and supportive societal regulations and systems. When families do not work well, protection and support from the wider systems of society become necessary. Since 1973, American middle-class families have steadily lost ground economically (National Commission on Children, 1993). The strain of child-rearing on families and the need for short- and long-term assistance from community systems have been great.

When resources are threatened or strained, definitions of access to resources often become issues. Thus, increasing variation in family forms and initiatives to change laws and regulations occur regarding family definition and access to resources. The families discussed in this chapter represent challenge and creativity as society struggles with these questions. These families are becoming increasingly evident as women and homosexuals seek independence and acceptance. While still a small minority, gay and lesbian experiences illustrate current struggles with gender roles and inclusiveness.

HISTORICAL BACKGROUND

There have probably been gay or lesbian families throughout the history of this country. In general though, this family form did not reach public discourse and debate until the 1970s and 1980s. When the 1948 Kinsey Report related that about 4 percent of males and 3 percent of females were exclusively homosexual, it was greeted with both surprise and discomfort by observers of American family life. In the 1950s, the McCarthy era of aggressive oppression of nonconformity coincided with witch hunts for and discrimination against homosexuals. A normal family life became the first line of defense against treason. The FBI and other agencies launched unprecedented intrusions into private lives under the guise of investigating traitors. Gay baiting became almost as widespread as red baiting (Boyer, 1985). Now it is known that some of our most prominent and respected citizens have been homosexuals.

In the 1980s, the White House Conference on the Family carried on a prolonged debate about an acceptable definition of family. In fact, this debate was so divisive that the 1990 conference was canceled. It is probable that an ongoing discussion about variation and inclusiveness in family forms would have been helpful in developing a kinder and gentler society. More recent figures show the incidence of homosexuality as 6 percent (Briggs, 1994). Documenting exclusive homosexual behavior and bisexual behavior is difficult. The gay rights movement and advocacy actions of the 1960s and 1970s led to an increase in acceptance by the general American public of gay and lesbian lifestyles. Briggs reported that, between 1979 and 1993, the percentage of Americans that preferred not to have a homosexual as a friend declined from 54 percent to 41 percent. In general, those respondents who were female, more highly educated or resided in major metropolitan areas were more liberal in their attitudes toward homosexuals. Blue collar workers were the only demographic group that showed a decrease in tolerance, a trend documented in the 1988 through 1993 studies.

In 1970, a half million Americans reported that they were cohabiting with an adult of the same sex. By 1988, there were 2.6 million persons cohabitating with someone of the same sex. It is likely that a significant portion of these couples have a homosexual relationship (Hare and Richards, 1993).

Because a homosexual lifestyle sometimes follows a period of heterosexual experience, approximately one-third of homosexual households contain children (Moses and Hawkins, 1982). Hoeffer (1981) estimated that there were 1.5 to 3 million lesbian mothers with 1.25 children per household in the United States. In addition, up to 10,000 lesbians have borne children through sperm donations or other such procedures, and many gay and lesbian couples have won the right to adopt children. On July 4, 1990, an article in *The New York Times* declared that there were 2 million gay mothers and fathers in America.

Part of the reality of living as a homosexual in American society is facing the tremendous negative implications of the chosen lifestyle. Many young men and women report years of denial or hiding of their homosexual orientation while engaging in a heterosexual lifestyle. Researchers have reported that adolescent homosexuals are six times more likely to attempt suicide than heterosexual adolescents (Mercer and Berger, 1989). The actual number of people who successfully live a bisexual lifestyle with both homosexual and heterosexual periods is not known.

SOCIO-CULTURAL FOUNDATIONS

Probably no other family lifestyle variation has caused as much debate and negative publicity as gay and lesbian families. Long-standing prejudice and misunderstanding have prevented an accurate perception of these families and denied them positive support from society. Nevertheless, a gay and lesbian advocacy movement emerged out of the political and sexual revolution in

America during the 1960s. A desire to be honest and to explore variation and individual freedom has been part of this movement. However, Bozette (1988) has documented a general devaluing of homosexuality in the United States.

There is evidence of differences in gay and lesbian lifestyles. A number of studies have found that lesbians tend to enter a sustained lover relationship after meeting as friends (Tanner, 1978). In fact, 75 percent of lesbian couples live together and tend to have more stable relationships than do gay lovers (Weston, 1992). Gay partners more often report entering the relationship because of sexual attraction, and then building a friendship and a sustaining affection. Only a little over 50 percent of gay lovers reside together, and there tends to be a greater disparity in their ages than among lesbian or heterosexual couples (Weston, 1992).

Within the homosexual community, there is a great diversity of values and political commitments. Nowhere is this illustrated more clearly than in the adaption of public celebrations or marriage ceremonies for gay and lesbian partners. Particularly for homosexuals with affiliations in a religious community, a ceremony that offers spiritual support for their union can be very important. Other homosexuals view marriage ceremonies as public property declarations and, therefore, too reflective of traditional heterosexual dominance-submission practices to be appropriate. Contrasting arguments on this point are eloquently made in Suzanne Sherman's book, *Lesbian and Gay Marriage: Private Commitments, Public Ceremonies* (1992).

One clear message in these discussions is the struggle of homosexuals to decide whether to adopt practices associated with a heterosexual lifestyle for their own personal meanings and purposes, or to view all practices of the heterosexual community as inappropriate for their use. Like many minority groups, homosexuals search for practices that may increase their acceptance without compromising their identity and values.

While the homosexual couple has a minority sexual orientation in American society, most practicing homosexuals resent society's extreme focus on their sexual behavior. While some observers see this as indicative of Americans' fascination with human sexuality in general, it may also represent the presence of homophobia or fear of one's own and others' homosexual tendencies (Buxton, 1991).

Many people try to understand homosexual couples by assuming they mimic a traditional power relationship found in heterosexual couples with one person playing a dominant, traditionally male role. Practicing homosexuals stress the full range of their interests, capabilities, and behaviors that go beyond the portion of their lives devoted to sexual relationships. Research shows that most homosexual couples have a balanced, comfortable relationship similar to that of best friends or roommates.

The values present in a homosexual household are a combination of values, like many other family types, with a clear decision to act on one's sexual orientation in an intimate and honest way. Coupled with these commitments and values is an interest in personal freedom or right to express one's individualism and uniqueness. Many homosexuals also place a high value on social criticism, or activism, and standards of justice and equity. The gay rights movement has built upon societal concern for democratic principles of equality, justice, and equal protection. The contrast of their sexual orientation with the dominant culture's patterns encourages values clarification and discussion.

Status

The status of homosexual families in this country has sexual, economic and social implications. In Briggs' (1994) study of homosexuals, the demographics of the gay/lesbian sample mirrored the heterosexual population's distribution by age, gender and ethnicity. The gay/lesbian sample reported significantly higher levels of education than the heterosexual sample but this did not translate into expected higher levels of income. The gay/lesbian sample reported slightly lower incomes than the heterosexual population, driven largely by the lower income of gay men in comparison to heterosexual men. According to traditional definitions of the family by blood or legal ties, the homosexual family is viewed as deviant and less valued. Some of this negative definition relates to a general misunderstanding of homosexuality and the reasons people are homosexual.

Reasons for Homosexuality

At various times in the history of the sexual revolution, a variety of theories have been used to explain the cause of homosexuality. It has been suggested that homosexuals are products of disturbed or inappropriate relationships with domineering mothers or weak fathers. Other explanations include experimentation with same-sex relationships in childhood and becoming obsessed with their attractiveness, a psychological disturbance that makes heterosexual relationships unsuccessful, or a genetic predisposition toward homosexuality. Each of these "causes" suggests a theoretical position toward human development and variation, with some variations valued less than others.

Recent researchers believe that there is not one primary reason an individual becomes a homosexual, but that there are a number of contributing factors. There is some evidence that a small portion of homosexuals are genetically predisposed toward homosexuality, from development as early as during gestation. Prenatal hormonal conditions have a powerful influence on the emergence of sexual characteristics. All fertilized eggs begin life as nonsexual organisms in which the presence of the XX or XY chromosome pair does not influence development until during the second to fifth month of gestation. Given the complexities of interaction in development, it is logical that some homosexuals are responding to some basic physiological events in their own development (Ellis and Ames, 1987).

While there is inadequate research to pinpoint the exact causes of homosexuality, scientists are becoming increasingly clear about what does not cause homosexuality. For example, children raised by gay or lesbian parents seem no more likely to become homosexuals in adulthood than children raised by heterosexual parents. The theory of a weak father and a dominant mother leading to homosexuality has not been confirmed. Likewise, the idea that females become homosexuals by choosing male role models has not been substantiated through research (Kirkpatrick, 1987).

Some researchers do believe that adolescent behaviors play a significant role in lifelong sexual patterns. Some findings have indicated that participation in homosexual behavior in adolescence and intense and compelling relationships during this period can encourage an adult homosexual orientation.

What we may be seeing, however, is adolescents recognizing their sexual orientation at an earlier age in a culture that has allowed more public discussion of this issue. One finding from research is that both researchers and clinicians have found it very difficult to change someone's sexual orientation, even when the individual has been motivated to do so. These findings would suggest both powerful reinforcing satisfactions with a homosexual orientation and the presence of physiological determinants of homosexuality.

Legal Status

The status of homosexual couples today is ambiguous in the legal system. Wisenkale and Heckart (1993) report that, as of 1992, only two states had even considered the possibility of allowing the category of domestic partnerships to be applied to homosexual households. Thus, homosexual partners who form family relationships have no legal, publicly sanctioned relationship such as marriage. In view of this, committed homosexual couples generally make wills that name each other as heir and write health care powers of attorney so that they may take appropriate action for their partner in a health crisis.

It is interesting that a number of communities, businesses, and cooperatives have included homosexual couples as domestic partnerships and have initiated policies that allow for insurance benefits and inheritance among homosexual couples. Wisenkale and Heckart (1993) comment that it is in more individualized environments, like communities and neighborhoods, that an understanding of homosexual families leads to the initiation of local regulations in support of their rights.

Among members of the gay community, there are strong differences of opinion about the advantages of "domestic partnerships" as a classification. Some activists view domestic partnership legislation as a breakthrough in policy definition of family. They appreciate the protection of property and the support for inheritance that domestic partnership statutes may provide. Other homosexuals resent domestic partnership legislation as an unnecessary intrusion into their private lives. It is interesting that in Wisenkale and Heckart's (1993) study of communities with domestic partnership policies, six of these communities are in California, five are towns that contain major universities, and three are in coastal metropolitan areas. It is probable that these areas support more liberal values toward regulation and contain a greater variation in household composition.

One-third of American states legally recognize informal or common-law marriages, and some homosexual couples have attempted to gain legal rights under these statutes in those states. Recent health costs and the need for services surrounding the AIDS epidemic have prompted a number of court cases that provide some precedents for changing the definition of family. Wisenkale and Heckart (1993) describe the *Marvin v. Marvin* (1976) case, which was heard after the death of one partner in a homosexual couple with a personal contract. In the *Braschi v. Stahl Associated Company* (1989) case in New York, the survivor of a gay couple who owned a home jointly was able to inherit the home. In the *Marvin* case, a New York judge commented, "The definition of family should find its foundation in the reality of daily family life" (Wisenkale and Heckart, 1993). A clear statement about the financial struggles of homosexual households was made by the selection of the IRS building in Washington as the setting for a public marriage ceremony for approximately 10,000 gay and lesbian partners during the 1987 March on Washington for Gay and Lesbian Rights (Sherman, 1992). Benkov (1994) summarized significant legal conflicts beginning in the early 1970s as homosexual partners sought protection of rights for each other and their children.

Public Disclosure

For committed homosexual couples, the issues of inheritance, benefits from the workplace, child support, costs of child care and legal standing after entering into contracts are troublesome. Those partners who are able to solve their legal questions and problems often still have to struggle with status in relation to friendships and families of origin. During the 1970s' gay rights movement, a great deal of publicity was given to the process of "coming out" to one's family of origin.

In the years since then, health reasons have compelled a number of homosexuals to return to their family of origin to seek assistance and support in dealing with sexually transmitted diseases, especially AIDS. After an initial shock, many of these families have created supportive environments for their homosexual sons and daughters. Simultaneously, these families have reported their struggles with the wider community's prejudice toward homosexuals, and the family's need to seek strength and support from new relationships. Working for AIDS information networks, becoming active in one of Parents and Friends of Lesbians and Gays' (PFLAG) 300 local chapters, and seeking help from a variety of counseling and support services have enabled some of these families to express their caring, and work in a supportive and positive environment for their family members (Sherman, 1992).

In the 1992 presidential election, homosexuality became a hotly debated topic among politicians. President Clinton's efforts to integrate the armed services by reducing barriers to homosexuals resulted in a damaging and difficult political fight early in his presidency. Media reports of the debate, subsequent decisions and initial court challenges repeatedly showed the public's fears and misunderstanding about how homosexual behavior might affect the military. In a traditionally male-dominated organization with the responsibility of aggressive military defense, a dialogue about homosexual rights and behavior was very difficult. It was clear that the most moving testimonies in the debate were from fathers, or commanding officers and friends of homosexuals who had been deeply influenced by their positive personal experiences with professionals who had declared themselves homosexual. Some observers compared the discussions to those President Harry Truman faced with the military when he ordered the integration of African-Americans into the military services after World War II.

The power of these experiences and the importance of support from one's own family and friends reflect the fundamental power of family as an institution. Gays and lesbians frequently comment on the power of their family's responses to their sexual orientation to influence their happiness and balance in a homosexual family. Many gays and lesbians struggle to share honestly with coworkers and bring their partners to work-related events. They find that many of their interactions with the wider community involve an ongoing balance between risk-taking and education. Thus, some homosexual couples call each other "spouse," "wife," or "husband" after marriage ceremonies. Others use the term "partner" or "companion." Some couples write "married" on enrollment forms and others write "single." Both responses are often coupled with feelings of frustration or anger and may include notes in the margin in an attempt to educate the bureaucracy represented (Sherman, 1992).

Support Groups

Like most minority groups that experience prejudice, homosexual families have created support groups and communities in which they can feel comfortable. In some larger urban areas, child care cooperatives or day care centers run by homosexual families have provided a place of nurturance and support for these parents and their children. A particularly important ongoing debate among gays and lesbians is whether, in seeking bondedness and connection with others, a new form of family or relationship can be created.

As with any minority rights movement, some members of the homosexual community are uncomfortable with the extremism of some of the leaders' actions. Some homosexuals have criticized gays and lesbians for creating a family lifestyle that resembles a heterosexual lifestyle and have suggested that kinship should be emphasized only within the broader homosexual community. Consequently, bonded intimate relationships that resemble a heterosexual couple family are discouraged by these leaders.

A number of national support groups, national information data bases, and local affiliate groups are now available. Most American college and university campuses include gay/lesbian activist groups. As with any minority advocacy groups, a range of political positions may be represented in these groups. When an extreme position is taken by the leadership, some members of the community may not feel welcome and/or may need to initiate an open discussion of policies and positions. Since these groups operate in very different environments of acceptance and support, this ongoing discussion or process of education is important to all of us.

Feminist scholars have been particularly critical of the nuclear family as an environment in which power relationships discriminate toward women, and have recommended more permeable boundaries for all homosexual families. Radical feminists have tended to discount lesbians who advocate or practice a more conservative lifestyle. In addition, feminists have pointed out that gay men are more often victims of the AIDS epidemic. When gay/lesbian advocacy groups form to promote homosexual rights, it is most often the rights of men that take precedence. Feminists have encouraged professionals to ask homosexual families how they define their own group, and what family means to them, in order to act positively in their behalf.

CHANGING ROLES OF FEMALES

A lesbian family clearly represents a changing role for females in the creation of family form. In an article by Koepke et al. (1992), lesbian couples with children scored significantly higher in relationship satisfaction and sexual relationship satisfaction than lesbian couples without children. There were no differences in satisfaction between child-free lesbian couples and lesbian couples with children based on the longevity of the relationship, or whether or not they had disclosed their sexual relationship to others. This issue of disclosure causes less pressure among lesbians than among gay men.

These couples did not show the depression of satisfaction scores, due to the presence of children, that is often found in the heterosexual community. Koepke et al. (1992) suggest that, since women are often the relationship builders or kinkeepers, lesbian couples may find more relationship satisfaction in jointly parenting than do lesbian couples without children. In contrast, though, the authors also point out that the lesbian partners risk substantial consequences in order to form their relationships. Rejection by their children or an attempt by ex-spouses to change custody relationships were listed as possible dangers. Their parenting roles were viewed as stable and deeply committed in an environment that could be threatening to less mature partners. Lesbian couples, for obvious reasons, more often consider becoming parents in their relationships. Artificial insemination, private arrangements with an acquaintance, or adoption are all choices made by lesbians. Sometimes the choice of which woman should become pregnant is obvious; sometimes both women wish to become pregnant at different times and raise both children together. Sherman (1992) illustrates this decision faced by a number of homosexual couples.

An interesting finding in a study by Hare and Richards (1993) is that lesbian parents had more positive relationships with male friends and more concern for good male models than did women in heterosexual families. The lesbian mothers spent more time and were more comfortable in their interactions with their male friends. These friendships may provide positive role models for the children of lesbians by showing male and female friendships without the struggles that exist in sexual relationships. Thorne's (1993) description of social relationships between male and female children at school illustrates the number of ways in which society emphasizes differences, and keeps the two sexes separated. In addition, Thorne documents a number of ways in which gender is a powerful divider, unless adults intervene and establish other ways for persons to relate. Children viewing the friendships between lesbian women and their male acquaintances may see a more comfortable friendship role that is part of an evolving understanding of male/female relationships.

CHANGING ROLES OF MALES

There are fewer gay families than lesbian families, and there are fewer gay families with custody of children. However, one quarter of gay men have been previously married and there are a number of gay men who are non-custodial parents, or who seek to adopt or provide foster care for children. Studies of gay fathers show little evidence that these men had originally married and procreated as a means to hide their homosexuality. Rather, they had genuine affection for their wives and children and only gradually realized the power of their homosexuality.

Gay men have been most dramatically impacted by the health risks surrounding AIDS in the gay community. Since multiple partners have traditionally been associated with the gay lifestyle rather than the lesbian lifestyle, and drug use has been historically higher among men than women, gay men have been particularly vulnerable to the AIDS epidemic. In many large urban areas, one-third to one-half of gay men have been directly affected by the death of someone in their intimate-friend circle.

In the *Braschi v. Stahl Association Company* (1989) case referred to above, that awarded a couple's home to the surviving gay member of a long-term couple, the court set four standards for the definition of a family:

1. Exclusivity and longevity of a relationship.
2. The level of emotional and financial commitment of the partners.
3. How the couple conducted their everyday lives in society.
4. The couple's reliance on each other for daily services. (Wisenkale and Heckart, 1993)

This definition of family was made after a judge's careful consideration of the gay couple's relationship and resources after one member died from AIDS. Recently, the state of California created a task force that settled on a functional definition of family that includes the following:

1. Maintaining physical health and safety.
2. Shaping a belief system and values and goals.
3. Teaching social skills.
4. Creating a haven or recuperation from stress in the wider system. (Wisenkale and Heckart, 1993)

These definitions reflect a change in the meaning of family, with a stronger appreciation for the social and psychological comforts of the family.

For gay men who are fathering children, the comfort and regenerative functions of the family are particularly important. Gay fathers have reported that revealing their homosexuality outside the family causes negative consequences for their children, but not revealing it deprives them of the support of the homosexual community (Crosbie-Burnett and Helmbrecht, 1993).

SOCIALIZATION OF CHILDREN

Homosexual couples report the same goals for children as do heterosexual couples, except for heightened interest in the child's right to choose. Since adults create families by choosing certain relationships, they want to be very clear about the rights of their children to do likewise. Most homosexual couples deliberately arrange for their children to know and interact with both male and female friends. In fact, some research suggests that the children of homosexual couples experience both males and females as significant-other adults in their lives more so than children of heterosexual couples. Benkov (1994) describes the rich variety of supportive friendships and family structures that homosexual couples have created to help with their socialization goals for their children.

This is probably a reflection of the permeability of family boundaries in a homosexual family with a supportive friend system, or the more extended nature of some homosexual families. Children raised in homosexual families may learn more about the variation and freedom for both men and women to engage in instrumental and expressive roles.

Active researchers of homosexual families report that the children deal with their parents' homosexuality by boundary control or attempts to control their parents' behavior, nondisclosure, or selective disclosure to trusted friends (Sears, 1994; and Benkov, 1994). The younger the children are when they learn of their parents' sexual orientation, the more comfortable they are with this information.

As mentioned above, homosexuals do not believe that their sexual orientation should be the determining variable in how they are treated by the wider society. In fact, for both gay and lesbian couples, who are rearing children either in their own custody or in the custody of former partners, the model is really a stepparent model. Yet homosexual couples are rarely included in stepfamily meetings, only recently being referred to in the literature as stepparents. In the 1990s, counselors are beginning to initiate training in how to support homosexual couples and the stepparents living as homosexual couples.

THE ROLE OF GRANDPARENTS AND OTHERS

There is limited research on the role of extended family members of homosexual families. Contact with the family of origin is common during a health crisis. In lesbian families, there have been some reports of extended family members being key sources of energy in the process of birth and parenting. Most discussion of extended family members involves the conflict and struggle by the parent generation to accept their children and grandchildren's family structure. Once these families have been confronted with their offspring's homosexual lifestyle, professionals can play a key role in helping with fears and supportive relationships.

The importance of political activism and advocacy among grandparents and extended family members cannot be overestimated. The support and education made available through the chapters of Parents and Friends of Lesbians and Gays (PFLAG) and the National Federation of Parents and Friends of Gays have assisted extended family members with information to support their private and public actions. Addresses of these organizations are given at the end of the chapter.

ECOLOGICAL CONSIDERATIONS

Many of the most important ecological factors surrounding homosexual families relate to the environment created by social relationships and belief systems. Where these environments are supportive, sharing is possible for homosexual families. Where environments are extremely critical, or the homosexual partners feel their professional and economic position does not allow them to reveal their family definition, then families can feel quite isolated and stressed. Every homosexual couple has significant developmental tasks in defining and maintaining their relationship in a way that is satisfying for both partners and the children involved. The fact that an unknown number of homosexuals is bisexual, or has had different periods of heterosexual lifestyle during their own development, emphasizes the complexity of these decisions.

Like other minorities, homosexual families often resent the wider society's focus on one variable in their lives. In the 1990s, there were repeated references to homosexuals receiving more physical and psychological attacks than racial minorities. The Gay and Lesbian Task Force completed a national study revealing that more than one third of individuals surveyed had suffered direct violence due to their sexual identities (Elia, 1993). Herek and Berrill (1992) reported that teenagers surveyed on their attitudes toward minorities reacted more negatively to gays than any other group of minorities. In addition, the conservative political climate of the 1990s has encouraged the passing of a number of deliberately discriminatory community and state statutes against the rights of homosexuals. Obviously, many of these will be challenged in the courts. However, growing religious fundamentalism, increasing fear of sexually transmitted diseases, and the tightening economic climate for the American family create pressures that conflict with a general societal concern for equal justice and human rights for all human beings.

Another particularly difficult reality for homosexual families is the continual ambiguity and stress of a lifestyle that carries clear risks for disclosure. In contrast to ethnic, racial, or physically challenged minorities, homosexuals form a minority which is revealed by the behavior choices of individuals themselves. When these behaviors are acted upon by adults in a caring relationship, it is difficult to understand how such families can be treated negatively within American society. The homosexual community has particularly reaped the grief and trauma of the AIDS epidemic. In addition, they are often in the position of a "blame the victim" mentality in the wider American society. When AIDS and other sexually transmitted diseases are treated as events that the homosexual community brought upon itself, it is difficult for homosexual individuals to feel accepted, respected, or protected. Homosexual couples who parent children need the assistance of the wider community systems to co-parent with them.

Religious Communities

The ten percent of Americans who are homosexuals include many people with strong religious and spiritual values. For many of them, one of the heaviest burdens has been the lack of support from their religious community. Americans have a strong pattern of public celebration of family events in religious communities. Thus, weddings, baptisms, and other family transitions are often shared with a congregation.

Yet religion has struggled with theological and political acceptance of homosexual rights. From Biblically referenced prejudicial statements against a homosexual lifestyle to investigations of sexual abuse among homosexual members of the clergy, religious communities reveal themselves as very human institutions. Both religious leaders and members of religious communities have struggled to create an open dialogue about religion's role in supporting homosexual couples.

These conflicts have been expressed through clergy leaving their congregation or the ministry entirely, or finding ways to begin changing practices. Sherman (1992) quotes a number of homosexual couples who were married by a member of the clergy known to them, but in a location different from where the congregation normally met. Other couples were already members of denominations that provided specific ceremonies and recognition within their faith. Sherman's research included interviews with rabbis, priests, ministers, and a Wiccan high priestess who conducted services for homosexual couples in a variety of settings.

A number of religious leaders have engaged in support for homosexuals whose partners are dying of AIDS. Their acknowledgement of the importance of spiritual values in this process has challenged conservative religious practices.

Some lesbians have been particularly concerned that mainstream religious groups have been marked by male chauvinist practices that conflict with lesbian values. While some of them have, therefore, resisted engaging in any public practices used by the heterosexual religious community, others have joined alternative religious communities. Native American Indian traditions and ancient Wiccan practices are two examples.

All of these efforts by traditional and alternative spiritual communities involve support for personal reflection, caring, and choice. The homosexual lifestyle perhaps provides one of the deepest challenges to the effectiveness of religious faith, compassion, love, and community.

CHANGES AND ADAPTATIONS

Some homosexual families have created strong connections to a wider community that is respectful and supportive of their life choices. With the increased publicity surrounding legal challenge and homosexuality, individuals have taken a variety of positions on disclosing their homosexuality to friends and community. The conflict described by gay fathers, who felt that disclosure brought censuring from some individuals in their children's community, but that the lack of disclosure robbed fathers of support from the gay community, is a typical conflict for many homosexual families.

There is evidence among the gay community that the AIDS epidemic has resulted in more conservative sexual behavior and more stable relationships. In the context of caring for the terminally ill, a number of homosexuals have reconfirmed the affectionate and supportive elements in their community. Difficult issues remain concerning the need to continue research that results in both the prevention and cure of AIDS. In addition, it is likely that for some time there will be misunderstanding and confusion about the relationship of homosexuality to the AIDS epidemic.

SERVING THESE FAMILIES

Compassion and sensitivity are qualities needed by all professionals supporting and serving the homosexual family. Homosexual families engage in their lifestyles at great personal risk and cost, and their commitment to parenting commands respect. Since many members of the homosexual community have experienced death and grief, it is important to be sensitive to the importance of the relationships, and to provide comfort and the means of expressing grief with these transitions.

Most homosexual parents are particularly concerned by society's portrayal of very rigid models of gender behavior, and are interested in a broader and more equitable experience for their own children. In a dramatic essay, Rofes

(1994) describes our cultural pattern of the hypermasculine "bully" in school. He identifies the harassment of the "sissy" in an educational environment that refuses to acknowledge this reality of male socialization. As professionals working with homosexual families, you can educate yourself about the language, illustrations, and activities planned in order to respect their interests. Many homosexuals act out strong values of individual freedom and responsibility through their lifestyle. Therefore, they are concerned that their children learn these same values and have an opportunity to practice them. Rules or regulations may be questioned more frequently than by other parents. A strong sense of justice and sensitivity to prejudice may be seen. In co-parenting with these families, it is important to see opportunities for growth and for expressing more universal values in the nurturing of children and youth.

In counseling sessions or conferences with these parents, you should certainly ask and remember what their children call each member of the homosexual couple. In addition, you can make certain that all adults who are important to the child's or youth's development are included in information sessions and are invited to significant celebrations. If a homosexual family is somewhat isolated from the opposite-sex group, you might facilitate friendship and support with other adults, particularly since the children of homosexual families may experience negative behaviors toward them or toward their parents. It is also helpful to give children self-protective behaviors to deal with negative situations. In an early childhood, elementary or middle school setting, instilling ways to "Say No," or "throw off" negative messages is an important part of learning life skills for these young people.

Staff in human service professions need to have agencies for referrals that are sensitive to and have an understanding of the homosexual family. As you provide in-service training, make certain that staff members have an opportunity to talk with homosexual members of the community and ask honest and frank questions that will help them in working with both children and parents.

CONCLUSIONS

People and family structures are diverse. Families are formed in many different ways, a few having been highlighted throughout this book. Families choose to relate to each other, forming alliances that give their members a sanctuary of emotional and economic support. Privacy rights protect families from the intrusion of others. The communal family may be a version of the extended family or it might be an unusual group. Same-sex partnerships are another form of family that has been in the news. Rights properly associated with these family forms are currently being clarified. Children and adults in these family forms are entitled to services of helping professionals without fear of discrimination. In working with families with a lifestyle that differs from your own, you must feel the obligation to seek understanding, to provide needed services, and to avoid being judgmental.

STUDY QUESTIONS

1. Define communal or chosen families. Describe the origins of these families at different stages in history.
2. When was the United States culture particularly critical of homosexuality?
3. Approximately how many individuals in the United States are estimated to be homosexual?
4. Approximately how many homosexual families are there in the United States?
5. Describe some differences between gay and lesbian families.
6. List different ways gay and lesbian persons can become parents.
7. How can gay or lesbian couples provide legal protection for their rights or the rights of a partner?
8. Define homophobia and give its causes.
9. List unresolved legal issues for the people in gay and lesbian families.

APPLICATIONS

1. Investigate whether there is a gay and lesbian rights organization on your campus. Arrange an interview with an officer of this organization, and summarize their basic organizational objectives. Ask your informant to evaluate the institutional support for the organization. Give examples of this support, or lack of support.
2. Investigate whether there is a family law committee within the Bar Association in your state. If there is such a committee, contact the chairperson or an officer of that group, and ask how gay and lesbian families legally protect themselves and their rights in this state.
3. Interview five of your fellow students on campus about their views of gay and lesbian families. Have they had any experiences with such families? What do they view as the positive and negative challenges for these families?
4. Contact a member of the local ministerial alliance or council. Ask if there are marriage ceremonies conducted by members of various religious groups for gay or lesbian couples. If possible, talk with a member of the clergy or priesthood about the kinds of ceremonies provided. Summarize these resources in a two-page report.
5. Write a position paper on the advantages of disclosure of homosexual lifestyle. What are the private, social and economic implications of disclosure? Would you advocate it or not? For what reasons?
6. Write a list of recommendations for homosexual partners who are also parents. These recommendations should include the following topics:

       a.   Disclosure of lifestyle to children.
       b.   Each partner's parenting role with the children.
       c.   Economic support for the children.
       d.   Relationship with extended family members.
       e.   Relationships with school systems and youth organizations.

7. Recently, some urban newspapers have changed their engagement and marriage social pages to read "celebrations." Write a letter to the editor suggesting the advantages of this policy and encouraging a change in this section of your local newspaper.

8. If there is a chapter of the Parents and Friends of Lesbians and Gays in your town, attend a meeting and interview an officer of the organization about their objectives and activities. Summarize your findings to share with classmates.

REFERENCES

Belcastro, Phillip A., Giamlich, Theresa, Nicholson, Thomas, Price, Jimmie, and Wilson, Richard. (1988). A review of data based studies addressing the effects of homosexual parenting on children's sexual and social functioning. *Journal of Divorce and Remarriage, 20*(1/2), 105–122.

Benkov, Laura. (1994). *Reinventing the family.* New York, NY: Crown Publishers, Inc.

Boyer, Paul. (1985). *By the bomb's early light: American thought and culture at the dawn of the atomic age.* New York, NY: Pantheon Books.

Bozette, F. (1989). Gay fathers: A review of the literature. In F. Bozette (Ed.), *Homosexuality and the family* (pp. 137–162). New York, NY: Haworth Press.

Bozette, F. (1988). Social control of identity by children of gay fathers. *Western Journal of Nursing Research, 10,* 550–595.

Braschi v. Stahl Association Co. (1989). New York Court of Appeals, WL.73109.

Briggs, J. Rex. (1994). *A Yankelovich monitor perspective on gays/lesbians.* Norwalk, CT: Yankelovich Partners, Inc.

Buxton, A. P. (1991). *The other side of the closet: The coming out crisis for straight spouses.* Santa Monica, CA: IBS Press.

Children's Defense Fund. (1987). *Declining earnings of young men: Their relation to poverty, teenaged pregnancy and family formation* (CDF Reports). Washington, DC: CDF Adolescent Pregnancy Prevention Clearinghouse.

Crosbie-Burnett, M., and Helmbrecht, L. (1993). A descriptive empirical study of gay male stepfamilies. *Family Relations, 42*(3), 256–262.

Downing, Christine. (1991). *Myths and mysteries of same sex love.* New York, NY: Continuum Publishing Co.

Elia, John P. (1993). Homophobia in the high school: A problem in need of resolution. *The High School Journal, 77*(1/2), 177–185.

Ellis, L., and Ames, M. A. (1987). Neurohormonal functioning and sexual orientation: A theory of homosexuality-heterosexuality. *Psychological Bulletin, 101,* 233–258.

Hare, J., and Richards, L. (1993). Children raised by lesbian couples: Does context of birth affect father and partner involvement? *Family Relations, 42*(3), 249–253.

Harry, Joseph. (1983). Gay male and female lesbian relationships. In Eleanor D. Macklin, and Roger H. Rubio (Eds.), *Contemporary families and alternative lifestyles* (pp. 216–234). Beverly Hills, CA: Sage Publications.

Herek, G. M., and Berrill, K. T. (Eds.). (1992). *Hate crimes: Confronting violence against lesbians and gay men.* London: Sage Publications.

Kirkpatrick, M. (1987). Clinical implications of lesbian mother studies. *Journal of Homosexuality, 14,* 120–211.

Koepke, L., Hare, J., and Moran, P. (1992). Relationship quality in a sample of lesbian couples with children and child-free lesbian couples. *Family Relations, 41,* 224–229.

Marcus, Eric. (1992). *Making history: The struggle for gay and lesbian equal rights.* New York, NY: HarperCollins Publishers.

Marvin v. Marvin. (1976). Supreme Court of CA, 18 Cal. 3d 660, 1348 Cal. Reports. 815, 557 P.2d 106.

Mercer, L. R., and Berger, R. M. (1989). Social service needs of lesbian and gay adolescents: Telling it their way. *Journal of Social Work and Human Sexuality, 8*(1), 75–95.

Moses, A., and Hawkins, R. (1982). *Counseling lesbian women and gay men.* Englewood Cliffs, NJ: Merrill/Prentice-Hall.

National Commission on Children. (1993). *Just the facts.* Washington, DC:

Rofes, Eric E. (1994). Making our schools safe for sissies. *The High School Journal, 77*(1/2), 37–40.

Sears, James T. (1994). Challenges for educators: Lesbian, gay and bisexual families. *The High School Journal, 77*(1/2), 138–156.

Seligman, Jean. (1993). Variations on a theme. *Newsweek,* Special Issue on the Family, pp. 38–41.

Sherman, Suzanne. (Ed.). (1992). *Lesbian and gay marriage.* Philadelphia, PA: Temple University Press.

Tanner, D. (1978). *The lesbian couple.* Lexington, MA: D. C. Heath.

The 21st Century Family. (1990, July 4). *The New York Times,* pp. 1, 10.

Thorne, Barrie. (1993). *Gender play: Girls and boys together.* New Brunswick, NJ: Rutgers University Press.

Weston, K. (1992). The politics of gay families. In Barrie Thorne (Ed.), *Rethinking the family: Some feminist questions* (pp. 119–139). Boston, MA: Northeastern University Press.

Wisenkale, Steven K. (1992). *Domestic partnerships: Issues and legislation*. New York, NY: Lambda Legal Defense and Education Fund.

Wisenkale, Steven K., and Heckart, Kathryn, E. (1993). Domestic partnerships. *Family Relations, 42,* 199–204.

FURTHER READING

Alpert, H. (1988). *We are everywhere: Writings by and about lesbian parents*. Freedom, CA: Crossing Press.

Berzon, Betty. (1988). *Permanent partners: Building gay and lesbian relationships that last*. New York, NY: E. P. Dutton.

Bozette, Frank. (Ed.). (1987). *Gay and lesbian parents*. Westport, CT: Perager.

Bozette, F. (Ed.). (1989). *Homosexuality and the family*. New York, NY: Haworth Press.

Clifford, Dennis, and Curry, Hayden. (1988). *A legal guide for lesbian and gay couples* (5th ed.). Berkeley, CA: Nolo Press.

Gantz, Joe. (1983). *Whose child cries: Children of gay parents talk about themselves*. Rolling Hills Estate, CA: Jolmar.

Hoeffer, Beverly. (1981). Children's acquisition of sex-role behavior in lesbian-mother families. *American Journal of Ortho-psychiatry, 51*(3), pp. 50–65.

Perry, Rev. Troy. (1990). *Don't be afraid anymore*. New York, NY: St. Martin's Press.

Preston, J. (Ed.). (1992). *A member of the family*. New York, NY: Dutton.

Rafkin, L. (1990). *Different mothers: Sons and daughters of lesbians talk about their lives*. Pittsburgh, PA: Cleis.

Schulenburg, J. (1985). *Gay parenting: A complete guide for gay men and lesbians with children*. Garden City, NY: Anchor.

MEDIA RESOURCES

Silent Pioneers: Gay and Lesbian Elders. (1985). (42 min.). Pioneer Films, NY: Filmmakers Library.

OTHER BOOKS

Brogan, Jim. (1986). *Casey: The bi-coastal kid*. Salinas, CA: Equanimity Press.

Ecker, B. A. (1983). *Independence day*. New York, NY: Avon Books.

Fricke, Aeron. (1981). *Confessions of a rock lobster*. Boston, MA: Alyson.

Garden, Nancy. (1982). *Annie on my mind*. New York, NY: Farrar, Straus and Giroux.

PERIODICALS

Empathy: An interdisciplinary journal for persons working to end oppression based on sexual identities. P.O. Box 5085, Columbia, SC 29250.

The high school journal, 77(1/2). Special Double Issue on The Gay Teenager. October/November, 1993; December/January, 1994.

Journal of Homosexuality. Haworth Press, Inc. 10 Alice St., Binghamton, NY 13904. 1-800-342-9678.

Quarterly research journal published on topics related to homosexuality.

Partners Magazine for Gay and Lesbian Couples. P.O. Box 9685, Seattle, WA 98109.

Quarterly magazine includes information in supporting same-sex relationships. A bi-monthly newsletter is also available.

Teaching Tolerance. Published twice a year since 1992 by the Southern Poverty Law Center at 400 Washington Ave., Montgomery, AL 36104.

Free to educators, it covers *all* forms of intolerance.

ORGANIZATIONS

AARP Grandparent Information Center. 601 East St. NW, Washington, DC 20049 (202) 434-2296

American Civil Liberties Union (ACLU). Lesbian and Gay Rights Project, 132 West 43rd St., New York, NY 10036. (212) 944-9800, ext. 545.

Children of Gay/Lesbians. 8306 Wilshire Blvd., Suite 222, Beverly Hills, CA 90211.

Family Diversity Project EEO Seminars. P.O. Box 65756, Los Angeles, CA 90065. (213) 258-8955, ext. 5931.

Lambda Legal Defense and Education Fund (LLDEF). 666 Broadway, 12th Floor, New York, NY 10012. (212) 995-8585.

National Coalition of Grandparents. 137 Larkin St., Madison, WI 53705 (608) 238-8751.

National Gay Task Force. 80 Fifth Ave., Room 506, New York, NY 10011.

National Federation of Parents and Friends of Gays (PFOG). 8020 Eastern Ave., N.W., Washington, DC 20012. (202) 726-3223.

Parents and Friends of Lesbians and Gays (PFLAG). P.O. Box 27605, Washington, DC 20038-7605.

ORGANIZATIONAL RESOURCES

Friends of Project 10. (1991). *Project 10 Handbook: Addressing Lesbian and Gay Issues in Our Schools*. 3rd edition. Los Angeles, CA: Author. ERIC Reproduction No. ED337567.

PART IV

Conclusions

CHAPTER 15

Serving Families

Key Concepts

- ◆ Advocacy
- ◆ Humility
- ◆ Dedication
- ◆ Service

There are no boundaries in the real Planet Earth. No United States, no Soviet Union, no China, no Taiwan, East Germany or West. Rivers flow unimpeded across the swaths of continents. The Persistent Tides—the pulse of the sea—do not discriminate, they push against all the varied shores on Earth.

— Jacques Yves Cousteau, Oceanographer and Explorer

As the ocean tides pulse against our shores, we can gain strength from their boundless energy to strengthen families everywhere. Families in America are a mere microcosm of the families of the world. There are many common threads of diversity and of common purpose among all the world's people. . . . As President Clinton said in his proclamation for the International Year of the Family, 1994:

> The fabric of the United States and the world is woven together from many diverse ethnic and cultural family threads. Each family's unique traditions and teachings blend together to build the very foundation upon which we, as an international family, have grown and will continue to grow.

In designating 1994 as the International Year of the Family, the United Nations hoped to encourage the people of the world to focus on the hopes and needs of the many diverse families living in their own communities as well as those in the global apartment house, the Earth. The year highlighted the fact that, although diverse, families are the basic social unit of all societies. Though families have structural and value differences, they are the builders of the human capital of the world. You, as a helping professional, have a solemn duty to assist in this noble endeavor.

REMEMBERING GOALS

A major goal for most families, stated in many ways, is to be together while learning values and virtues within the family circle. Another important goal of families is to learn to grow and develop together and to relate harmoniously to each other and to the outside world. As you have learned, the family circle is defined differently by various cultural groups. Much of family life is within the home, out of view of neighbors and others. In America, the home is the most private of environments, protected by law and rules of decorum from infringement by others, and especially protected from invasion by governmental authorities.

Family support systems, agencies that serve families, and helping professionals in their many community roles must become attuned to families, helping where families need help and when called upon. Empowering all families to achieve a high-quality life in their community must be the major goal of every helping professional serving families.

GIVING SERVICE

Service orientation for helping professionals focuses on empowering individuals and families to obtain the best assistance available to meet their needs and to create a harmonious and peaceful society. As graduates entering the professional arena, you will be able to serve diverse people from the youngest to the eldest. An orientation toward service means that the clients' needs are paramount, that their satisfaction is important, and that you will go the extra mile to assist each of them. While you cannot do for them what they might do for themselves, you must provide a needed high-quality service as mandated by your employer as well as your personal standards.

An excellent example of a service orientation was seen in an airport waiting room by a woman selling hot dogs. The people waiting for planes were tired and hungry. She took a personal interest in each person who wanted a hot dog, checking to be sure that each had all the mustard, pickle, and catsup desired. In their tired and hungry state, she brought smiles to their faces and made the wait go more quickly. We've all experienced vendors who seemed to hate doing us a favor; this woman enjoyed pleasing her patrons and performing a needed service.

Your college years will prepare you to be professionals, developing the skills and expertise to serve families in many respects. Not only will you be professionally prepared as a teacher, social worker, physician, or the like, but you will become skillful in meeting and speaking with clients of many different age, ethnic, and challenged groups. Initially, your education and skill development may be elementary, but throughout your career you will continue to learn and develop new skills. You may already be browsing college catalogs for additional professional and graduate studies. Many of you, wishing to serve families in the years ahead, should plan for further professional education.

You will become advocates for your clients as you provide needed services. In many respects you must be creative as you seek to pull together the collage of clients' personal characteristics, the family's needs, the professional know-how, the state of the art knowledge, and the resources available. Like an artist weaving a landscape, you will fashion a wonderful tapestry for each client you serve.

WELCOMING DIVERSITY

As you have learned throughout this book, people and their families are diverse in many ways. No two individuals or families are alike. Even clients from your own community will differ from you in many respects. You must learn to recognize differences between yourself and your clients and not let those differences impact the quality of your service. You must serve equally well people of any family, no matter what group—ethnic, racial, age, gender, disabled, regional, religious, or other. Your professional preparation for high-quality service and your commitment to serve with distinction should always be a priority. Upon meeting new clients, make them feel accepted, regardless of their particular group, and remember that, although we all have unique aspects, we are all human beings deserving respect.

You may feel uncertain because of your own characteristics, especially if you are new to your job. Will you receive the recognition and acceptance you have rightly earned? Hopefully, because of your advanced level of knowledge and understanding, people will accept your skills and abilities and disregard the fact that you may not be like them in some ways. A great deal has been learned in recent years about welcoming diverse people into our midst. Of course, there is still much to be learned. Your study of diversity in this book is a step in that direction. What you've learned will allow you to be a role model, welcoming diversity, as you conscientiously do your job. Little by little, those clients who have doubts will be persuaded that your skills, abilities, dedication, and human qualities are more important than superficial differences. In other words, the differences won't make a difference—diversity will be accepted and respected!

APPLYING ECOLOGICAL SYSTEM CONCEPTS

In studying about the ecological system that helps us plan services for families, you've learned that one of the three divisions of the ecological system is the natural physical-biological environment consisting of the various natural resources of a region. The richness of this natural resource base affects the level of goods and services the private and government sectors can provide.

A second part of the ecological system is the human-built environment. This environment includes the accumulation of capital in industrial factories, roads, institutions, and structural systems that a country develops to meet the needs and desires of individuals and families. Though each new person born brings a new pair of hands to produce food and well-being, the output will be meager and life will be bleak and barren of opportunity unless there is an adequate accumulation of private and public capital for those new hands to utilize in productive work. We've seen examples of the development of systems in government, education, health, social services, business, agriculture, religion, and the like. Understanding how families interact with the various systems gives us important information to help plan services for a particular group.

The third part of the ecological system is the sociocultural environment, which is where the people, their cultural values, and their family structures are considered—including family size and the total numbers of a population in relation to resources available in a given region or country. To assure that every new birth is a planned one would help reduce violence within families and communities.

In the sociocultural environment, we find what people value, how they operate social systems, and how families learn to use those systems and guide their children to learn to function adequately. Through overt teaching as well as through modeling behavior, families teach their children to use the education or health system.

All areas of the ecological system must be considered as you analyze the services proposed for families. As you endeavor to improve systems, you may interact with policy makers at the local, state, national, and international levels. If you observe barriers that might interfere with a family's access to a system, you can help break up or remove those barriers. Many of your families are too vulnerable to become activists.

FOCUSING ON ECONOMIC CONCERNS

Your study of various family groups has taught you about some families' economic views. In discussing the Amish people, for example, you learned that they are content to be economically and politically independent. They practice sustainability, frugal living, and seek no assistance from outside their communities. They desire to be left alone. You may find other groups equally adamant in their desire for privacy.

On the other hand, the teen-aged mothers discussed in another chapter generally look to the community, state, and nation for economic and emotional support, such as support for housing, health care, food, and education for themselves and their children. If any of those services are withdrawn, the mothers often face real financial difficulties both in the present and in the future. Many teen mothers have made decisions, including desiring and permitting themselves to become pregnant, causing them and their children to face many trials in life. The human capital—skills, knowledge, abilities, etc.— of these young women must be developed to ensure that they and their children do not spend a lifetime on public assistance. Studies show that investing in their education in the present will pay off in their children's future contributions to society.

Poverty and its related problems affect housing, nutrition, health, education, employment, and the social and cultural quality of life. Recalling our ecological system, remember that all systems are linked and that pressure or movement in one system can affect the other systems. The current political climate favors a punitive effort to control the teen-age pregnancy phenomenon.

The U.S. is currently in a period of economic belt-tightening. No matter how worthy some programs appear, taxpayers are concerned about spending and legislators are voting to hold the line and even make cuts. Such budget constraints have caused many health and social service providers to look elsewhere for funding or find ways to economize and provide services more efficiently.

There is a strong ethic in the country that responsibility for children rests solely with their parents. Many governmental programs today are being designed to help put people to work, in part by providing care for children so parents can become trained to become productive wage earners. Absent parents are being sought so they can assume full financial responsibility for their children.

Various social systems are attempting to strengthen families in different ways. Churches have a renewed commitment to the families in their midst. Families are being encouraged to save money by doing things at home—cooking, sewing, mending, laundering, as well as entertaining. Urging families to omit items like soft drinks and other "junk foods" from the grocery cart because of their expense in relation to the lack of useful nutrition they contribute to the diet is another way families can be taught to economize. Family labor is often abundant and the skills learned in home production sometimes can be transferred to outside employment. Part of children's human capital development should include learning to manage their home services.

Finding good jobs for the breadwinners of the families is still the best guarantee of adequate services for families. In a full-employment economy, families can purchase needed services with income earned. Most people want to be independent of public welfare. Modern societies are finding, even encouraging, that both men and women become breadwinners in many families. Because many families are financially overextended, parents attempting to raise a family on one paycheck are disadvantaged and especially vulnerable if layoffs occur. While the government attempts to create an economic safety net, there is a growing sentiment that people must face the reality of possible financial difficulties if they don't take responsibility for themselves. The old-fashioned virtues of hard work and personal responsibility are expected of everyone. Children are the economic responsibility of parents. More and more, authorities are requiring both parents to assume this financial responsibility. Computer lists of absent parents—mostly fathers who abdicate their responsibilities—are being developed so these parents can be located and made to pay child support. The double standard, wherein fathers accept no responsibility for pregnancies and children and place all blame and burden on mothers, appears to be ending as women demand empowerment and equality.

ACTING WITH HUMILITY

Humility is a characteristic of temperament that every person needs when dealing with people, especially in the helping professions. Science has shown us a great deal about people, and while studies may tell us about averages and norms, they may not give us much insight into a specific individual who may be far from the norm or average. Your role as a professional will be to study each client and apply what you know from science to help solve problems being presented by the individual family. At times you will be forced to admit that there are things you really don't know, that you'll try to find out, or that you may have to try possible solutions. Feigning knowledge you don't have is both unethical and dangerous.

Some professionals assume guises of authority—authority that is often not warranted by present-day information, especially about individual cases. Readily admit when you are wrong or may not know something. For example, a college counselor once told a young male student that his entrance test scores showed that "people with scores like yours have generally NOT made it through this college." The student arrived each term and showed his high grades to the counselor. Consequently, the counselor reminded the student that data may not always apply in individual cases. Was the test wrong? Had the student just had a bad day when he took the test? Or, had the counselor, by leveling with the student, motivated him to tackle the task of his classes with increased energy and determination to prove the counselor and scores wrong?

It is helpful to bring clients along with you in the discovery process. That is what empowerment means. Clients are the ones whose efforts will most likely bring success to the family. A specified diet is only as good as the decision-making of the person eating the food; the disciplinary method only as good as the parent or teacher putting it into operation. Each of your clients can help design the treatment and then be motivated to take pride in its success.

BEING HONEST

You will need to be honest with those you serve. They will be expecting honest, clear, and forthright advice and leadership from you. Many people in difficult circumstances are tough enough to take honest answers. Their imaginations can always conjure up worse scenarios than your honesty might present. Before advising clients, take time to plan your session. Make information clear. Go over it a number of times with clients, perhaps on various days to be sure they understand. Allow clients to call you on the telephone for information. Parents of disabled children, for example, are tired of what they call "the runaround." Make it possible for them to receive honest assistance from you.

BEING ENERGETIC

A great amount of energy is needed in working with families. You will need energy to seek information, inform your clients, and see if they carry out the plan you've worked out with them. You'll need energy to go the extra mile when you recognize that families won't get the assistance they need and deserve unless you help them through the bureaucratic maze. The effort you make will prove tiring but satisfying.

If you recognize that you are having difficulties, you may want to consult with experts or consider more advanced education. Every science and service is progressing so fast that your early college degree will soon become outdated if you don't make plans to attend refresher workshops, do professional reading, and seek advanced degrees along the way. Advanced degrees will take money and energy, especially if you have to work to support yourself, like many graduate students today.

ACTING WITH DEDICATION

Experiencing a satisfied dedication to your career is a pleasant outcome of study, hard work, and commitment. You'll find yourself tackling your work because you enjoy it, rather than merely to satisfy a boss or receive a paycheck.

Being dedicated means you'll eagerly look for new information, attend conferences, develop professional connections, and read continuously to be assured of the latest knowledge.

Being dedicated doesn't mean giving up a life of your own, only that you become focused and learn to decide what your priorities are. However, you should also know that every year many people change careers, even after working in one field for a number of years. Technologies change, people reassess their decisions, family commitments shift, all making it important to confront a decision made earlier. Some career counselors are now predicting that most people will change careers to some extent at least three times during a working lifetime. Every university has career specialists available to guide you in new choices in your world of work. Always seek information and career advice before making career changes.

USING ADVOCACY

Advocating for families may mean championing the cause of a single family as a route to societal improvement. Helping to improve society may mean taking responsibility in a political campaign, such as working for efficiency and equity in needed human services. In that sense, as a committed professional, you'll become an advocate for the families you serve. Dedication to your job and a desire to see a society that works more effectively may prompt you to seek advocacy work as an adjunct to your job description. Advocacy may mean that you take a leadership role in promoting societal improvement.

You may see an inequity in a service that reduces societal productivity. Consequently, you may become an advocate for improving procedures to move toward equity for diverse groups. Advocacy requires you to keep in touch with leaders of your profession, become one of them, and confer as needed to improve societal functioning on the local, national, and global levels.

CORRECTING PROBLEMS OF DISCRIMINATION

Gender, age, race, ethnicity, sexual-orientation, disability, religion, and family forms are types of diversity that have been discussed in previous chapters. Efforts to achieve equity concerning these diversities have been ongoing for centuries. Many groups have struggled for rights to education, jobs, and equal pay in the workplace. Some of the groups discussed in this book may have made you aware of the powerful male patriarchy that exists in many homes. There may be youths born into those families who are discontented with that situation and wish to change it. Some Americans have succeeded in making changes in oppressive situations in the past. The history of efforts toward equal rights for boys and girls, brothers and sisters, men and women, and husbands and wives, is well worth reading about. Some of the strongest advocates of these efforts to end discrimination are persons who have taken action when they found themselves severely discriminated against.

CONCLUSIONS

Families with many cultural, ethnic, and structural variations will continue to be formed in the U.S. and around the world. Modern communication has facilitated improved understanding within families as well as within the entire global human family. Familiarity and understanding will continue to develop over the years ahead with respect to diversity. In a world of diverse peoples, in some situations, each of you will be classified as a minority. It is apparent that harmful discrimination and intolerance is not an appropriate response. Let us recognize that diversity adds strength to our global society and is something to be cherished. Peaceful, enlightened dialogue within national and global democratic structures must replace violence and war if the human family is to survive and thrive.

The United Nations, representing all the diverse people of the world, endeavors to promote dialogues, utilizing the talents of all the world's people and bringing to bear new perspectives from all points of the globe. To encourage a peaceful dialogue leading to more harmonious relationships within families and among families all around the world, the United Nations proclaimed the year 1994 as the International Year of the Family. Reflecting the crucial role played by the family in promoting the well-being of society, the year's motto was, "Building the smallest democracy at the heart of society." May we all contribute to that motto at home and abroad as we remember this line from South African Archbishop Desmond Tutu's 1984 Nobel Peace Prize statement:

My humanity is bound up in yours, for we can only be human together.

STUDY QUESTIONS

1. What was the reason the United Nations designated 1994 as the International Year of the Family?
2. List ten personal temperament characteristics needed by helping professionals for empowering families. Briefly describe these characteristics in a two-page report.
3. Review the application of the ecological systems framework and tell how it applies to serving families in your community.
4. Read the opening and closing quotations of the chapter and tell how they apply to the objectives of this book.

APPLICATIONS

1. Ask your librarian to assist you in finding documents of the United Nations and other countries relating to families during the 1994 International Year of the Family. Analyze the content and, in a two-page essay, discuss how the recommendations or major concepts relate to American families.

2. Write a two-page essay on the International Year of the Family motto, "Building the smallest democracy at the heart of society." Discuss how that motto is incongruent or may not be accepted by some of the cultures you have studied and give examples.
3. Study the ten personal temperament characteristics for helping professionals. Write a two-page essay on how difficult or easy it will be for you to put these characteristics into practice. Give examples of professional people you know and rate them on these characteristics.

FURTHER READING

Brown, Lester, Kane, Hal, and Roodman, David M. (1994). *Vital signs 1994: The trends that are shaping our future*. New York, NY: W. W. Norton & Company, and Washington, DC: Worldwatch Institute.

Ferencz, Benjamin C. (1991). *Planethood: The key to your future*. Coos Bay, OR: Love Line Books.

Ferencz, Benjamin C. (1994). *New legal foundations for global survival*. Dobbs Ferry, NY: Oceana Publications, Inc.

Keyes, Ken, Jr. (1987). *The hundredth monkey*. Coos Bay, OR: Vision Books.

Name Index

Abalos, David T., 72, 74, 76, 77, 80
Abd al-Auhir al Jurjani, 128
Ahmed, Ismael, 119, 121
Ahrons, C. R., 217, 242
Akiko, Yasano, 93
Albert, Linda, 244
Allen, R., 63
Allen, W., 57
Allen-Meares, Paula, 174
Amato, Paul, 223
Ames, M. A., 305
Amiruddin, B., 125
Amman, Jakob, 156
Apfel, N. H., 181
Arbuthnot, Jack, 230
Aswad, Barbara, 123, 124, 125
Austin, 222

Bagbee, B. H., 218
Barrow, L., 61
Baumrind, D., 199
Bean, Frank, 72, 77
Baruch, Bernard, 299
Beavers, Jeanette, 269
Bell, Derrick, 64
Bell, R., 58
Benkov, Laura, 307, 311
Berger, M., 125
Berger, R. M., 303
Berger, S. H., 242
Bernado, Stephanie, 129
Bernal, Guillermo, 73
Bernea, E., 125
Berrill, K. T., 312
Bezirgan, B., 125

Biagini, J., 111
Billingsley, A., 55, 57
Booth, Alan, 223
Boyer, Paul, 302
Bozette, F., 304
Bray, J. M., 242
Briggs, J. Rex, 303, 305
Britsch, Susan, 74, 75
Bronfenbrenner, Urie, 36, 37
Broom, L., 101
Brown, A., 58
Brown, G., 110
Brown, P., 222
Bubolz, M. M., 18, 19, 37, 38
Buehler, Cheryl, 212
Burton, L. M., 197
Buxton, A. P., 304

Cabezas, A., 108
Caldwell, Bettye, 6
Carlin, J., 111, 112
Cassatt, Mary, 184
Chan, S., 95
Chavez, Linda, 75, 84
Cherlin, A. J., 245
Chilman, Catherine, 274
Chung, D., 96
Coleman, M., 242, 243, 247, 250
Coles, R., 141
Collier, J., 150
Confucius, 96
Coontz, Stephanie, 58, 60, 175, 176, 179, 182, 189, 211, 224, 231, 240, 244
Cox, M., 217, 228
Cox, R., 217, 228

Subject Index